Sociology Matters

Also available from McGraw-Hill
by Richard T. Schaefer
Sociology: A Brief Introduction, 9th edition (2011)
Sociology in Modules (2011)
Sociology, 12th edition (2010)

Sociology Matters

Fifth Edition

Richard T. Schaefer

DePaul University

McGraw Hill
Connect
Learn
Succeed™

Connect
Learn
Succeed™

SOCIOLOGY MATTERS, FIFTH EDITION

Published by McGraw-Hill, a business unit of The McGraw-Hill Companies, Inc., 1221 Avenue of the
Americas, New York, NY 10020. Copyright ©2012 by The McGraw-Hill Companies, Inc. All rights
reserved. Previous editions © 2009, 2008, and 2006. No part of this publication may be reproduced or
distributed in any form or by any means, or stored in a database or retrieval system, without the prior
written consent of The McGraw-Hill Companies, Inc., including, but not limited to, in any network or
other electronic storage or transmission, or broadcast for distance learning.

Some ancillaries, including electronic and print components, may not be available to customers outside
the United States.

This book is printed on acid-free paper.

1 2 3 4 5 6 7 8 9 0 DOC/DOC 1 0 9 8 7 6 5 4 3 2 1

ISBN 978-0-07-352825-0
MHID 0-07-352825-0

Vice President & Editor-in-Chief: *Michael Ryan*
Vice President EDP/Central Publishing Services: *Kimberly Meriwether David*
Publisher: *William Glass*
Senior Sponsoring Editor: *Gina Boedeker*
Executive Marketing Manager: *Pamela S. Cooper*
Managing Developmental Editor: *Meghan Campbell*
Project Manager: *Erin Melloy*
Design Coordinator: *Brenda A. Rolwes*
Cover Designer: *Studio Montage, St. Louis, Missouri*
Cover Image: *© James Lauritz/Getty Images*
Buyer: *Susan K. Culbertson*
Media Project Manager: *Sridevi Palani*
Compositor: *Laserwords Private Limited*
Typeface: *10/12 Times Roman*
Printer: *R. R. Donnelley*

All credits appearing on page 371–372 are considered to be an extension of the copyright page.

Library of Congress Cataloging-in-Publication Data

Schaefer, Richard T.
  Sociology matters / Richard T. Schaefer.—5th ed.
    p. cm.
  ISBN-13: 978-0-07-352825-0 (alk. paper)
  ISBN-10: 0-07-352825-0
  1. Sociology. 2. Cultural relations. 3. Social stratification. I. Title.
  HM447.S33 2012
  301—dc22

                                    2010052473

www.mhhe.com

Dedication

To my students, for their contributions every term

About the Author

Richard T. Schaefer
Professor, DePaul University
BA Northwestern University
MA PhD University of Chicago

Growing up in Chicago at a time when neighborhoods were going through transitions in ethnic and racial composition, Richard T. Schaefer found himself increasingly intrigued by what was happening, how people were reacting, and how these changes were affecting neighborhoods and people's jobs. His interest in social issues caused him to gravitate to sociology courses at Northwestern University, where he eventually received a BA in sociology.

"Originally as an undergraduate I thought I would go on to law school and become a lawyer. But after taking a few sociology courses, I found myself wanting to learn more about what sociologists studied, and fascinated by the kinds of questions they raised." This fascination led him to obtain his MA and PhD in sociology from the University of Chicago. Dr. Schaefer's continuing interest in race relations led him to write his master's thesis on the membership of the Ku Klux Klan and his doctoral thesis on racial prejudice and race relations in Great Britain.

Dr. Schaefer went on to become a professor of sociology, and now teaches at DePaul University in Chicago. In 2004 he was named to the Vincent DePaul professorship in recognition of his undergraduate teaching and scholarship. He has taught introductory sociology for over 35 years to students in colleges, adult education programs, nursing programs, and even a maximum-security prison. Dr. Schaefer's love of teaching is apparent in his interaction with his students. "I find myself constantly learning from the students who are in my classes and from reading what they write. Their insights into the material we read or current events that we discuss often become part of future course material and sometimes even find their way into my writing."

Dr. Schaefer is the author of the ninth edition of *Sociology: A Brief Introduction* (McGraw-Hill, 2011), *Sociology in Modules* (McGraw-Hill, 2011), and the twelfth edition of *Sociology* (McGraw-Hill, 2010). He is also the author of *Racial and Ethnic Groups*, now in its twelfth edition census update (McGraw-Hill, 2011), and *Race and Ethnicity in the United States*, sixth edition, both published by Pearson. Together with William Zellner, he coauthored the ninth edition of *Extraordinary Groups,* published by Worth in 2011. Dr. Schaefer served as the general editor of the three-volume *Encyclopedia of Race, Ethnicity, and Society,* published by Sage in 2008. His articles and book reviews have appeared in many journals, including *American Journal of Sociology; Phylon: A Review of Race and Culture; Contemporary Sociology; Sociology and Social Research; Sociological Quarterly;* and *Teaching Sociology.* He served as president of the Midwest Sociological Society in 1994–1995.

Dr. Schaefer's advice to students is to "look at the material and make connections to your own life and experiences. Sociology will make you a more attentive observer of how people in groups interact and function. It will also make you more aware of people's different needs and interests—and perhaps more ready to work for the common good, while still recognizing the individuality of each person."

Preface

Sociology has been my life's work for several decades. In the classroom and in the pages of my textbooks, I have tried to spark students' interest in the discipline by showing them its real-life implications. My aim has been to convince students that sociology is more than just another academic pursuit, an exercise in scholarship for the sake of scholarship. Sociology illuminates the world around us—our families, schools, neighborhoods, and other familiar institutions we have lived with all our lives. It puts into larger perspective our culture and our socialization—the way we come to be the way we are. Sociology makes us think deeply about the divide between ourselves and those of different races, classes, and ethnicities. It forces us to recognize the effects of power, technological advances, electronic media, and the increasingly rapid process of social change on our own lives. Sociology matters—to you, me, and everyone with a stake in the society we live in.

This concise volume stresses the same theme, in fewer pages and with fewer illustrations and study aids. *Sociology Matters* is intended for instructors who desire an especially short, relatively inexpensive introductory text. This text covers the essential content in *Sociology: A Brief Introduction,* Ninth Edition, in much the same depth. Its 11 chapters can be covered easily in a quarter- or semester-long course, together with other materials instructors might wish to add.

Major Emphases

Like the brief ninth edition of *Sociology,* this volume includes comprehensive, balanced coverage of the major theoretical perspectives. Chapter 1 introduces, defines, and contrasts the functionalist, conflict, and interactionist perspectives as well as the increasingly important feminist approach. Later chapters use these distinctive viewpoints to explore topics such as deviance (Chapter 4); social stratification (Chapter 5); race and ethnicity (Chapter 6); gender (Chapter 7); social institutions (Chapters 8 and 9); population, communities, health, and the environment (Chapter 10); and social movements, social change, and technology (Chapter 11).

This volume also includes strong coverage of gender, race, ethnicity, and social class. Three entire chapters are devoted to these topics: Chapter 5, on stratification in the United States and global inequality; Chapter 6, on race and ethnicity; and Chapter 7, on gender. Related discussions appear throughout the book. For instance, Chapter 3 examines race and gender as ascribed statuses; Chapter 4, racial profiling and the perceived seriousness of white-collar crime; Chapter 10, the connection between health and a person's social class, race, ethnicity, and gender; and Chapter 11, the role of gender in social movements.

Finally, this volume includes considerable cross-cultural coverage. Chapter 2 covers the development of culture around the world. Chapter 4 covers international crime rates. Chapter 5 treats social stratification from a global perspective, including coverage of world-systems analysis, dependency theory, modernization theory, the development of multinational corporations, and the global economy. Chapter 7 covers cross-cultural differences in gender roles. Chapter 8 takes a global view of the family. Chapter 10, which opens with a vignette on global population growth, treats global environmental issues. And Chapter 11 covers global social change.

Special Features

This volume offers a variety of learning aids designed to help students understand and review basic concepts, including:

- Chapter outline
- Chapter-opening vignette with chapter overview
- Use Your Sociological Imagination sections, which prompt students to apply their knowledge of sociology to the world around them
- Tables and figures, some with sticker-style captions and Think About It questions. Many tables are presented as *Summing Up* to aide in learning.
- Photographs and cartoons
- Online Learning Center icons, which alert students to relevant material on the book's companion website
- Boldfaced key terms
- *Sociology Matters* sections at the end of each chapter, which point out the relevance of a chapter's content to students' lives
- Numbered 10-point chapter summary
- End-of-chapter key terms list with page references
- End-of-book Appendix, "Careers in Sociology"
- End-of-book glossary with page references

What's New in the Fifth Edition?

The most important changes in this edition include the following (refer as well to the chapter-by-chapter list of changes on pages xi–xiv).

CONTENT

- Four new key terms have been added, along with related coverage: W. E. B. DuBois's concept of *double consciousness,* as well as *macrosociology and microsociology* (Chapter 1) and *White privilege* (Chapter 6).
- Coverage of numerous other topics has been augmented or added, including: public sociology (Chapter 1); Charles Darwin's theory of natural selection (Chapter 2); cross-cultural differences in social interaction and social reality (Chapter 3); the role of reference groups in anticipatory socialization (Chapter 3); recent replication of Milgram's obedience experiment (Chapter 4); income inequality in the United States (Chapter 5); the federal government's new Supplemental Poverty Measure (SPM) (Chapter 5); the proposed Development, Relief, and Education for Alien Minors (DREAM) Act (Chapter 6); student research on gender norm transgressions (Chapter 7); single-parent families and households headed by a same-sex couple (Chapter 8); the transformative effect of educational programs for the disadvantaged (Chapter 9); capitalism in China (Chapter 9); the accelerating effect of the extended economic downturn that began in 2008 on the processes of deindustrialization and downsizing (Chapter 9); passage of the Patient Protection and Affordable Care Act (Chapter 10); the 2010 BP Deepwater Horizon oil spill in the Gulf of Mexico (Chapter 10); the 2009 climate change summit in Copenhagen (Chapter 10); occupations most vulnerable to offshoring (Chapter 11); and the controversy over the use of GPS and handheld devices to locate cars and people (Chapter 11).
- An Appendix, "Careers in Sociology," has been added at the end of the book.

PEDAGOGY

- Nineteen new Use Your Sociological Imagination exercises challenge students to apply what they have learned to their own life experiences.
- Seven new figures illustrate important sociological trends and developments.
- Seven new cartoons highlight sociological issues.
- Three new Think About It exercises.
- Two new chapter-opening passages spark student interest.
- Two new tables help students to make broad comparisons across time and across the globe.
- A new Summing Up table pulls together coverage of the major theoretical perspectives.

Supplements and Internet Resources

A wealth of complimentary teaching and learning resources is available to students and instructors who use *Sociology Matters*. Students will benefit from the free study aids and topical activities accessible to them at McGraw-Hill's website, www.mhhe.com/schaefersm5e. Among these features are:

- Student Self-Quizzes
- Internet Connection
- Learning Objectives

Instructors also have an Online Learning Center devoted to their needs. They may choose from the following resources:

- Instructor's Manual
- Test Bank
- Chapter PowerPoint slides

What's New in Each Chapter?

CHAPTER 1   THE SOCIOLOGICAL VIEW

- Chapter-opening discussion of the Gulf Coast oil spill and its social effects
- Discussion of how sociologists might study the effects of the Gulf Coast oil spill and the earthquake in Haiti
- Key term treatment of W. E. B. DuBois's concept of double consciousness
- Key term treatment of macrosociology and microsociology
- Discussions of how the Gulf Coast oil spill might be viewed using the functionalist, conflict, and interactionist perspectives
- Use of data from the Bureau of the Census's Current Population Survey to illustrate sampling
- Updated figure, "Impact of a College Education on Income"
- Discussion of Barbara Ehrenreich's book *Nickel and Dimed* as an example of the participant observation method
- Use Your Sociological Imagination exercise
- Coverage of public sociology
- Coverage of the Community Health Assets and Needs Assessment (CHANA) as an example of applied sociology

CHAPTER 2 CULTURE AND SOCIALIZATION

- Streamlined organization for increased readability
- Chapter-opening passage on the struggle to revive native languages in the United States
- Discussion of varying attitudes toward the practice of children marrying adults as an illustration of cultural relativism
- Discussion of McDonald's move toward local development of menus and marketing strategies at overseas restaurants
- Expanded discussion of changes in U.S. college students' values, including environmental values, with figure, "Life Goals of First-Year College Students in the United States, 1966–2009"
- Use Your Sociological Imagination exercise
- Expanded section on sociobiology, with discussion of Charles Darwin's theory of natural selection
- Figure, "The New Normal: Internet at Home"

CHAPTER 3 SOCIAL INTERACTION, GROUPS, AND SOCIAL STRUCTURE

- Discussion of cross-cultural differences in social interaction and social reality
- Discussion of the role of reference groups in anticipatory socialization
- Discussion of how online social networks served as a morale booster for the unemployed during the recent economic downturn
- Discussion of the benefits of participating in virtual worlds
- Use Your Sociological Imagination exercise

CHAPTER 4 DEVIANCE AND SOCIAL CONTROL

- Discussion of a recent replication of Milgram's obedience experiment

CHAPTER 5 STRATIFICATION IN THE UNITED STATES AND GLOBAL INEQUALITY

- Expanded discussion of income inequality in the United States, with figure, "Mean Household Income by Quintile"
- Revision of figure, "Distribution of Wealth in the United States," to emphasize wealth of the top 10 percent of the population
- Discussion of the effect of the recent economic recession on income inequality

- Discussion of the federal government's new Supplemental Poverty Measure (SPM)
- Figure, "Multinational Corporations Compared to Nations"
- Three Use Your Sociological Imagination exercises

CHAPTER 6   INEQUALITY BY RACE AND ETHNICITY

- Coverage of the Development, Relief, and Education for Alien Minors (DREAM) Act in the chapter-opening discussion
- Key term treatment of *White privilege*
- Two Use Your Sociological Imagination exercises

CHAPTER 7   INEQUALITY BY GENDER

- Student research on gender norm transgressions, with table, "An Experiment in Gender Norm Violation by College Students"
- Discussion of investors' reaction to the installation of women on corporate boards of directors
- Use Your Sociological Imagination exercise

CHAPTER 8   SOCIAL INSTITUTIONS: FAMILY AND RELIGION

- Discussion of the Inauguration of President Barack Obama as an example of the institutional function of providing and maintaining a sense of purpose
- Summing Up table, "Sociological Perspectives on Social Institutions"
- Coverage of single-parent families and households headed by a same-sex couple, with cartoon

CHAPTER 9   SOCIAL INSTITUTIONS: EDUCATION, GOVERNMENT, AND THE ECONOMY

- Discussion of the transformative effect of educational programs for the disadvantaged, with figure, "Annual Median Earnings by Educational Level"
- Section, "Capitalism in China," with cartoon
- Discussion of the accelerating effect of the extended economic downturn that began in 2008 on the processes of deindustrialization and downsizing
- Three Use Your Sociological Imagination exercises

CHAPTER **10**   POPULATION, COMMUNITY, HEALTH, AND
THE ENVIRONMENT

- Discussion of passage of the Patient Protection and Affordable Care Act
- Coverage of the BP Deepwater Horizon oil spill in the Gulf of Mexico
- Discussion of conflict over water in Africa
- Coverage of the 2009 climate change summit in Copenhagen
- Discussion of the creation of "green-collar jobs" in green industries
- Five Use Your Sociological Imagination exercises

CHAPTER **11**   SOCIAL MOVEMENTS, SOCIAL CHANGE,
AND TECHNOLOGY

- Figure, "Largest Societies, Real and Virtual"
- Discussion of congressional opposition to President Obama's decision to abandon manned space flights to the moon as an example of vested interests
- Table, "Occupations Most Vulnerable to Offshoring"
- Discussion of the controversy over the use of GPS and handheld devices to locate cars and people
- Two Use Your Sociological Imagination exercises

Acknowledgments

Elizabeth Morgan, who collaborated with me on the first edition, as well as on several editions of my longer introductory textbooks for undergraduates, brought her experience and knowledge to the fifth edition of *Sociology Matters*.

I deeply appreciate the contributions my editors made to this book. Kate Scheinman and Erin Melloy helped to shape this fresh approach to sociology for undergraduates. This edition also benefits from past work by Gina Boedeker, senior sponsoring editor and Meghan Campbell, managing developmental editor, who lent their expertise and experience to its development. I received strong support and encouragement from William Glass, publisher; Patrick Brown, director of marketing; and Sridevi Palani, media project manager. Additional guidance and support came from Erin Melloy, project manager; Brenda Rolwes, design coordinator; Sue Culbertson, buyer; Judy Brody, permissions editor; and Rebecca Lazure with Laserwords for the composition of the fifth edition.

As is evident from these acknowledgments, the preparation of a textbook is truly a team effort. The most valuable member of this effort continues to be my wife, Sandy, who provides the support so necessary to my creative and scholarly activities.

I have had the good fortune to be able to introduce students to sociology for many years. Those students have been enormously helpful in spurring my own sociological imagination. In ways I can fully appreciate but cannot fully acknowledge, their questions in class and queries in the hallway have found their way into this textbook.

Richard T. Schaefer
www.schaefersociology.net
schaeferrt@aol.com

As a full-service publisher of quality educational products, McGraw-Hill does much more than just sell textbooks to your students. We create and publish an extensive array of supplements to support instruction on your campus. Orders of new (versus used) textbooks help us to defray the cost of developing such supplements, which is substantial. Please consult your local McGraw-Hill representative to learn about the availability of the supplements that accompany Sociology Matters. *If you are not sure who your representative is, you can find him or her by using the Rep Locator at www.mhhe.com.*

Academic Reviewers

Many sociologists reviewed this book and offered constructive and thorough evaluations of its content. I would like to thank the following reviewers for their thoughtful comments on the manuscript and its features:

Todd E. Bernhardt
Broward Community College

Rosemarie Best
Warren County Community College

Henry Borne
Holy Cross College

Gayle Gordon Bouzard
Texas State University—San Marcos

Junell Chapman
Ohio Northern University

Cynthia Crisel
Arkansas State University—Mountain Home

Raymond De Vries
St. Olaf College

Furjen Deng
Sam Houston State University

Charles Edgley
University of Arkansas at Little Rock

Barbara Feldman
Seton Hall University

Cynthia Ganote
Vanderbilt University

William Gronfein
*Indiana University—Purdue
University Indianapolis*

Bram Hamovitch
Lakeland Community College

Kristen Hefley
University of Oklahoma, Norman

Michelle Jacob
MiraCosta College

A. J. Jacobs
East Carolina University

Judy G. Kairath
*College of the Desert and
Copper Mountain College*

Ho Hon Leung
SUNY College at Oneonta

Kathleen S. Lowney
Valdosta State University

Scott Lukas
Lake Tahoe College

Derek Martin
*Southern Illinois University—
Carbondale*

Stephanie M. McClure
University of Georgia

Dennis McGrath
Community College of Philadelphia

Jenny McIver
South Georgia College

Melanie Moore
*University of Northern
Colorado*

Angela Orend
University of Louisville

Nelson Pichardo
Central Washington University

James R. Robinson
Oklahoma State University

Josephine Ruggiero
Providence College

Claudia Scholz
*University of Texas at
San Antonio*

Julia Spence
*Johnson County Community
College*

Jim Spickard
University of Redlands

Alison M. St. John
*Moraine Valley Community
College*

Leonard A. Steverson
South Georgia College

Laurel Tripp
University of Maine

Mary Valentine
College of the Canyons

Meifang Zhang
Midlands Technical College

Brief Contents

Contents

The Sociological View

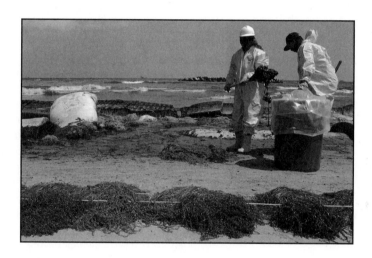

In mid-July 2010, the National Commission on the BP Deepwater Horizon Oil Spill and Offshore Drilling held its first meeting in New Orleans. Although presidential commissions are nothing new, the circumstances of this particular meeting were unusual. Events were still unfolding in the Gulf of Mexico and the surrounding communities even as commission members began to deliberate. On shore, small business owners and workers in the fishing and tourist industries were grappling with the spill's implications for their own livelihoods, as well as for the region as a whole. Workers in the oil industry, still reeling from a government-ordered moratorium on oil drilling throughout the Gulf, were wondering whether they had a future in oil. All were struggling to put food on the table and pay their bills.

In the committee room, there was much disagreement about both the scope of the problem and the spill's consequences. Estimates of the amount of oil that was gushing from the well varied widely. It was obvious, however, that the extent of the contamination dwarfed that of the Exxon *Valdez* spill off the coast of Alaska 20 years earlier. The environmental catastrophe had begun in April with a spectacular explosion on one of BP's drilling platforms, which was followed by a devastating fire. Eleven workers had died in the blast. Since then, Americans had watched helplessly as BP made one unsuccessful attempt after another to cap the damaged well. Although the spill was located far off the coast in extremely deep water, oil slicks soon began to wash up on the shores of Alabama, Louisiana, Mississippi, Florida, and Texas. Photos of oil-soaked birds and dirty beaches filled the news.

What had caused this man-made disaster? What would its economic and environmental impact be? In the months to come, members of the national commission would debate these and other questions. During the course of their investigation, they would call on experts in energy, oceanography, economics, and the environment. Each expert would view the spill through the lens of his or her field of inquiry.

If called, how would a sociologist react to the events just described? Taking a sociological perspective, he or she would ask questions about the people affected by the oil spill. Sociologists are especially interested in how people cluster together in groups based on similar backgrounds or characteristics, such as age, gender, social class, race, or ethnic group. In this case, sociologists would be particularly interested in the occupational groups affected by the disaster—the fishermen, waiters, hotel staffers, and others thrown out of work in the aftermath—as well as in the groups that promote environmental protection.

Sociologists also examine how social patterns change from one generation to the next. The environmental movement began with the first Earth Day in 1970. Although many people today were born well after 1970, a significant percentage of them embrace environmentalism. How did they learn to value the environment—what transmitted that view from one generation to the next? Equally important, why do some people in their age group reject environmentalism?

Finally, sociologists study the organizations that promote certain values, such as environmentalism, as well as the business organizations—some of which are global in scope—whose pursuit of profit so often clashes with environmental protection. How do these organizations contribute to the wise or unwise use of natural resources?

Whatever the subject, sociologists study social patterns that are shared by many people. This focus on the group rather than on the individual is a distinguishing feature of sociology. As the sociologist C. Wright Mills wrote more than half a century ago, if one person is unemployed, his difficulty is a personal problem, but if thousands of people are unemployed, their difficulty is a social problem. Sociologists look for the root causes of such social patterns in the way society is organized and governed (Mills [1959] 2000a).

As a field of study, sociology is extremely broad in scope. You'll see throughout this book the tremendous range of topics sociologists investigate—from tattooing to tweeting, from neighborhood groups to global economic patterns, from peer pressure to class consciousness. Sociologists look at how other people influence your behavior; how the government, religion, and the economy affect you; and how you yourself affect others. These aren't just academic questions. Sociology matters because it illuminates your life and your world, whether you are going to school, working for pay, or raising a family.

This first chapter introduces sociology as a social science, one that is characterized by a special skill called the *sociological imagination*. We'll meet four pioneering thinkers—Émile Durkheim, Max Weber, Karl Max, and W.E.B. DuBois—and discuss the concepts and theoretical perspectives that grew out of their work. We'll see how sociologists use the scientific method to investigate the many questions they pose. Sociologists use surveys, observation, experiments, and existing sources in their research; they often wrestle with ethical issues that arise during their studies. We'll examine some practical uses for their research at the end of the chapter.

What Is Sociology?

Sociology is the scientific study of social behavior and human groups. It focuses primarily on the influence of social relationships on people's attitudes and behavior and on how societies are established and change. This textbook deals with such varied topics as families, the workplace, street gangs, business firms, political parties, genetic engineering, schools, religions, and labor unions. It is concerned with love, poverty, conformity, discrimination, illness, technology, and community.

THE SOCIOLOGICAL IMAGINATION

In attempting to understand social behavior, sociologists rely on a unique type of creative thinking. C. Wright Mills described such thinking as the *sociological imagination*—an awareness of the relationship between an individual and the wider society, both today and in the past. This awareness allows all of us (not just sociologists) to comprehend the links between our immediate, personal social settings and the remote, impersonal social world that surrounds us and helps to shape us (Mills [1959] 2000a).

A key element in the sociological imagination is the ability to view one's own society as an outsider would, rather than only from the perspective of personal experiences and cultural biases. Consider something as simple as the practice of eating while walking. In the United States people think nothing of consuming coffee or chocolate as they walk along the street. Sociologists would see this as a pattern of acceptable behavior because others regard it as acceptable. Yet sociologists need to go beyond one culture to place the practice in perspective. This "normal" behavior is quite unacceptable in some other parts of the world. For example, in Japan people do not eat while walking. Streetside sellers and vending machines dispense food everywhere, but the Japanese will stop to eat or drink whatever they buy before they continue on their way. In their eyes, to engage in another activity while eating shows disrespect for the food preparers, even if the food comes out of a vending machine.

The sociological imagination allows us to go beyond personal experiences and observations to understand broader public issues. Divorce, for example, is unquestionably a personal hardship for a husband and wife who split apart. However, C. Wright Mills advocated using the sociological imagination to view divorce not simply as the personal problem of a particular man or woman but rather as a societal concern. From this perspective, an increase in the divorce rate serves to redefine a major social institution, the family. Today, households frequently include step-parents and half-sisters or -brothers whose parents have divorced and remarried. Through the complexities of the blended family, this private concern becomes a public issue that affects schools, government agencies, businesses, and religious institutions.

The sociological imagination is an empowering tool. It allows us to look beyond a limited understanding of things to see the world and its people in a new way and through a broader lens than we might otherwise use. It may be as simple as understanding why a roommate prefers country music to hip-hop, or it may open up a whole different way of understanding whole populations. For example, in the aftermath of the terrorist attacks on the United States on September 11, 2001, many citizens wanted to understand how Muslims throughout the world perceived their country, and why. From time to time this textbook will offer you the chance to exercise your own sociological imagination in a variety of situations. We'll begin with one that may be close to home for you.

SOCIOLOGY AND THE SOCIAL SCIENCES

Is sociology a science? The term *science* refers to the body of knowledge obtained by methods based on systematic observation. Like researchers in other scientific disciplines, sociologists engage in organized, systematic study of phenomena (in this case, human behavior) in order to enhance understanding. All scientists, whether studying mushrooms or murderers, attempt to collect precise information through methods of study that are as objective as possible. They rely on careful recording of observations and accumulation of data.

Of course, there is a great difference between sociology and physics, between psychology and astronomy. For this reason, the sciences are commonly divided into natural and social sciences. *Natural science* is

Use Your Sociological Imagination

You are walking down the street in your city or hometown. Looking around, you can't help noticing that half or more of the people you see are overweight. How do you explain your observation? If you were C. Wright Mills, how do you think you would explain it?

the study of the physical features of nature and the ways in which they interact and change. Astronomy, biology, chemistry, geology, and physics are all natural sciences. *Social science* is the study of various aspects of human society. The social sciences include sociology, anthropology, economics, history, psychology, and political science.

These social science disciplines have a common focus on the social behavior of people, yet each has a particular orientation. Anthropologists usually study past cultures and preindustrial societies that continue today, as well as the origins of men and women. Economists explore the ways in which people produce and exchange goods and services, along with money and other resources. Historians are concerned with the peoples and events of the past and their significance for us today. Political scientists study international relations, the workings of government, and the exercise of power and authority. Psychologists investigate personality and individual behavior. So what does *sociology* focus on? It emphasizes the influence that society has on people's attitudes and behavior and the ways in which people shape society. Humans are social animals; therefore, sociologists scientifically examine our social relationships with others.

Let's consider how different social sciences would study the impact of the Gulf Coast oil spill, described at the beginning of the chapter. Historians would compare it to the damage done by other oil spills. Economists would conduct research on the economic impact of the damage, not just in the Southeast but throughout the nation and the world. Psychologists would study individual cases to assess the emotional stress of the event. And political scientists would study the stances taken by different elected officials, along with their implications for the government's response to the spill.

What approach would sociologists take? They might look at the spill's impact on different communities, as well as on different social classes. Some might undertake neighborhood studies, to determine how to maintain the integrity of communities hit hard by unemployment. Others might focus on the spill's impact on marginalized groups, such as Vietnamese Americans: a third of all Gulf Coast shrimp fishermen come from that ethnic group. The strength of the social impact would not surprise sociologists, for the affected areas are among the poorest in the United States. In Louisiana and Mississippi in particular, coastal communities were still recovering from the effects of Hurricane Katrina, which had destroyed or severely damaged 300,000 homes five years earlier. When the oil spill left countless families without an income, most residents had no savings left to fall back on—no way to tide themselves over until the next paycheck.

Sociologists would take a similar approach in studying the earthquake that hit Port-au-Prince, the capital of Haiti, in 2010. They might consider the possibility of reversing Haitians' generation-long migration from the countryside to the capital city, by making life in rural areas more sustainable. They might study the use of new media, such as Twitter, to funnel donations to charities. They might conduct short- and long-term research on the adoption of Haitian orphans by U.S. families, many of them White. Or they might evaluate current and potential U.S. policy toward Haitian immigrants, refugees, and deportees.

Sociologists put their sociological imaginations to work in a variety of areas—including gender, the family, human ecology, and religion. Throughout this textbook, you will see how sociologists develop theories and conduct research to study and better understand societies. And you will be encouraged to use your own sociological imagination to examine the United States (and other societies) from the viewpoint of a respectful but questioning outsider.

SOCIOLOGY AND COMMON SENSE

Sociology focuses on the study of human behavior. Yet we all have experience with human behavior and at least some knowledge of it. All of us might well have theories about why people buy lottery tickets, for example, or why people become homeless. Our theories and opinions typically come from "common sense"—that is, from our experiences and conversations, from what we read, from what we see on television, and so forth.

In our daily lives, we rely on common sense to get us through many unfamiliar situations. However, this commonsense knowledge, while sometimes accurate, is not always reliable, because it rests on commonly held beliefs rather than on systematic analysis of facts. It was once considered "common sense" to accept the idea that the earth was flat—a view rightly questioned by Pythagoras and Aristotle. Incorrect commonsense notions are not just a part of the distant past; they remain with us today.

Contrary to the saying "The love of money is the root of all evil," for example, sociologists have found that in reality, affluence brings not only nicer cars and longer vacations but also better health and a significantly reduced exposure to pollution of all types. Another commonsense belief, "Love knows no reason," does not stand up to sociological research on courtship and marriage. The choice of a lifetime partner is generally limited by societal expectations and confined within boundaries defined by age, money, education, ethnicity, religion, and even height. Cupid's arrow flies only in certain directions (Ruane and Cerulo 2004).

Contrary to the common notion that women tend to be chatty compared to men, furthermore, researchers have found little difference between the sexes in terms of their talkativeness. Over a five-year period they placed unobtrusive microphones on 396 college students in various fields, at campuses in Mexico as well as the United States. They found that both men and women spoke about 16,000 words per day (Mehl et al. 2007).

Similarly, "common sense" tells us that in the United States today, military marriages are more likely to end in separation or divorce than in the past due to the strain of long deployments in Iraq and Afghanistan. Yet a study released in 2007 shows no significant increase in the divorce rate among U.S. soldiers over the last decade. In fact, the rate of marital dissolution among members of the military is comparable to that of nonmilitary families. Interestingly, this is not the first study to disprove the widely held notion that military service strains the marital bond. Two generations earlier, during the Vietnam era, researchers came to the same conclusion (Call and Teachman 1991; Karney and Crown 2007).

Like other social scientists, sociologists do not accept something as a fact because "everyone knows it." Instead, each piece of information must be tested and recorded, then analyzed in relation to other data. Sociologists rely on scientific studies in order to describe and understand a social environment. At times, the findings of sociologists may seem like common sense, because they deal with familiar facets of everyday life. The difference is that such findings have been *tested* by researchers. Common sense now tells us that the earth is round. But this particular commonsense notion is based on centuries of scientific work that began with the breakthroughs made by Pythagoras and Aristotle.

What Is Sociological Theory?

Why do people commit suicide? One traditional commonsense answer is that people inherit the desire to kill themselves. Another view is that sunspots drive people to take their own lives. These explanations may not seem especially convincing to contemporary researchers, but they represent beliefs widely held as recently as 1900.

Sociologists are not particularly interested in why any one individual commits suicide; they are more concerned with identifying the social forces that systematically cause some people to take their own lives. In order to undertake this research, sociologists develop a theory that offers a general explanation of suicidal behavior.

We can think of theories as attempts to explain events, forces, materials, ideas, or behavior in a comprehensive manner. Within sociology, a ***theory*** is a set of statements that seeks to explain problems, actions, or behavior. An effective theory may have both explanatory and predictive power. That is, it can help us to see the relationships among seemingly isolated phenomena, as well as to understand how one type of change in an environment leads to other changes.

The World Health Organization (2010) estimates that nearly 1 million people commit suicide each year. More than a hundred years ago, a sociologist tried to look at suicide data scientifically. Émile Durkheim

([1897] 1951) developed a highly original theory about the relationship between suicide and social factors. He was primarily concerned not with the personalities of individual suicide victims but rather with suicide *rates* and how they varied from country to country. As a result, when he looked at the number of reported suicides in France, England, and Denmark in 1869, he noted the total population of each country so that he could determine the rate of suicide in each. He found that whereas England had only 67 reported suicides per million inhabitants, France had 135 per million and Denmark had 277 per million. The question then became: "Why did Denmark have a comparatively high rate of reported suicides?"

Durkheim went much deeper into his investigation of suicide rates; the result was his landmark work *Suicide,* published in 1897. He refused to automatically accept unproven explanations regarding suicide, including the beliefs that cosmic forces or inherited tendencies caused such deaths. Instead, he focused on such problems as the cohesiveness or lack of cohesiveness of religious, social, and occupational groups.

Durkheim's research suggested that suicide, while a solitary act, is related to group life. Protestants had much higher suicide rates than Catholics; the unmarried had much higher rates than married people; soldiers were more likely to take their lives than civilians. In addition, there seemed to be higher rates of suicide in times of peace than in times of war and revolution, and in times of economic instability and recession rather than in times of prosperity. Durkheim concluded that the suicide rate of a society reflected the extent to which people were or were not integrated into the group life of the society.

Émile Durkheim, like many other social scientists, developed a theory to explain how individual behavior can be understood within a social context. He pointed out the influence of groups and societal forces on what had always been viewed as a highly personal act. Clearly, Durkheim offered a more *scientific* explanation for the causes of suicide than that of sunspots or inherited tendencies. His theory has predictive power, since it suggests that suicide rates will rise or fall in conjunction with certain social and economic changes.

Of course, a theory—even the best of theories—is not a final statement about human behavior. Durkheim's theory of suicide is no exception. Sociologists continue to examine factors that contribute to differences in suicide rates around the world and to a particular society's rate of suicide. For example, although the overall rate of suicide in New Zealand is only marginally higher than the rate in the United States, the suicide rate among young people is 41 percent higher in New Zealand. Sociologists and psychiatrists from that country suggest that their remote, sparsely populated society maintains exaggerated standards of masculinity that are especially difficult for young males. Gay adolescents who fail to conform to their peers' preference for sports are particularly vulnerable to suicide (Shenon 1995).

The Development of Sociology

People have always been curious about sociological matters—such as how we get along with others, what we do for a living, and whom we select as our leaders. Philosophers and religious authorities of ancient and medieval societies made countless observations about human behavior. They did not test or verify their observations scientifically; nevertheless, those observations often became the foundation for moral codes. Several of the early social philosophers predicted that a systematic study of human behavior would one day emerge. Beginning in the 19th century, European theorists made pioneering contributions to the development of a science of human behavior.

EARLY THINKERS: COMTE, MARTINEAU, AND SPENCER

The 19th century was an unsettled time in France. The French monarchy had been deposed in the revolution of 1789, and Napoleon had subsequently suffered defeat in his effort to conquer Europe. Amid this chaos, philosophers considered how society might be improved. Auguste Comte (1798–1857), credited with being the most influential of the philosophers of the early 1800s, believed that a theoretical science of society and a systematic investigation of behavior were needed to improve French society. He coined the term *sociology* to apply to the science of human behavior.

Writing in the 1800s, Comte feared that the excesses of the French Revolution had permanently impaired France's stability. Yet he hoped that the systematic study of social behavior would eventually lead to more rational human interactions. In Comte's hierarchy of sciences, sociology was at the top. He called it the "queen," and its practitioners "scientist-priests." This French theorist did not simply give sociology its name; he also presented a rather ambitious challenge to the fledgling discipline.

Scholars learned of Comte's works largely through translations by the English sociologist Harriet Martineau (1802–1876). As a sociologist, Martineau was a pathbreaker in her own right. She offered insightful observations of the customs and social practices of both her native Britain and the United States. Martineau's book *Society in America* ([1837] 1962) examines religion, politics, child rearing, and immigration in the young nation. This groundbreaking book gives special attention to social class distinctions and to such factors as gender and race. Martineau ([1838] 1989) also wrote the first book on sociological methods.

Martineau's writings emphasized the impact that the economy, law, trade, health, and population could have on social problems. She spoke out in favor of the rights of women, the emancipation of slaves, and religious tolerance. Later in life, deafness did not keep her from being

Use Your Sociological Imagination

If you were Durkheim's successor in his research on suicide, how would you investigate the factors that may explain the increase in suicide rates among young people in the United States today?

an activist. In Martineau's ([1837] 1962) view, intellectuals and scholars should not simply offer observations of social conditions; they should *act* on their convictions in a manner that will benefit society. That is why Martineau conducted research on the nature of female employment and pointed to the need for further investigation of the issue (Deegan 2003; Hill and Hoecker-Drysdale 2001).

Another important contributor to the discipline of sociology is Herbert Spencer (1820–1903). A relatively prosperous Victorian Englishman, Spencer (unlike Martineau) did not feel compelled to correct or improve society; instead, he merely hoped to understand it better. Drawing on Charles Darwin's study *On the Origin of Species,* Spencer applied the concept of evolution of the species to societies in order to explain how they change, or evolve, over time. Similarly, he adapted Darwin's evolutionary view of the "survival of the fittest" by arguing that it is "natural" that some people are rich while others are poor.

Spencer's approach to societal change was extremely popular in his own lifetime. Unlike Comte, Spencer suggested that since societies are bound to change eventually, one need not be highly critical of present social arrangements or work actively for social change. This viewpoint appealed to many influential people in England and the United States who had a vested interest in the status quo and were suspicious of social thinkers who endorsed change.

ÉMILE DURKHEIM

As discussed earlier, Émile Durkheim made many pioneering contributions to sociology, including his important theoretical work on suicide. The son of a rabbi, Durkheim (1858–1917) was educated in both France and Germany. He established an impressive academic reputation and was appointed one of the first professors of sociology in France. Above all, Durkheim will be remembered for his insistence that behavior must be understood within a larger social context, not just in individualistic terms.

To give one example of this emphasis, Durkheim ([1912] 2001) developed a fundamental thesis to help understand all forms of society. Through intensive study of the Arunta, an Australian tribe, he focused on the functions that religion performs and underscored the role that group life plays in defining what we consider to be religious. Durkheim concluded that, like other forms of group behavior, religion reinforces a group's solidarity.

Like many other sociologists, Durkheim did not limit his interests to one aspect of social behavior. Later in this book, we will consider his thinking on crime and punishment, religion, and the workplace. Few sociologists have had such a dramatic impact on so many different areas within the discipline.

MAX WEBER

Another important early theorist is Max Weber (pronounced "VAY-ber"). Born in Germany in 1864, Weber studied legal and economic history, but he gradually developed an interest in sociology. Eventually, he became a professor at various German universities. Weber taught his students that they should employ *Verstehen* (pronounced "Fair-SHTAY-en"), the German word for "understanding" or "insight," in their intellectual work. He pointed out that we cannot analyze much of our social behavior by the same criteria we use to measure weight or temperature. To fully comprehend behavior, we must learn the subjective meanings people attach to their actions—how they themselves view and explain their behavior.

We also owe credit to Weber for a key conceptual tool: the ideal type. An *ideal type* is a construct, a made-up model that serves as a measuring rod against which actual cases can be evaluated. In his own works, Weber identified various characteristics of bureaucracy as an ideal type (discussed in detail in Chapter 3). In presenting this model of bureaucracy, Weber was not describing any particular organization, nor was he using the term *ideal* in a way that suggested a positive evaluation. Instead, his purpose was to provide a useful standard for measuring how bureaucratic an actual organization is (Gerth and Mills 1958). Later in this textbook, we will use the concept of an ideal type to study the family, religion, authority, and economic systems and to analyze bureaucracy.

KARL MARX

Karl Marx (1818–1883) shared with Durkheim and Weber a dual interest in abstract philosophical issues and the concrete reality of everyday life. Unlike them, Marx was so critical of existing institutions that a conventional academic career was impossible for him. He spent most of his life in exile from his native Germany.

Marx's personal life was a difficult struggle. When a paper that he had written was suppressed, he fled to France. In Paris, he met Friedrich Engels (1820–1895), with whom he formed a lifelong friendship. The two lived at a time when European and North American economic life was increasingly dominated by the factory rather than the farm.

In 1847, in London, Marx and Engels attended secret meetings of an illegal coalition of labor unions known as the Communist League. The following year, they prepared a platform called *The Communist Manifesto,* in which they argued that the masses of people who have no resources other than their labor (whom they referred to as the *proletariat*) should unite to fight for the overthrow of capitalist societies.

In Marx's analysis, society was fundamentally divided between classes that clash in pursuit of their own class interests. When he examined the industrial societies of his time, such as Germany, England, and the United States, he saw the factory as the center of conflict between the exploiters (the owners of the means of production) and the exploited (the workers). Marx viewed these relationships in systematic terms; that is, he believed that an entire system of economic, social, and political relationships maintained the power and dominance of the owners over the workers. Consequently, Marx and Engels argued, the working class needed to *overthrow* the existing class system. Marx's influence on contemporary thinking has been dramatic. His writings inspired those who were later to lead communist revolutions in Russia, China, Cuba, Vietnam, and elsewhere.

Even apart from the political revolutions that his work fostered, Marx's significance is profound. Marx emphasized the *group* identifications and associations that influence an individual's place in society. This area of study is the major focus of contemporary sociology. Throughout this textbook, we will consider how membership in a particular gender classification, age group, racial group, or economic class affects a person's attitudes and behavior. In an important sense, we can trace this way of understanding society back to the pioneering work of Karl Marx.

W.E.B. DUBOIS

Marx's work encouraged sociologists to view society through the eyes of those segments of the population that rarely influence decision making. In the United States, some early Black sociologists, including W.E.B. DuBois (1868–1963), conducted research that they hoped would assist in the struggle for a racially egalitarian society. DuBois (pronounced doo-BOYSS) believed that knowledge was essential in combating prejudice and achieving tolerance and justice. Sociologists, he contended, needed to draw on scientific principles to study social problems such as those experienced by Blacks in the United States. To separate opinion from fact, he advocated basic research on the lives of Blacks. Through his in-depth studies of urban life, both White and Black, in cities such as Philadelphia and Atlanta, DuBois ([1899] 1995) made a major contribution to sociology.

Like Durkheim and Weber, DuBois saw the importance of religion to society. However, he tended to focus on religion at the community level and the role of the church in the lives of its members ([1903] 2003). DuBois had little patience with theorists such as Herbert Spencer, who seemed content with the status quo. He believed that the granting of full political rights to Blacks was essential to their social and economic progress.

Because many of his ideas challenged the status quo, DuBois did not find a receptive audience within either the government or the academic world. As a result, he became increasingly involved with organizations whose members questioned the established social order. In 1909 he helped to found the National Association for the Advancement of Colored People, better known today as the NAACP (Wortham 2008).

DuBois's insights have been lasting. In 1897 he coined the term *double consciousness* to refer to the division of an individual's identity into two or more social realities. He used the term to describe the experience of being Black in White America. Today, an African American holds the most powerful office in the nation, President of the United States. Yet for millions of African Americans, the reality of being Black in the United States typically is not one of power ([1903] 1961).

MODERN DEVELOPMENTS

Sociology today builds on the firm foundation developed by Émile Durkheim, Max Weber, Karl Marx, and W.E.B. DuBois. However, the discipline has certainly not remained stagnant over the last 100 years. While Europeans have continued to make contributions, sociologists from throughout the world, and especially the United States, have advanced sociological theory and research. Their new insights have helped us to better understand the workings of society.

Charles Horton Cooley Charles Horton Cooley (1864–1929) is typical of the sociologists who came to prominence in the early 1900s. Born in Ann Arbor, Michigan, Cooley received his graduate training in economics but later became a sociology professor at the University of Michigan. Like other early sociologists, he had become interested in this "new" discipline while pursuing a related area of study.

Cooley shared the desire of Durkheim, Weber, W.E.B. DuBois, and Marx to learn more about society. But to do so effectively, he preferred to use the sociological perspective to look first at smaller units—intimate, face-to-face groups such as families, gangs, and friendship networks. He saw these groups as the seedbeds of society, in the sense that they shape people's ideals, beliefs, values, and social nature. Cooley's work increased our understanding of groups of relatively small size.

Jane Addams In the early 1900s, many leading sociologists in the United States saw themselves as social reformers dedicated to systematically studying and then improving a corrupt society. They were genuinely concerned about the lives of immigrants in the nation's growing cities, whether those immigrants came from Europe or from the rural American south. Early female sociologists, in particular, often took active roles in poor urban areas as leaders of community centers known as *settlement houses*. For example, Jane Addams (1860–1935), a member of the American Sociological Society, cofounded the famous Chicago settlement, Hull House.

Addams and other pioneering female sociologists commonly combined intellectual inquiry, social service work, and political activism—all with the goal of assisting the underprivileged and creating a more egalitarian society. For example, working with the Black journalist and educator Ida Wells-Barnett, Addams successfully prevented racial segregation in the Chicago public schools. Addams's efforts to establish a juvenile court system and a women's trade union also reveal the practical focus of her work (Addams 1910, 1930; Deegan 1991; Lengermann and Niebrugge-Brantley 1998).

By the middle of the 20th century, however, the focus of the discipline had shifted. Sociologists for the most part restricted themselves to theorizing and gathering information; the aim of transforming society was left to social workers and others. This shift away from social reform was accompanied by a growing commitment to scientific methods of research and to value-free interpretation of data. Not all sociologists were happy with this emphasis. A new organization, the Society for the Study of Social Problems, was created in 1950 to deal more directly with social inequality and other social ills.

Robert Merton   Sociologist Robert Merton (1910–2003) made an important contribution to the field by successfully combining theory and research. Born in 1910 to Slavic immigrant parents in Philadelphia, Merton subsequently won a scholarship to Temple University. He continued his studies at Harvard, where he acquired his lifelong interest in sociology. Merton's teaching career was based at Columbia University.

Merton produced a theory that is one of the most frequently cited explanations of deviant behavior. He noted different ways in which people attempt to achieve success in life. In his view, some may deviate from the socially agreed-upon goal of accumulating material goods or the socially accepted means of achieving that goal. For example, in Merton's classification scheme, "innovators" are people who accept the goal of pursuing material wealth but use illegal means to do so, including robbery, burglary, and extortion. Merton based his explanation of crime on individual behavior—influenced by society's approved goals and means—yet it has wider applications. It helps to account for the high crime rates among the nation's poor, who may see no hope of advancing themselves through traditional roads to success. Chapter 4 discusses Merton's theory in greater detail.

Merton also emphasized that sociologists should strive to bring together the "macro-level" and "micro-level" approaches to studying society. *Macrosociology* concentrates on large-scale phenomena or entire civilizations. For example, Emile Durkheim's cross-cultural study of suicide was a macro-level analysis. In contrast, *microsociology* concentrates on small groups, often through experimental means. Micro-level investigations are particularly useful to sociologists who study everyday forms of social interaction, such as routine encounters on the job and in public places.

Pierre Bourdieu   Increasingly, scholars in the United States have been drawing on the insights of sociologists in other countries. The ideas of the late French sociologist Pierre Bourdieu (1930–2002) have found a broad following both in North America and elsewhere. As a young man, Bourdieu did fieldwork in Algeria during its struggle for independence from France. Today, scholars study Bourdieu's research techniques as well as his conclusions.

Bourdieu wrote about how capital in its many forms sustains individuals and families from one generation to the next. To Bourdieu, *capital* included not just material goods, but the accumulation of knowledge, prestige, culture, and formal schooling. Capital can also be social in nature, from social connections such as friendship networks to the support of family and kinfolk. In this respect, Bourdieu's work represents a continuation of the insights of such early social thinkers as Marx and Weber (Bourdieu and Passerson 1990; Sallaz and Zavisca 2007).

Today sociology reflects the diverse contributions of earlier theorists. As sociologists approach such topics as divorce, drug addiction, and religious cults, they can draw on the theoretical insights of the discipline's pioneers. A careful reader can hear Comte, Durkheim, Weber, Marx, DuBois, Cooley, Addams, and many others speaking through the pages of current research. Sociology has also broadened beyond the intellectual confines of North America and Europe. Contributions to the discipline now come from sociologists studying and researching human behavior in other parts of the world. In describing the work of today's sociologists, it is helpful to examine a number of influential theoretical approaches (also known as *perspectives*).

Major Theoretical Perspectives

Sociologists view society in different ways. Some see the social world basically as a stable, ongoing entity. They are impressed with the endurance of the family, organized religion, and other social institutions. Some see society in terms of many conflicting groups, competing for scarce resources. To other sociologists, the most fascinating aspects of the social world are the everyday, routine interactions among individuals, which we often take for granted. These three views, the ones most widely used by sociologists, are the functionalist, conflict, and interactionist perspectives. Together, they will provide an introductory look at the discipline.

FUNCTIONALIST PERSPECTIVE

Think of society as a living organism in which each part of the organism contributes to its survival. This view is the *functionalist perspective* (also referred to as the *structural functionalist approach*).

The functionalist perspective emphasizes the way that the parts of a society are structured to maintain its stability. In examining any aspect of society, then, functionalists emphasize the contribution that it makes to overall social stability.

In evaluating the effects of the Gulf oil spill, for example, functionalists would stress society's supportive function. They might expect a revitalization of the environmental movement, as happened in the early 1900s after the damming of Hetch Hetchy Valley, just outside Yosemite, as well as in the 1990s after wildfires swept through the Everglades. Functionalists might also note full employment in selected occupations, such as the manufacture of containment booms, even when jobs in other industries were scarce. They would observe that churches and charity groups provided spiritual and material support to households affected by the oil spill. And they would not be surprised that because offshore oil drilling is an integral part of the Gulf Coast economy, the Governor of Louisiana strongly opposed a moratorium on deep-sea drilling, despite concern about its safety.

Talcott Parsons (1902–1979), a Harvard University sociologist, was a key figure in the development of functionalist theory. Parsons had been greatly influenced by the work of Émile Durkheim, Max Weber, and other European sociologists. For over four decades, Parsons dominated sociology in the United States with his advocacy of functionalism. He saw any society as a vast network of connected parts, each of which helps to maintain the system as a whole. According to the functionalist approach, if an aspect of social life does not contribute to a society's stability or survival—if it does not serve some identifiably useful function or promote value consensus among members of a society—it will not be passed on from one generation to the next.

Dysfunctions Functionalists acknowledge that not all parts of a society contribute to its stability all the time. A *dysfunction* refers to an element or process of a society that may actually disrupt the social system or reduce its stability.

We view many dysfunctional behavior patterns, such as homicide, as undesirable. Yet we should not automatically interpret them in this way. The evaluation of a dysfunction depends on one's own values, or as the saying goes, on "where you sit." For example, the official view in prisons in the United States is that inmate gangs should be eradicated because they are dysfunctional to smooth operations. Yet some guards have actually come to view prison gangs as a functional part of their jobs. The danger posed by gangs creates a "threat to security," requiring increased surveillance and more overtime work for guards, as well as requests for special staffing to address gang problems (G. Scott 2001).

Manifest and Latent Functions A college catalog typically states various functions of the institution. It may inform you, for example, that the university intends to "offer each student a broad education in classical and contemporary thought, in the humanities, in the sciences, and in the arts." However, it would be quite a surprise to find a catalog that declared, "This university was founded in 1895 to assist people in finding a marriage partner." No college catalog will declare this as the purpose of the university. Yet societal institutions serve many functions, some of them quite subtle. The university, in fact, *does* facilitate mate selection.

Robert Merton (1968) made an important distinction between manifest and latent functions. **Manifest functions** of institutions are open, stated, conscious functions. They involve the intended, recognized consequences of an aspect of society, such as the university's role in certifying academic competence and excellence. By contrast, **latent functions** are unconscious or unintended functions that may reflect hidden purposes of an institution. One latent function of universities is to serve as a meeting ground for people seeking marital partners.

CONFLICT PERSPECTIVE

In contrast to the functionalists' emphasis on stability and consensus, conflict sociologists see the social world in continual struggle. Proponents of the **conflict perspective** assume that social behavior is best understood in terms of conflict or tension between competing groups. Such conflict need not be violent; it can take the form of labor negotiations, party politics, competition between religious groups for members, or disputes over the federal budget.

Because conflict theorists see the social order in this way, they would emphasize the coercion and exploitation that underlies relations between the oil industry and Gulf Coast communities. The oil industry, they would note, is a form of big business, in which profits are considered more important than the health and safety of workers. Conflict theorists would also emphasize the often-overlooked effect of the Gulf Coast oil spill on minority groups living in inland communities, including Vietnamese Americans, American Indian tribal groups, and African Americans. These groups, which were living a marginal existence before the spill, endured particularly significant economic setbacks after the spill. Finally, conflict theorists would note that although news outlets tend to focus on oil spills that affect wealthy industrial countries, often the worst spills afflict communities in less well-off developing nations, such as Nigeria.

Throughout most of the 1900s, advocates of the functionalist perspective had the upper hand among sociologists in the United States. However, proponents of the conflict approach have become increasingly persuasive since the late 1960s. The widespread social unrest resulting from battles over civil rights, bitter divisions over the war in Vietnam, the rise of the feminist and gay liberation movements, the Watergate scandal, urban riots, and confrontations at abortion clinics offered support for the conflict approach—the view that our social world is characterized by continual struggle between competing groups. Currently, sociologists accept conflict theory as one valid way to gain insight into a society.

The Marxist View   As we saw earlier, Karl Marx viewed the struggle between social classes as inevitable, given the exploitation of workers under capitalism. Expanding on Marx's work, sociologists and other social scientists have come to see conflict not merely as a class phenomenon but as a part of everyday life in all societies. In studying any culture, organization, or social group, sociologists want to know who benefits, who suffers, and who dominates at the expense of others. They are concerned with the conflicts between women and men, parents and children, cities and suburbs, and Whites and Blacks, to name only a few. Conflict theorists are interested in how society's institutions—including the family, government, religion, education, and the media—may help to maintain the privileges of some groups and keep others in a subservient position. Their emphasis on social change and the redistribution of resources makes conflict theorists more "radical" and "activist" than functionalists (Dahrendorf 1959).

Feminist Perspective   Sociologists began embracing the feminist perspective in the 1970s, although it has a long tradition in many other disciplines. Proponents of the *feminist perspective* view inequity based on gender as central to all behavior and organization. Because this perspective clearly focuses on one aspect of inequality, it is often allied with the conflict perspective. But unlike conflict theorists, those who hold to the feminist perspective tend to focus on the relationships of everyday life, just as interactionists would. Drawing on the work of Marx and Engels, many contemporary feminist theorists view women's subordination as inherent in capitalist societies. Some radical feminist theorists, however, view the oppression of women as inevitable in *all* male-dominated societies, whether capitalist, socialist, or communist.

An early example of this perspective (long before the label came into use by sociologists) can be seen in the life and writings of Ida Wells-Barnett (1862–1931). Following her groundbreaking publications in the 1890s on the practice of lynching Black Americans, she became an advocate in the women's rights campaign, especially the struggle to win the vote for women. Like feminist theorists who succeeded her, Wells-Barnett used her analysis of society as a means of resisting oppression. In her case, she researched what it meant to be African American, a woman in the United States, and a Black woman in the United States (Wells-Barnett 1970).

Feminist scholarship has broadened our understanding of social behavior by extending the analysis beyond the male point of view. In the past, studies of physical violence typically failed to include domestic violence, in which women are the chief victims. Not only was there a void in the research; in the field, law enforcement agencies were ill-prepared to deal with such violence. Similarly, feminists have complained that studies of "children having children" focus almost entirely on the characteristics and behavior of unwed teenage mothers, ignoring the unwed father's role. They have called for more scrutiny of boys and their behavior, as well as their parents and their role models. In sum, the feminist approach moves women from the margins of scientific inquiry to the center (Ferree 2005; Fields 2005; hooks 1994).

You are a sociologist who uses the conflict perspective to study various aspects of our society. How do you think you would interpret the practice of prostitution? Contrast this view with the functionalist perspective. Do you think your comments would differ if you took the feminist view, and if so, how?

INTERACTIONIST PERSPECTIVE

Workers interacting on the job, encounters in public places like bus stops and parks, behavior in small groups—these are all aspects of microsociology that catch the attention of interactionists. Whereas functionalist and conflict theorists both analyze large-scale, societywide patterns of behavior, proponents of the *interactionist perspective* generalize about everyday forms of social interaction in order to understand society as a whole. In the 1990s, for example, the workings of juries became a subject of public scrutiny. High-profile trials ended in verdicts that left some people shaking their heads. Long before jury members were being interviewed on their front lawns following trials, interactionists tried to better understand behavior in the small-group setting of a jury deliberation room.

In studying the social order, interactionists are especially interested in shared understandings of everyday behavior. They would examine the Gulf Coast oil spill on a micro level, by focusing on how it shaped personal relations and day-to-day social behavior. Difficult times, for example, often strengthen ties among neighbors and family members, who depend on one another for help. At the same time, stressful events can contribute to social breakdowns, from divorce to suicide. Observations like these were made two decades ago in the aftermath of the Exxon *Valdez* oil spill.

Though the functionalist and conflict approaches were initiated in Europe, interactionism developed first in the United States. George Herbert Mead (1863–1931) is widely regarded as the founder of the interactionist perspective. Mead taught at the University of Chicago from 1893 until his death. His sociological analysis, like that of Charles Horton Cooley, often focused on human interactions within one-to-one situations and small groups. Mead was interested in observing the most minute forms of communication—smiles, frowns, the nodding of one's head—and in understanding how such individual behavior was influenced by the larger context of a group or society. Despite his innovative views, Mead only occasionally wrote articles, and never a book. He was an extremely popular teacher; in fact, most of his insights have come to us through edited volumes of lectures that his students published after his death.

Interactionism is a sociological framework in which human beings are seen to be living in a world of meaningful objects. These "objects" may include material things, actions, other people, relationships, and even symbols. The interactionist perspective is sometimes referred to as the *symbolic interactionist perspective,* because interactionists see symbols as an especially important part of human communication. Symbols carry shared social meanings that are generally recognized by all members of a society. However, some symbols carry different meanings for different groups of people. To some people in the United States, for example, the Confederate flag symbolizes respect for their rich cultural heritage; to others, it represents the subjugation of their civil rights.

Different cultures may use different symbols to convey the same idea. For example, consider the different ways various societies portray suicide without the use of words. People in the United States point a finger at the head (shooting); urban Japanese bring a fist against the stomach (stabbing); and the South Fore of Papua, New Guinea, clench a hand at the throat (hanging). These symbolic interactions are classified as a form of ***nonverbal communication,*** which can include many other gestures, facial expressions, and postures (Masuda et al. 2008).

What symbols at your college or university have special meaning for students?

THE SOCIOLOGICAL APPROACH

Which perspective should a sociologist use in studying human behavior—functionalist, conflict, interactionist, feminist? Despite their differences, proponents of these viewpoints have much in common. All would agree, for example, that disasters are worthy subjects of investigation. All would admit that there is much more to be learned about the Gulf Coast oil spill than can be addressed from a single theoretical perspective. In fact, sociologists make use of all the perspectives summarized in Table 1–1, since each offers unique insights into the same issue. We can gain the broadest understanding of our society, then, by drawing on all the major perspectives, noting where they overlap and where they diverge.

Although no one approach is "correct," and sociologists draw on all of them for various purposes, many sociologists tend to favor one particular perspective over others. A sociologist's theoretical orientation influences his or her approach to a research problem in important ways. The choice of what to study, how to study it, and what questions to pose (or not to pose) can all be influenced by a researcher's theoretical orientation. In the next part of this chapter, we will see how sociologists have adapted the scientific method to their discipline and how they apply that method in surveys, case observations, and experiments. Bear in mind, though, that even with meticulous attention to all the steps in the scientific method, a researcher's work will always be guided by his or her theoretical viewpoint. Research results, like theories, shine a spotlight on one part of the stage, leaving other parts in relative darkness.

Table 1–1 Comparing Major Theoretical Perspectives

	Functionalist	Conflict	Interactionist	Feminist
View of society	Stable, well integrated	Characterized by tension and struggle between groups	Active in influencing and affecting everyday social interaction	Characterized by gender inequality, whose causes and solutions vary
View of the individual	People are socialized to perform societal functions	People are shaped by power, coercion, and authority	People manipulate symbols and create their social worlds through interaction	People differ according to their social class, race, ethnicity, age, sexual orientation, and physical ability
View of the social order	Maintained through cooperation and consensus	Maintained through force and coercion	Maintained by shared understanding of everyday behavior	Maintained by views that exclude women
View of social change	Change is predictable and reinforcing	Change takes place all the time and may have positive consequences	Reflected in people's social positions and their communications with others	Essential in order to bring about equality
Example	Public punishments reinforce the social order	Laws reinforce the positions of those in power	People respect laws or disobey them based on their own past experience	Domestic violence, date rape, and economic inequality must be eliminated

What Is the Scientific Method?

Like all of us, sociologists are interested in the central questions of our time. Is the family falling apart? Why is there so much crime in the United States? Is the world lagging behind in its ability to feed the population? Such issues concern most people, whether or not they have academic training. However, unlike the typical citizen, the sociologist is committed to using the scientific method in studying society. The *scientific method* is a systematic, organized series of steps that ensures maximum objectivity and consistency in researching a problem.

Many of us will never actually conduct scientific research. Why, then, is it important that we understand the scientific method? Because it plays a major role in the workings of our society. Residents of the United States are constantly being bombarded with "facts" or "data." A television reporter informs us that "one in every two marriages in this country now ends in divorce." An advertiser cites supposedly scientific studies to prove that a particular product is superior. Such claims may be accurate or exaggerated. We can better evaluate such information—and will not be fooled so easily—if we are familiar with the standards of scientific research. These standards are quite stringent and demand as strict adherence as possible.

The scientific method requires precise preparation in developing useful research. Otherwise, the research data collected may not prove accurate. Sociologists and other researchers follow five basic steps in the scientific method: (1) defining the problem, (2) reviewing the literature, (3) formulating the hypothesis, (4) selecting the research design and then collecting and analyzing data, and (5) developing the conclusion (see Figure 1–1). We'll use an actual example to illustrate the workings of the scientific method.

DEFINING THE PROBLEM

Does it "pay" to go to college? Some people make great sacrifices and work hard to get a college education. Parents borrow money for their children's tuition. Students work part-time jobs or even take full-time positions while attending evening or weekend classes. Does it pay off? Are there monetary returns for getting that degree?

The first step in any research project is to state as clearly as possible what you hope to investigate—that is, *define the problem.* In this instance, we are interested in knowing how schooling relates to income. We want to find out the earnings of people with different levels of formal schooling. Early on, any social science researcher must develop an operational definition of each concept being studied. An **operational definition** is an explanation of an abstract concept that is specific enough to allow a researcher to assess the concept. For example, a sociologist interested in status might use membership in exclusive social clubs as an operational definition of status. Someone studying prejudice might consider a person's unwillingness to hire or work with members of minority groups as an operational definition of prejudice. In our example, we need to develop two operational definitions—one for education and the other for earnings—in order to study whether it pays to get an advanced educational degree.

Initially, we will take a functionalist perspective (although we may end up incorporating other approaches). We will argue that opportunities

Figure 1–1
The Scientific Method

for more earning power are related to level of schooling and that schools prepare students for employment.

REVIEWING THE LITERATURE

By conducting a *review of the literature*—the relevant scholarly studies and information—researchers refine the problem under study, clarify possible techniques to be used in collecting data, and eliminate or reduce avoidable mistakes. In our example, we would examine information about the salaries for different occupations. We would see if jobs that require more academic training are better rewarded. It would also be appropriate to review other studies on the relationship between education and income.

The review of the literature would soon tell us that many other factors besides years of schooling influence earning potential. For example, we would learn that the children of richer parents are more likely to go to college than are those from modest backgrounds. As a result, we might consider the possibility that the richer parents may also help their children to secure better-paying jobs after graduation.

FORMULATING THE HYPOTHESIS

After reviewing earlier research and drawing on the contributions of sociological theorists, the researchers may then *formulate the hypothesis.* A **hypothesis** is a speculative statement about the relationship between two or more factors known as *variables.* Income, religion, occupation, and gender can all serve as variables in a study. We can define a **variable** as a measurable trait or characteristic that is subject to change under different conditions.

Researchers who formulate a hypothesis generally must suggest how one aspect of human behavior influences or affects another. The variable hypothesized to cause or influence another is called the **independent variable.** The second variable is termed the **dependent variable** because its action "depends" on the influence of the independent variable.

Our hypothesis is that the higher one's educational degree, the more money a person will earn. The independent variable that is to be measured is the level of educational degree. The variable that is thought to "depend" on it—income—must also be measured.

Identifying independent and dependent variables is a critical step in clarifying cause-and-effect relationships. **Causal logic** involves the relationship between a condition or variable and a particular consequence, with one event leading to the other. Under causal logic, being less integrated into society (the independent variable) may be directly related to or produce a greater likelihood of suicide (the dependent variable). Similarly, parents' income levels (an independent variable) may affect the likelihood that their children will enroll in college (a dependent variable). Later in life, the level of education their children achieve (independent variable) may be directly related to their children's income levels (dependent variable). Note that income level can be either an independent or a dependent variable, depending on the causal relationship.

A *correlation* exists when a change in one variable coincides with a change in the other. Correlations are an indication that causality *may* be present; they do not necessarily indicate causation. For example, data indicate that working mothers are more likely to have delinquent children than are mothers who do not work outside the home. But this correlation is actually *caused* by a third variable: family income. Lower-class households are more likely than others to have a full-time working mother; at the same time, reported rates of delinquency are higher in that class than in other economic levels. Consequently, while having a mother who works outside the home is correlated with delinquency, it does not *cause* delinquency. Sociologists seek to identify the *causal* link between variables; they generally describe the causal link in their hypotheses.

COLLECTING AND ANALYZING DATA

How do you test a hypothesis to determine if it is supported or refuted? You need to collect information, using one of the research designs described later in the chapter. The research design guides the researcher in collecting and analyzing data.

Selecting the Sample   In most studies, social scientists must carefully select what is known as a *sample*. A *sample* is a selection from a larger population that is statistically representative of that population. There are many kinds of samples, but the one social scientists use most frequently is the random sample. In a *random sample,* every member of an entire population being studied has the same chance of being selected. Thus, if researchers want to examine the opinions of people listed in a city directory (a book that, unlike the telephone directory, lists all households), they might use a computer to randomly select names from the directory. This selection would constitute a random sample. The advantage of using specialized sampling techniques is that sociologists do not need to question everyone in a population.

It is all too easy to confuse the careful scientific techniques used in representative sampling with the many *nonscientific* polls that receive much more media attention. For example, television viewers and radio listeners are encouraged to e-mail their views on today's headlines or on political contests. Such polls reflect nothing more than the views of those who happened to see the television program (or hear the radio broadcast) and took the time, perhaps at some cost, to register their opinions. These data do not necessarily reflect (and indeed may distort) the views of the broader population. Not everyone has access to a television or radio, the time to watch or listen to a program, or the means and/or inclination to send e-mail. Similar problems are raised by the "mail-back" questionnaires found in many magazines and by "mall intercepts," in which shoppers are asked about some issue. Even when these techniques include answers from tens of thousands of people, they will be far less accurate than a carefully selected representative sample of 1,500 respondents.

For the purposes of our research example, we will use information collected in the Current Population Survey conducted by the Bureau of the Census. Each year the Census Bureau surveys approximately 54,000 households across the United States. Technicians at the bureau then use the data to estimate the nation's entire population.

Ensuring Validity and Reliability   The scientific method requires that research results be both valid and reliable. *Validity* refers to the degree to which a measure or scale truly reflects the phenomenon under study. A valid measure of income depends on the gathering of accurate data. Various studies show that people are reasonably accurate in reporting how much money they earned in the most recent year. If a question is written unclearly, however, the resulting data might not be accurate. For example, respondents to an unclear question about income might report their parents' or spouse's income instead of their own. *Reliability* refers to the extent to which a measure produces consistent results. One problem of reliability is that some people may not *disclose* accurate information, but most do.

DEVELOPING THE CONCLUSION

Scientific studies, including those conducted by sociologists, do not aim to answer all the questions that can be raised about a particular subject. Therefore, the conclusion of a research study represents both an end and a beginning. It terminates a specific phase of the investigation, but it should also generate ideas for future study.

Supporting Hypotheses   In our example, we find that the data support our hypothesis: People with more formal schooling *do* earn more money. As Figure 1–2 shows, as a group, those with a high school diploma earn more than those who failed to complete high school, but those with an associate's degree earn more than high school graduates. The relationship continues through more advanced levels of schooling; those with graduate degrees earn the most.

Sociological studies do not always generate data that support the original hypothesis. In many instances, a hypothesis is refuted, and researchers must reformulate their conclusions. Unexpected results may also lead sociologists to reexamine their methodology and make changes in the research design.

Figure 1–2

Impact of a College Education on Income

Half of all people with a high school diploma or less (left) earn under $25,000 a year, while 26 percent earn $40,000 or more. In contrast, 56 percent of those with an associate's degree or higher (right) earn $40,000 or more, while 24 percent earn less than $25,000.

SOURCE: Author's analysis of DeNavas-Walt et al. 2009, Detailed Table PINC-03.

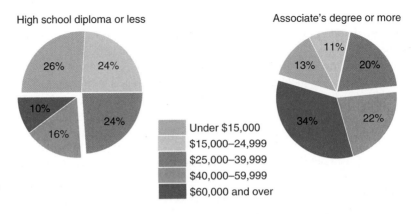

High school diploma or less   Associate's degree or more

Under $15,000
$15,000–24,999
$25,000–39,999
$40,000–59,999
$60,000 and over

Think About It
What kinds of knowledge and skills do people with an associate's degree or higher possess, compared to those with a high school education or less? Why would employers value those kinds of knowledge and skills?

Controlling for Other Factors A *control variable* is a factor held constant to test the relative impact of the independent variable. For example, if researchers wanted to know how adults in the United States feel about restrictions on smoking in public places, they would probably attempt to use a respondent's smoking behavior as a control variable. That is, how do smokers versus nonsmokers feel about smoking in public places? The researchers would compile separate statistics on how smokers and nonsmokers feel about antismoking regulations.

Our study of the influence of education on income suggests that not everyone enjoys equal educational opportunities, a disparity that is one of the causes of social inequality. Since education affects a person's income, we may wish to call on the conflict perspective to explore this topic further. What impact does a person's race or gender have? Is a woman with a college degree likely to earn as much as a man with similar schooling? Later in this textbook we will consider these other factors and variables. We will examine the impact that education has on income, while controlling for variables such as gender and race.

IN SUMMARY: THE SCIENTIFIC METHOD

Let's summarize the process of the scientific method through a review of our example. We *defined a problem* (the question of whether it pays to get a higher educational degree). We *reviewed the literature* (other studies of the relationship between education and income) and *formulated a hypothesis* (the higher one's educational degree, the more money a person will earn). We *collected and analyzed the data,* making sure the sample was representative and the data were valid and reliable. Finally, we *developed the conclusion:* The data do support our hypothesis about the influence of education on income.

Major Research Designs

An important aspect of sociological research is deciding how to collect the data. A ***research design*** is a detailed plan or method for obtaining data scientifically. Selection of a research design requires creativity and ingenuity. This choice will directly influence both the cost of the project and the amount of time needed to collect the results of the research. Research designs that sociologists use regularly to generate data include surveys, observation, experiments, and existing sources.

What might be the effects of a college education on society as a whole? Think of some potential effects on the family, government, and the economy.

SURVEYS

Almost all of us have responded to surveys of one kind or another. We may have been asked what kind of detergent we use, which presidential candidate we intend to vote for, or what our favorite television program is. A ***survey*** is a study, generally in the form of an interview or questionnaire, that provides researchers with information about how people think and act. Among the United States' best-known surveys of opinion are the Gallup poll and the Harris poll. As anyone who watches the news knows, these polls have become a staple of political life.

In preparing to conduct a survey, sociologists must not only develop a representative sample; they must exercise great care in the wording of questions. An effective survey question must be simple and clear enough for people to understand it. It must also be specific enough so that there are no problems in interpreting the results. Open-ended questions ("What do you think of the programming on educational television?") must be carefully phrased to solicit the type of information desired. Surveys can be indispensable sources of information, but only if the sampling is done properly and the questions are worded accurately and without bias.

There are two main forms of the survey: the ***interview,*** in which a researcher obtains information through face-to-face or telephone questioning, and the ***questionnaire,*** a printed or written form used to obtain information from a respondent. Each of these has its own advantages. An interviewer can obtain a high response rate, because people find it more difficult to turn down a personal request for an interview than to throw away a written questionnaire. In addition, a skillful interviewer can go beyond written questions and probe for a subject's underlying feelings and reasons. On the other hand, questionnaires have the advantage of being cheaper, especially in large samples.

Surveys are an example of ***quantitative research,*** in which scientists collect and report data primarily in numerical form. Most of the survey research discussed so far in this book has been quantitative. While this type of research is appropriate for large samples, it doesn't offer great depth and detail on a topic. That is why researchers also make use of **qualitative research,** which relies on what scientists see in field and naturalistic settings. Qualitative research often focuses on small groups and communities rather than on large groups or whole nations. The most common form of qualitative research is *observation.*

OBSERVATION

Investigators who collect information through direct participation and/or by closely watching a group or community are engaged in **observation.** This method allows sociologists to examine certain behaviors and communities that could not be investigated through other research techniques. Though observation may seem a relatively informal method compared to surveys or experiments, researchers are careful to take detailed notes while observing their subjects.

An increasingly popular form of qualitative research in sociology today is ethnography. **Ethnography** refers to the study of an entire social setting through extended systematic observation. Typically, the emphasis is on how the subjects themselves view their social life in some setting (P. Adler and Adler 2003, 2004, 2008a).

In some cases, the sociologist actually joins a group for a period, to get an accurate sense of how it operates. This approach is called *participant observation.* In Barbara Ehrenreich's widely read book, *Nickel and Dimed: On (Not) Getting By in America,* the author was a participant observer. Disguising herself as a divorced, middle-aged housewife without a college degree, Ehrenreich set out to see what life was like for low-wage workers. Her book chronicles her own and others' experiences trying to make ends meet on a minimum wage (Ehrenreich 2001).

During the late 1930s, in a classic example of participant-observation research, William F. Whyte moved into a low-income Italian neighborhood in Boston. For nearly four years he was a member of the social circle of "corner boys" that he describes in *Street Corner Society.* Whyte revealed his identity to these men and joined in their conversations, bowling, and other leisure-time activities. His goal was to gain greater insight into the community that these men had established. As Whyte (1981:303) listened to Doc, the leader of the group, he "learned the answers to questions I would not even have had the sense to ask if I had been getting my information solely on an interviewing basis." Whyte's work was especially valuable, since at the time, the academic world had little direct knowledge of the poor, and tended to rely on the records of social service agencies, hospitals, and courts for information (P. Adler et al. 1992).

The initial challenge that Whyte faced—and that every participant observer encounters—was to gain acceptance into an unfamiliar group. It is no simple matter for a college-trained sociologist to win the trust of a religious cult, a youth gang, a poor Appalachian community, or a circle of skid row residents. Doing so requires a great deal of patience and an accepting, nonthreatening personality on the part of the observer.

Observation research poses other complex challenges for the investigator. Sociologists must be able to fully understand what they are observing. In a sense, then, researchers must learn to see the world as the group sees it in order to fully comprehend the events taking place around them.

EXPERIMENTS

When sociologists want to study a possible cause-and-effect relationship, they may conduct experiments. An *experiment* is an artificially created situation that allows the researcher to manipulate variables.

In the classic method of conducting an experiment, two groups of people are selected and matched for similar characteristics, such as age or education. The researchers then assign one of the groups to be the experimental group and the other to be the control group. The *experimental group* is exposed to an independent variable; the *control group* is not. Thus, if scientists were testing a new type of antibiotic drug, they would administer that drug to an experimental group but not to a control group.

In some experiments, just as in observation research, the presence of a social scientist or other observer may affect the behavior of the people being studied. The recognition of this phenomenon grew out of an experiment conducted during the 1920s and 1930s at the Hawthorne plant of the Western Electric Company. A group of researchers set out to determine how to improve the productivity of workers at the plant. The investigators manipulated such variables as the lighting and working hours to see what impact the changes would have on productivity. To their surprise, they found that *every* step they took seemed to increase productivity. Even measures that seemed likely to have the opposite effect, such as reducing the amount of lighting in the plant, led to higher productivity.

Why did the plant's employees work harder even under less favorable conditions? Their behavior apparently was influenced by the greater attention being paid to them in the course of the research and by the novelty of being subjects in an experiment. Since that time sociologists have used the term *Hawthorne effect* to refer to the unintended influence of observers or experiments on subjects of research, who deviate from their typical behavior because they realize that they are under observation (Franke and Kaul 1978).

You are a researcher interested in the effect of TV-watching on schoolchildren's grades. How would you go about setting up an experiment to measure the effect?

USE OF EXISTING SOURCES

Sociologists do not necessarily need to collect new data in order to conduct research and test hypotheses. The term *secondary analysis* refers to a variety of research techniques that make use of previously collected and publicly accessible information and data. Generally, in conducting secondary analysis, researchers utilize data in ways unintended by the initial collectors of information. For example, census data that were compiled for specific uses by the federal government are also valuable to marketing specialists in locating everything from bicycle stores to nursing homes.

Sociologists consider secondary analysis to be *nonreactive,* since it does not influence people's behavior. For example, Émile Durkheim's statistical analysis of suicide neither increased nor decreased human self-destruction. Researchers, then, can avoid the Hawthorne effect by using secondary analysis.

Many social scientists find it useful to study cultural, economic, and political documents, including newspapers, periodicals, radio and television tapes, the Internet, scripts, diaries, songs, folklore, and legal papers, to name some examples (see Table 1–2). In examining these sources, researchers employ a technique known as **content analysis,** which is the systematic coding and objective recording of data, guided by some rationale.

summingUP

Table 1–2   Existing Sources Used in Sociological Research

Most Frequently Used Sources
Census data
Crime statistics
Birth, death, marriage, divorce, and health statistics

Other Sources
Newspapers and periodicals
Personal journals, diaries, e-mail, and letters
Records and archival material of religious organizations, corporations, and other organizations
Transcripts of radio programs
Motion pictures and television programs
Video tapes
Web pages, blogs, and chat rooms
Song lyrics
Scientific records (such as patent applications)
Speeches of public figures (such as politicians)
Votes cast in elections or by elected officials on specific legislative proposals
Attendance records for public events
Videotapes of social protests and rallies
Literature, including folklore

Table 1–3 Major Research Designs

Method	Examples	Advantages	Limitations
Survey	Questionnaires Interviews	Yields information about specific issues	Can be expensive and time-consuming
Observation	Ethnography	Yields detailed information about specific groups or organizations	Involves months if not years of labor-intensive data gathering
Experiment	Deliberate manipulation of people's social behavior	Yields direct measures of people's behavior	Ethical limitations on the degree to which subjects' behavior can be manipulated
Existing sources/ secondary analysis	Analysis of census or health data	Cost-efficiency	Limited to data collected for some other purpose
	Analysis of films or TV commercials		

Researchers today are analyzing the nature and extent of violence contained in children's television programming. In a recent study, they found that 69 percent of the shows specifically intended for children ages 12 and under contained violence. Though a comparison with non-children's programming showed little difference in the total amount of time devoted to violence, it did show that children's programs contain more scenes of violence than other programs (B. Wilson et al. 2002).

Table 1–3 summarizes the advantages and limitations of the four major research designs.

Ethics of Research

A biochemist cannot inject a drug into a human being unless the drug has been thoroughly tested and the subject agrees to the shot. To do otherwise would be both unethical and illegal. Sociologists must also abide by certain specific standards in conducting research, called a ***code of ethics.*** The professional society of the discipline, the American Sociological Association (ASA), first published its *Code of Ethics* in 1971 (revised most recently in 1997), which put forth the following basic principles:

1. Maintain objectivity and integrity in research.
2. Respect the subject's right to privacy and dignity.
3. Protect subjects from personal harm.
4. Preserve confidentiality.

5. Seek informed consent when data are collected from research participants or when behavior occurs in a private context.

6. Acknowledge research collaboration and assistance.

7. Disclose all sources of financial support. (American Sociological Association 1997)

Most sociological research uses *people* as sources of information—as respondents to survey questions, subjects of observation, or participants in experiments. In all cases, sociologists need to be certain that they are not invading the privacy of their subjects. Generally, they handle this responsibility by assuring them anonymity and by guaranteeing the confidentiality of personal information.

We have examined the process of sociological research, including related ethical considerations, in detail. But not all sociologists are researchers. Some practice what is known as *applied sociology,* or the application of sociological knowledge to real-world social problems.

You are a sociological researcher who is having difficulty maintaining a neutral attitude toward your research topic. Your topic isn't racism or sexism. What is it?

Applied and Clinical Sociology

Sociology matters because it addresses real issues that affect people's lives. Many early sociologists—notably, Jane Addams and George Herbert Mead—were strong advocates for social reform. They wanted their theories and findings to be relevant to policy makers and to people's lives in general. For instance, Mead was the treasurer of Hull House, where for many years he used his theory to improve the lives of those who were powerless (especially immigrants). He also served on committees dealing with Chicago's labor problems and with public education.

Today, ***applied sociology*** is defined as the use of the discipline of sociology with the specific intent of yielding practical applications for human behavior and organizations. By extension, Michael Burawoy (2005), in his presidential address to the American Sociological Association, endorsed what he called *public sociology,* encouraging scholars to engage a broader audience in bringing about positive outcomes. In effect, the applied sociologist reaches out to others and joins them in their efforts to better society.

Often, the goal of such work is to assist in resolving a social problem. For example, in the past 50 years, eight presidents of the United States have established commissions to delve into major societal concerns facing our nation. Sociologists are often asked to apply their expertise to studying such issues as violence, pornography, crime, immigration, and population. In Europe, both academic and government research departments are offering increasing financial support for applied studies.

One example of applied sociology is the growing interest in community health care. Rather than focusing on social problems, sociologists and others have begun to emphasize the assets a community can offer its residents. For example, sociologist P. Raphael Hernández-Arias developed the Community Health Assets and Needs Assessment (CHANA) to study four low-income immigrant communities on the South Side of Chicago. The idea was to identify existing resources that could be used to address residents' health needs, from medical clinics to fresh produce markets. CHANA showed that, from one neighborhood to another, and even within a single neighborhood, the resources available to residents varied considerably. One community had plenty of sources for fresh produce; another, next to none. One had sixteen social service organizations; another, just two. The number of health clinics and doctors' offices also varied widely. Hernández-Arias is sharing the data from CHANA with community activists and with Chicago's Department of Public Health, in an effort both to maximize existing resources and to develop new ones (Velásquez and P. Hernández-Arias 2009).

The growing popularity of applied sociology has led to the rise of the specialty of clinical sociology. Louis Wirth (1931) wrote about clinical sociology more than 70 years ago, but the term itself has become popular only in recent years. While applied sociologists may simply evaluate social issues, *clinical sociology* is dedicated to altering social relationships (as in family therapy) or to restructuring social institutions (as in the reorganization of a medical center).

Applied sociologists generally leave it to others to act on their evaluations. By contrast, clinical sociologists take direct responsibility for implementation and view those with whom they work as their clients. This specialty has become increasingly attractive to graduate students in sociology because it offers an opportunity to apply intellectual learning in a practical way. Up to now, a shrinking job market in the academic world has made such alternative career routes appealing.

Applied and clinical sociology can be contrasted with *basic* (or *pure*) *sociology,* which seeks a more profound knowledge of the fundamental aspects of social phenomena. This type of research is not necessarily meant to generate specific applications, although such ideas may result once findings are analyzed. When Durkheim studied suicide rates, he was not primarily interested in discovering a way to eliminate suicide. In this sense, his research is an example of basic rather than applied sociology.

Use Your Sociological Imagination

What issues facing your local community would you like to address with applied sociological research?

Sociology Matters

Sociology matters because it offers new insights into what is going on around you, in your own life as well as in the larger society. Consider the purpose of a college education:

- What are your own reasons for going to college? Are you interested only in academics, or did you enroll for the social life as well? Does your college encourage you to pursue both, and if so, why?

- How does your pursuit of a college education impact society as a whole? What are the social effects of your decision to become a student, both now and later in life, after you receive your degree?

Sociology also matters because sociologists follow a scientific research design to reach their conclusions. Consider the importance of careful research:

- Have you ever acted on incomplete information, or even misinformation? What were the results?

- What might be the result if legislators or government policy makers were to base their actions on faulty research?

CHAPTER RESOURCES

Summary

Sociology is the scientific study of social behavior and human groups. This chapter presented a brief history of the discipline and introduced the concept of the **sociological imagination.** It surveyed sociological **theory,** including contemporary perspectives, and suggested some practical uses for theory. This chapter also presented the principles of the **scientific method** and showed how sociologists use them in their research.

1. The **sociological imagination** is an awareness of the relationship between an individual and the wider society. It is based on an ability to view society as an outsider might, rather than from the perspective of an insider.

2. Sociologists employ **theory** to explain problems, actions, or behavior. Nineteenth-century thinkers who contributed to the development of sociological theory include Émile Durkheim, who pioneered work on suicide; Max Weber, a German thinker who taught the need for *Verstehen,* or "insight," in intellectual work; Karl Marx, a German intellectual who emphasized the importance of class conflict; and W.E.B. DuBois, who emphasized the importance of race.

3. Today, several theoretical perspectives guide sociological research. The **functionalist perspective** holds that society is structured in ways that maintain social stability, so that social change tends to be slow and evolutionary.

4. The **conflict perspective,** on the other hand, emphasizes the importance of conflict between competing social groups, so that social change tends to be swift and revolutionary. A related perspective, the *feminist perspective,* stresses conflict based on gender inequality.

5. The **feminist perspective** stresses gender as the key to understanding social interactions. Feminist sociologists charge that too often, scholars concentrate on male social roles, ignoring male–female differences in behavior.

6. The **interactionist perspective** is concerned primarily with the everyday ways in which individuals shape their society and are shaped by it. Interactionists see social change as an ongoing and very personal process.

7. The **scientific method** includes five steps: defining the problem; reviewing the literature; formulating the *hypothesis;* selecting the **research design** and collecting and analyzing data; and developing the conclusion. The **hypothesis** states a possible relationship between two or more variables, usually one **independent variable** and a **dependent variable** that is thought to be related to it.

8. To avoid having to test everyone in a population, sociologists use a **sample** that is representative of the general population. Using a representative sample lends **validity** and **reliability** to the results of scientific research.

9. Sociologists use four major research designs in their work: **surveys** of the population; personal **observation** of behaviors and communities; **experiments** that test hypothetical cause-and-effect relationships; and analysis of existing sources.

10. **Applied sociology**—the practical application of the discipline to problems in human behavior and organizations—is a growing field that includes community research and **clinical sociology.**

www.mhhe.com/schaefersm5e
Visit the Online Learning Center for *Sociology Matters* to access quizzes, review activities, and other learning tools.

Key Terms

applied sociology, 32

basic sociology, 33

causal logic, 23

clinical sociology, 33

code of ethics, 31

conflict perspective, 17

content analysis, 30

control group, 29

control variable, 26

correlation, 24

dependent variable, 23

double consciousness, 13

dysfunction, 16

ethnography, 28

experiment, 29

experimental group, 29

feminist perspective, 18

functionalist perspective, 15

Hawthorne effect, 29

hypothesis, 23

ideal type, 11

independent variable, 23

interactionist perspective, 19

interview, 27

latent function, 17

macrosociology, 14

manifest function, 17

microsociology, 14

natural science, 4

nonverbal communication, 20

observation, 28

operational definition, 22

qualitative research, 28

quantitative research, 27

questionnaire, 27

random sample, 24

reliability, 25

research design, 27

sample, 24

science, 4

scientific method, 21

secondary analysis, 29

social science, 5

sociological imagination, 3

sociology, 3

survey, 27

theory, 7

validity, 25

variable, 23

Verstehen, 11

Culture and Socialization

What Is Culture?

Development of Culture around the World

Cultural Variation

Language and Culture

Norms and Values

Global Culture War

Culture and the Dominant Ideology

Culture and Socialization

The Self and Socialization

Agents of Socialization

Socialization throughout the Life Course

When Ryan Wilson enters the *Hinono' Eitiino' Oowu'*—that is, the Arapaho Language Lodge—in Riverton, Wyoming, he is on a survival mission. His task is to teach both children and adults their native language. Because the Arapaho language is no longer spoken fluently by anyone under age 55, it is in danger of dying out with its few surviving speakers.

Among the Shinnecock people of Long Island, the situation is even more dire. As best as anyone can tell, the native language has not been spoken for almost two centuries. Linguists do have a vocabulary list that Thomas Jefferson compiled while visiting the tribe in 1791, when three elder women could still speak the language. Drawing on this and other historical documents, they are attempting to reintroduce the language to the tribe's 1,700 members.

The short-term outlook is brighter at the Miccosukee Indian School, on the edge of the Everglades in Florida, and in other locations around the country. All told, such efforts are expected to increase significantly the more than 370,000 native peoples in the United States who speak their native language at home. Although that number may seem large, more than five in six self-identified Native Americans cannot speak their native language (Cohen 2010; Frosch 2008; Shin and Kominski 2010; Sturtevant and Cattelino 2004).

The struggle to maintain native languages is a global effort. Around the world, people recognize that language is a vital element of both culture and socialization. However, language can also act as a barrier. In many places in the United States, medical practitioners are trying to make language a tool rather than an obstacle in their visits with patients. They are becoming sensitive not just to language but to the values and understandings behind it. In many hospitals, signs on the doors of Muslim patients now ask staff and visitors to knock and wait for permission to enter, so female patients have enough time to cover themselves. And doctors are finding that they need extra patience, as well as a willingness to learn about alternative medicine, to treat immigrants from Asia and Latin America, many of whom are unfamiliar with Western health care (Buchanan 2008; Pennachio 2004, 2005).

As social service workers who care for and police the immigrant community know, culture is fundamental to any society. Yet too many Americans fail to adjust to the growing diversity in the United States, as well as to the cultural mores of the foreign markets they seek to serve. In this chapter we will learn that all societies share certain basic cultural elements, even though they may express those elements differently. We will see how cultures change, whether from within or in response to outside influences, such as multinational corporations. And we will learn how culture reinforces the power of the dominant classes in society.

Culture also affects the basic attitudes, values, and behaviors that children learn through a process called **socialization.** It can even affect a child's **personality**—the individual characteristics, attitudes, needs, and behaviors that set one person apart from another. Throughout the life course, culture prescribes the roles people take and the ceremonies they participate in as they pass from one life stage to another. It molds the most fundamental institutions of society, from the family, schools, and peer groups to the mass media, the workplace, and the state. Culture, in other words, is all-encompassing.

What Is Culture?

Culture is the totality of learned, socially transmitted customs, knowledge, material objects, and behavior. It includes the ideas, values, customs, and artifacts (for example, iPods, comic books, and birth control devices) of groups of people. Patriotic attachment to the flag of the United States is an aspect of culture, as is a national passion for the tango in Argentina.

Sometimes people refer to a particular person as "very cultured" or to a city as having "lots of culture." That use of the term *culture* is different from our use in this textbook. In sociological terms, *culture* does not refer solely to the fine arts and refined intellectual taste. It consists of *all* objects and ideas within a society, including ice cream cones, rock music, and slang words. Sociologists consider both a portrait by Rembrandt and a portrait by a billboard painter to be aspects of a culture. A tribe that cultivates soil by hand has just as much culture as a people that relies on computer-operated machinery. Each people has a distinctive culture with its own characteristic ways of gathering and preparing food, constructing homes, structuring the family, and promoting standards of right and wrong.

The fact that you share a similar culture with others helps to define the group or society to which you belong. A fairly large number of people are said to constitute a **society** when they live in the same territory, are relatively independent of people outside it, and participate in a common culture. The city of Los Angeles is more populous than many nations of the world, yet sociologists do not consider it a society in its own right. Rather, it is part of—and dependent on—the larger society of the United States.

A society is the largest form of human group. It consists of people who share a common heritage and culture. Members of the society learn this culture and transmit it from one generation to the next. They even preserve their distinctive culture through literature, art, video recordings, and other means of expression.

Sociologists have long recognized the many ways in which culture influences human behavior. Through what has been termed a toolkit of habits, skills, and styles, people of a common culture construct their acquisition of knowledge, their interactions with kinfolk, their entrance into the job market—in short, the way in which they live. If not for the social transmission of culture, each generation would have to reinvent television, not to mention the wheel (Swidler 1986).

Having a common culture also simplifies many day-to-day interactions. For example, when you buy an airline ticket, you know you don't need to bring along hundreds of dollars in cash. You can pay with a credit card. When you are part of a society, you can take many small (as well as more important) cultural patterns for granted. You assume that theaters will provide seats for the audience, that physicians will not disclose confidential information, and that parents will be careful when crossing the street with young children. All these assumptions reflect basic values, beliefs, and customs of the culture of the United States.

Today, when text, sound, and video can be transmitted around the world instantaneously, some aspects of culture transcend national borders.

The German philosopher Theodor Adorno and others have spoken of the worldwide *culture industry* that standardizes the goods and services demanded by consumers. Adorno contends that globally, the primary effect of popular culture is to limit people's choices. Yet others have shown that the culture industry's influence does not always permeate international borders. Sometimes it is embraced; at other times, soundly rejected (Adorno [1971] 1991:98–106; Horkheimer and Adorno [1944] 2002).

CULTURAL UNIVERSALS

All societies, despite their differences, have developed certain general practices known as *cultural universals.* Many cultural universals are, in fact, adaptations to meet essential human needs, such as people's need for food, shelter, and clothing. Anthropologist George Murdock (1945:124) compiled a list of cultural universals that includes athletic sports, cooking, funeral ceremonies, medicine, and sexual restrictions.

The cultural practices listed by Murdock may be universal, but the manner in which they are expressed varies from culture to culture. For example, one society may let its members choose their own marriage partners. Another may encourage marriages arranged by the parents.

Not only does the expression of cultural universals vary from one society to another; it may also change dramatically over time within a society. Each generation, and each year for that matter, most human cultures change and expand through the processes of *innovation* and *diffusion* (see pages 42–44).

ETHNOCENTRISM

Many everyday statements reflect our attitude that our own culture is best. We use terms such as *underdeveloped, backward,* and *primitive* to refer to other societies. What "we" believe is a religion; what "they" believe is superstition and mythology.

It is tempting to evaluate the practices of other cultures from our own perspective. Sociologist William Graham Sumner (1906) coined the term *ethnocentrism* to refer to the tendency to assume that one's own culture and way of life represent the norm or are superior to all others. The ethnocentric person sees his or her own group as the center or defining point of culture and views all other cultures as deviations from what is "normal."

Recently, ethnocentric value judgments have complicated U.S. efforts at democratic reform of the Iraqi government. Before the 2003 war in Iraq, U.S. planners had assumed that Iraqis would adapt to a new form of government in the same way the Germans and Japanese did following World War II. But in the Iraqi culture, unlike the German and Japanese cultures, loyalty to the family and the extended clan comes before patriotism and the common good. In a country in which almost half of all people, even those in the cities, marry a first or second cousin, citizens are predisposed to favor their own kin in government and business dealings. Why trust a stranger from outside the family? What Westerners would criticize as nepotism, then, is actually an acceptable, even admirable, practice to Iraqis (Tierney 2003).

Conflict theorists point out that ethnocentric value judgments serve to devalue groups and to deny equal opportunities. Functionalists, on the other hand, point out that ethnocentrism serves to maintain a sense of solidarity by promoting group pride. Denigrating other nations and cultures can enhance our own patriotic feelings and belief that our way of life is superior. Yet this type of social stability is established at the expense of other peoples. Of course, ethnocentrism is hardly limited to citizens of the United States. Visitors from many African cultures are surprised at the disrespect that children in the United States show their parents. People from India may be repelled by our practice of living in the same household with dogs and cats. Many Islamic fundamentalists in the Arab world and Asia view the United States as corrupt, decadent, and doomed to destruction. All these people may feel comforted by membership in cultures that in their view are superior to ours.

CULTURAL RELATIVISM

While ethnocentrism is the evaluation of foreign cultures using the familiar culture of the observer as a standard of correct behavior, *cultural relativism* is the evaluation of a people's behavior from the perspective of their own culture. Medical practitioners who seek to adapt to their patients' cultural expectations are exhibiting this approach. Cultural relativism places a priority on understanding other cultures rather than dismissing them as "strange" or "exotic." Unlike ethnocentrism, cultural relativism employs a kind of *value neutrality* in scientific study, which Max Weber saw as being extremely important.

Cultural relativism stresses that different social contexts give rise to different norms and values. Thus, we must examine practices such as polygamy, bullfighting, and monarchy within the particular contexts of the cultures in which they are found. While cultural relativism does not suggest that we must unquestionably *accept* every cultural variation, it does require a serious and unbiased effort to evaluate norms, values, and customs in light of their distinctive culture.

How one views a culture—whether from an ethnocentric point of view or through the lens of cultural relativism—has important consequences for social policy. Consider the practice of children marrying adults. Most people in North America cannot fathom the idea of a 12-year-old girl marrying. The custom, which is illegal in the United States, is common in West Africa and South Asia. Should the United States respect such marriages? The apparent answer is no. In 2006 the

U.S. government spent $623 million to discourage the practice in many of the countries with the highest child-marriage rates.

From the perspective of cultural relativism, we might ask whether one society should spend its resources to dictate the norms of another. However, federal officials have defended the government's actions. They contend that child marriage deprives girls of education, threatens their health, and weakens public health efforts to combat HIV/AIDS (Jain and Kurz 2007; B. Slavin 2007).

Development of Culture around the World

We've come a long way from our prehistoric heritage. The human species has produced such achievements as the novels of Leo Tolstoy, the art of Pablo Picasso, and the films of Ang Lee. As we begin a new millennium, we can transmit an entire book around the world via the Internet, clone cells, and prolong lives through organ transplants. We can peer into the outermost reaches of the universe or analyze our innermost feelings. In all these ways, we are remarkably different from other species of the animal kingdom. Though cultures differ in their customs, artifacts, and languages, they all share certain basic characteristics. In this section we will see how those characteristics change as cultures develop and how cultures influence one another through their technological, commercial, and artistic achievements.

INNOVATION

The process of introducing a new idea or object to a culture is known as *innovation.* Innovation interests sociologists because of the potential social consequences of introducing something new. There are two forms of innovation: discovery and invention. A *discovery* involves making known or sharing the existence of some aspect of reality. The finding of the DNA molecule and the identification of a new moon of Saturn are both acts of discovery. A significant factor in the process of discovery is the sharing of newfound knowledge with others. By contrast, an *invention* results when existing cultural items are combined into a form that did not exist before. The bow and arrow, the automobile, and the Internet are all examples of inventions, as are Protestantism and democracy.

GLOBALIZATION, DIFFUSION, AND TECHNOLOGY

The familiar green Starbucks logo beckons you into a comfortable coffee shop where you can order decaf latte and a cinnamon ring. What's unusual about that? This Starbucks happens to be located in the heart of Beijing's Forbidden City, just outside the Palace of Heavenly

Purity, former residence of Chinese emperors. In 2002 it was one of 25 Starbucks stores in China; eight years later there were more than 375. The success of Starbucks in a country in which coffee drinking is still a novelty (most Chinese are tea drinkers) has been striking (Sanchanta 2010).

The emergence of Starbucks in China illustrates a rapidly escalating trend called *globalization. **Globalization*** may be defined as the world-wide integration of government policies, cultures, social movements, and financial markets through trade and the exchange of ideas. While public discussion of globalization is relatively recent, intellectuals have been pondering its social consequences for a long time. Karl Marx and Friedrich Engels warned in *The Communist Manifesto* (written in 1848) of a world market that would lead to production in distant lands, sweeping away existing working relationships. Today, more and more cultural expressions and practices are crossing national borders, transforming the traditions and customs of the societies exposed to them. Sociologists use the term ***diffusion*** to refer to the process by which a cultural item spreads from group to group or society to society. Diffusion can occur through a variety of means, among them exploration, military conquest, missionary work, the influence of the mass media, tourism, and the Internet.

Sociologist George Ritzer (2011) coined the term ***McDonaldization*** to describe the process through which the principles of the fast-food restaurant have come to dominate certain sectors of society, both in the United States and throughout the world. For example, hair salons and medical clinics now take walk-in appointments. In Hong Kong, sex selection clinics offer a menu of items, from fertility enhancement to methods of increasing the likelihood of producing a child of the desired sex. Religious groups—from evangelical preachers on local stations or websites to priests at the Vatican Television Center—use marketing techniques similar to those that are used to sell Happy Meals.

McDonaldization is associated with the melding of cultures, through which we see more and more similarities in cultural expression. In Japan, for example, African entrepreneurs have found a thriving market for hip-hop fashions popularized by teens in the United States. Similarly, the familiar Golden Arches of McDonald's can be seen around the world. Yet corporations like McDonald's have had to make some adjustments of their own. Until 2001, McDonald's ran its overseas operations from corporate headquarters in suburban Chicago. After a few false starts, executives recognized the need to develop the restaurant's menus and marketing strategies overseas, relying on advice from local people. Now, at over 3,700 restaurants in Japan, customers can enjoy the Mega Tamago Burger—beef, bacon, and fried egg with special sauces. In India, patrons who don't eat beef can order a double chicken-patty sandwich known as the Maharaja Mac. And in Austria, the locals' love of coffee, cake, and conversation has inspired the McCafe (Hughlett 2008; Ritzer 2002).

Use Your Sociological Imagination

If you grew up in your parents' generation—without computers, e-mail, the Internet, and cell phones—how would your daily life differ from the one you lead today?

Technology in its many forms has increased the speed of cultural diffusion and broadened the distribution of cultural elements. Sociologist Gerhard Lenski has defined *technology* as "cultural information about how to use the material resources of the environment to satisfy human needs and desires" (Nolan and Lenski 2009:37). Today's technological developments no longer need await publication in journals with limited circulation. Press conferences, often carried simultaneously on the Internet, now trumpet new developments.

Sociologist William F. Ogburn (1922) made a useful distinction between the elements of material and nonmaterial culture. *Material culture* refers to the physical or technological aspects of our daily lives, including food items, houses, factories, and raw materials. *Nonmaterial culture* refers to ways of using material objects and to customs, beliefs, philosophies, governments, and patterns of communication. Generally, the nonmaterial culture is more resistant to change than the material culture. Ogburn introduced the term *culture lag* to refer to the period of maladjustment when the nonmaterial culture is still struggling to adapt to new material conditions. For example, the ethics of using the Internet, particularly issues concerning privacy and censorship, have not yet caught up with the explosion in Internet use and technology.

Cultural Variation

Each culture has a unique character. Inuit tribes in northern Canada—wrapped in furs and dining on whale blubber—have little in common with farmers in Southeast Asia, who dress for the heat and subsist mainly on the rice they grow in their paddies. Cultures adapt to meet specific sets of circumstances, such as climate, level of technology, population, and geography. Thus, despite the presence of cultural universals such as courtship and religion, great diversity exists among the world's many cultures. Moreover, even *within* a single nation, certain segments of the populace develop cultural patterns that differ from the patterns of the dominant society.

SUBCULTURES

Rodeo riders, residents of a retirement community, workers on an offshore oil rig—all are examples of what sociologists refer to as *subcultures.* A *subculture* is a segment of society that shares a distinctive pattern of customs, rules, and traditions that differs from the pattern of the larger society. In a sense, a subculture can be thought of as a culture existing within a larger, dominant culture. The existence of many subcultures is characteristic of complex societies such as the United States.

Members of a subculture participate in the dominant culture while at the same time engaging in unique and distinctive forms of behavior.

Frequently, a subculture will develop an ***argot,*** or specialized language, that distinguishes it from the wider society. Athletes who play *parkour,* an extreme sport that combines forward running with fence leaping and the vaulting of walls, water barriers, and even moving cars, speak an argot they devised especially to describe their feats. Parkour runners talk about doing *King Kong vaults*—diving arms first over a wall or grocery cart and landing in a standing position. They may follow this maneuver with a *tic tac*—kicking off a wall to overcome some kind of obstacle (Wilkinson 2007).

Argot allows "insiders," the members of the subculture, to understand words with special meanings. It also establishes patterns of communication that "outsiders" can't understand. Sociologists associated with the interactionist perspective emphasize that language and symbols offer a powerful way for a subculture to feel cohesive and maintain its identity.

In India, a new subculture has developed among employees at the international call centers established by multinational corporations. To serve customers in the United States and Europe, the young men and women who work there must be fluent speakers of English. But the corporations that employ them demand more than proficiency in a foreign language; they expect their Indian employees to adopt Western values and work habits, including the grueling pace U.S. workers take for granted. In return they offer perks such as Western-style dinners, dances, and coveted consumer goods. Significantly, they allow employees to take the day off only on U.S. holidays, like Labor Day and Thanksgiving—not on Indian holidays like Diwali, the Hindu festival of lights. While most Indian families are home celebrating, call center employees see only each other; when they have the day off, no one else is free to socialize with them. As a result, these employees have formed a tight-knit subculture based on hard work and a taste for Western luxury goods and leisure-time pursuits.

Increasingly, call center workers are becoming the object of criticism from Indians who live a more conventional lifestyle centered on family and holiday traditions. In response to such negative public opinion, the government of the Indian state where call centers are located has banned schools from teaching English rather than Kannada, the local language. Beginning in 2008, some 300,000 students were affected by the ban (Chu 2007; Kalita 2006).

COUNTERCULTURES

By the end of the 1960s, an extensive subculture had emerged in the United States, composed of young people turned off by a society they believed was too materialistic and technological. This group included primarily political radicals and "hippies" who had "dropped out" of mainstream social institutions. These young men and women rejected the pressure to accumulate more and more cars, larger and larger homes, and an endless array of material goods. Instead, they expressed a desire to live in a culture based on more humanistic values, such as sharing, love, and coexistence with the environment. As a political force, this subculture opposed the United States' involvement in the war in Vietnam and encouraged draft resistance (Flacks 1971; Roszak 1969).

When a subculture conspicuously and deliberately *opposes* certain aspects of the larger culture, it is known as a ***counterculture.*** Countercultures typically thrive among the young, who have the least investment in the existing culture. In most cases, a 20-year-old can adjust to new cultural standards more easily than someone who has spent 60 years following the patterns of the dominant culture (Zellner 1995).

In the wake of the World Trade Center and Pentagon attacks of September 11, 2001, people around the United States learned of the existence of terrorist groups operating as a counterculture within their country. This was a situation that generations have lived with in Northern Ireland, Israel, the Palestinian Territory, and many other parts of the world. Worldwide, terrorist cells are not necessarily fueled only by outsiders. Frequently, people become disenchanted with the policies of their own country, and a few take very violent steps.

CULTURE SHOCK

You arrive in a developing African country as a Peace Corps volunteer. What aspects of this very different culture do you think would be the hardest to adjust to? What might the citizens of that country find shocking about your culture?

Anyone who feels disoriented, uncertain, out of place, even fearful when immersed in an unfamiliar culture may be experiencing ***culture shock.*** For example, a resident of the United States who visits certain areas in China and wants local meat for dinner may be stunned to learn that the specialty is dog meat. Similarly, someone from a strict Islamic culture may be shocked upon first seeing the comparatively provocative dress styles and open displays of affection common in the United States and Europe.

All of us, to some extent, take for granted the cultural practices of our *society.* As a result, it can be surprising and even disturbing to realize that other cultures do not follow our "way of life." The fact is, customs that seem strange to us are considered normal and proper in other cultures, which may see *our* customs as odd.

Language and Culture

The English language makes extensive use of words dealing with war. We speak of "conquering" space, "fighting the battle" of the budget, "waging war" on drugs, making a "killing" on the stock market, and "bombing" an examination; something monumental or great is "the bomb." An observer from an entirely different and warless culture could gauge the importance of war and the military in our lives simply by recognizing the prominence that militaristic terms have in our language.

Similarly, cattle are so important to the Nuer of southern Sudan that they have more than 400 words to describe the animals (Haviland et al. 2005).

Language is, in fact, the foundation of every culture. **Language** is an abstract system of word meanings and symbols for all aspects of culture. It includes speech, written characters, numerals, symbols, and gestures and expressions of nonverbal communication.

Though language is a cultural universal, striking differences are evident in its use. For decades, the Navajo have referred to cancer as *lood doo na'dziihii*. Now, through a project funded by the National Cancer Institute, the tribal college is seeking to change the phrase. Why? Literally, the word means "the sore that does not heal," and health educators are concerned that tribal members who have been diagnosed with cancer view it as a death sentence. Their effort to change the Navajo language, not easy in itself, is complicated by the Navajo belief that to talk about the disease is to bring it on one's people (Fonseca 2008).

The thumbs-up gesture is an example of *nonverbal communication,* or the use of gestures, facial expressions, and other visual images to communicate. If you are in the midst of a friendly meeting and one member suddenly sits back, folds his arms, and turns down the corners of his mouth, you know at once that trouble has arrived. When you see a friend in tears, you may give her a quick hug. After winning a big game, you probably high-five your teammates. These are all examples of nonverbal communication.

We are not born with these expressions. We learn them, just as we learn other forms of language, from people who share our culture. That is as true for the basic expressions of happiness and sadness as it is for more complex emotions, such as shame or distress (Fridlund et al. 1987).

Like other forms of language, nonverbal communication is not the same in all cultures. For example, sociological research done at the micro level documents that people from various cultures differ in the degree to which they touch others during the course of normal social interactions. Even experienced travelers are sometimes caught off guard by these differences. In Saudi Arabia, a middle-aged man may want to hold hands with a partner after closing a business deal. The gesture, which would shock an American businessman, is considered a compliment in that culture. The meaning of hand signals is another form of nonverbal communication that can differ from one culture to the next. In Australia, the thumbs-up sign is considered rude (Passero 2002).

Still, some gestures, such as the basic emotional expressions—a smile, a look of horror—may be close to universal. Not long ago, a team of linguists, social scientists, and physical scientists collaborated on a system for communicating with those who will live thousands of years from now, long after people have ceased to speak our languages. The challenge was to create a series of signs and explanations that would warn future generations of the dangers posed by the Waste Isolation

Figure 2–1
A Timeless Alert

The symbols on this subsurface marker at the Waste Isolation Pilot Plant in New Mexico are an attempt to communicate the presence of hazardous waste to people who may live 10,000 years from now. Would these symbols convince you not to dig? Might future generations misinterpret them?

Pilot Plant (WIPP), a nuclear waste repository in New Mexico. For the next few centuries, warning signs engraved in English, Spanish, Russian, French, Chinese, Arabic, and Navajo will alert those in the area to the presence of the underground dump, which will remain highly radioactive for at least 10,000 years. But the signs also include pictographs that researchers hope will be understandable to people who live millennia from now, no matter what their language; see Figure 2–1 (Department of Energy 2004; Piller 2006).

Norms and Values

"Wash your hands before dinner." "Thou shalt not kill." "Respect your elders." All societies have ways of encouraging and enforcing what they view as appropriate behavior while discouraging and punishing what they consider to be improper behavior. They also have a collective idea of what is good and desirable in life—or not. In this section we will learn to distinguish between the closely related concepts of norms and values.

NORMS

Norms are the established standards of behavior maintained by a society. For a norm to become significant, it must be widely shared and understood. For example, in movie theaters in the United States, we typically expect that people will be quiet while the film is shown. Of course, the application of this norm can vary, depending on the particular film and type of audience. People who are viewing a serious artistic film will be more likely to insist on the norm of silence than those who are watching a slapstick comedy or horror movie.

Types of Norms Sociologists distinguish between norms in two ways. First, norms are classified as either formal or informal. ***Formal norms*** generally have been written down and specify strict punishment of violators. In the United States, we often formalize norms into laws, which must be very precise in defining proper and improper behavior. Sociologist Donald Black (1995) has termed ***law*** "governmental social control," meaning formal norms that are enforced by the state. Laws are just one example of formal norms. The requirements for a college major and the rules of a card game are also considered formal norms.

By contrast, ***informal norms*** are generally understood but are not precisely recorded. Standards of proper dress are a common example of informal norms. Our society has no specific punishment or sanction for a person who comes to school, say, wearing a monkey suit. Making fun of the nonconforming student is usually the most likely response.

Norms are also classified by their relative importance to society. When classified in this way, they are known as *mores* and *folkways*. ***Mores*** (pronounced "MOR-ays") are norms deemed highly necessary to the welfare of a society, often because they embody the most cherished principles of a people. Each society demands obedience to its mores; violations can lead to severe penalties. Thus, the United States has strong mores against murder, treason, and child abuse, which have been institutionalized into formal norms.

Folkways are norms governing everyday behavior. Folkways play an important role in shaping the daily behavior of members of a culture. Still, society is less likely to formalize folkways than mores, and their violation raises comparatively little concern. For example, walking up a "down" escalator in a department store challenges our standards of appropriate behavior, but it will not result in a fine or a jail sentence.

In many societies around the world, folkways exist to reinforce patterns of male dominance. In traditional Buddhist areas of Southeast Asia, various folkways reveal men's hierarchical position above women. On trains, women do not sleep in upper berths above men. Hospitals that house men on the first floor do not place women patients on the second floor. Even on clotheslines, folkways dictate male dominance: Women's attire is hung lower than that of men (Bulle 1987).

Acceptance of Norms People do not follow norms, whether mores or folkways, in all situations. In some cases, they can evade a norm because they know it is weakly enforced. It is illegal for U.S. teenagers to drink alcoholic beverages, yet drinking by minors is common throughout the nation. In fact, teenage alcoholism is a serious social problem.

Use Your Sociological Imagination

You are a high school principal. What norms would you want to govern students' behavior? How might those norms differ from those typical of college students?

Norms are violated in some instances because one norm conflicts with another. For example, suppose one night you hear the screams of the woman next door, who is being beaten by her husband. If you decide to intervene by ringing their doorbell or calling the police, you are violating the norm of "minding your own business," while at the same time following the norm of assisting a victim of violence.

Even when norms do not conflict, there are always exceptions. Under different circumstances, the same action can cause one to be viewed as either a hero or a villain. Secretly taping telephone conversations is normally considered illegal and abhorrent. However, it can be done with a court order to obtain valid evidence for a criminal trial. We would heap praise on a government agent who uses such methods to convict an organized crime boss or detect a planned terrorist attack. Similarly, we tolerate killing another human being in self-defense, and we actually reward killing in warfare.

Acceptance of norms is subject to change as the political, economic, and social conditions of a culture are transformed. Until the 1960s, for example, formal norms throughout much of the United States prohibited the marriage of people from different racial groups. Over the last half century, however, such legal prohibitions were cast aside. The process of change can be seen today in the increasing acceptance of single parents and growing support for the legalization of marriage between same-sex couples (see Chapter 8).

SANCTIONS

Suppose a football coach sends a 12th player onto the field. Or imagine a college graduate showing up in shorts for a job interview at an accounting firm. Consider a driver who neglects to put any money into a parking meter. These people have violated widely shared and understood norms. So what happens? In each of these situations, the person will receive sanctions if his or her behavior is detected.

Sanctions are penalties and rewards for conduct concerning a social norm. Note that the concept of *reward* is included in this definition. Conformity to a norm can lead to positive sanctions such as a pay raise, a medal, a word of gratitude, or a pat on the back. Negative sanctions include fines, threats, imprisonment, and stares of contempt.

Table 2–1 summarizes the relationship between norms and sanctions. As you can see, the sanctions associated with formal norms (those that are written down and codified) tend to be formal as well. If a coach sends too many players onto the field, the team will be penalized 15 yards. The driver who fails to put money in the parking meter will be ticketed and expected to pay a fine. But sanctions for violations of informal norms can vary. The college graduate who comes to the job interview in shorts will probably lose any chance of getting the job; on the other hand, he or she might be so brilliant, the interviewer will overlook the unconventional attire.

Table 2–1 Norms and Sanctions

Norms	Sanctions	
	Positive	**Negative**
Formal	Salary bonus	Demotion
	Testimonial dinner	Firing from a job
	Medal	Jail sentence
	Diploma	Expulsion
Informal	Smile	Frown
	Compliment	Humiliation
	Cheers	Bullying

The entire fabric of norms and sanctions in a culture reflects that culture's values and priorities. The most cherished values will be most heavily sanctioned; matters regarded as less critical will carry light and informal sanctions.

VALUES

Though we all have our own personal sets of standards—which may include caring, fitness, or success in business—we also share a general set of objectives as members of a society. Cultural *values* are collective conceptions of what is considered good, desirable, and proper—or bad, undesirable, and improper. They indicate what people in a given culture prefer, as well as what they find important and morally right or wrong. Values may be specific, such as honoring one's parents and owning a home, or they may be more general, such as health, love, and democracy. Of course, the members of a society do not uniformly share its values. Angry political debates and billboards promoting conflicting causes tell us that much.

Values influence people's behavior and serve as criteria for evaluating the actions of others. There is often a direct relationship among a culture's values, norms, and sanctions. For example, if a culture highly values the institution of marriage, it may have norms (and strict sanctions) that prohibit the act of adultery. If a culture views private property as a basic value, it will probably have stiff laws against theft and vandalism.

Socially shared, intensely felt values are a fundamental part of life in the United States. Even so, our values can and do change. Each year more than 219,864 entering college students at 297 of the nation's four-year colleges fill out a questionnaire about their attitudes. Because this survey focuses on an array of issues, beliefs, and life goals, it is commonly cited as a barometer of the nation's values. The respondents are asked what values are personally important to them. Over the past 40 years, the value of "being very well-off financially" has shown the strongest gain in popularity; the proportion of first-year college students who endorse this value as "essential" or "very important" rose from 44 percent in 1967 to 78.1 percent in 2009 (see Figure 2–2). In contrast, the value that has shown the most striking decline in endorsement by students is "developing a meaningful philosophy of life." While this value was the most popular in the 1967 survey, endorsed by more than 80 percent of the respondents, it had fallen to seventh place on the list by 2009, when it was endorsed by 48 percent of students entering college.

During the 1980s and 1990s, support for values having to do with money, power, and status grew. At the same time, support for certain values having to do with social awareness and altruism, such as "helping others," declined. According to the 2009 nationwide survey, only 42.1 percent of first-year college students stated that "influencing social values" was an "essential" or "very important" goal. The proportion of students for whom "helping to promote racial understanding" was an essential or very important goal reached a record high of 42 percent in 1992, then fell to 33.1 in 2009—a decline from 2008, the year the nation

Figure 2–2

Life Goals of First-Year College Students in the United States, 1966–2009
SOURCES: UCLA Higher Education Research Institute, as reported in Astin et al. 1994; Pryor et al. 2007, 2009.

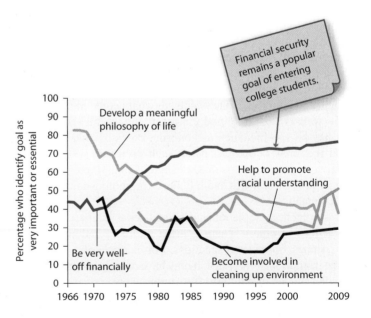

Financial security remains a popular goal of entering college students.

Develop a meaningful philosophy of life

Help to promote racial understanding

Be very well-off financially

Become involved in cleaning up environment

Think About It
Why do you think values have shifted among college students in the past few decades? Which of these values is important to you?

elected Barack Obama president. Like other aspects of culture, such as language and norms, a nation's values are not necessarily fixed.

Whether the slogan is "Plant a Tree" or "Think Green," students have been exposed to values associated with environmentalism. How many of them accept those values? Poll results over the past 40 years show fluctuations, with a high of nearly 46 percent of students indicating a desire to become involved in cleaning up the environment. Beginning in the 1980s, student support for embracing this objective dropped to around 20 percent or even lower (see Figure 2–2). Even with recent attention to global warming, the proportion remains level at only 26.9 percent of first-year students in 2009.

Global Culture War

When people's cultural values clash, social conflict may follow. For almost a generation, public attention in the United States has focused on *culture war,* or the polarization of society over controversial elements of culture. Originally, in the 1990s, the term referred to political debates over heated issues such as abortion, religious expression, gun control, and sexual orientation. Soon, however, it took on a global meaning—especially after 9/11, as Americans wondered, "Why do they hate us?" Through 2000, global studies of public opinion had reported favorable views of the United States in countries as diverse as Morocco and Germany. But by 2003, in the wake of the U.S. invasion of Iraq, foreign opinion of the United States had become quite negative (J. Hunter 1991; Kohut et al. 2005, 2007).

In the last 20 years, extensive efforts have been made to compare values in different nations, recognizing the challenges in interpreting value concepts in a similar manner across cultures. Psychologist Shalom Schwartz has measured values in more than 60 countries. Around the world, certain values are widely shared, including benevolence, which is defined as "forgiveness and loyalty." In contrast, power, defined as "control or dominance over people and resources," is a value that is endorsed much less often (Hitlin and Piliavin 2004; S. Schwartz and Bardi 2001).

Despite this evidence of shared values, some scholars have interpreted the terrorism, genocide, wars, and military occupations of the early 21st century as a "clash of civilizations." According to this thesis, cultural and religious identities, rather than national or political loyalties, are becoming the prime source of international conflict. Critics of this thesis point out that conflict over values is nothing new; only our ability to create havoc and violence has grown. Furthermore, speaking of a clash of "civilizations" disguises the sharp divisions that exist within large groups. Christianity, for example, runs the gamut from Quaker-style pacifism to certain elements of the Ku Klux Klan's ideology (Berman 2003; Huntington 1993; Said 2001).

Culture and the Dominant Ideology

Functionalist and conflict theorists agree that culture and society are mutually supportive, but for different reasons. Functionalists maintain that social stability requires a consensus and the support of society's members; strong central values and common norms provide that support. This view of culture became popular in sociology beginning in the 1950s. It was borrowed from British anthropologists who saw cultural traits as a stabilizing element in a culture. From a functionalist perspective, a cultural trait or practice will persist if it performs functions that society seems to need or contributes to overall social stability and consensus.

Conflict theorists agree that a common culture may exist, but they argue that it serves to maintain the privileges of certain groups. Moreover, in protecting their own self-interest, powerful groups may keep others in a subservient position. The term ***dominant ideology*** describes the set of cultural beliefs and practices that help to maintain powerful social, economic, and political interests. This concept was first used by Hungarian Marxist Georg Lukacs (1923) and Italian Marxist Antonio Gramsci (1929); it did not gain an audience in the United States until the early 1970s. In Karl Marx's view, a capitalist society has a dominant ideology that serves the interests of the ruling class.

From a conflict perspective, the dominant ideology has major social significance. Not only do a society's most powerful groups and institutions control wealth and property; even more important, they control the means of producing beliefs about reality through religion, education, and the media. From a feminist perspective, if all a society's most important institutions tell women they should be subservient to men, that dominant ideology will help to control women and keep them in a subordinate position.

A growing number of social scientists believe it is not easy to identify a "core culture" in the United States. For support, they point to the lack of consensus on national values, the diffusion of cultural traits, the diversity within our culture, and the changing views of young people. Yet there is no way of denying that certain expressions of values have greater influence than others, even in so complex a society as the United States.

Table 2–2 summarizes the major theoretical perspectives on culture.

Use Your Sociological Imagination

Look around your campus. Do the people you see suggest that the United States has a core culture with a dominant ideology, or a diverse culture with differing values and ideologies? What about the city or town where your college or university is located—does it suggest the same conclusion?

Culture and Socialization

What makes us who we are? Is it the genes we are born with, or the environment we grow up in? Researchers have traditionally clashed over the relative importance of biological and environmental factors in human development, a conflict called the *nature versus nurture* (or

Table 2–2 Sociological Perspectives on Culture

	Functionalist Perspective	Conflict Perspective	Feminist Perspective	Interactionist Perspective
Cultural Variation	Ethnocentrism reinforces group solidarity; subcultures serve the interests of subgroups	Ethnocentrism devalues groups; countercultures question the dominant social order	Cultural relativism respects variations in the way men and women are viewed in different societies	Customs and traditions are transmitted through intergroup contact and through the media
Norms	Reinforce societal standards	Reinforce patterns of dominance	Reinforce roles of men and women	Are maintained through face-to-face interaction
Values	Are collective conceptions of what is good	May perpetuate social inequality	May perpetuate men's dominance	Are defined and redefined through social interaction
Culture and Society	Culture reflects a society's strong central values	Culture reflects a society's dominant ideology	Culture reflects society's view of men and women	A society's core culture is perpetuated through daily social interactions

heredity versus environment) debate. Today, most social scientists have moved beyond this debate, acknowledging instead the *interaction* of the two variables in shaping human development. However, we can better appreciate how heredity and environment interact to influence the socialization process if we first examine situations in which one factor operates almost entirely without the other (Homans 1979).

SOCIOBIOLOGY: THE IMPACT OF HEREDITY

While sociology emphasizes diversity and change in the expression of culture, another school of thought, sociobiology, stresses the universal aspects of culture. **Sociobiology** is the systematic study of how biology affects human social behavior. Sociobiologists assert that many of the cultural traits humans display, such as the almost universal expectation that women will be nurturers and men will be providers, are not learned but are rooted in our genetic makeup.

Sociobiology is founded on the naturalist Charles Darwin's (1859) theory of evolution. In traveling the world, Darwin had noted small variations in species from one location to another. He theorized that over hundreds of generations, random variations in genetic makeup had helped certain members of a species to survive in a particular environment. The species was slowly adapting to its environment. Darwin called this process of adaptation to the environment through random genetic variation *natural selection.*

Sociobiologists apply Darwin's principle of natural selection to the study of social behavior. They assume that particular forms of behavior become genetically linked to a species if they contribute to its fitness to survive (van den Berghe 1978). In its extreme form, sociobiology suggests that *all* behavior is the result of genetic or biological factors and that social interactions play no role in shaping people's conduct.

Some researchers insist that intellectual interest in sociobiology will only deflect serious study of the more significant influence on human behavior, the social environment. Yet Lois Wladis Hoffman (1985), in her presidential address to the Society for the Psychological Study of Social Issues, argued that sociobiology poses a valuable challenge to social scientists to better document their research. Interactionists, for example, could show how social behavior is not programmed by human biology, but instead adjusts continually to the attitudes and responses of others.

Certainly most social scientists would agree that there is a biological basis for social behavior. But there is less support for the extreme positions taken by certain advocates of sociobiology. Like interactionists, conflict theorists and functionalists believe that people's behavior rather than their genetic structure defines social reality. Conflict theorists fear that the sociobiological approach could be used as an argument against efforts to assist disadvantaged people, such as schoolchildren who are not competing successfully (Freese 2008; Machalek and Martin 2010; E. Wilson 2000).

SOCIAL ENVIRONMENT: THE IMPACT OF ISOLATION

In the 1994 movie *Nell,* Jodie Foster played a young woman hidden from birth by her mother in a backwoods cabin. Raised without normal human contact, Nell crouches like an animal, screams wildly, and speaks or sings in a language all her own. The movie was drawn from the actual account of an emaciated 16-year-old boy who appeared mysteriously in 1828 in the town square of Nuremberg, Germany (Lipson 1994).

Some viewers may have found the story of Nell difficult to believe, but the painful childhood of a girl called Isabelle was all too real. For the first six years of her life, Isabelle lived in almost total seclusion in a darkened room. She had little contact with other people, with the exception of her mother, who could neither speak nor hear. Isabelle's grandparents had been so deeply ashamed of her illegitimate birth that they kept her hidden away from the world. Ohio authorities finally discovered the child in 1938, when Isabelle's mother escaped from her parents' home, taking her daughter with her.

When Isabelle was discovered at age six, she could not speak; she could merely make various croaking sounds. Her only communications with her mother were simple gestures. Isabelle had been largely deprived of the typical interactions and socialization experiences of childhood. Since she had seen few people, she initially showed a strong fear of strangers and reacted almost like a wild animal when confronted with an unfamiliar person. As she became accustomed to seeing certain individuals, her reaction changed to one of extreme apathy. At first, observers believed that Isabelle was deaf, but she soon began to react to nearby sounds. On tests of maturity, she scored at the level of an infant rather than a six-year-old.

Specialists developed a systematic training program to help Isabelle adapt to human relationships and socialization. After a few days of training, she made her first attempt to verbalize. Although she started slowly, Isabelle passed quickly through six years of development. In a little over two months, she was speaking in complete sentences. Nine months later she could identify both words and sentences. Before Isabelle reached the age of nine, she was ready to attend school with other children. By her 14th year she was in 6th grade, doing well in school, and was emotionally well-adjusted.

Yet without an opportunity to experience socialization in her first six years, Isabelle had been hardly human in the social sense when she was first discovered. Her inability to communicate at the time of her discovery—despite her physical and cognitive potential to learn—and her remarkable progress over the next few years underscore the impact of socialization on human development (K. Davis 1940, 1947).

Unfortunately, other children who have been locked away or severely neglected have not fared so well as Isabelle. In many instances, the consequences of social isolation have proved much more damaging. For example, in 1970 a 14-year-old Californian named Genie was discovered in a room where she had been confined since the age of 20 months. During her years of isolation, no family member had spoken to her, nor could she hear anything other than swearing. Since there was no television or radio in her home, she had never heard the sounds of normal human speech. One year after beginning extensive therapy, Genie's grammar resembled that of a typical 18-month-old. Though she made further advances with continued therapy, she never achieved full language ability. Figure 2–3 shows a sketch Genie made of her teacher five years after she was discovered (Curtiss 1977, 1985; Rymer 1993).

Isabelle's and Genie's experiences are important to researchers because there are only a few cases of children reared in total isolation. Unfortunately, however, there are many cases of children raised in extremely neglectful social circumstances. Recently, attention has focused on infants and young children from orphanages in the formerly communist countries of Eastern Europe. In Romanian orphanages, babies once lay in their cribs for 18 to 20 hours a day, curled against their feeding bottles and receiving little adult care. Such minimal attention continued for the first five years of their lives. Many of them were fearful of human contact and prone to unpredictable antisocial behavior. This situation came to light as families in North America and Europe

Figure 2–3
Genie's Sketch

This sketch was made in 1975 by Genie—a girl who had been isolated for most of her 14 years, until she was discovered by authorities in 1970. In her drawing, her linguist friend (on the left) plays the piano while Genie listens. Genie was 18 when she drew this picture.
SOURCE: Curtiss 1977:274.

began adopting thousands of the children. The adjustment problems for about 20 percent of them were often so dramatic that the adopting families suffered guilty fears of being ill-fit adoptive parents. Many of them have asked for assistance in dealing with the children. Slowly, efforts are being made to introduce the deprived youngsters to feelings of attachment that they have never experienced before (Groza et al. 1999; M. Talbot 1998).

Increasingly, researchers are emphasizing the importance of early socialization experiences for children who grow up in more normal environments. We know now that it is not enough to care for an infant's physical needs; parents must also concern themselves with children's social development. If, for example, children are discouraged from having friends, they will miss out on social interactions that are critical for emotional growth.

Use Your
Sociological Imagination

What events in your life have had a strong influence on who you are?

The Self and Socialization

We all have various perceptions, feelings, and beliefs about who we are and what we are like. How do we come to develop these ideas? Do they change as we age?

We were not born with these understandings. Building on the work of George Herbert Mead (1964b), sociologists recognize that we create our own designation: the *self*. The **self** is a distinct identity that sets one apart from others. It is not a static phenomenon, but continues to develop and change throughout our lives.

Sociologists and psychologists alike have expressed interest in how the individual develops and modifies the sense of self as a result of social interaction. The work of sociologists Charles Horton Cooley and George Herbert Mead, pioneers of the interactionist approach, has been especially useful in furthering our understanding of these important issues.

COOLEY: LOOKING-GLASS SELF

In the early 1900s, Charles Horton Cooley advanced the belief that we learn who we are by interacting with others. Our view of ourselves, then, comes not only from direct contemplation of our personal qualities but also from our impressions of how others perceive us. Cooley used the phrase *looking-glass self* to emphasize that the self is the product of our social interactions with other people.

The process of developing a self-identity or self-concept has three phases. First, we imagine how we present ourselves to others—to relatives, friends, even strangers on the street. Then we imagine how others evaluate us (attractive, intelligent, shy, or strange). Finally, we develop some sort of feeling about ourselves, such as respect or shame, as a result of these impressions (Cooley 1902).

A subtle but critical aspect of Cooley's looking-glass self is that it results from an individual's "imagination" of how others view him or her. As a result, we can develop self-identities based on *incorrect* perceptions of how others see us. A student may react strongly to a teacher's criticism and decide (wrongly) that the instructor views him or her as stupid. This misperception can easily be converted into a negative self-identity through the following process: (1) The teacher criticized me, (2) the teacher must think that I'm stupid, (3) I *am* stupid. Yet self-identities are also subject to change. If the student receives an A at the end of the course, he or she will probably no longer feel stupid.

MEAD: STAGES OF THE SELF

George Herbert Mead continued Cooley's exploration of interactionist theory. Mead (1934, 1964a) developed a useful model of the process by which the self emerges, defined by three distinct stages: the preparatory stage, the play stage, and the game stage.

The Preparatory Stage   During the *preparatory stage,* children imitate the people around them, especially family members with whom they continually interact. Thus, a small child will bang on a piece of wood while a parent is engaged in carpentry work, or will try to throw a ball if an older sibling is doing so nearby.

As they grow older, children become more adept at using symbols to communicate with others. *Symbols* are the gestures, objects, and language that form the basis of human communication. By interacting with relatives and friends, as well as by watching cartoons on television and looking at picture books, children in the preparatory stage begin to understand the use of symbols.

In multicultural societies, cultural differences in the meaning of symbols create the potential for conflict. For example, the symbolic headscarf that Muslim women wear recently became a major social issue in France. For years French public schools have banned overt signs of religion, such as large crosses, skullcaps, and headscarves. Muslim students who violated the informal dress code were expelled. In 2003, amid growing controversy, a government advisory panel recommended that the French Parliament strengthen the ban by writing it into law. The issue is a particularly thorny one because of the conflicting cultural meanings these symbols carry. To many of the French, the headscarf symbolizes the submission of women—an unwelcome connotation in a society that places a high value on egalitarianism. To others it represents a challenge to the French way of life. Thus, 69 percent of the French surveyed on the issue supported the ban. But to Muslims, the headscarf symbolizes modesty and respectability. Muslim schoolchildren take this symbol very seriously (*The Economist* 2004).

The Play Stage   Mead was among the first to analyze the relationship of symbols to socialization. As children develop skill in communicating through symbols, they gradually become more aware of social relationships. As a result, during the *play stage,* the child begins to pretend to be other people. Just as an actor "becomes" a character, a child becomes a doctor, parent, superhero, or ship captain.

In fact, Mead noted that an important aspect of the play stage is role playing. **Role taking** is the process of mentally assuming the perspective of another in order to respond from that imagined viewpoint. Through this process, a young child will gradually learn when it is best to ask a parent for favors. If the parent usually comes home from work in a bad mood, the child will wait until after dinner, when the parent is more relaxed and approachable.

The Game Stage   In Mead's third stage, the *game stage,* the child of about eight or nine years old no longer just plays roles but begins to consider several tasks and relationships simultaneously. At this point in development, children grasp not only their own social positions but also those of others around them—just as in a football game the players must understand their own and everyone else's positions. Consider a girl or boy who is part of a scout troop out on a weekend hike in the mountains. The child must understand what he or she is expected to do but must also recognize the responsibilities of other scouts and of the leaders. This is the final stage of development in Mead's model; the child can now respond to numerous members of the social environment.

Mead uses the term **generalized other** to refer to the attitudes, viewpoints, and expectations of society as a whole that a child takes into account in his or her behavior. Simply put, this concept suggests that when an individual acts, he or she takes into account an entire group of people. For example, a child will not act courteously merely to please a particular parent. Rather, the child comes to understand that courtesy is a widespread social value endorsed by parents, teachers, and religious leaders.

In the game stage, children can take a more sophisticated view of people and their social environment. They now understand what specific occupations and social positions are and no longer equate Mr. Williams only with the role of "librarian" or Ms. Franks only with "principal." It has become clear to the child that Mr. Williams can be a librarian, a parent, and a marathon runner at the same time, and that Ms. Franks is one of many principals in our society. Thus, the child has reached a new level of sophistication in his or her observations of individuals and institutions. Table 2–3 summarizes the three stages of the self outlined by George Herbert Mead.

MEAD: THEORY OF THE SELF

Mead is best known for his theory of the self. According to Mead (1964b), the self begins as the privileged center of a person's world. Young children picture themselves as the focus of everything around them and find it difficult to consider the perspectives of others. When shown a mountain scene and asked to describe what an observer on the opposite side of the mountain sees (such as a lake or hikers), they describe only objects visible from their own vantage point. This childhood tendency to place ourselves at the center of events never entirely disappears. Many people with a fear of flying automatically assume that if any plane goes down, it will be the one they are on. And who reads the horoscope section in the paper without looking at their own horoscope first? Why else do we buy lottery tickets, if we don't imagine ourselves winning?

Nonetheless, as people mature, the self changes and begins to reflect greater concern for the reactions of others. Mead used the term *significant others* to refer to those individuals who are most important in

Table 2–3 Mead's Stages of the Self

Stage	Self Present?	Definition	Example
Preparation	No	Child imitates the actions of others	When adults laugh and smile, child laughs and smiles
Play	Developing	Child takes the role of a single other, as if he or she were the other	Child first takes the role of doctor, then the role of patient
Game	Yes	Child considers the roles of two or more others simultaneously	In game of hide-and-seek, child takes into account the roles of both hider and seeker

summingUP

the development of the self. Parents, friends, co-workers, coaches, and teachers are often among those who play a major role in shaping a person's self. Many young people, for example, find themselves drawn to the same kind of work their parents engage in (H. Sullivan [1953] 1968).

In some instances, studies of significant others have generated controversy among researchers. For example, some researchers contend that African American adolescents are more "peer-oriented" than their White counterparts because of presumed weaknesses in Black families. However, investigations indicate that this hasty conclusion is based on limited studies focused on less affluent Blacks. In fact, there appears to be little difference in the people African Americans and Whites from similar economic backgrounds regard as their significant others (Giordano et al. 1993; Juhasz 1989).

GOFFMAN: PRESENTATION OF THE SELF

How do we manage our "self"? How do we display to others who we are? Erving Goffman, a sociologist associated with the interactionist perspective, suggested that many of our daily activities involve attempts to convey impressions of who we are.

Early in life, the individual learns to slant his or her presentation of the self in order to create distinctive appearances and satisfy particular audiences. Goffman (1959) refers to this altering of the presentation of the self as ***impression management.*** In analyzing such everyday social interactions, Goffman makes so many explicit parallels to the theater that his view has been termed the ***dramaturgical approach.*** According to this perspective, people resemble performers in action. For example, a clerk may try to appear busier than he or she actually is if a supervisor happens to be watching. A customer in a singles' bar may try to look as if he or she is waiting for a particular person to arrive.

Use Your Sociological Imagination

Who have been your significant others? Are you someone else's significant other?

People judge us by our appearance, attire, body language, demeanor, and mannerisms. Knowing that they do, most of us alter the way we present ourselves to others, a strategy that Goffman called impression management.

Goffman's work on the self represents a logical progression of the sociological work begun by Cooley and Mead on how personality is acquired through socialization and how we manage the presentation of the self to others. Cooley stressed the process by which we come to create a self; Mead focused on how the self develops as we learn to interact with others; Goffman emphasized the ways in which we consciously create images of ourselves for others.

PSYCHOLOGICAL APPROACHES TO THE SELF

Psychologists have shared the interest of Cooley, Mead, and other sociologists in the development of the self. Early work in psychology, such as that of Sigmund Freud (1856–1939), stressed the role of inborn drives—among them the drive for sexual gratification—in channeling human behavior. More recently, psychologists such as Jean Piaget have emphasized the stages through which human beings progress as the self develops.

Like Charles Horton Cooley and George Herbert Mead, Freud believed that the self is a social product and that aspects of one's personality are influenced by other people (especially one's parents). However, unlike Cooley and Mead, he suggested that the self has components that work in opposition to each other. According to Freud, our natural impulsive instincts are in constant conflict with societal constraints. Part of us seeks limitless pleasure, while another part favors rational behavior. By interacting with others, we learn the expectations of society and then select behavior most appropriate to our own culture. (Of course, as Freud was well aware, we sometimes distort reality and behave irrationally.)

Research on newborn babies by the Swiss child psychologist Jean Piaget (1896–1980) has underscored the importance of social interactions in developing a sense of self. Piaget found that newborns have no self in the sense of a looking-glass image. Ironically, though, they are quite self-centered; they demand that all attention be directed toward them. Newborns have not yet separated themselves from the universe of which they are a part. For these babies, the phrase "you and me" has no meaning: They understand only "me." However, as they mature, children are gradually socialized into social relationships, even within their rather self-centered world.

In his well-known *cognitive theory of development,* Piaget (1954) identified four stages in the development of children's thought processes. In the first, or *sensorimotor,* stage, young children use their senses to make discoveries. For example, through touching they discover that their hands are actually a part of themselves. During the second, or *preoperational,* stage, children begin to use words and symbols to distinguish objects and ideas. The milestone in the third, or *concrete operational,* stage is that children engage in more logical thinking. They learn that even when a formless lump of clay is shaped into a snake, it is still the same clay. Finally, in the fourth, or *formal operational,* stage, adolescents become capable of sophisticated abstract thought and can deal with ideas and values in a logical manner.

Piaget suggested that moral development becomes an important part of socialization as children develop the ability to think more abstractly. When children learn the rules of a game such as checkers or jacks, they are learning to obey societal norms. Those under eight years old display a rather basic level of morality: Rules are rules, and there is no concept of "extenuating circumstances." As they mature, children become capable of greater autonomy and begin to experience moral dilemmas and doubts as to what constitutes proper behavior.

According to Jean Piaget, social interaction is the key to development. As children grow older, they pay increasing attention to how other people think and why they act in particular ways. In order to develop a distinct personality, each of us needs opportunities to interact with others. As we saw earlier, Isabelle was deprived of the chance for normal social interactions, and the consequences were severe (Kitchener 1991).

We have seen that a number of thinkers considered social interaction the key to the development of an individual's sense of self. As is generally true, we can best understand this topic by drawing on a variety of theory and research. Table 2–4 summarizes the rich literature, both sociological and psychological, on the development of the self.

summingUP

Table 2–4 Theoretical Approaches to Development of the Self

Scholar	Key Concepts and Contributions	Major Points of Theory
Charles Horton Cooley 1864–1929 sociologist (USA)	Looking-glass self	Stages of development not distinct; feelings toward ourselves developed through interaction with others
George Herbert Mead 1863–1931 sociologist (USA)	The self Generalized other	Three distinct stages of development; self develops as children grasp the roles of others in their lives
Erving Goffman 1922–1982 sociologist (USA)	Impression management Dramaturgical approach Face-work	Self developed through the impressions we convey to others and to groups
Sigmund Freud 1856–1939 psychotherapist (Austria)	Psychoanalysis	Self influenced by parents and by inborn drives, such as the drive for sexual gratification
Jean Piaget 1896–1980 child psychologist (Switzerland)	Cognitive theory of development	Four stages of cognitive development; moral development linked to socialization

Agents of Socialization

We have seen that each culture considers its own distinctive ways of handling basic societal tasks to be "natural." Yet methods of education, marital ceremonies, religious doctrines, and other aspects of culture differ markedly from one society to another. Parents in India are accustomed to arranging marriages for their children; parents in the United States leave marital decisions up to their offspring. Lifelong residents of Naples consider it natural to speak Italian; lifelong residents of Buenos Aires feel the same way about Spanish. These cultural preferences are learned and transmitted through the process of socialization.

The continuing and lifelong socialization process involves many different social forces that influence our lives and alter our self-images. The family is the most important agent of socialization in the United States, especially for children. We'll also give particular attention in this section to six other agents of socialization: the school, the peer group, the mass media, the workplace, religion, and the state.

FAMILY

Children in Amish communities are raised in a highly structured and disciplined manner. But they are not immune to the temptations posed by their peers in the non-Amish world—"rebellious" acts such as dancing, drinking, and riding in cars. Still, Amish families don't get too concerned; they know the strong influence they ultimately exert over their offspring. The same is true for the family in general. It is tempting to say that the "peer group" or even the "media" really raise children these days, especially when the spotlight falls on young people involved in shooting sprees and hate crimes. Almost all available research, however, shows that the role of the family in socializing a child cannot be overestimated (Schaefer and Zellner 2011).

The lifelong process of learning begins shortly after birth. Since newborns can hear, see, smell, taste, and feel heat, cold, and pain, they are constantly orienting themselves to the surrounding world. Human beings, especially family members, constitute an important part of their social environment. People minister to the baby's needs by feeding, cleansing, carrying, and comforting the baby.

The term *gender role* refers to expectations regarding the proper behavior, attitudes, and activities of males or females. For example, we traditionally think of "toughness" as masculine—and desirable in men but not women—while we view "tenderness" as feminine. Yet other cultures do not necessarily assign these qualities to each gender in the way that our culture does.

The existence of gender roles does not imply that inevitably, males and females will assume certain roles, nor does it imply that those roles are quite distinct from each other. Rather, gender roles emphasize the fact that males and females are not genetically predetermined to occupy certain roles.

As the primary agents of childhood socialization, parents play a critical role in guiding children into those gender roles deemed appropriate in a society. Other adults, older siblings, the mass media, and religious and educational institutions also have a noticeable impact on a child's socialization into feminine and masculine norms. A culture or subculture may require that one sex or the other take primary responsibility for the socialization of children, economic support of the family, or religious or intellectual leadership.

Interactionists remind us that socialization concerning not only masculinity and femininity but also marriage and parenthood begins in childhood as a part of family life. Children observe their parents as they express affection, deal with finances, quarrel, complain about in-laws, and so forth. These experiences represent an informal process of anticipatory socialization. The child develops a tentative model of what being married and being a parent are like.

SCHOOL

Where did you learn the national anthem? Who taught you about the heroes of the American Revolution? Where were you first tested on your knowledge of your culture? Like the family, schools have an explicit mandate to socialize people in the United States—and especially children—into the norms and values of our culture.

As conflict theorists Samuel Bowles and Herbert Gintis (1976) have observed, schools in this country foster competition through built-in systems of reward and punishment, such as grades and evaluations by teachers. Consequently, a child who is working intently to learn a new skill can sometimes come to feel stupid and unsuccessful. However, as the self matures, children become capable of increasingly realistic assessments of their intellectual, physical, and social abilities.

Functionalists point out that as agents of socialization, schools fulfill the function of teaching children the values and customs of the larger society. Conflict theorists agree but add that schools can reinforce the divisive aspects of society, especially those of social class. For example, higher education in the United States is costly despite the existence of financial aid programs. Students from affluent backgrounds have an advantage in gaining access to universities and professional training. At the same time, less affluent young people may never receive the preparation that would qualify them for the best-paying and most prestigious jobs.

In other cultures as well, schools serve socialization functions. During the 1980s, for example, Japanese parents and educators were distressed to realize that children were gradually losing the knack of eating with chopsticks. The trend became a national issue in 1997, when school lunch programs introduced plastic "sporks" (combined fork and spoon, used frequently in the United States). National leaders, responding to the public outcry, banished sporks in favor of *hashi* (chopsticks). On a more serious note, Japanese schools have come under increasing pressure in recent years as working parents have abdicated more and more responsibility to educational institutions. To rectify the imbalance, the Japanese government in 1998 promoted a guide to better parenting, calling on parents to read more with their children, allow for more playtime, limit TV watching, and plan family activities (Gauette 1998).

PEER GROUP

Ask 13-year-olds who matters most in their lives and they are likely to answer "friends." As a child grows older, the family becomes somewhat less important in a person's social development, and peer groups increasingly assume the role of Mead's significant others. Within the peer group, young people associate with others who are approximately their own age and who often enjoy a similar social status (Giordano 2003).

We can see how important peer groups are to young people when their social lives are strained by war or disaster. In Baghdad, the overthrow of Saddam Hussein has profoundly changed teenagers' world, casting doubt on their future. Some young people have lost relatives or friends; others have become involved with fundamentalist groups or fled with their families to safer countries. Those youths who are left behind can suffer intense loneliness and boredom. Confined to their homes by crime and terrorism, those fortunate enough to have computers turn to Internet chat rooms or immerse themselves in their studies. Through e-mail, they struggle to maintain old friendships interrupted by wartime dislocation (Sanders 2004).

Peers can be the source of harassment as well as support, as news stories around the world have shown. This problem has received considerable attention in Japan, where bullying in school is a constant fact of life. Groups of students act together to humiliate, disgrace, or torment a specific student, a practice known in Japan as *ijime*. Most students go along with the bullying out of fear that they themselves might become the target. In some cases the *ijime* has led to a child's suicide. In 1998 the situation became so desperate that a volunteer association set up a 24-hour telephone hotline in Tokyo just for children. The success of the effort convinced the government to sponsor a nationwide hotline system (Matsushita 1999; Sugimoto 1997).

MASS MEDIA AND TECHNOLOGY

In the past 80 years, media innovations—radio, motion pictures, recorded music, television, and the Internet—have become important agents of socialization. Television, and increasingly the Internet, are critical forces in the socialization of children in the United States. One national survey indicates that 68 percent of U.S. children have a television in their bedroom, and nearly 50 percent of all youths ages 8 to 18 use the Internet every day (see Figure 2–4).

These media, however, are not always a negative socializing influence. Television programs and even commercials can introduce young people to unfamiliar lifestyles and cultures. Not only do children in the United States learn about life in "faraway lands," but inner-city children learn about the lives of farm children, and vice versa. The same thing happens in other countries.

Sociologists and other social scientists have begun to consider the impact of technology on socialization. They are particularly interested in the online social media networks, like Facebook. Does this way of

Figure 2–4
The New Normal:
Internet at Home
SOURCE: Rideout et al.
2010.

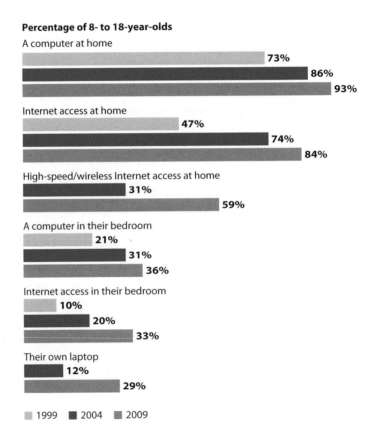

Percentage of 8- to 18-year-olds

A computer at home — 73%, 86%, 93%

Internet access at home — 47%, 74%, 84%

High-speed/wireless Internet access at home — 31%, 59%

A computer in their bedroom — 21%, 31%, 36%

Internet access in their bedroom — 10%, 20%, 33%

Their own laptop — 12%, 29%

1999   2004   2009

Think About It
How did your use of the Internet when you were younger compare to these survey results?

communicating resemble face-to-face interaction, or does it represent a new form of social interaction?

Not just in industrial nations, but in Africa and other developing areas, people have been socialized into relying on new communications technologies. Not long ago, if Zadhe Iyombe wanted to talk to his mother, he had to make an eight-day trip from the capital city of Kinshasa up the Congo River by boat to the rural town where he was born. Now both he and his mother have access to a cell phone, and they send text messages to each other daily. Iyombe and his mother are not atypical. Although cell phones aren't cheap, 1.4 billion owners in developing countries have come to consider them a necessity. Today, there are more cell phones in developing nations than in industrial nations—the first time in history that developing nations have outpaced the developed world in the adoption of a telecommunications technology (K. Sullivan 2006).

WORKPLACE

Learning to behave appropriately in the workplace is a fundamental aspect of human socialization. In the United States, working full-time confirms one's adult status; it indicates to all that one has passed out of adolescence. In a sense, socialization into an occupation can represent both a harsh reality ("I have to work in order to buy food and pay the rent") and the realization of an ambition ("I've always wanted to be an airline pilot") (Moore 1968:862).

Once, "going to work" began with the end of one's formal schooling, but that is no longer the case, at least not in the United States. More and more young people work today, and not just for a parent or relative. Adolescents generally seek jobs in order to make spending money; 80 percent of high school seniors say that little or none of what they earn goes to family expenses. They rarely look on their employment as a means of exploring vocational interests or getting on-the-job training (R. Cooper 1998).

RELIGION AND THE STATE

Increasingly, social scientists are recognizing the importance of both government ("the state") and religion as agents of socialization, because of their impact on the life course. Traditionally, family members have served as the primary caregivers in our culture, but in the 20th century, the family's protective function was steadily transferred to outside agencies such as hospitals, mental health clinics, and child care centers. Many of these agencies are run by the state or by groups affiliated with certain religions.

Both government and organized religion have impacted the life course by reinstituting some of the rites of passage once observed in agricultural communities and early industrial societies. For example, religious organizations stipulate certain traditional rites that may bring together all the members of an extended family, even if they never meet for any other reason. And government regulations stipulate the ages at which a person may drive a car, drink alcohol, vote in elections, marry without parental permission, work overtime, and retire. These regulations do not constitute strict rites of passage: Most 18-year-olds choose not to vote, and most people choose their age of retirement without reference to government dictates.

Socialization throughout the Life Course

THE LIFE COURSE

Among the Kota people of the Congo, adolescents paint themselves blue. Mexican American girls go on a daylong religious retreat before dancing the night away. Egyptian mothers step over their newborn infants seven times, and students at the U.S. Naval Academy throw their hats in the air. These are all ways of celebrating *rites of passage,* a means of dramatizing and validating changes in a person's status. The Kota rite marks the passage to adulthood. The color blue, viewed as the color of death, symbolizes the death of childhood. Hispanic girls celebrate reaching womanhood at age 15 with a *quinceañera* ceremony. In many Latino communities in the United States, the popularity of the *quinceañera* supports a network of party planners, caterers, dress designers, and the Miss Quinceañera Latina pageant.

These specific ceremonies mark stages of development in the life course. They indicate that the process of socialization continues through all stages

What was the last rite of passage you participated in? Was it formal or informal?

of the life cycle. In fact, some researchers have chosen to concentrate on socialization as a lifelong process. Sociologists and other social scientists who take such a *life-course approach* look closely at the social factors that influence people throughout their lives, from birth to death. They recognize that biological changes mold but do not dictate human behavior.

ANTICIPATORY SOCIALIZATION AND RESOCIALIZATION

The development of a social self is literally a lifelong transformation that begins in the crib and continues even as one prepares for death. Two types of socialization occur at many points throughout the life course: anticipatory socialization and resocialization.

Anticipatory socialization refers to the processes of socialization in which a person "rehearses" for future positions, occupations, and social relationships. A culture can function more efficiently and smoothly if members become acquainted with the norms, values, and behavior associated with a social position before actually assuming that status. Preparation for many aspects of adult life begins with anticipatory socialization during childhood and adolescence and continues throughout our lives as we prepare for new responsibilities.

Occasionally, assuming new social and occupational positions requires us to *unlearn* an established orientation. *Resocialization* refers to the process of discarding former behavior patterns and accepting new ones as part of a transition in one's life. Often resocialization occurs when there is an explicit effort to transform an individual, as happens in reform schools, therapy groups, prisons, religious conversion settings, and political indoctrination camps. The process of resocialization typically involves considerable stress for the individual, much more so than socialization in general or even anticipatory socialization (Gecas 1982).

Resocialization is particularly effective when it occurs within a total institution. Erving Goffman (1961) coined the term *total institution* to refer to institutions such as prisons, the military, mental hospitals, and convents, which regulate all aspects of a person's life under a single authority. Because the total institution is generally cut off from the rest of society, it provides for all the needs of its members. Quite literally, the crew of a merchant vessel at sea becomes part of a total institution. So elaborate are its requirements, so all-encompassing its activities, a total institution often represents a miniature society.

Goffman (1961) identified four common traits of total institutions, as follows:

1. All aspects of life are conducted in the same place under the control of a single authority.
2. Any activities within the institution are conducted in the company of others in the same circumstances—for example, army recruits or novices in a convent.

3. The authorities devise rules and schedule activities without consulting the participants.

4. All aspects of life within a total institution are designed to fulfill the purpose of the organization. Thus, all activities in a monastery might be centered on prayer and communion with God.

People often lose their individuality within total institutions. For example, a person entering prison may experience the humiliation of a *degradation ceremony* as he or she is stripped of clothing, jewelry, and other personal possessions. From this point onward, scheduled daily routines allow for little or no personal initiative. The individual becomes secondary and rather invisible in the overbearing social environment (Garfinkel 1956).

Sociology Matters

Sociology matters because it raises your awareness of cultural patterns you would otherwise take for granted.

- What culture and/or subcultures do you belong to? Have you ever questioned your culture's norms and values?
- How does your culture relate to cultures in other societies? Do you feel comfortable in mainstream society?

Sociology matters, too, because it shows you how you became who you are.

- How do you view yourself as you interact with others around you? How do you think you formed this view of yourself?
- What people, groups, or social institutions have been particularly important in helping you to define who you are?

Summary

Culture is the totality of learned, socially transmitted customs, knowledge, material objects, and behavior that defines the group or **society** to which we belong. People learn these elements of culture through the lifelong process of **socialization.** This chapter presented the basic elements that are common to all cultures, as well as variations that distinguish one culture from another. It examined the role of socialization in human development, including the way in which people develop their concept of the **self.** It closed with a description of the major agents of socialization and the life-course approach to socialization.

1. **Cultural universals** are general practices that are found in every **culture,** including courtship, family, games, language, medicine, religion, and sexual restrictions. The manner in which these universal practices are expressed varies from one culture to the next, however.

2. Most people use their own culture as the standard for evaluating other cultures, a perspective that is called **ethnocentrism.** Some sociologists attempt to see other cultures as members of those cultures see them, a perspective called **cultural relativism.**

3. In recent decades, international trade and the exchange of ideas have accelerated cultural change. Sociologists use the term **globalization** to refer to the resulting worldwide integration of government policies, cultures, social movements, and financial markets.

4. **Language,** an important element of culture, includes speech, writing, and symbols as well as gestures and other forms of **nonverbal communication.** Language both describes and shapes culture.

5. **Norms** are the standards of behavior members of a society are expected to uphold. Norms may be **formal**—written down—or **informal**—generally understood. **Sanctions** are the rewards and punishments meted out to those who comply with or violate social norms.

6. Every culture has a **dominant ideology**—a set of beliefs and practices that reinforce powerful social, economic, and political interests. Large cultures may include **subcultures**—groups of people who share norms and values that differ from those of the larger society and may contradict the dominant ideology.

7. The process of **socialization** to a society's cultural values is influenced both by the environment and by heredity. The study of the biological bases of social behavior is called **sociobiology.**

8. Charles Horton Cooley asserted that we learn who we are by interacting with others, a phenomenon he called the **looking-glass self.** Another interactionist, George Herbert Mead, proposed a three-stage theory of the development of the **self.**

9. Erving Goffman showed that many of our daily activities involve attempts to convey distinct impressions of who we are, a process he called **impression management.**

10. Sociologists who take a **life-course approach** to the study of socialization are interested in the social factors that influence people throughout their lives, from birth to death. The primary agents in this process are the family, schools, peer groups, the mass media and technology, the workplace, religion, and the state.

Key Terms

anticipatory
    socialization, 71

argot, 45

cognitive theory of
    development, 63

counterculture, 46

cultural relativism, 41

cultural universal, 40

culture, 38

culture industry, 40

culture lag, 44

culture shock, 46

culture war, 53

degradation
    ceremony, 72

diffusion, 43

discovery, 42

dominant ideology, 54

dramaturgical
    approach, 62

ethnocentrism, 40

folkway, 49

formal norm, 49

gender role, 65

generalized other, 60

globalization, 43

impression
    management, 62

informal norm, 49

innovation, 42

invention, 42

language, 47

law, 49

life-course
    approach, 71

looking-glass self, 59

material culture, 44

McDonaldization, 43

mores, 49

nonmaterial
    culture, 44

norm, 48

personality, 38

resocialization, 71

rite of passage, 70

role taking, 60

sanction, 50

self, 58

significant other, 61

socialization, 38

society, 39

sociobiology, 55

subculture, 44

symbol, 59

technology, 44

total institution, 71

value, 51

Social Interaction, Groups, and Social Structure

Social Interaction
and Reality

Elements of Social Structure

Social Structure in Global
Perspective

Understanding
Organizations

In the early 1970s, social psychologist Philip Zimbardo asked 70 male students at Stanford University to participate in an unorthodox experiment: a mock prison he had set up in the basement of a campus building. Using a coin toss, Zimbardo assigned half the subjects to play the role of prisoner and half to act as prison guards. He told the "guards" to make up their own rules for running the prison, then waited to see what would happen.

The results both astonished and frightened Zimbardo. Virtually overnight, the guards became tough enforcers of the rules, shouting curt commands at the prisoners. Some became cruel and abusive; one even forced a prisoner into "solitary confinement" in a closet. The prisoners reacted just as swiftly: some became depressed, apathetic, and helpless; others, rebellious and angry. In just six days, the situation became so intolerable that Zimbardo was forced to abandon the study. Given the anxiety and distress he had observed in the student prisoners, continuing the experiment would have been unethical (Zimbardo 2007).

In this study, college students adopted predictable patterns of behavior (those expected of guards and prisoners) when they were placed together in a mock prison. Sociologists use the term *social interaction* to refer to the ways in which people respond to one another. Social interaction need not be face-to-face; talking over the telephone and communicating via e-mail are also forms of social interaction. In Zimbardo's mock prison experiment, the social interactions between guards and prisoners were highly impersonal. Guards wore reflective sunglasses that made eye contact impossible and addressed prisoners by number rather than by name.

As in many real-life prisons, the simulated prison at Stanford had a social structure in which guards held virtually total control over prisoners. Formally defined, *social structure* is the way in which a society is organized into predictable relationships. Clearly, the prison's social structure influenced how the guards and prisoners interacted. As Zimbardo (et al. 2009:516) noted, it was a real prison "in the minds of the jailers and their captives." The experiment, conducted 40 years ago, has since been repeated—with similar findings—both in the United States and in other countries.

Zimbardo's experiment took on new relevance in 2004, in the wake of shocking revelations of prisoner abuse at the U.S.-run Abu Ghraib military facility in Iraq. Graphic photos showed U.S. soldiers humiliating naked Iraqi prisoners and threatening to attack them with police dogs. The structure of the wartime prison, coupled with intense pressure on military intelligence officers to secure information regarding terrorist plots, contributed to the breakdown in the guards' behavior. But Zimbardo himself noted that the guards' depraved conduct could have been predicted simply on the basis of his research (Zimbardo 2007:324–379).

The two concepts of social interaction and social structure are closely linked to groups and organizations. Often, social interactions take place in groups of friends, relatives, or co-workers or in formal organizations such as universities and prisons. Whatever the setting, an underlying social structure dictates the relationships among members of the group or organization and the ways in which they respond to one another. In this chapter we will study the five basic elements of social structure: statuses, social roles, groups, social networks, and social institutions such as the family, religion, and government. We'll also touch on a new element of social structure, *virtual worlds*. We'll see that functionalists, conflict theorists, and interactionists approach these institutions quite differently. Next, we'll examine how and why formal organizations, such as a corporation or the college you attend, came into existence, touching on Max Weber's model of the modern bureaucracy in the process. And we'll compare our modern social structure with simpler forms, using typologies developed by Émile Durkheim, Ferdinand Tönnies, and Gerhard Lenski.

Social Interaction and Reality

How do we define our social reality? As an example, let's consider something as simple as how we regard tattoos. Even as recently as a few years ago, most people in the United States considered tattoos to be "weird" or "kooky." Tattoos were associated with fringe countercultural groups, such as punk rockers, biker gangs, and skinheads. Among many people, a tattoo elicited an automatic negative response. Now, however, there are so many tattooed people, including society's trendsetters and major sports figures, and the ritual of getting a tattoo has become so legitimized, that people regard tattoos differently. At this point, as a result of increased social interactions with tattooed people, tattoos look perfectly at home to us in a number of settings.

The nature of social interaction and what constitutes reality varies across cultures. In Western societies, with their emphasis on romantic love, couples see marriage as a relationship as well as a social status. From Valentine's Day flowers to more informal, everyday gestures, professions of love are an expected part of marriage. In Japan, however, marriage is considered more a social status than a relationship. Although many or most Japanese couples undoubtedly do love each other, saying "I love you" does not come easily to them, especially not to husbands. Nor do most husbands call their wives by name (they prefer "Mother") or look them in the eyes. In 2006, in an effort to change these restrictive customs, some Japanese men formed the Devoted Husband Organization, which has been sponsoring a new holiday, Beloved Wives Day. Recently, the group organized an event called Shout Your Love from the Middle of a Cabbage Patch Day. Dozens of men stood in a cabbage patch north of Tokyo and shouted, "I love you!" to their wives, some of whom had never heard their husbands say those words (Kambayashi 2008).

The ability to define social reality reflects a group's power within a society. In fact, one of the most crucial aspects of the relationship between dominant and subordinate groups is the ability of the dominant or majority group to define a society's values. Sociologist William I. Thomas (1923), an early critic of theories of racial and gender differences, recognized that the "definition of the situation" could mold the thinking and personality of the individual. Writing from an interactionist perspective, Thomas observed that people respond not only to the objective features of a person or situation but also to the *meaning* the person or situation has for them. For example, in Philip Zimbardo's mock prison experiment, student "guards" and "prisoners" accepted the definition of the situation (including the traditional roles and behavior associated with being a guard or prisoner) and acted accordingly.

Let's take a closer look at the elements of social structure that help to define social reality.

Elements of Social Structure

We can examine predictable social relationships in terms of five elements: statuses, social roles, groups, social networks, and social institutions. These elements make up a social structure just as a foundation, walls, and ceilings make up a building's structure. The elements of social structure are developed through the lifelong process of socialization, described in Chapter 2.

STATUSES

We normally think of a person's "status" as having to do with influence, wealth, and fame. However, sociologists use the term *status* to refer to any of the full range of socially defined positions within a large group or society, from the lowest to the highest position. Within our society, a person can occupy the status of president of the United States, fruit picker, son or daughter, violinist, teenager, resident of Minneapolis, dental technician, or neighbor. A person can hold several statuses at the same time.

Ascribed and Achieved Status   Sociologists view some statuses as *ascribed* and others as *achieved* (see Figure 3–1). An *ascribed status* is "assigned" to a person by society without regard for the person's unique talents or characteristics. Generally, this assignment takes place at birth; thus, a person's racial background, gender, and age are all considered ascribed statuses. Though these characteristics are biological in origin, they are significant mainly because of the *social* meanings they have in our culture. Conflict theorists are especially interested in ascribed statuses, since they often confer privileges or reflect a person's membership in a subordinate group. The social meanings of race, ethnicity, and gender will be analyzed more fully in Chapters 6 and 7.

In most cases, we can do little to change an ascribed status. But we can attempt to change the traditional constraints associated with such statuses. For example, the Gray Panthers—an activist political group founded in 1971 to work for the rights of older people—have tried to modify society's negative and confining stereotypes of the elderly. As a result of their work and that of other groups supporting older citizens, the ascribed status of "senior citizen" is no longer as difficult for millions of older people.

Unlike ascribed statuses, an *achieved status* comes to us largely through our own efforts. Both "bank president" and "prison guard" are achieved statuses, as are "lawyer," "pianist," "sorority member," "convict," and "social worker." You must do something to acquire an achieved status—go to school, learn a skill, establish a friendship, or invent a new product. As we will see in the next section, our ascribed status heavily

Figure 3–1
Social Statuses

Ascribed statuses   Achieved statuses

Think About It
The person in this figure—"me"—occupies many positions in society, each of which involves distinct statuses. How would you define *your* statuses? Which have the most influence in your life?

influences our achieved status. Being male, for example, decreases the likelihood that a person will consider becoming a child care worker.

Master Status   Each person holds many different and sometimes conflicting statuses; some may connote higher social positions and some, lower positions. How, then, do others view one's overall social position? According to sociologist Everett Hughes (1945), societies deal with such inconsistencies by agreeing that certain statuses are more important than others. A *master status* is a status that dominates others and thereby determines a person's general position within society. For example, Arthur Ashe, who died of AIDS in 1993, had a remarkable career as a tennis star, but at the end of his life, his status as a well-known personality with AIDS may have outweighed his statuses as a retired athlete, an author, and a political activist. Throughout the world, many people with disabilities find that their status as "disabled" receives undue weight and overshadows their actual ability to perform successfully in meaningful employment.

Our society gives so much importance to race and gender that they often dominate our lives. These ascribed statuses frequently influence achieved status. The African American activist Malcolm X (1925–1965), an eloquent and controversial advocate of Black power and Black pride in the early 1960s, recalled that his feelings and perspectives changed dramatically when he was in eighth grade. His English teacher, a White man, advised him that his goal of becoming a lawyer was "no realistic goal for a nigger" and encouraged him instead to become a carpenter. Malcolm X (1964:37) found that his position as a Black man (ascribed status) was an obstacle to his dream of becoming a lawyer (achieved status). In the United States, the ascribed statuses of race and gender can function as master statuses that impact one's potential to achieve a desired professional and social status.

SOCIAL ROLES

What Are Social Roles?   Throughout our lives, we acquire what sociologists call *social roles*. A ***social role*** is a set of expectations for people who occupy a given social position or status. Thus, in the United States, we expect that cab drivers will know how to get around a city, that receptionists will be reliable in handling phone messages, and that police officers will take action if they see a citizen being threatened. With each distinctive social status—whether ascribed or achieved—come particular role expectations. However, actual performance varies from individual to individual. One secretary may assume extensive administrative responsibilities, while another may focus on clerical duties. Similarly, in Philip Zimbardo's mock prison experiment, some students were brutal and sadistic guards, but others were not.

Roles are a significant component of social structure. Viewed from a functionalist perspective, roles contribute to a society's stability by enabling members to anticipate the behavior of others and to pattern their own actions accordingly. Yet social roles can also be dysfunctional, by restricting people's interactions and relationships. If we view a person only as a "police officer" or a "supervisor," it will be difficult to relate to the person as a friend or neighbor.

Role Conflict   Imagine the delicate situation of a woman who has worked for a decade on an assembly line in an electrical plant, and has recently been named supervisor of her unit. How is this woman expected to relate to her longtime friends and co-workers? Should she still go out to lunch with them, as she has done almost daily for years? Is it her responsibility to recommend the firing of an old friend who cannot keep up with the demands of the assembly line?

Role conflict occurs when incompatible expectations arise from two or more social positions held by the same person. Fulfillment of the roles associated with one status may directly violate the roles linked to a second status. In the example just given, the newly promoted supervisor will most likely experience a sharp conflict between her social and occupational roles. Role conflicts call for important ethical choices. The new supervisor will have to make a difficult decision about how much allegiance she owes her friend and how much she owes her employers, who have given her supervisory responsibilities.

Another type of role conflict occurs when individuals move into occupations that are not common among people with their ascribed status. Male preschool teachers and female police officers experience this type of role conflict. In the latter case, female officers must strive to reconcile their workplace role in law enforcement with the societal view of a woman's role, which does not embrace many skills needed in police work. And while female police officers encounter sexual harassment, as women do throughout the labor force, they must also deal with the "code of silence," an informal norm that precludes their implicating fellow officers in wrongdoing (Fletcher 1995; S. Martin 1994).

Role Strain   Role conflict describes the situation of a person dealing with the challenge of occupying two social positions simultaneously. However, even a single position can cause problems. Sociologists use the term *role strain* to describe the situation that occurs when the same social position imposes conflicting demands and expectations.

People who belong to minority cultures may experience role strain while working in the mainstream culture. Criminologist Larry Gould (2002) interviewed officers of the Navajo Nation Police Department about their relations with conventional law enforcement officials, such as sheriffs and FBI agents. Besides enforcing the law, Navajo Nation officers practice an alternative form of justice known as Peacemaking, in which they seek reconciliation between the parties to a crime. The officers expressed great confidence in Peacemaking, but worried that if they did not make arrests, other law enforcement officials would think they were too soft, or "just taking care of their own." Regardless of the strength of their ties to traditional Navajo ways, all felt the strain of being considered "too Navajo" or "not Navajo enough."

If you were a male nurse, what aspects of role conflict would you need to consider? Now imagine you are a professional boxer and a woman. What conflicting role expectations might that involve? In both cases, how well do you think you would handle role conflict?

GROUPS

In sociological terms, a *group* is any number of people with similar norms, values, and expectations who interact with one another on a regular basis. The members of a women's basketball team, of a hospital's business office, or of a symphony orchestra constitute a group. However, the residents of a suburb would not be considered a group, since they rarely interact with one another at one time.

Every society is composed of many groups in which daily social interaction takes place. People seek out groups to establish friendships, to accomplish certain goals, and to fulfill the social roles they have acquired. Groups, then, play a vital part in a society's social structure. Much of our social interaction takes place within groups and is influenced by their norms and sanctions. Being a teenager or a retired person takes on special meaning when you interact within a group designed for people with that particular status. The expectations associated with many social roles, including those accompanying the statuses of brother, sister, and student, become more clearly defined in the context of a group.

Primary and Secondary Groups   Charles Horton Cooley (1902) coined the term *primary group* to refer to a small group characterized by intimate, face-to-face association and cooperation. The members of a street gang constitute a primary group; so do members of a family living in the same household, as well as a group of "sisters" in a college sorority.

Primary groups play a pivotal role both in the socialization process (see Chapter 2) and in the development of roles and statuses. Indeed, primary groups can be instrumental in a person's day-to-day existence. When we find ourselves identifying closely with a group, it is probably a primary group.

We also participate in many groups that are not characterized by close bonds of friendship, such as large college classes and business associations. The term *secondary group* refers to a formal, impersonal group in which there is little social intimacy or mutual understanding (see Table 3-1). The distinction between primary and secondary groups is not always clear-cut. Some social clubs may become so large and impersonal that they no longer function as primary groups.

In-Groups and Out-Groups   A group can hold special meaning for members because of its relationship to other groups. People in one group sometimes feel antagonistic to or threatened by another group, especially if that group is perceived as being different culturally or racially. Sociologists explain these "we" and "they" feelings using two

Table 3–1 Comparison of Primary and Secondary Groups

Primary Group	Secondary Group
Generally small	Usually large
Relatively long period of interaction	Relatively short duration, often temporary
Intimate, face-to-face association	Little social intimacy or mutual understanding
Some emotional depth in relationships	Relationships generally superficial
Cooperative, friendly	Formal and impersonal

terms first employed by William Graham Sumner (1906): *in-group* and *out-group.*

An ***in-group*** can be defined as any group or category to which people feel they belong. Simply put, it comprises everyone who is regarded as "we" or "us." The in-group may be as narrow as a teenage clique or as broad as an entire society. The very existence of an in-group implies that there is an out-group viewed as "they" or "them." An ***out-group*** is a group or category to which people feel they do *not* belong.

Conflict between in-groups and out-groups can turn violent. In 1999 two disaffected students at Columbine High School in Littleton, Colorado, launched an attack on the school that left 15 students and teachers dead, including themselves. The gunmen, members of an out-group that other students referred to as the Trenchcoat Mafia, apparently resented the taunting of an in-group referred to as the Jocks. Similar episodes have occurred in schools across the nation, where rejected adolescents, overwhelmed by personal and family problems, peer group pressure, academic responsibilities, or media images of violence, have struck out against more popular classmates.

Try putting yourself in the shoes of an out-group member. What does your in-group look like from that perspective?

Reference Groups Both in-groups and primary groups can dramatically influence the way an individual thinks and behaves. Sociologists call any group that individuals use as a standard in evaluating themselves and their own behavior a ***reference group.*** For example, a high school student who aspires to join a social circle of hip-hop music devotees will pattern his or her behavior after that of the group. The student will begin dressing like these peers, downloading the same music, and hanging out at the same stores and clubs.

Reference groups have two basic purposes. First, they serve a normative function by setting and enforcing standards of conduct and belief. The high school student who wants the approval of the hip-hop crowd will have to follow the group's dictates, at least to some extent. Second, reference groups perform a comparison function by serving as a standard against which people can measure themselves and others. An actor will evaluate himself or herself against a reference group composed of others in the acting profession (Merton and Kitt 1950).

Reference groups may help the process of anticipatory socialization. For example, a college student majoring in finance may read the *Wall Street Journal,* study the annual reports of corporations, and listen to midday stock market news on the radio. Such a student is using financial experts as a reference group to which he or she aspires.

SOCIAL NETWORKS

Groups do not merely serve to define other elements of the social structure, such as roles and statuses; they also link the individual with the larger society. We all belong to a number of different groups and, through our acquaintances, make connections with people in different social circles. These connections are known as a ***social network***—a series of social relationships that links a person directly to others, and through them, indirectly to still more people. Social networks can center on virtually any activity, from sharing job information to exchanging news and gossip or sharing sex. Some networks may constrain people by limiting the range of their interactions, yet networks can also empower people by making vast resources available to them (Christakis and Fowler 2009).

Involvement in social networks—commonly known as *networking*—is especially valuable in finding employment. Albert Einstein was successful in finding a job only when a classmate's father put him in touch with his future employer. These kinds of contacts—even those that are weak and distant—can be crucial in establishing social networks and facilitating the transmission of information.

In the workplace, networking pays off more for men than for women because of the traditional presence of men in leadership positions. One survey of executives found that 63 percent of the men used networking to find new jobs, compared to 41 percent of the women. Women were more likely than men to rely on classified advertisements to find jobs. Still, women at all levels of the paid labor force are beginning to make effective use of social networks. Now that many job advertisements have migrated to the Internet, new research is needed to determine whether gender differences will persist in both in-person and online networking (L. Flynn 2008; Henly 1999).

During the recent economic downturn, electronic social networks served a new purpose, encouraging the jobless. Websites and chat rooms that could not locate jobs for those who had been thrown out of work concentrated instead on helping them to stick together, support one another, and maintain a positive attitude. For the unemployed, online conversations with friends or even strangers in the same predicament can be an invaluable morale booster (Scherer 2010b).

VIRTUAL WORLDS

Today, with recent advances in technology, people can maintain their social networks electronically; they don't need face-to-face contacts. Whether through text-messaging, handheld devices, or social networking sites like Facebook, a significant amount of networking occurs online. Adolescents can now interact freely with distant friends, even under close scrutiny by parents or teachers. Without leaving their cubicles, employees with a taste for adventure can escape their work environments.

The future of virtual networking is difficult to imagine. Consider *Second Life* (SL), an Internet-based virtual world that included about 12 million networked "players" as of January 2008. Nearly 400,000 of those players were active over a seven-day period. Participants in such a virtual world typically go about their virtual lives in the virtual world, attending college, establishing a business, even buying and decorating a home (Bainbridge 2007; *Second Life* 2008).

Just like real worlds, however, virtual worlds have become politicized and consumer-oriented. MySpace has been purchased by the global media giant News Corp, which has added targeted advertising to the site. If a MySpace user confesses to liking tacos, a banner ad for Taco Bell may appear at the top of the page. And *Second Life* is now open to real-world corporations that want to "build" their stores in SL. The commercialization of these spaces has been met with a good deal of antagonism: Reebok has weathered a virtual nuclear bomb attack, and "customers" have been "shot" outside the American Apparel store. Elsewhere in SL, virtual protesters have paraded on behalf of a far-right French group in a confrontation with anti-Nazi protesters. And in 2007, Sweden became the first real-world country to place an "embassy" in SL (Burkeman 2007; A. Hamilton 2007; Semuels 2007).

Virtual life can and does migrate into real life. In 2007, college housing officials became worried when freshmen and their parents began checking out the Facebook profiles of prospective roommates. Soon,

Even though you may not be totally sure whom you are "talking to" online, the Internet has added a massive new dimension to social interaction.

colleges were fielding requests for new roommates before students even arrived on campus. Concerns went far beyond tastes in music; the reservations expressed most often by parents included a potential roommate's race, religion, and sexual orientation (Collura 2007).

Online socialization may not necessarily reinforce people's prejudices, however. Researchers at Pennsylvania State University argue that participating in the *Second Life* virtual world opens us up to people from different cultural and linguistic backgrounds. In their view, such online friendships may enhance cross-cultural encounters and friendships in the first life—that is, the real world (Diehl and Prins 2008).

Sociologist Manuel Castells (2010a, 2010b, 2010c) views these emerging electronic social networks as fundamental to new organizations and the growth of existing businesses and associations. With other scholars, sociologists are now scrambling to understand these environments and their social processes. *Second Life* went public in 2003—a millennium ago in the world of cyberspace. Scholars worry that after the current period of transition, given the absence of a historical record, reconstructing these worlds as they existed when they were populated by only a hundred avatars, much less tens of thousands, will be impossible.

Finally, virtual networks can help to preserve real-world networks interrupted by war and other dislocations. In 2003, the deployment of U.S. troops in the Middle East increased many people's reliance on e-mail. Today, digital photos and sound files accompany e-mail messages between soldiers and their families and friends. GIs can even view siblings' graduations or children's birthday parties live, via Webcams. And U.S. soldiers and Iraqi citizens have begun to post their opinions of the war in Iraq in online journals called Weblogs, or blogs. Though critics are skeptical of the identity of some of the authors, these postings have become yet another source of news about the war (Faith 2005; O'Connor 2004; Sisson 2007).

If you were deaf, what impact might instant messaging over the Internet have on you?

SOCIAL INSTITUTIONS

The mass media, the government, the economy, the family, and the health care system are all examples of social institutions found in our society. *Social institutions* are organized patterns of beliefs and behavior centered on basic social needs, such as replacing personnel (the family) and preserving order (the government).

A close look at social institutions gives sociologists insight into the structure of a society. Consider religion, for example. The institution of religion adapts to the segment of society that it serves. Church work has very different meanings for ministers who serve a skid row area or a middle-class suburban community. Religious leaders assigned to a skid row mission will focus on tending to the ill and providing food and shelter. Clergy in the suburbs will focus on counseling those considering marriage and divorce, arranging youth activities, and overseeing cultural

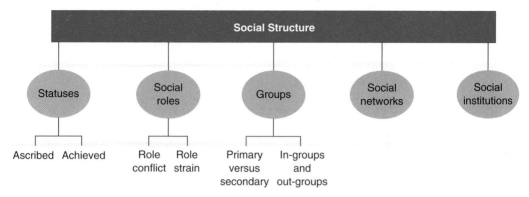

Figure 3–2
Social Structure: An Overview

events. We will examine social institutions in more detail in Chapters 8 and 9. Figure 3–2 summarizes the five major elements of social structure.

Social Structure in Global Perspective

Modern societies are complex, especially when compared with earlier social arrangements. Sociologists Émile Durkheim, Ferdinand Tönnies, and Gerhard Lenski have offered three ways to contrast modern societies with simpler forms of social structure.

DURKHEIM'S MECHANICAL AND ORGANIC SOLIDARITIES

In his *Division of Labor* ([1893] 1933), Durkheim argued that social structure depends on the division of labor in a society—in other words, on the manner in which tasks are performed. Thus, a task such as providing food can be carried out almost totally by one individual, or it can be divided among many people. The latter pattern is typical of modern societies, in which the cultivation, processing, distribution, and retailing of a single food item are performed by literally hundreds of people.

In societies in which there is minimal division of labor, a collective consciousness develops that emphasizes group solidarity. Durkheim termed this collective frame of mind ***mechanical solidarity,*** implying that all individuals perform the same tasks. In this type of society, no one needs to ask, "What do your parents do?" since all are engaged in similar work. Each person prepares food, hunts, makes clothing, builds homes, and so forth. Because people have few options regarding what to do with their lives, there is little concern for individual needs. Instead, the group is the dominating force in society. Both social interaction and negotiation are based on close, intimate, face-to-face social contacts. Since there is little specialization, there are few social roles.

As societies become more advanced technologically, they rely on greater division of labor. The person who cuts down timber is not the same person who puts up your roof. With increasing specialization, many different tasks must be performed by many different individuals—even in manufacturing a single item, such as a radio or stove. In general, social interactions become less personal than in societies characterized by mechanical solidarity. People begin relating to others on the basis of their social positions ("butcher," "nurse") rather than their distinctive human qualities. Because the overall social structure of the society continues to change, statuses and social roles are in perpetual flux.

Once society has become more complex and division of labor is greater, no individual can go it alone. Dependence on others becomes essential for group survival. In Durkheim's terms, mechanical solidarity is replaced by **organic solidarity,** a collective consciousness resting on the need a society's members have for one another. Durkheim chose the term *organic solidarity* because in his view, individuals become interdependent in much the same way as organs of the human body.

TÖNNIES'S *GEMEINSCHAFT* AND *GESELLSCHAFT*

Ferdinand Tönnies (1855–1936) was appalled by the rise of an industrial city in his native Germany during the late 1800s. In his view, the city marked a dramatic change from the ideal type of a close-knit community, which Tönnies termed *Gemeinschaft,* to that of an impersonal mass society, or *Gesellschaft* (Tönnies [1887] 1988).

The **Gemeinschaft** (pronounced guh-MINE-shoft) community is typical of rural life. It is a small community in which people have similar backgrounds and life experiences. Virtually everyone knows one another, so that social interactions are intimate and familiar, almost as one might find among kinfolk. A commitment to the larger social group and a sense of togetherness characterize the community. People relate to others in a personal way, not just as "clerk" or "manager." With this personal interaction, however, comes little privacy.

Social control in the *Gemeinschaft* community is maintained through informal means, such as moral persuasion, gossip, and even gestures. These techniques work effectively because people genuinely care about how others feel toward them. Social change is relatively limited in the *Gemeinschaft;* the lives of members of one generation may be quite similar to those of their grandparents.

By contrast, the **Gesellschaft** (pronounced guh-ZELL-shoft) is an ideal type characteristic of modern urban life. Most people are strangers and feel little in common with other community residents. Relationships are governed by social roles that grow out of immediate tasks, such as purchasing a product or arranging a business meeting. Self-interest dominates, and little consensus exists concerning values or commitment to the group. As a result, social control must rely on more formal techniques, such as laws and legally defined punishments. Social change is an important aspect of life in the *Gesellschaft;* it can be strikingly evident, even within a single generation.

Table 3–2 summarizes the differences between the *Gemeinschaft* and the *Gesellschaft.* Sociologists have used these terms to compare social structures that stress close relationships with those that emphasize less personal ties. It is easy to view the *Gemeinschaft* with nostalgia, as a far better way of life than the rat race of contemporary existence. However, the more intimate relationships of the *Gemeinschaft* come at a price. The prejudice and discrimination found there can be quite confining; ascribed statuses such as family background often outweigh a person's unique talents and achievements. In addition, the *Gemeinschaft* tends to distrust individuals who seek to be creative or just to be different.

LENSKI'S SOCIOCULTURAL EVOLUTION

Sociologist Gerhard Lenski takes a very different view of society and social structure. Rather than distinguishing between two opposite types of society, as Tönnies did, Lenski sees human societies as undergoing

summingUP

Table 3–2 Comparison of the *Gemeinschaft* and *Gesellschaft*

Gemeinschaft	*Gesellschaft*
Rural life typifies this form	Urban life typifies this form
People share a feeling of community that results from their similar backgrounds and life experiences	People have little sense of commonality; their differences appear more striking than their similarities
Social interactions are intimate and familiar	Social interactions are likely to be impersonal and task-specific
People maintain a spirit of cooperation and unity of will	Self-interest dominates
Tasks and personal relationships cannot be separated	The task being performed is paramount; relationships are subordinate
People place little emphasis on individual privacy	Privacy is valued
Informal social control predominates	Formal social control is evident
People are not very tolerant of deviance	People are more tolerant of deviance
Emphasis is on ascribed statuses	Emphasis is on achieved statuses
Social change is relatively limited	Social change is very evident, even within a generation

Think About It
How would you classify the communities with which you are familiar? Are they more *Gemeinschaft* or *Gesellschaft*?

a process of change characterized by a dominant pattern known as *sociocultural evolution.* This term refers to long-term trends in societies resulting from the interplay of continuity, innovation, and selection (Nolan and Lenski 2009).

In Lenski's view, a society's level of technology is critical to the way it is organized. Lenski defines *technology* as "cultural information about how to use the material resources of the environment to satisfy human needs and desires" (Nolan and Lenski 2009:37). The available technology does not completely define the form that a particular society and its social structure take. Nevertheless, a low level of technology may limit the degree to which a society can depend on such things as irrigation or complex machinery. As technology advances, society evolves from a preindustrial to an industrial and then a postindustrial stage.

Preindustrial Societies   How does a preindustrial society organize its economy? If we know that, it is possible to categorize the society. The first type of preindustrial society to emerge in human history is the *hunting-and-gathering society,* in which people simply rely on whatever foods and fibers are readily available. Technology in such societies is minimal. Organized in groups, people move constantly in search of food. There is little division of labor into specialized tasks.

Hunting-and-gathering societies are composed of small, widely dispersed groups. Each group consists almost entirely of people related to one another. As a result, kinship ties are the source of authority and influence, and the social institution of the family takes on a particularly important role. Tönnies would certainly view such societies as examples of *Gemeinschaft.*

Since resources are scarce, there is relatively little inequality in hunting-and-gathering societies in terms of material goods. Social differentiation is based on ascribed statuses such as gender, age, and family background. By the close of the 20th century, the last hunting-and-gathering societies had virtually disappeared.

Horticultural societies, in which people plant seeds and crops rather than merely subsist on available foods, emerged about 12,000 years ago. Members of horticultural societies are much less nomadic than hunters and gatherers. They place greater emphasis on the production of tools and household objects. Yet their technology remains rather limited: They cultivate crops with the aid of digging sticks or hoes (Wilford 1997).

The last stage of preindustrial development is the *agrarian society,* which emerged about 5,000 years ago. As in horticultural societies, members of agrarian societies are engaged primarily in the production of food. However, the introduction of technological innovations such as the plow allows farmers to dramatically increase their crop yields. Farmers can cultivate the same fields over generations, allowing the emergence of still larger settlements.

Industrial Societies   Although the Industrial Revolution did not topple monarchs, it produced changes every bit as significant as those resulting from political revolutions. The Industrial Revolution, which took place largely in England during the period 1760 to 1830, was a scientific revolution focused on the application of nonanimal (mechanical) sources of power to labor tasks. An *industrial society* is a society that depends on mechanization to produce its goods and services. Industrial societies rely on inventions that facilitate agricultural and industrial production, and on new sources of energy, such as steam.

As the Industrial Revolution proceeded, a new form of social structure emerged. Many societies underwent an irrevocable shift from an agrarian-oriented economy to an industrial base. No longer did a typical individual or a family make an entire product. Instead, specialization of tasks and manufacturing of goods became increasingly common. Workers, generally men but also women and even children, left their family homesteads to work in central locations such as factories.

The process of industrialization had distinctive social consequences. Families and communities could not continue to function as self-sufficient units. Individuals, villages, and regions began to exchange goods and services and to become interdependent. As people came to rely on the labor of members of other communities, the family lost its unique position as the source of power and authority. The need for specialized knowledge led to more formalized education, and education emerged as a social institution distinct from the family.

Postindustrial and Postmodern Societies   When the concept of sociocultural evolution first appeared in the 1960s, sociologists paid relatively little attention to how maturing industrialized societies may change with the emergence of even more advanced forms of technology. Since then Lenski and other sociologists have studied the significant changes in the occupational structure of industrial societies as they shift from manufacturing to service economies. Social scientists call these technologically advanced nations *postindustrial societies,* defined by sociologist Daniel Bell (1999) as societies whose economic systems are engaged primarily in the processing and control of information. The main output of a postindustrial society is services rather than manufactured goods. Large numbers of people become involved in occupations devoted to the teaching, generation, or dissemination of ideas.

Bell views this transition from industrial to postindustrial society as a positive development. He sees a general decline in organized working-class groups and a rise in interest groups concerned with such national issues as health, education, and the environment. Bell's outlook is functionalist because he portrays postindustrial society as basically consensual. Organizations and interest groups, he predicts, will engage in an open and competitive process of decision making. The level of conflict between diverse groups will diminish, strengthening social stability.

More recently, sociologists have gone beyond discussion of post-industrial societies to the postmodern society. A ***postmodern society*** is a technologically sophisticated society that is preoccupied with consumer goods and media images. Such societies consume goods and information on a mass scale. Postmodern theorists take a global perspective, noting the ways that aspects of culture cross national boundaries. For example, residents of the United States may listen to reggae music from Jamaica, eat sushi and other types of Japanese food, and wear clogs from Sweden. Table 3–3 summarizes the six stages of sociocultural evolution.

Durkheim, Tönnies, and Lenski present three visions of society's social structure. While they differ, each is useful, and this textbook will draw on all three. The sociocultural evolutionary approach emphasizes a historical perspective. It does not picture different types of social structure coexisting within the same society. Consequently, one would not expect a single society to include hunters and gatherers along with a post-modern culture. In contrast, Durkheim's and Tönnies's theories allow for the existence of different types of community—such as a *Gemeinschaft* and a *Gesellschaft*—in the same society. Thus, a rural New Hampshire community located 100 miles from Boston can be linked to the city by modern information technology. The main difference between these two theories is a matter of emphasis. While Tönnies emphasized the overriding concern in each type of community—one's own self-interest or the well-being of the larger society—Durkheim emphasized the division (or lack of division) of labor.

Table 3–3 Stages of Sociocultural Evolution

Societal Type	First Appearance	Characteristics
Hunting-and-gathering	Beginning of human life	Nomadic; reliance on readily available food and fibers
Horticultural	About 10,000 to 12,000 years ago	More settled; development of agriculture and limited technology
Agrarian	About 5,000 years ago	Larger, more stable settlements; improved technology and increased crop yields
Industrial	1760–1850	Reliance on mechanical power and new sources of energy; centralized workplaces; economic interdependence; formal education
Postindustrial	1960s	Reliance on services, especially the processing and control of information; expanded middle class
Postmodern	Latter 1970s	High technology; mass consumption of consumer goods and media images; cross-cultural integration

summingUP

The work of these three thinkers reminds us that a major focus of sociology has been to identify changes in social structure and the consequences for human behavior. At the macro level, we see society shifting to more advanced forms of technology. The social structure becomes increasingly complex, and new social institutions emerge to assume some functions that once were performed by the family. On the micro level, these changes affect the nature of social interactions. Each individual takes on multiple social roles, and people come to rely more on social networks and less on kinship ties. As the social structure becomes more complex, people's relationships become more impersonal, transient, and fragmented. The development of formal organizations and bureaucracies, the subject of the next section, is another outcome of this process.

Use Your Sociological Imagination

Describe any personal experiences you have had with a nonindustrial, or developing, society. If you have not had that kind of experience, how do you think you would prepare for it?

Understanding Organizations

FORMAL ORGANIZATIONS AND BUREAUCRACIES

As industrial and postmodern societies have shifted to more advanced forms of technology and their social structures have become more complex, our lives have become increasingly dominated by large secondary groups referred to as *formal organizations*. A ***formal organization*** is a group designed for a special purpose and structured for maximum efficiency. The United States Postal Service, the McDonald's fast-food chain, the Boston Pops orchestra, and the college you attend are all examples of formal organizations. Organizations vary in their size, specificity of goals, and degree of efficiency, but all are structured to facilitate the management of large-scale operations. All have a bureaucratic form of organization.

In our society, formal organizations fulfill an enormous variety of personal and societal needs, shaping the lives of every one of us. In fact, formal organizations have become such a dominant force that we must create organizations to supervise other organizations, such as the Securities and Exchange Commission (SEC), which regulates the stock market. Though it sounds much more exciting to say that we live in a "computer age" than in an "age of formal organizations," the latter is probably a more accurate description of our times (Azumi and Hage 1972; Etzioni 1964).

CHARACTERISTICS OF A BUREAUCRACY

A ***bureaucracy*** is a component of formal organization in which rules and hierarchical ranking are used to achieve efficiency. Rows of desks staffed by seemingly faceless people, endless lines and forms, impossibly complex language, and frustrating encounters with red tape—all these unpleasant images have combined to make *bureaucracy* a dirty word and an easy target in political campaigns. As a result, few people want to identify their occupation as "bureaucrat," despite the fact that all of us perform various bureaucratic tasks. Elements of bureaucracy enter into almost every occupation in an industrial society.

Max Weber ([1913–1922] 1947) first directed researchers to the significance of bureaucratic structure. In an important sociological advance, Weber emphasized the basic similarity of structure and process found in the otherwise dissimilar enterprises of religion, government, education, and business. Weber saw bureaucracy as a form of organization quite different from the family-run business. For analytical purposes, he developed an ideal type of bureaucracy that would reflect the most characteristic aspects of all human organizations. By *ideal type* Weber meant a construct or model that serves as a measuring rod against which actual cases can be evaluated. In actuality, perfect bureaucracies do not exist; no real-world organization corresponds exactly to Weber's ideal type.

Weber proposed that whether the purpose is to run a church, a corporation, or an army, the ideal bureaucracy displays five basic characteristics. A discussion of those characteristics, as well as the dysfunctions (or potential negative consequences) of a bureaucracy, follows. (Table 3–4 summarizes the discussion.)

1. *Division of Labor.*   Specialized experts perform specific tasks. In your college bureaucracy, the admissions officer does not do the job of registrar; the dean doesn't see to the maintenance of buildings. By working at a specific task, people are more likely to become highly skilled and carry out a job with maximum efficiency. This emphasis

summingUP

Table 3–4 Characteristics of a Bureaucracy

Characteristic	Positive Consequence	Negative Consequence	
		For the Individual	For the Organization
Division of labor	Produces efficiency in large-scale organizations	Produces trained incapacity	Produces a narrow perspective
Hierarchy of authority	Clarifies who is in command	Deprives employees of a voice in decision making	Permits concealment of mistakes
Written rules and regulations	Let workers know what is expected of them	Stifle initiative and imagination	Lead to goal displacement
Impersonality	Reduces bias	Contributes to cold and uncaring atmosphere	Discourages loyalty to company
Employment based on technical qualifications	Discourages favoritism and reduces petty rivalries	Discourages ambition to improve oneself elsewhere	Fosters Peter Principle

on specialization is so basic a part of our lives that we may not realize it is a fairly recent development in Western culture.

Although the division of labor has certainly enhanced the performance of many complex bureaucracies, in some cases it can lead
to *trained incapacity.* That is, workers become so specialized that
they develop blind spots and fail to notice obvious problems. Even
worse, they may not care about what is happening in the next department. Some observers believe that such developments have caused
workers in the United States to become less productive on the job.

In some cases, the bureaucratic division of labor can have tragic
results. In the wake of the coordinated attacks on the World Trade
Center and the Pentagon on September 11, 2001, Americans wondered aloud how the FBI and CIA could have failed to detect the terrorists' elaborately planned operation. The problem, in part, turned
out to be the division of labor between the FBI, which focuses on
domestic matters, and the CIA, which operates overseas. Officials at
these intelligence-gathering organizations, both of which are huge
bureaucracies, are well known for jealously guarding information
from one another. Subsequent investigations revealed that they
knew about Osama bin Laden and his al-Qaeda terrorist network
in the early 1990s. Unfortunately, five federal agencies—the CIA,
FBI, National Security Agency, Defense Intelligence Agency, and
National Reconnaissance Office—failed to share their leads on the
network. Although the hijacking of the four commercial airliners
used in the massive attacks may not have been preventable, the
bureaucratic division of labor definitely hindered efforts to defend
against terrorism and actually undermined U.S. national security.

2. *Hierarchy of Authority.* Bureaucracies follow the principle of
   hierarchy; that is, each position is under the supervision of a higher
   authority. A president heads a college bureaucracy; he or she selects
   members of the administration, who in turn hire their own staff.
   In the Roman Catholic Church, the pope is the supreme authority;
   under him sit cardinals, bishops, and so forth.

3. *Written Rules and Regulations.* What if your sociology professor gave your classmate an A for having such a friendly smile?
   You might think that wasn't fair—that it was "against the rules."
   Through written rules and regulations, bureaucracies generally offer
   employees clear standards for an adequate (or exceptional) performance. In addition, procedures provide a valuable sense of continuity in a bureaucracy. Individual workers will come and go, but the
   organization's structure and past records give it a life of its own that
   outlives the services of any one bureaucrat.

   Of course, rules and regulations can overshadow the larger goals
   of an organization to the point that they become dysfunctional.
   What if a hospital emergency room physician failed to treat a seriously injured person because he or she had no valid proof of U.S.

citizenship? If blindly applied, rules no longer serve as a means to achieving an objective but instead become important (and perhaps too important) in their own right. Robert Merton (1968) has used the term **goal displacement** to refer to overzealous conformity to official regulations.

4. *Impersonality.*   Max Weber wrote that in a bureaucracy, work is carried out *sine ira et studio,* "without hatred or passion." Bureaucratic norms dictate that officials perform their duties without the personal consideration of people as individuals. Although this approach is intended to guarantee equal treatment for each person, it also contributes to the often cold and uncaring feeling associated with modern organizations. We typically think of big government and big business when we think of impersonal bureaucracies. But today even small firms use electronically automated menus to screen callers.

5. *Employment Based on Technical Qualifications.*   Within the ideal bureaucracy, hiring is based on technical qualifications rather than on favoritism, and performance is measured against specific standards. Written personnel policies dictate who gets promoted; people often have a right to appeal if they believe that particular rules have been violated. Such procedures protect bureaucrats against arbitrary dismissal, provide a measure of security, and encourage loyalty to the organization.

   Although ideally any bureaucracy will value technical and professional competence, personnel decisions do not always follow this ideal pattern. Bureaucratic dysfunctions have become well publicized,

A hierarchy of authority may deprive individuals of a voice in decision making, but it does clarify who supervises whom.

"Frankly, at this point in the flow chart, we don't know what happens to these people..."

particularly because of the work of Laurence J. Peter. According to the *Peter Principle,* every employee within a hierarchy tends to rise to his or her level of incompetence (Peter and Hull 1969).

These five characteristics of bureaucracy, developed by Max Weber more than 90 years ago, describe an ideal type rather than offering a precise definition of an actual bureaucracy. Not every formal organization will possess all five of Weber's characteristics. In fact, actual bureaucratic organizations can vary widely.

BUREAUCRACY AND ORGANIZATIONAL CULTURE

How does bureaucratization affect the average individual who works in an organization? Early theorists of formal organizations tended to neglect this question. Max Weber, for example, focused on managerial personnel within bureaucracies but had little to say about workers in industry or clerks in government agencies.

According to the *classical theory* of formal organizations, also known as the *scientific management approach,* workers are motivated almost entirely by economic rewards. This theory stresses that only the physical constraints on workers limit their productivity. Therefore, workers are treated as a resource, much like the machines that began to replace them in the 20th century. Management attempts to achieve maximum work efficiency through scientific planning, established performance standards, and careful supervision of workers and production. Under the scientific management approach, planning includes efficiency studies but not studies of workers' attitudes or job satisfaction.

Not until workers organized unions—and forced management to recognize that they were not objects—did theorists of formal organizations begin to revise the classical approach. Along with management and administrators, social scientists became aware that informal groups of workers have an important impact on organizations. An alternative way of considering bureaucratic dynamics, the *human relations approach,* emphasizes the roles of people, communication, and participation within a bureaucracy. This type of analysis reflects the interest of interactionist theorists in small-group behavior. Unlike planning under the scientific management approach, planning based on the human relations perspective focuses on workers' feelings, frustrations, and emotional need for job satisfaction (Perrow 1986).

Today, research on formal organizations is following new avenues. Among them are:

- The recent arrival of a small number of women and minority group members in high-level management

- In large corporations, the decision-making role of groups that lie outside the top ranks of leadership

- The loss of fixed boundaries in organizations that have outsourced key functions
- The role of the Internet and virtual worlds in influencing business and consumer preferences

Though research on organizations still embraces Max Weber's insights, it has gone well beyond them (Hamm 2007; Kleiner 2003; W. R. Scott 2008).

Sociology Matters

Sociology matters because it defines your social status in terms of a variety of social characteristics and groups.

- What is your ascribed status? What do you hope your achieved status will be someday? Do you have a master status, and if so, how might it impact your achievements?
- What primary and secondary groups do you belong to, and why? How do those groups affect your behavior?
- What social networks and institutions are you involved in? Do you belong to any virtual networks? What are the functions of those networks, and how can they help you?

CHAPTER RESOURCES

Summary

Through **social structure,** society is organized into predictable relationships that facilitate **social interaction.** The transmission of culture and even the survival of society depend on social interaction. This chapter has presented the basic elements of social structure, from individual **statuses** and the **social roles** that go with them to **groups, social networks,** and **social institutions.** It has examined several theories of social structure and **formal organizations,** including **bureaucracies.**

1. An **ascribed status** is generally assigned to a person at birth, whereas an **achieved status** is attained largely through one's own effort. In the United States, ascribed statuses such as race and gender can function as **master statuses** that affect one's potential for achievement.

2. The statuses people carry determine the **social roles** they play. People who play more than one social role often suffer from **role conflict,** but even a single role can create **role strain.**

3. Much of our social behavior takes place within **groups.** When we find ourselves identifying closely with a group, it is probably a **primary group.** A **secondary group** is more formal and impersonal.

4. People tend to see the world in terms of **in-groups** (groups to which they belong) and **out-groups** (groups they do not belong to or identify with). **Reference groups** set and enforce standards of social conduct, allowing members to compare themselves to others.

5. Groups serve as links to **social networks** and their vast resources. Today, more and more networking is being done online, some of it in virtual worlds that exist only on the Internet.

6. **Social institutions,** such as government and the family, fulfill essential social functions that other groups cannot, such as preserving order and perpetuating society.

7. Émile Durkheim thought that social structure depends on the division of labor in a society. According to Durkheim, societies with minimal division of labor have a collective consciousness called **mechanical solidarity;** those with greater division of labor show an interdependence called **organic solidarity.**

8. The sociologist Ferdinand Tönnies contrasted the close-knit type of community that characterizes rural life, which he called *Gemeinschaft,* with the impersonal type of mass society that characterizes urban life, which he called *Gesellschaft.*

9. In his theory of **sociocultural evolution,** Gerhard Lenski linked the historical development of societies to the technological advances they achieved. Lenski traced their evolution from primitive **hunting-and-gathering societies** to modern-day **postindustrial** and **postmodern societies.**

10. As societies have become more complex, large **formal organizations** and **bureaucracies** have become more powerful and pervasive. Max Weber theorized that in its **ideal type,** every bureaucracy has five basic characteristics: division of labor, hierarchical authority, written rules and regulations, impersonality, and employment based on technical qualifications.

www.mhhe.com/schaefersm5e
Visit the Online Learning Center for *Sociology Matters* to access quizzes, review activities, and other learning tools.

Key Terms

achieved status, 78

agrarian society, 90

ascribed status, 78

bureaucracy, 93

classical theory, 97

formal
    organization, 93

Gemeinschaft, 88

Gesellschaft, 88

goal displacement, 96

group, 81

horticultural
    society, 90

human relations
    approach, 97

hunting-and-gathering
    society, 90

ideal type, 94

industrial society, 91

in-group, 83

master status, 79

mechanical
    solidarity, 87

organic solidarity, 88

out-group, 83

Peter Principle, 97

postindustrial
    society, 91

postmodern
    society, 92

primary group, 82

reference group, 83

role conflict, 80

role strain, 81

scientific
    management
    approach, 97

secondary group, 82

social institution, 86

social interaction, 76

social network, 84

social role, 80

social structure, 76

sociocultural
    evolution, 90

status, 78

technology, 90

trained incapacity, 95

Deviance and Social Control

Social Control

What Is Deviance?

Sociological Perspectives on Deviance

Crime

Rachel came from a happy family. She began wounding herself with a coat hanger when her friends turned against her. She stayed home from school for a week, couldn't stop crying, after they began spreading malicious rumors about her. Natalie, a college student, started injuring herself in eighth grade. She was hanging around the bridge with a group of stoners and punks, smoking and taking drugs, when she began imitating the ones who cut themselves.

These descriptions of the covert practice of self-injury are taken from Patricia A. Adler and Peter Adler's extensive research on the little-known behavior and its social underpinnings. Over a six-year period, the Adlers conducted lengthy, emotionally intense interviews with self-injurers, becoming friends with many. They met others in virtual space, through Internet-based support groups and Web postings. "Rather than remaining strictly detached from our subjects, we became involved in their lives, helping them and giving voice to their experiences and beliefs," the Adlers admit (2007:542).

The Adlers' work on self-injury reflects all three major sociological approaches. For self-injurers, who rarely come into contact with others like themselves, the Internet functions as a meeting place, a refuge from their self-imposed social isolation. As conflict theorists would point out, their unconventional behavior marginalizes them, preventing them from receiving assistance even when they would welcome it. Interactionists would recognize the critical nature of self-injurers' interpersonal contacts, in person and often online.

Though many people would like to ignore the phenomenon of self-injury, believing that those who practice it will eventually "grow out of it," the Adlers' research allows us to consider it intelligently and scientifically, within the social context. Self-injurers, the Adlers found, are a diverse group, most of whom have never been treated for psychological problems. They include older adults, who communicate with one another online, as well as teens and young adults. Far from being impulsive or pathological, self-injury is a carefully planned and considered behavior. Surprisingly, members often begin to injure themselves in the company of others rather than in secret. They have recently begun to coalesce as a subculture (Adler and Adler 2007:544–545, 559–560; 2008b).

Who decides what is and is not normal behavior, and how does society attempt to control what people say and do? In this chapter we will study various mechanisms of *social control,* both formal and informal. We will examine several theoretical explanations for *deviance* from social norms. And we will discuss one form of deviance that is subject to strict formal controls: *crime.*

Social Control

As we saw in Chapter 2, each culture, subculture, and group has distinctive norms governing what is deemed appropriate behavior. Laws, dress codes, organizational bylaws, course requirements, and the rules of sports and games all express social norms.

How does a society bring about acceptance of basic norms? The term **social control** refers to the techniques and strategies for preventing deviant behavior in any society. Social control occurs on all levels of society. In the family, we are socialized to obey our parents simply because they are our parents. Peer groups introduce us to informal norms, such as dress codes, that govern the behavior of members. Colleges establish standards they expect their students to meet. In bureaucratic organizations, workers encounter a formal system of rules and regulations. Finally, the government of every society legislates and enforces social norms.

Most of us respect and accept basic social norms and assume that others will do the same. Even without thinking, we obey the instructions of police officers, follow the day-to-day rules at our jobs, and move to the rear of elevators when people enter. Such behavior reflects an effective process of socialization to the dominant standards of a culture. At the same time, we are well aware that individuals, groups, and institutions *expect* us to act "properly." This expectation carries with it **sanctions,**

No death penalty
0 executions
1–5
6–10
11–25
26–50
Over 50

Figure 4–1
Executions by State Since 1976

NOTE: *Number of executions carried out from January 17, 1977, to January 2, 2008, as of November 5, 2010. Three federal executions not shown on map.*
SOURCE: Death Penalty Information Center 2010.

Think About It
Why is there so much variation in the number of executions from one state to the next? What might cause that variation?

penalties and rewards for conduct concerning a social norm. If we fail to live up to the norm, we may face punishment through informal sanctions such as fear and ridicule or formal sanctions such as jail sentences or fines.

The ultimate formal sanction is the death penalty, which has been the subject of much controversy recently. As Figure 4–1 shows, 1,233 people were executed in the United States from 1976 through 2010. Much of the controversy centers on the effectiveness of this sanction as a form of social control. Other than eliminating the person who is executed, what does the death penalty accomplish? Does it actually control others' behavior by deterring them from committing a capital offense? To answer this question, researchers must consider the motivation behind capital crimes as well as the criminal's understanding of the resulting penalties. Taking these factors into consideration, researchers have found little evidence that execution is any more a deterrent to capital crimes than an extended prison term (Rosenfeld 2004; Sorenson et al. 1999).

The challenge to effective social control is that people often receive competing messages about how to behave. While the state or government may clearly define acceptable behavior, friends or fellow employees may encourage quite different behavior patterns. Binge drinking in college is the perfect example. The larger society frowns on underage drinking and has laws on the books against it. But within the college peer group, binge drinking is generally accepted, with no sanctions attached. Half the men, 41 percent of the women, and over 80 percent of those living in fraternity and sorority houses engage in binge drinking (Wechsler et al. 2002, 2004).

Dramatic breakdowns in social control tend to highlight society's complicated and often conflicting influences on deviant behavior. In April 2007, just as college students were beginning to focus on the impending end of the semester, tragedy struck on the campus of Virginia Tech. In a two-hour shooting spree, a mentally disturbed senior armed with semi-automatic weapons killed a total of 32 students and faculty at Virginia's largest university. Observers struggled to describe the events and place them in some social context. For sociologists in particular, the event raised numerous issues and topics for study, including the media's role in describing such attacks, the presence of violence in our educational institutions, the gun control debate, the inadequacy of the nation's mental health care system, and the stereotyping and stigmatization of people who suffer from mental illness.

As with other topics, sociologists who study social control tend to speak from one of the major theoretical perspectives. Functionalists contend that people must respect social norms if a group or society is to survive. In their view, societies literally could not function if massive numbers of people defied standards of appropriate conduct. By contrast, conflict theorists maintain that "successful functioning" of a society will consistently benefit the powerful and work to the disadvantage of other groups. They point out, for example, that in the United States, widespread resistance to social norms was necessary to overturn the institution of slavery, to win independence from England, to secure civil rights, to allow women to vote, and to force an end to the war in Vietnam.

CONFORMITY AND OBEDIENCE

Techniques for social control operate on both the group level and the societal level. People we think of as peers or equals influence us to act in particular ways; the same is true of people who hold authority over us or occupy awe-inspiring positions. Stanley Milgram (1975) made a useful distinction between these two important levels of social control.

Milgram defined *conformity* as going along with peers—individuals of our own status, who have no special right to direct our behavior. By contrast, *obedience* is defined as compliance with higher authorities in a hierarchical structure. Thus, a recruit entering military service will typically *conform* to the habits and language of other recruits and will *obey* the orders of superior officers. Students will *conform* to the drinking behavior of their peers and will *obey* the requests of campus security officers.

If ordered to do so, would you comply with an experimenter's instruction to give people increasingly painful electric shocks? Most people would say no, yet the research of social psychologist Stanley Milgram (1963, 1975) suggests that most of us *will* obey such orders. In Milgram's words (1975:xi), "Behavior that is unthinkable in an individual . . . acting on his own may be executed without hesitation when carried out under orders."

Milgram placed advertisements in New Haven, Connecticut, newspapers to recruit subjects for what was described as a learning experiment at Yale University. Participants included postal clerks, engineers, high school teachers, and laborers. They were told that the purpose of the research was to investigate the effects of punishment on learning. The experimenter, dressed in a gray technician's coat, explained that in each testing, one subject would be randomly selected as the "learner" and another would function as the "teacher." However, the experiment was rigged so that the "real" subject would always be the teacher, while an associate of Milgram's served as the learner.

At this point, the learner's hand was strapped to an electric apparatus. The teacher was taken to an electronic "shock generator" with 30 graduated lever switches labeled from 15 to 450 volts. Before beginning the experiment, all subjects were given sample shocks of 45 volts, to convince them of the authenticity of the experiment. The experimenter then instructed the teacher to apply shocks of increasing voltage each time the learner gave an incorrect answer on a memory test. Teachers were told that "although the shocks can be extremely painful, they cause no permanent tissue damage." In reality, the learner did not receive any shocks.

The learner acted out a prearranged script, deliberately giving incorrect answers and pretending to be in pain. For example, at 150 volts, the learner would cry out, "Get me out of here!" At 270 volts, the learner would scream in agony. When the shock reached 350 volts, the learner would fall silent. If the teacher wanted to stop the experiment, the experimenter would insist that the teacher continue, using such statements as "The experiment requires that you continue" and "You have no other choice; you *must* go on" (Milgram 1975:19–23).

The results of this unusual experiment stunned and dismayed Milgram and other social scientists. Almost *two-thirds* of participants fell into the category of "obedient subjects." Why did these subjects obey? Why were they willing to inflict seemingly painful shocks on innocent victims who had never done them any harm? There is no evidence that these subjects were unusually sadistic; few seemed to enjoy administering the shocks. Instead, in Milgram's view, the key to obedience was the experimenter's social role as a "scientist" and "seeker of knowledge."

If you were a participant in Milgram's research on obedience, how far do you think you would go in carrying out "orders"? Do you see any ethical problem with the experimenter's manipulation of the subjects?

Milgram pointed out that in the modern industrial world, we are accustomed to submitting to impersonal authority figures whose status is indicated by a title (professor, lieutenant, doctor) or a uniform (the technician's coat). Because we view the authority as larger and more important than the individual, we shift responsibility for our behavior to the authority figure. Milgram's subjects frequently stated, "If it were up to me, I would not have administered shocks." They saw themselves as merely doing their duty (Milgram 1975).

From a conflict perspective, our obedience may be affected by the value we place on those whom our behavior affects. While Milgram's experiment shows that in general, people are willing to obey authority figures, other studies show that they are even more willing to obey if they feel the "victim" is deserving of punishment. Sociologist Gary Schulman (1974) re-created Milgram's experiment and found that White students were significantly more likely to shock Black "learners" than White "learners." By a margin of 70 percent to 48 percent, they imposed more shocks on the Black learners than on the White learners.

From an interactionist perspective, one important aspect of Milgram's findings is the fact that in follow-up studies, subjects were less likely to inflict the supposed shocks as they were moved physically closer to their victims. Moreover, interactionists emphasize the effect of *incrementally* administering additional dosages of 15 volts. In effect, the experimenter gradually persuaded the teacher to continue inflicting higher levels of punishment. It is doubtful that anywhere near the two-thirds rate of obedience would have been reached had the experimenter told the teachers to immediately administer 450 volts to the learners (Allen 1978; Katovich 1987).

How willing would participants in this experiment be to shock learners today? Although many people may be skeptical of the high levels of conformity Milgram found, recent replications of his experiment confirm his findings. In 2006, using additional safeguards to protect participants' welfare, psychologist Jerry Burger (2009) repeated part of Milgram's experiment with college undergraduates. To avoid biasing the participants, Burger was careful to screen out students who had heard of Milgram's study. The results of the replication were startlingly similar to Milgram's: participants showed a high level of willingness to shock the learner, just as the participants in Milgram's experiment had almost half a century earlier. At the most comparable point in the two studies, Burger measured a rate of 70 percent full obedience—lower, but not significantly so, than the rate of 82.5 percent measured two generations earlier (Twenge 2009).

INFORMAL AND FORMAL SOCIAL CONTROL

The sanctions used to encourage conformity and obedience—and to discourage violation of social norms—are carried out through both informal and formal social control. As the term implies, people use *informal social control* casually to enforce norms. Examples include smiles, laughter, a raised eyebrow, and ridicule.

In the United States and many other cultures, adults often view spanking, slapping, or kicking children as a proper and necessary means of informal social control. Child development specialists counter that such corporal punishment is inappropriate because it teaches children to solve problems through violence. They warn that slapping and spanking can escalate into more serious forms of abuse. Yet, despite a 1998 policy statement by the American Academy of Pediatrics that corporal punishment is not effective and can indeed be harmful, 59 percent of pediatricians support the use of corporal punishment, at least in certain situations. Our culture widely accepts this form of informal social control (Chung et al. 2009).

Formal social control is carried out by authorized agents, such as police officers, physicians, school administrators, employers, military officers, and managers of movie theaters. It can serve as a last resort when socialization and informal sanctions do not bring about desired behavior. An increasingly significant means of formal social control in the United States is to imprison people. Though the United States has less than 5 percent of the world's population, it houses almost a quarter of the world's prisoners. At any given time of the year, 1,000 out of every 100,000 adults in the United States are in jail or prison, compared to 627 in Russia, 151 in England, and 88 in Germany (Liptak 2008).

LAW AND SOCIETY

Some norms are so important to a society that they are formalized into laws controlling people's behavior. *Law* may be defined as governmental social control (Black 1995). Some laws, such as the prohibition against murder, are directed at all members of society. Others, such as fishing and hunting regulations, affect particular categories of people. Still others govern the behavior of social institutions (corporate law and laws regarding the taxation of nonprofit enterprises).

Sociologists see the creation of laws as a social process. Laws are created in response to a perceived need for formal social control. Sociologists have sought to explain how and why such perceptions arise. In their view, law is not merely a static body of rules handed down from generation to generation. Rather, it reflects continually changing standards of what is right and wrong, how violations are to be determined, and what sanctions are to be applied (Schur 1968).

Sociologists representing varying theoretical perspectives agree that the legal order reflects the values of those in a position to exercise authority. Therefore, the creation of criminal law can be a most controversial matter. Should it be against the law to employ illegal immigrants in a factory or to have an abortion? Such issues have been bitterly debated because they require a choice among competing values. Not surprisingly, laws that are unpopular—such as the prohibition of alcohol under the 18th Amendment in 1919 and the widespread establishment of a 55-mile-per-hour speed limit on the highway—become difficult to enforce when there is no consensus supporting the underlying norms.

Socialization is actually the primary source of conforming and obedient behavior, including obedience to law. Generally, it is not external pressure from a peer group or authority figure that makes us go along with social norms. Rather, we have internalized such norms as valid and desirable and are committed to observing them. In a profound sense, we want to see ourselves (and to be seen) as loyal, cooperative, responsible, and respectful of others. In the United States and other societies around the world, people are socialized both to want to belong and to fear being viewed as different or deviant.

What Is Deviance?

For sociologists, the term *deviance* does not mean perversion or depravity. Rather, **deviance** is behavior that violates the standards of conduct or expectations of a group or society (Wickman 1991:85). In the United States, alcoholics, compulsive gamblers, and the mentally ill would all be classified as deviants. Being late for class is a deviant act; the same is true of wearing jeans to a formal wedding. On the basis of the sociological definition, we are all deviant from time to time. Each of us violates common social norms in certain situations.

Is being overweight an example of deviance? In the United States and many other cultures, unrealistic standards of appearance and body image place a huge strain on people, especially women and girls. Journalist Naomi Wolf (1992) has used the term *beauty myth* to refer to an exaggerated ideal of beauty, beyond the reach of all but a few females. The beauty myth can have unfortunate consequences. In order to shed their "deviant" image and conform to (unrealistic) societal norms, many women and girls become consumed with adjusting their appearance. Yet what is deviant in one culture may be celebrated in another.

Deviance involves the violation of group norms, which may or may not be formalized into law. It is a comprehensive concept that includes not only criminal behavior but also many actions not subject to prosecution. The public official who takes a bribe has defied social norms, but so has the high school student who refuses to sit in an assigned seat or cuts class. Of course, deviation from norms is not always negative, let alone criminal. A member of an exclusive social club who speaks out against a traditional policy of excluding women, Blacks, and Jews from admittance is deviating from the club's norms. So is a police officer who blows the whistle on police corruption or brutality.

A person can acquire a deviant identity in many ways. Because of physical or behavioral characteristics, some people are unwillingly cast in negative social roles. Once they have been assigned a deviant role, they have trouble presenting a positive image to others and may even experience lowered self-esteem. Whole groups of people—for instance, "short people" or "redheads"—may be labeled in this way. The interactionist Erving Goffman coined the term *stigma* to describe the labels society uses to devalue members of certain social groups (Goffman 1963; Heckert and Best 1997).

Prevailing expectations about beauty and body shape may prevent people who are regarded as ugly or obese from advancing as rapidly as their abilities permit. Both overweight and anorexic people are assumed to be weak in character, slaves to their appetites or to media images. Because they do not conform to the beauty myth, these people may be viewed as "disfigured" or "strange" in appearance, bearers of what Goffman calls a "spoiled identity." However, what constitutes disfigurement is a matter of interpretation. Of the 1 million cosmetic procedures done every year in the United States alone, many are performed on women who would be objectively defined as having a normal appearance. And while feminist sociologists have accurately noted that the beauty myth makes many women feel uncomfortable with themselves, men too lack confidence in their appearance. The number of males who choose to undergo cosmetic procedures has risen sharply in recent years; men now account for 20 percent of such surgeries (American Academy of Cosmetic Surgery 2008).

Often people are stigmatized for deviant behaviors they may no longer engage in. The labels "compulsive gambler," "ex-convict," "recovering alcoholic," and "ex–mental patient" can stick to a person for life. Goffman draws a useful distinction between a prestige symbol that calls attention to a positive aspect of one's identity, such as a wedding band or a badge, and a stigma symbol that discredits or debases one's identity, such as a conviction for child molestation. While stigma symbols may not always be obvious, they can become a matter of public knowledge. Since 1994, many states have required convicted sex offenders to register with local police departments. Some communities publish the names and addresses, and in some instances even the pictures, of convicted sex offenders on the Web.

You are a reporter who is investigating gambling activities in your community. How do you find people react to those who engage in highly stigmatized forms of gambling? How do you see them encourage other forms of gambling?

Sociological Perspectives on Deviance

Why do people violate social norms? We have seen that deviant acts are subject to both informal and formal sanctions. The nonconforming or disobedient person may face disapproval, loss of friends, fines, or even imprisonment. Why, then, does deviance occur?

Early explanations for deviance blamed supernatural causes or genetic factors (such as "bad blood" or evolutionary throwbacks to primitive ancestors). In the 1800s, substantial efforts were made to identify biological factors that lead to deviance and especially to criminal activity.

Although such research was discredited in the 20th century, contemporary researchers, primarily biochemists, have sought to isolate genetic factors connected to certain personality traits. Although criminality (much less deviance) is hardly a personality characteristic, researchers have focused on traits that might lead to crime, such as aggression. Of course, aggression can also lead to success in the corporate world, professional sports, and other pursuits.

The contemporary search for biological roots of criminality is but one aspect of the larger sociobiology debate. In general, sociologists reject any emphasis on genetic roots of crime and deviance. The limitations of current knowledge, the possibility of reinforcing racist and sexist assumptions, and the disturbing implications for the rehabilitation of criminals have led sociologists to draw largely on other approaches to explain deviance (Sagarin and Sanchez 1988).

FUNCTIONALIST PERSPECTIVE

According to functionalists, deviance is a common part of human existence, with positive (as well as negative) consequences for social stability. Deviance helps to define the limits of proper behavior. Children who see one parent scold the other for belching at the dinner table learn about approved conduct. The same is true of the driver who receives a speeding ticket, the department store cashier who is fired for yelling at a customer, and the college student who is penalized for handing in papers weeks overdue.

Durkheim's Legacy   Émile Durkheim ([1895] 1964) focused his sociological investigations mainly on criminal acts, yet his conclusions have implications for all types of deviant behavior. In Durkheim's view, the punishments established within a culture (including both formal and informal mechanisms of social control) help to define acceptable behavior and thus contribute to social stability. If improper acts were not sanctioned, people might stretch their standards of what constitutes appropriate conduct. Recently, for example, the gradual intensification of violence in professional wrestling, which has gone unsanctioned, has led to much greater tolerance of what was once considered deviant behavior.

Durkheim ([1897] 1951) introduced the term *anomie* into sociological literature to describe the loss of direction felt in a society when social control of individual behavior has become ineffective. Anomie is a state of normlessness that typically occurs during a period of profound social change and disorder, such as a time of economic collapse. People become more aggressive or depressed, which results in higher rates of violent crime and suicide. Since there is much less agreement on what constitutes proper behavior during times of revolution, sudden prosperity, or economic depression, conformity and obedience become less significant as social forces. Stating exactly what constitutes deviance also becomes much more difficult.

Merton's Theory of Deviance   What do a mugger and a teacher have in common? Each is "working" to obtain money that can be exchanged for desired goods. As this example illustrates, behavior that violates accepted norms (such as mugging) may be performed with the same basic objectives in mind as those of people who pursue conventional lifestyles.

On the basis of this kind of analysis, sociologist Robert Merton (1968) adapted Durkheim's concept of anomie to explain why people accept or reject the goals of a society, the socially approved means of meeting those goals, or both. Merton maintained that one important cultural goal in the United States is success, measured largely in terms of money. In addition to setting this goal for people, our society offers specific instructions on how to reach it—go to school, work hard, do not quit, take advantage of opportunities, and so forth.

What happens in a society with a heavy emphasis on wealth as a basic symbol of success? Merton reasoned that people adapt in certain ways, by conforming to or deviating from such cultural expectations. In his *anomie theory of deviance,* he posited five basic forms of adaptation (see Table 4–1).

Conformity to social norms, the most common adaptation in Merton's typology, is the opposite of deviance. It involves acceptance of both the overall societal goal ("become affluent") and the approved means ("work hard"). In Merton's view, there must be some consensus regarding accepted cultural goals and legitimate means for attaining them. Without such consensus, societies could exist only as collectives of people rather than as unified cultures, and might experience continual chaos.

summingUP

Table 4–1 Merton's Modes of Individual Adaptation

Mode	Institutionalized Means (Hard Work)	Societal Goal (Acquisition of Wealth)
Nondeviant		
Conformity	+	+
Deviant		
Innovation	−	+
Ritualism	+	−
Retreatism	−	−
Rebellion	±	±

NOTE: + indicates acceptance; − indicates rejection; ± indicates replacement with new means and goals.

SOURCE: Merton 1968:194.

You are a young person growing up in a poor neighborhood. You yearn for the flashy, expensive lifestyle you see on *The Apprentice* or MTV. How will you get it?

Of course, in a varied society such as the United States, conformity is not universal. For example, the means for realizing objectives are not equally distributed. People in the lower social classes often identify with the same goals as those of more powerful and affluent citizens, yet they lack equal access to high-quality education and training for skilled work. Moreover, even within a society, institutionalized means for realizing objectives vary. For instance, it is legal to win money by playing roulette or poker in Nevada, but not in neighboring Utah.

The other four types of behavior represented in Table 4–1 all involve some departure from conformity. The "innovator" accepts society's goals but pursues them with means regarded as improper. For example, a professional thief who specializes in safecracking may see his criminal lifestyle as an adaptation to the goal of material success.

In Merton's typology, the "ritualist" has abandoned the goal of material success and become compulsively committed to the institutional means. Work becomes simply a way of life rather than a means to achieving success. An example is the bureaucratic official who blindly applies rules and regulations without remembering the larger goals of an organization. Such would be true of a welfare caseworker who refuses to assist a homeless family because their last apartment was in another district.

The "retreatist," as described by Merton, has basically withdrawn (or "retreated") from both the goals *and* the means of society. In the United States, drug addicts and vagrants are typically portrayed as retreatists. Some social workers worry that adolescents who are addicted to alcohol will become retreatists at an early age.

The final adaptation identified by Merton reflects people's attempts to create a new social structure. The "rebel" who feels alienated from dominant means and goals may seek a dramatically different social order. Members of a revolutionary political organization, such as a militia group, can be categorized as rebels according to Merton's model.

Although Merton's theory of deviance is popular, it has not been applied systematically to real-world crime. Nevertheless, Merton made a key contribution to the sociological understanding of deviance by pointing out that deviants (such as innovators and ritualists) share a great deal with conforming people. The convicted felon may hold many of the same aspirations as people with no criminal background. Thus, the theory helps us to understand deviance as socially created behavior, rather than as the result of momentary pathological impulses.

INTERACTIONIST PERSPECTIVE

The functionalist approach to deviance explains why rule violation continues to exist in societies, despite pressure to conform and obey. However, functionalists do not indicate how a given person comes to commit a deviant act, or why on some occasions crimes do or do not occur. The emphasis on everyday behavior that is the focus of the interactionist perspective provides two such explanations of crime: cultural transmission and social disorganization theory.

Cultural Transmission   In the course of studying graffiti writing by gangs in Los Angeles, sociologist Susan A. Phillips (1999) discovered that the writers learned from one another. In fact, Phillips was surprised by how stable their focus was over time. She also noted how other ethnic groups built on the models of the African American and Chicano gangs, superimposing Cambodian, Chinese, or Vietnamese symbols.

These teenagers demonstrate that humans *learn* how to behave in social situations, whether properly or improperly. There is no natural, innate manner in which people interact with one another. Though these simple ideas are not disputed today, such was not the case when sociologist Edwin Sutherland (1883–1950) first advanced the argument that an individual undergoes the same basic socialization process whether learning conforming or deviant acts.

Sutherland, whose ideas have been the dominating force in criminology, drew on the ***cultural transmission*** school, which emphasizes that people learn criminal behavior through their social interactions. Such learning includes not only the techniques of lawbreaking (for example, how to break into a car quickly and quietly) but also the motives, drives, and rationalizations of criminals. The cultural transmission approach can also be used to explain the behavior of those who habitually abuse alcohol or drugs.

Sutherland maintained that people acquire their definitions of proper and improper behavior through interactions with a primary group and significant others. He used the term ***differential association*** to describe the process through which exposure to attitudes *favorable* to criminal acts leads to rule violations. Research suggests that this process also applies to such noncriminal deviant acts as smoking, truancy, and early sexual behavior (E. Jackson et al. 1986).

To what extent will a given person engage in activity regarded as proper or improper? For each individual, it will depend on the frequency, duration, and importance of two types of social interactions: those that endorse deviant behavior and those that promote acceptance of social norms. People are more likely to engage in norm-defying behavior if they are part of a group or subculture that stresses deviant values, such as a street gang.

Sutherland offers the example of a boy who is sociable, outgoing, and athletic and who lives in an area with a high delinquency rate. The youth is very likely to come into contact with peers who commit acts of vandalism, fail to attend school, and so forth and may come to adopt such behavior. However, an introverted boy living in the same neighborhood may stay away from his peers and avoid delinquency. In another community, an outgoing and athletic boy may join a Little League baseball team or a scout troop because of his interactions with peers. Thus, Sutherland views deviant behavior as the result of the types of groups to which one belongs and the kinds of friendships one has.

According to critics, though the cultural transmission approach may explain the deviant behavior of juvenile delinquents or graffiti artists, it fails to explain the conduct of the first-time impulsive shoplifter or the impoverished person who steals out of necessity. While the theory is not a precise statement of the process through which one becomes a criminal, it does stress the paramount role of social interaction in increasing a person's motivation to engage in deviant behavior (E. Jackson et al. 1986; Sutherland, Cressey, and Luckenbill 1992).

Social Disorganization Theory   The social relationships that exist in a community or neighborhood affect people's behavior. Philip Zimbardo (2007:24–25), author of the mock prison experiment described in Chapter 3, once did an experiment that demonstrated the power of communal relationships. He abandoned a car in each of two different neighborhoods, leaving its hood up and removing its hubcaps. In one neighborhood, people started to strip the car for parts before Zimbardo had finished setting up a remote video camera to record their behavior. In the other neighborhood, weeks passed without the car being touched, except for a pedestrian who stopped to close the hood during a rainstorm.

What accounts for the strikingly different outcomes of Zimbardo's experiment in the two communities? According to *social disorganization theory,* increases in crime and deviance can be attributed to the absence or breakdown of communal relationships and social institutions, such as the family, school, church, and local government. This theory was developed at the University of Chicago in the early 1900s to describe the apparent disorganization that occurred as cities expanded with rapid immigration and migration from rural areas. Using the latest survey techniques, Clifford Shaw and Henry McKay literally mapped the distribution of social problems in Chicago. They found high rates of social problems in neighborhoods where buildings had deteriorated and the population had declined. Interestingly, the patterns persisted over time, despite changes in the neighborhoods' ethnic and racial composition.

This theory is not without its critics. To some, social disorganization theory seems to "blame the victim," leaving larger societal forces, such as the lack of jobs or high-quality schools, unaccountable. Critics also argue that even troubled neighborhoods have viable, healthy organizations, which persist despite the problems that surround them.

More recently, social disorganization theorists have taken to emphasizing the effect of social networks on communal bonds. These researchers acknowledge that communities are not isolated islands. Residents' bonds may be enhanced or weakened by their ties to groups outside the immediate community (Jensen 2003; Sampson and Groves 1989; Shaw and McKay 1942).

LABELING THEORY

The Saints and Roughnecks were two groups of high school males continually engaged in excessive drinking, reckless driving, truancy, petty theft, and vandalism. There the similarity ended. None of the Saints was ever arrested, but every Roughneck was frequently in trouble with police and townspeople. Why the disparity in their treatment? On the basis of his observation research in their high school, sociologist William Chambliss (1973) concluded that social class played an important role in the varying fortunes of the two groups.

The Saints hid behind a facade of respectability. They came from "good families," were active in school organizations, planned on attending college, and received good grades. People generally viewed their delinquent acts as isolated cases of "sowing wild oats." By contrast, the Roughnecks had no such aura of respectability. They drove around town in beat-up cars, were generally unsuccessful in school, and aroused suspicion no matter what they did.

We can understand such discrepancies by using an approach to deviance known as *labeling theory.* Unlike Sutherland's work, labeling theory does not focus on why some individuals come to commit deviant acts. Instead, it attempts to explain why certain people (such as the Roughnecks) are *viewed* as deviants, delinquents, "bad kids," "losers," and criminals, while others whose behavior is similar (such as the Saints) are not seen in such harsh terms. Reflecting the contribution of interactionist theorists, labeling theory emphasizes how a person comes to be labeled as deviant or to accept that label. Sociologist Howard Becker (1963:9; 1964), who popularized this approach, summed it up with this statement: "Deviant behavior is behavior that people so label."

Labeling theory is also called the *societal-reaction approach,* reminding us that it is the *response* to an act, not the behavior itself, that determines deviance. For example, studies have shown that some school personnel and therapists expand educational programs designed for learning-disabled students to include those with behavioral problems. Consequently, a "troublemaker" can be improperly labeled as learning-disabled, and vice versa.

Labeling and Agents of Social Control   Traditionally, research on deviance has focused on people who violate social norms. In contrast, labeling theory focuses on police, probation officers, psychiatrists, judges, teachers, employers, school officials, and other regulators of social control. These agents, it is argued, play a significant role in creating the deviant identity by designating certain people (and not others) as "deviant." An important aspect of labeling theory is the recognition that some individuals or groups have the power to *define* labels and apply them to others. This view ties into the conflict perspective's emphasis on the social significance of power.

Use Your Sociological Imagination

You are a teacher. What kinds of labels, freely used in education, might be attached to your students?

In recent years, the practice of *racial profiling*, in which people are identified as criminal suspects purely on the basis of their race, has come under public scrutiny. Studies confirm the public's suspicions that in some jurisdictions, police officers are much more likely to stop African American males than White males for routine traffic violations, in the expectation of finding drugs or guns in their cars. Civil rights activists refer to these cases sarcastically as DWB ("Driving While Black") violations. After the September 11, 2001, attacks on the World Trade Center and the Pentagon, profiling took a new turn as people who appeared to be Arab or Muslim came under special scrutiny.

The labeling approach does not fully explain why certain people accept a label and others reject it. In fact, this perspective may exaggerate the ease with which societal judgments can alter our self-images. Labeling theorists do suggest, however, that how much power one has relative to others is important in determining a person's ability to resist an undesirable label. Competing approaches (including that of Sutherland) fail to explain why some deviants continue to be viewed as conformists rather than as violators of rules. According to Howard Becker (1973), labeling theory was not conceived as the *sole* explanation for deviance; its proponents merely hoped to focus more attention on the undeniably important actions of those people officially in charge of defining deviance (N. Davis 1975; compare with Cullen and Cullen 1978).

Labeling and Sexual Deviance   Labels have been applied to many types of deviance. Certainly one of the most visible examples has to do with human sexuality and gender. What is deviant sexual behavior? What is criminal sexual behavior? Labeling theory focuses on the process through which these behaviors come to be considered deviant.

The definition of deviant sexual behavior has varied significantly both over time and from culture to culture. Until 1973, the American Psychiatric Association considered homosexuality a "sociopathic personality disorder," which in effect meant that homosexuals should seek therapy. Two years later, however, the association removed homosexuality from its list of mental illnesses. Today, the organization publicly proclaims that "being gay is just as healthy as being straight." In Goffman's terms (see page 109), mental health professionals have removed the stigma from this form of sexual expression. As a result, in the United States and many other countries, consensual sex between same-sex adults is no longer a crime (American Psychological Association 2008; International Gay and Lesbian Human Rights Commission 2010).

Despite the change in health professionals' attitudes, the stigma of homosexuality lingers on. As a result, many people prefer the more positive terms *gay* and *lesbian*. Others, in defiance of the stigma, have proudly adopted the pejorative term *queer* in a deliberate reaction to the ridicule they have borne because of their sexual orientation. Still others maintain that constructing one's sexual orientation as either homosexual or heterosexual is too limiting. Indeed, such either-or language ignores those who are *bisexual,* or sexually attracted to both sexes.

Another group whose sexual orientation does not fit into the usual categories is *transgendered persons,* or those people whose current gender identity does not match their physical identity at birth. Some transgendered persons see themselves as both male and female. Others, called *transexuals,* may take hormones or undergo surgery in an effort to draw physically closer to their chosen gender identity. Transgendered persons are sometimes confused with *transvestites,* or cross-dressers who wear the clothing of the opposite sex. Transvestites are typically men, either gay or heterosexual, who choose to wear women's clothing.

The use of all these terms even in a positive or nonjudgmental way is problematic, because they imply that human sexuality can be confined in neat, mutually exclusive categories. Moreover, the destigmatization of these labels tends to reflect the influence of the socially privileged—that is, the affluent—who have the resources to overcome the stigma. In contrast, the traditional Native American concept of the *two spirit,* a personality that blends the masculine and the feminine, has been largely ridiculed or ignored (Gilley 2006; Wentling et al. 2008).

What does constitute sexual deviance, then? The answer to this question seems to change with each generation. Today, U.S. laws allow married women to accuse their husbands of rape, when a generation ago such an offense was not recognized. Similarly, *pedophilia*—an adult having sex with a minor—is generally regarded with disgust today, even when it is consensual. Yet in many countries, fringe groups now speak positively of "intergenerational sex," arguing that "childhood" is not a biological given (Hendershott 2002).

Though this and some other aspects of sexual expression are still against the law, then, the meaning of the labels is beginning to blur. Similarly, child pornography is both illegal and abhorrent to most people, yet many of the fashion advertisements in mainstream magazines seem to verge on it. And while sex work and sex trafficking seem wrong to most of us, society tolerates and even regulates many aspects of those activities (Barton 2006).

CONFLICT THEORY

Conflict theorists point out that people with power protect their own interests and define deviance to suit their own needs. Sociologist Richard Quinney (1974, 1979, 1980) is a leading proponent of the view that the criminal justice system serves the interests of the powerful. Crime, according to Quinney (1970), is a definition of conduct created by authorized agents of social control—such as legislators and law enforcement officers—in a politically organized society. Quinney and other conflict theorists argue that lawmaking is often an attempt by the powerful to coerce others into their own morality (see also Spitzer 1975).

Conflict theory helps to explain why our society has laws against gambling, drug usage, and prostitution, many of which are violated on a massive scale. (We will examine these "victimless crimes" later in the chapter.) According to the conflict school, criminal law does not represent a consistent application of societal values but instead reflects competing values and interests. Thus, marijuana is outlawed in the United States because it is alleged to be harmful to users, yet cigarettes and alcohol are sold legally almost everywhere.

Conflict theorists also contend that the entire criminal justice system of the United States treats suspects differently on the basis of their racial, ethnic, or social class background. In fact, researchers have found that discretionary differences in the way social control is exercised put deprived African Americans and Hispanics at a disadvantage in the justice system, both as juveniles and as adults (Hawkins et al. 2000; Steffensmeier and Demuth 2000).

The perspective advanced by labeling and conflict theorists forms quite a contrast to the functionalist approach to deviance. Functionalists view standards of deviant behavior as merely reflecting cultural norms, whereas conflict and labeling theorists point out that the most powerful groups in a society can shape laws and standards and determine who is (or is not) prosecuted as a criminal. Those groups would be unlikely to apply the label "deviant" to the corporate executive whose decisions lead to large-scale environmental pollution. In the opinion of conflict theorists, agents of social control and powerful groups can generally impose their own self-serving definitions of deviance on the general public.

FEMINIST PERSPECTIVE

Feminist criminologists such as Freda Adler and Meda Chesney-Lind have suggested that many of the existing approaches to deviance and crime were developed with only men in mind. For example, in the United States, for many years any husband who forced his wife to have sexual intercourse—without her consent and against her will—was not legally considered to have committed rape. The law defined rape as pertaining only to sexual relations between people who were not married to each other, reflecting the overwhelmingly male composition of state legislatures at the time.

It took repeated protests by feminist organizations to change the criminal law defining rape. Beginning in 1993, husbands in all 50 states could be prosecuted under most circumstances for the rape of their wives. There remain alarming exceptions in no fewer than 30 states, however. For example, the husband is exempt when he does not need to use force because his wife is asleep, unconscious, or mentally or physically impaired. These interpretations rest on the notion that the marriage contract entitles a husband to sex (Bergen 2006).

summingUP

Table 4–2 Approaches to Deviance

Approach	Perspective	Proponent	Emphasis
Anomie	Functionalist	Émile Durkheim	Adaptation to societal norms
		Robert Merton	
Cultural transmission/ differential association	Interactionist	Edwin Sutherland	Patterns learned through others
Social disorganization	Interactionist	Clifford Shaw	Communal relationships
		Henry McKay	
Labeling/Societal reaction	Interactionist	Howard Becker	Societal response to acts
		William Chambliss	
Conflict	Conflict	Richard Quinney	Dominance by authorized agents Discretionary justice
Feminist	Conflict/feminist	Freda Adler	Role of gender
		Meda Chesney-Lind	Women as victims and perpetrators

When it comes to crime and to deviance in general, society tends to treat women in a stereotypical fashion. For example, consider how women who have many and frequent sexual partners are more likely than men who are promiscuous to be viewed with scorn. Cultural views and attitudes toward women influence how they are perceived and labeled. In addition, feminist theorists such as Freda Adler and Meda Chesney-Lind emphasize that deviance, including crime, tends to flow from economic relationships.

Table 4–2 summarizes the various approaches sociologists have used in studying deviance.

Crime

Crime is a violation of criminal law for which some governmental authority applies formal penalties. It represents a deviation from formal social norms administered by the state. Laws divide crimes into various categories, depending on the severity of the offense, the age of the offender, the potential punishment that can be levied, and the court that holds jurisdiction over the case.

Nearly 1.4 million violent crimes were reported in the United States in 2008, including more than 16,200 homicides. The key ingredients in the incidence of street crime appear to have been drug use and the widespread presence of firearms. According to the FBI, 19 percent of all reported aggravated assaults, 40 percent of reported robberies, and 68 percent of reported murders involved a firearm. Even with a recent decline in major crime in the United States, current levels exceed the levels experienced in the 1960s (Department of Justice 2009).

TYPES OF CRIME

Rather than relying solely on legal categories, sociologists classify crimes in terms of how they are committed and how society views the offenses. In this section we will examine five types of crime differentiated by sociologists: victimless crimes, professional crime, organized crime, white-collar crime, and transnational crime.

Victimless Crimes   When we think of crime, we tend to think of acts that endanger people's economic or personal well-being against their will (or without their direct knowledge). By contrast, sociologists use the term *victimless crime* to describe the willing exchange among adults of widely desired, but illegal, goods and services. For example, prostitution is widely regarded as a victimless crime (Schur 1965, 1985).

Some activists are working to decriminalize many of these illegal practices. Supporters of decriminalization are troubled by the attempt to legislate a moral code of behavior for adults. In their view, it is impossible to prevent prostitution, drug abuse, gambling, and other victimless crimes. The already overburdened criminal justice system should instead devote its resources to "street crimes" and other offenses with obvious victims.

Despite the wide use of the term *victimless crime,* many people object to the notion that there is no victim other than the offender in such crimes. Excessive drinking, compulsive gambling, and illegal drug use contribute to an enormous amount of personal and property damage. A person with a drinking problem can become abusive to a spouse or children; a compulsive gambler or drug user may steal to pursue his obsession. And feminist sociologists contend that prostitution, as well as the more disturbing aspects of pornography, reinforce the misconception that women are "toys" who can be treated as objects rather than people. According to critics of decriminalization, society must not give tacit approval to conduct that has such harmful consequences.

The controversy over decriminalization reminds us of the important insights of labeling and conflict theorists presented earlier. Underlying this debate are two interesting questions: Who has the power to define gambling, prostitution, and public drunkenness as "crimes"? And who has the power to label such behaviors as "victimless"? The answer, in both cases, is generally the state legislatures and sometimes the police and the courts.

Professional Crime   Although the adage "crime doesn't pay" is familiar, many people do make a career of illegal activities. A *professional criminal* (or career criminal) is a person who pursues crime as a day-to-day occupation, developing skilled techniques and enjoying a certain degree of status among other criminals. Some professional criminals specialize in burglary, safecracking, hijacking of cargo, pickpocketing, and shoplifting. Such people have acquired skills that reduce the likelihood of arrest, conviction, and imprisonment. As a result, they may have long careers in their chosen "professions."

Edwin Sutherland (1937) offered pioneering insights into the behavior of professional criminals by publishing an annotated account written by a professional thief. Unlike the person who engages in crime only once or twice, professional thieves make a business of stealing. They devote their entire working time to planning and executing crimes, and sometimes travel across the nation to pursue their "professional duties." Like people in regular occupations, professional thieves consult with their colleagues concerning their work, becoming part of a subculture of similarly occupied individuals. They exchange information on good places to burglarize, outlets for stolen goods, and ways of securing bail bonds.

Organized Crime   A 1976 government report takes three pages to define the term *organized crime*. For our purposes, we will consider **organized crime** to be the work of a group that regulates relations between various criminal enterprises involved in various illegal activities, including the smuggling and sale of drugs, prostitution, and gambling. Organized crime dominates the world of illegal business just as large corporations dominate the conventional business world. It allocates territory, sets prices for goods and services, and arbitrates internal disputes. A secret, conspiratorial activity that generally evades law enforcement, it takes over legitimate businesses, gains influence over labor unions, corrupts public officials, intimidates witnesses in criminal trials, and even "taxes" merchants in exchange for "protection" (National Advisory Commission on Criminal Justice 1976).

There has always been a global element in organized crime. But law enforcement officials and policymakers now acknowledge the emergence of a new form of organized crime, one that takes advantage of advances in electronic communications. *Transnational* organized crime includes drug and arms smuggling, money laundering, and trafficking in illegal immigrants and stolen goods: see page 123 (Lumpe 2003; Office of Justice Programs 1999).

White-Collar and Technology-Based Crime   Income tax evasion, stock manipulation, consumer fraud, bribery and extraction of "kickbacks," embezzlement, and misrepresentation in advertising— these are all examples of **white-collar crime,** illegal acts committed in the course of business activities, often by affluent, "respectable" people. Edwin Sutherland (1949, 1983) likened these crimes to organized crime because they are often perpetrated through people's occupational roles (Friedrichs 1998).

A new type of white-collar crime has emerged in recent decades: computer crime. The use of high technology allows criminals to carry out embezzlement or electronic fraud, often leaving few traces, or to gain access to a company's inventory without leaving home. According to a study by the FBI and the National White Collar Crime Center, more than one million Internet crimes were reported in less than four years, ranging from scams to identity theft (Internet Crime Complaint Center 2007).

Sutherland (1940) coined the term *white-collar crime* in 1939 to refer to acts by individuals, but the term has been broadened recently to include offenses by businesses and corporations. *Corporate crime,* or any act by a corporation that is punishable by the government, takes many forms and includes individuals, organizations, and institutions among its victims. Corporations may engage in anticompetitive behavior, environmental pollution, tax fraud, accounting fraud, stock fraud and manipulation, the production of unsafe goods, bribery and corruption, and worker health and safety violations (Simpson 1993).

Given the economic and social costs of white-collar crime, one might expect the criminal justice system to take this problem quite seriously. Yet white-collar offenders are more likely to receive fines than prison sentences. Conviction for such illegal acts does not generally harm a person's reputation and career aspirations nearly so much as conviction for street crime would. Apparently, the label "white-collar criminal"

"BUT IF WE GO BACK TO SCHOOL AND GET A GOOD EDUCATION, THINK OF ALL THE DOORS IT'LL OPEN TO WHITE-COLLAR CRIME."

does not carry the stigma of the label "felon convicted of a violent crime." Conflict theorists don't find such differential labeling and treatment surprising. They argue that the criminal justice system largely disregards the white-collar crimes of the affluent, while focusing instead on crimes committed by the poor. If an offender holds a position of status and influence, his or her crime is treated as less serious, and the sanction is much more lenient (Maguire 1988).

As a newspaper editor, how might you treat front-page stories about corporate crime differently from those about violent crime?

Transnational Crime   More and more, scholars and police officials are turning their attention to *transnational crime,* or crime that occurs across multiple national borders. In the past, international crime was often limited to the clandestine shipment of goods across the border between two countries. But increasingly, crime is no more restricted by such borders than is legal commerce. Rather than concentrating on specific countries, international crime now spans the globe.

Historically, probably the most dreaded example of transnational crime has been slavery. At first, governments did not regard slavery as a crime but merely regulated it as they would the trade in goods. In the 20th century, transnational crime grew to embrace trafficking in endangered species, drugs, and stolen art and antiquities.

Transnational crime is not exclusive of some of the other types of crime we have discussed. For example, organized criminal networks are increasingly global. Technology definitely facilitates their illegal activities, such as trafficking in child pornography. In the 1990s, the United Nations began to categorize transnational crimes; Table 4–3 lists some of the more common types.

CRIME STATISTICS

Crime statistics are not as accurate as social scientists would like. However, since they relate to an issue of grave concern to the people of the United States, they are frequently cited as if they were completely reliable. Such data do serve as an indicator of police activity, as well as of the approximate level of certain crimes. Yet it would be a mistake to interpret these data as an exact representation of the incidence of crime.

Understanding Crime Statistics   Reported crime is very high in the United States, and the public continues to regard crime as a major social problem. However, there has recently been a significant decline in violent crime nationwide following many years of increases. A number of explanations have been offered, including:

- Community-oriented policing and crime prevention programs
- New gun control laws
- A massive increase in the prison population, which at least prevents inmates from committing crimes outside the prison

Table 4–3 Types of Transnational Crime

Bankruptcy and insurance fraud

Computer crime (treating computers as both a tool and a target of crime)

Corruption and bribery of public officials

Environmental crime

Hijacking of airplanes ("skyjacking")

Illegal drug trade

Illegal money transfers ("money laundering")

Illegal sales of firearms and ammunition

Infiltration of legal businesses

Intellectual property crime

Networking of criminal organizations

Sea piracy

Terrorism

Theft of art and cultural objects

Trafficking in body parts (includes illegal organ transplants)

Trafficking in human beings (includes sex trade)

SOURCE: Compiled by the author based on Mueller 2001 and United Nations Office on Drugs and Crime 2005.

It remains to be seen whether this pattern will continue, but even with current declines, reported crimes remain well above those of other nations, and yet current reported rates in the United States are still the lowest in about 40 years. Feminist scholars draw our attention to one significant variation: The proportion of major crimes committed by women has increased. In a recent 10-year period (1999–2008), female arrests for major reported crimes increased 12 percent, while comparable male arrests declined 19 percent (Department of Justice 2009:Table 33).

The crime index, published annually by the FBI as part of the *Uniform Crime Reports,* includes statistics on murder, rape, robbery, assault, burglary, larceny-theft, motor vehicle theft, and arson (see Table 4–4). Obviously, many serious offenses, such as white-collar crime, are not included in this index (although they are recorded elsewhere). In addition, the crime index is disproportionately devoted to property crimes, whereas most citizens are more worried about violent crimes. Thus, a significant decrease in the number of rapes and robberies could be overshadowed by a slightly larger increase in the number of automobiles stolen, leading to the mistaken impression that *personal* safety is more at risk than before.

The most serious limitation of official crime statistics is that they include only those crimes actually *reported* to law enforcement agencies. Because members of racial and ethnic minority groups often distrust law

Table 4–4 National Crime Rates and Percentage Change

Crime Index Offenses in 2008	Number Reported	Rate per 100,000 Inhabitants	Percentage Change in Rate Since 1999
Violent crime			
Murder	16,272	5	−6
Forcible rape	89,000	29	−11
Robbery	444,855	145	−3
Aggravated assault	834,885	275	−8
Total	1,382,012	455	−13
Property crime			
Burglary	2,222,196	731	−5
Larceny-theft	6,558,873	2,167	−15
Motor vehicle theft	956,846	315	−26
Total	9,767,915	3,213	−14

NOTES: Arson was designated an index offense beginning in 1979; data on arson were still incomplete as of 2008. Because of rounding, the offenses may not add to totals.

SOURCE: Department of Justice 2009: Tables 1, 1a.

enforcement agencies, they may not contact the police. Feminist sociologists and others have noted that many women do not report rape or spousal abuse out of fear that they will be blamed for the crime.

Partly because of these deficiencies in official statistics, the National Crime Victimization Survey was initiated in 1972. The Bureau of Justice Statistics, in compiling this annual report, seeks information from law enforcement agencies, but also interviews members of over 76,000 households and asks if they were victims of a specific set of crimes during the preceding year. In general, those who administer *victimization surveys* question ordinary people, not police officers, to determine whether they have been victims of crime.

Unfortunately, like other crime data, victimization surveys have particular limitations. They require that victims understand what has happened to them and are willing to disclose such information to interviewers. Fraud, income tax evasion, and blackmail are examples of crimes that are unlikely to be reported in victimization studies. Nevertheless, 91 percent of all households have been willing to cooperate with investigators for the National Crime Victimization Survey. As Figure 4–2 shows, data from these surveys reveal a fluctuating crime rate with significant declines in both the 1980s and 1990s.

International Crime Rates If developing reliable crime data in the United States is difficult, making useful cross-national comparisons

Figure 4–2
Victimization Rates,
1973–2007
SOURCES: Rand 2008;
Rennison 2002.

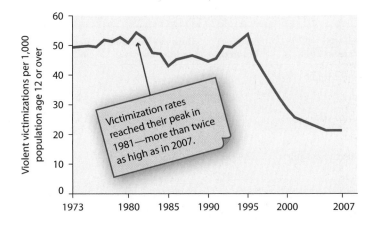

Think About It
What might have caused the victimization rate to drop so dramatically beginning in the mid-1990s?

is even more difficult. Nevertheless, with some care, we can offer preliminary conclusions about how crime rates differ around the world.

During the 1980s and 1990s, violent crimes were much more common in the United States than in Western Europe. Murders, rapes, and robberies were reported to the police at much higher rates in the United States. Yet the incidence of certain other types of crime appears to be higher elsewhere. For example, England, Italy, Australia, and New Zealand all have higher rates of car theft than the United States (International Crime Victim Survey 2004).

Why are violent crime rates so much higher in the United States? Sociologist Elliot Currie (1985, 1998) has suggested that our society places greater emphasis on individual economic achievement than other societies. At the same time, many observers have noted that the culture of the United States has long tolerated, if not condoned, many forms of violence. Coupled with sharp disparities between poor and affluent citizens, significant unemployment, and substantial alcohol and drug abuse, all these factors combine to produce a climate conducive to crime.

Disturbing increases in violent crime are evident in other Western societies, however. For example, crime has skyrocketed in Russia since the overthrow of Communist party rule (with its strict controls on guns and criminals) in 1991. In 1988 there were fewer than 260 homicides in Moscow; now there are more than 1,000 homicides per year. Organized crime has filled a power vacuum there since the end of communism; one result is that gangland shootouts and premeditated "contract hits" have become more common. Some prominent reformist politicians have been targeted as well (Winslow and Zhang 2008a, 2008b).

Sociology Matters

Sociology matters because it explains why you accept certain social norms almost without thinking—and why you pay a price if you break those norms.

- What social norms were you expected to conform to when you became a student at your college or university? Are they similar to or different from the norms you grew up with?

- What happens to students who do not conform to accepted social norms? Is social control on your campus stricter or more lenient than social control in other parts of society?

- Is crime a problem on your campus? If so, what social forces might underlie it?

CHAPTER RESOURCES

Summary

Conformity and **deviance** are two ways in which people respond to real or imagined pressure from others. This chapter examined the mechanisms of **social control** that society uses to encourage conformity to social norms. We defined deviance and offered several theories to explain its existence. The chapter closed with a discussion of **crime** and statistics on criminal activity in the United States and other nations.

1. Stanley Milgram defined **conformity** as going along with one's peers. **Obedience,** on the other hand, means compliance with higher authorities in a hierarchical structure.

2. Some norms are so important to a society that they are formalized in **law.** Socialization is the primary source of both conformity and obedience to law.

3. **Deviance** is behavior that violates any social norm, whether it concerns conduct or personal appearance. Some forms of deviance carry a negative social **stigma,** while others are more or less accepted.

4. The sociologist Robert Merton noted that people who engage in deviant behavior share many of the same goals and values as people who conform to social norms, though they may differ in the means by which they pursue their goals. Merton's theory is called the **anomie theory of deviance.**

www.mhhe.com/schaefersm5e
Visit the Online Learning Center for *Sociology Matters* to access quizzes, review activities, and other learning tools.

5. The interactionist theorist Edwin Sutherland believed that people learn criminal behavior by associating with others, an approach called **cultural transmission.** In his theory of **differential association,** Sutherland proposed that deviance results from a person's exposure to individuals who approve of criminal acts.

6. Other interactionists attribute increases in crime and deviance to the absence or breakdown of communal relationships and social institutions, such as the family, school, church, and local government. This approach is called **social disorganization theory.**

7. **Labeling theory** emphasizes that society brands some people who engage in a behavior as deviant, but not others, based largely on a person's social class, race, or ethnicity. This theory of deviance is also called the **societal-reaction approach.**

8. Conflict theorists stress that laws and the **sanctions** imposed on criminals for breaking them reflect the interests of the powerful. Feminists emphasize that in crimes involving women, such as rape and prostitution, crime is defined differently, and those involved are treated differently, depending on their gender.

9. **Crime** is a violation of criminal law for which some governmental authority applies formal penalties. Sociologists differentiate among **victimless crimes,** such as drug use and prostitution, **professional crime, organized crime, white-collar crime,** and **transnational crime.**

10. Crime statistics are among the least reliable social data, partly because many crimes are not reported to law enforcement agencies. Rates of violent crime are higher in the United States than in other Western societies.

Key Terms

anomie, 110

anomie theory of deviance, 111

conformity, 104

crime, 119

cultural transmission, 113

deviance, 108

differential association, 113

formal social control, 107

informal social control, 107

labeling theory, 115

law, 107

obedience, 104

organized crime, 121

professional criminal, 120

sanction, 102

social control, 102

social disorganization theory, 114

societal-reaction approach, 115

stigma, 109

transnational crime, 123

victimization survey, 125

victimless crime, 120

white-collar crime, 121

Stratification in the United States and Global Inequality

Systems of Stratification

Sociological Perspectives on Stratification

Is Stratification Universal?

Stratification by Social Class

Social Mobility

The Global Divide

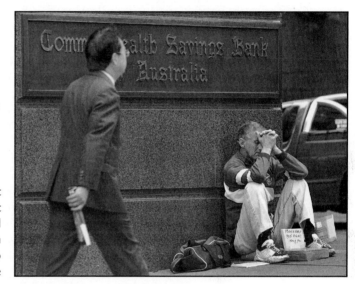

Apparently, $53 billion is not the sum it used to be. That was Microsoft co-founder Bill Gates's estimated worth in 2009, when he dropped to second richest person in the world. Mexican telecom owner Carlos Slim Helú's net worth that year was $53.5 billion, making him the world's richest person. Today, the world has at least 957 billionaires (a billion equals *one thousand million*) in 54 countries. Gates's fortune alone equals the entire gross national income of 13 African countries, home to 82 million people.

At the other end of this spectrum of wealth are the poor. World-wide, the gross national income per person is about $8,700. In low-income countries—home to nearly a billion people—people get by on less than $530 per person. Even in the relatively wealthy nation of the United States, nearly 37 million people are unable to fulfill their basic needs for food and shelter, no matter how many jobs they hold. The typical corporate head makes more by the end of the first day's lunch than the average U.S. worker makes in a year. In fact, the income gap between the highest- and lowest-paid workers in the United States is estimated to be wider now than it has been at any time since before the Great Depression of the 1930s (Edwards 2008:9; Forbes 2010; World Bank 2010a:32–34).

129

The condition in which members of a society enjoy different amounts of wealth, prestige, or power is termed **social inequality.** Every society manifests some degree of social inequality. Sociologists refer to the structured ranking of entire groups of people that perpetuates unequal economic rewards and power as **stratification.** In industrial societies, these unequal rewards are evident both in people's **income**—in their salaries and wages—and in their **wealth**—in material assets such as land, stocks, and other property. But the unequal rewards of stratification can also be seen in the mortality rates of different groups.

In this chapter we will examine four stratification systems, paying particular attention to the theories of Karl Marx and Max Weber. We will see how a person's social class affects his or her opportunities, including the chance to move up the social ladder. And we will look at stratification in developing countries, where multinational corporations based in developed nations have been charged with exploiting those who work in their factories.

Systems of Stratification

Not all societies are stratified in the same way. Sociologists have studied stratification in ancient as well as modern times, in Western and non-Western societies. In the following section we will compare four different general systems of stratification. Then we will discuss several theoretical approaches to stratification, its purpose and desirability.

Look at the four general systems of stratification examined here—slavery, castes, estates, and social classes—as ideal types useful for purposes of analysis. Any stratification system may include elements of more than one type. For example, prior to the Civil War, you could find in the southern states of the United States social classes dividing Whites as well as the institutionalized enslavement of Blacks.

To understand these systems better, it may be helpful to review the distinction between *achieved status* and *ascribed status,* discussed in Chapter 3. *Ascribed status* is a social position "assigned" to a person by society without regard for that person's unique talents or characteristics. By contrast, *achieved status* is a social position attained by a person largely through his or her own efforts. The two are closely linked. The nation's most affluent families generally inherit wealth and status, while many members of racial and ethnic minorities inherit disadvantaged status. Age and gender, as well, are ascribed statuses that influence a person's wealth and social position.

SLAVERY

The most extreme form of legalized social inequality for individuals or groups is *slavery.* What distinguishes this oppressive system of stratification is that enslaved individuals are *owned* by other people, who treat these human beings as property, just as if they were household pets or appliances.

Slavery has varied in the way it has been practiced. In ancient Greece, the main source of slaves was captives of war and piracy. Although succeeding generations could inherit slave status, it was not necessarily permanent. A person's status might change depending on which city-state happened to triumph in a military conflict. In effect, all citizens had the potential of becoming slaves or of being granted freedom, depending on the circumstances of history. By contrast, in the United States and Latin America, where slavery was an ascribed status, racial and legal barriers prevented the freeing of slaves.

CASTES

Castes are hereditary systems of rank, usually religiously dictated, that tend to be fixed and immobile. The caste system is generally associated with Hinduism in India and other countries. In India there are four major castes, called *varnas*. A fifth category of outcastes, referred to as *untouchables,* is considered to be so lowly and unclean as to have no place within this system of stratification. There are also many minor castes. Caste membership is an ascribed status (at birth, children automatically assume the same position as their parents). Each caste is quite sharply defined, and members are expected to marry within that caste.

In recent decades, industrialization and urbanization have taken their toll on India's rigid caste system. Many villagers have moved to urban areas, where their low-caste status is unknown. The anonymity of city life allows these families to take advantage of opportunities they would not otherwise have had, and eventually to move up the social ladder.

ESTATES

A third type of stratification system, called *estates,* was associated with feudal societies during the Middle Ages. The **estate system,** or *feudalism,* required peasants to work land leased to them by nobles in exchange for military protection and other services. The basis for the system was the nobles' ownership of land, which was critical to their superior and privileged status. As in systems based on slavery and caste, inheritance of one's position largely defined the estate system. The nobles inherited their titles and property; the peasants were born to a subservient position in an agrarian society.

SOCIAL CLASSES

A **class system** is a social ranking based primarily on economic position in which achieved characteristics can influence social mobility.

In contrast to slavery and the caste and estate systems, the boundaries between classes are imprecisely defined; one can move from one stratum, or level, of society to another. Yet class systems maintain stable stratification hierarchies and patterns of class divisions, and they, too, are marked by unequal distribution of wealth and power.

Sociologist Daniel Rossides (1997) uses a five-class model to describe the class system of the United States: the upper class, the upper-middle class, the lower-middle class, the working class, and the lower class. Although the lines separating social classes in his model are not so sharp as the divisions between castes, he shows that members of the five classes differ significantly in ways other than just income level.

Rossides categorizes about 1 to 2 percent of the people of the United States as *upper class,* a group limited to the very wealthy. These people associate in exclusive clubs and social circles. By contrast, the *lower class,* consisting of approximately 20 to 25 percent of the population, disproportionately consists of Blacks, Hispanics, single mothers with dependent children, and people who cannot find regular work or must make do with low-paying work. This class lacks both wealth and income and is too politically weak to exercise significant power.

Both these classes, at opposite ends of the nation's social hierarchy, reflect the importance of ascribed status and achieved status. Ascribed statuses such as race and disability clearly influence a person's wealth and social position. Sociologist Richard Jenkins (1991) has researched how being disabled marginalizes a person in the labor market of the United States. People with disabilities are particularly vulnerable to unemployment, are often poorly paid, and in many cases occupy the lower rungs of the occupational ladder. Regardless of their actual performance on the job, the disabled are stigmatized as not "earning their keep." Such are the effects of ascribed status.

Sandwiched between the upper and lower classes in Rossides's model are the upper-middle class, the lower-middle class, and the working class. The *upper-middle class,* numbering about 10 to 15 percent of the population, is composed of professionals such as doctors, lawyers, and architects. They participate extensively in politics and take leadership roles in voluntary associations. The *lower-middle class,* which accounts for approximately 30 to 35 percent of the population, includes less affluent professionals (such as elementary school teachers and nurses), owners of small businesses, and a sizable number of clerical workers. While not all members of this varied class hold degrees from a college, they share the goal of sending their children there.

Rossides describes the *working class*—about 40 to 45 percent of the population—as people holding regular manual or blue-collar jobs. Certain members of this class, such as electricians, may have higher incomes than people in the lower-middle class. Yet even if they have achieved some degree of economic security, they tend to identify with manual workers and their long history of involvement in the labor movement

Use Your Sociological Imagination

How can you tell someone's social class? What indicators can be misleading?

of the United States. Of Rossides's five classes, the working class is declining noticeably in size. In the economy of the United States, service and technical jobs are replacing positions involved in the actual manufacturing or transportation of goods.

Sociological Perspectives on Stratification

Sociologists have hotly debated stratification and social inequality and have reached varying conclusions. No theorist stressed the significance of class for society—and for social change—more strongly than Karl Marx. Marx viewed class differentiation as the crucial determinant of social, economic, and political inequality. By contrast, Max Weber questioned Marx's emphasis on the overriding importance of the economic sector and argued that stratification should be viewed as having many dimensions.

KARL MARX'S VIEW OF CLASS DIFFERENTIATION

Sociologist Leonard Beeghley (1978:1) aptly noted that "Karl Marx was both a revolutionary and a social scientist." Marx was concerned with stratification in all types of human societies, beginning with primitive agricultural tribes and continuing into feudalism. But his main focus was on the effects of economic inequality on all aspects of 19th-century Europe. The plight of the working class made him feel that it was imperative to strive for changes in the social class structure.

In Marx's view, social relations during any period of history depend on who controls the primary mode of economic production, such as land or factories. Differential access to scarce resources shapes the relationship between groups. Thus, under the estate system, most production was agricultural, and the land was owned by the nobility. Peasants had little choice but to work according to terms dictated by those who owned the land.

Using this type of analysis, Marx examined social relations within *capitalism*—an economic system in which the means of production are held largely in private hands, and the main incentive for economic activity is the accumulation of profits (Rosenberg 1991). Marx focused on the two classes that began to emerge as the estate system declined—the bourgeoisie and the proletariat. The *bourgeoisie,* or capitalist class, owns the means of production, such as factories and machinery; the *proletariat* is the working class. In capitalist societies, the members of the bourgeoisie maximize profit in competition with other firms. In the process, they exploit workers, who must exchange their labor for subsistence wages. In Marx's view, members of each class share a distinctive culture. He was most interested in the culture of the proletariat, but he also examined the ideology of the bourgeoisie, through which it justifies its dominance over workers.

The economic downturn that began in 2008 with the threatened failure of several major investment banks has brought public scrutiny of the salaries and bonuses awarded to financial executives.

According to Marx, exploitation of the proletariat will inevitably lead to the destruction of the capitalist system, because the workers will revolt. But first, the working class must develop ***class consciousness***—a subjective awareness of common vested interests and the need for collective political action to bring about social change. Workers must often overcome what Marx termed ***false consciousness,*** or an attitude held by members of a class that does not accurately reflect its objective position. A worker with false consciousness may adopt an individualistic viewpoint toward capitalist exploitation ("*I* am being exploited by *my* boss"). By contrast, the class-conscious worker realizes that *all* workers are being exploited by the bourgeoisie and have a common stake in revolution.

For Karl Marx, class consciousness is part of a collective process in which the proletariat comes to identify the bourgeoisie as the source of its oppression. Revolutionary leaders will guide the proletariat in its class struggle. Ultimately, the proletariat will overthrow the rule of the bourgeoisie and the government (which Marx saw as representing the interests of capitalists) and eliminate private ownership of the means of production. In Marx's rather utopian view, classes and oppression will cease to exist in the postrevolutionary workers' state.

How accurate were Marx's predictions? He failed to anticipate the emergence of labor unions, whose power in collective bargaining weakens the stranglehold that capitalists maintain over workers. Moreover, as contemporary conflict theorists note, he did not foresee the extent to which political liberties and relative prosperity could contribute to "false consciousness." Many people have come to view themselves as individuals striving for improvement within "free" societies that offer substantial mobility rather than as downtrodden members of a working class facing a collective fate. Finally, Marx did not predict that Communist party rule would be established and later overthrown in the former Soviet Union and Eastern Europe. Still, the Marxist approach to the study of class is useful in stressing the importance of stratification as a determinant of social behavior, and of the fundamental separation in many societies between two distinct groups, the rich and the poor.

MAX WEBER'S VIEW OF STRATIFICATION

Unlike Karl Marx, Max Weber insisted that no single characteristic (such as class) totally defines a person's position within the stratification system. Instead, writing in 1916, Weber identified three analytically distinct components of stratification: class, status, and power (Gerth and Mills 1958).

Weber used the term *class* to refer to a group of people who have a similar level of wealth and income. For example, certain workers in the United States try to support their families through minimum-wage jobs. According to Weber's definition, these wage earners constitute a class because they share the same economic position and fate. Although Weber agreed with Marx on the importance of this economic dimension of stratification, he argued that the actions of individuals and groups could not be understood *solely* in economic terms.

Weber used the term *status group* to refer to people who have the same prestige or lifestyle. An individual gains status through membership in a desirable group, such as the medical profession. But status is not the same as economic class standing. In our culture, a successful pickpocket may earn the same income as a college professor. Yet the thief is widely regarded as a member of a low-status group, whereas the professor holds high status.

For Weber, the third major component of stratification reflects a political dimension. *Power* is the ability to exercise one's will over others. In the United States, power stems from membership in particularly influential groups, such as corporate boards of directors, government bodies, and interest groups. Conflict theorists generally agree that two major sources of power—big business and government—are closely interrelated.

In Weber's view, then, each of us has not one rank in society but three. Our position in a stratification system reflects some combination of class, status, and power. Each factor influences the other two, and in fact the rankings on these three dimensions often tend to coincide. John F. Kennedy came from an extremely wealthy family, attended exclusive preparatory schools, graduated from Harvard University, and went on to become president of the United States. Like Kennedy, many people from affluent backgrounds achieve impressive status and power.

INTERACTIONIST VIEW OF STRATIFICATION

Both Karl Marx and Max Weber looked at inequality primarily from a macrosociological perspective, considering the entire society or even the global economy. Marx did suggest the importance of a more microsociological analysis, however, when he stressed the ways in which individuals develop a true class consciousness.

Interactionists, as well as economists, have long been interested in the importance of social class in shaping a person's lifestyle. The theorist Thorstein Veblen (1857–1929) noted that those at the top of the social hierarchy typically convert part of their wealth into *conspicuous consumption,* purchasing more automobiles than they can reasonably use and building houses with more rooms than they can possibly occupy. Or they may engage in *conspicuous leisure,* jetting to remote destinations and staying just long enough to have dinner or view a sunset over some historic locale (Veblen [1899] 1964).

At the other end of the spectrum, behavior that is judged to be typical of the lower class is subject not only to ridicule but even to legal action. Communities have, from time to time, banned trailers from people's front yards and sofas from their front porches. In some communities, it is illegal to leave a pickup truck in front of the house overnight.

Use Your Sociological Imagination

Give some examples of conspicuous consumption among your fellow college students. Which are obvious and which more subtle?

Is Stratification Universal?

Must some members of society receive greater rewards than others? Do people need to feel socially and economically superior to others? Can social life be organized without structured inequality? These questions have been debated for centuries, especially among political activists. Utopian socialists, religious minorities, and members of recent countercultures have all attempted to establish communities that to some extent or other would abolish inequality in social relationships.

Social science researchers have found that inequality exists in all societies—even the simplest. For example, when anthropologist Gunnar Landtman ([1938] 1968) studied the Kiwai Papuans of New Guinea, he initially noticed little differentiation among them. Every man in the village did the same work and lived in similar housing. However, on closer inspection, Landtman observed that certain Papuans—the men who were warriors, harpooners, and sorcerers—were described as "a little more high" than others. By contrast, villagers who were female, unemployed, or unmarried were considered "down a little bit" and were barred from owning land.

Stratification is universal, then, in that all societies maintain some form of social inequality among members. Depending on its values, a society may assign people to distinctive ranks based on their religious knowledge, skill in hunting, beauty, trading expertise, or ability to provide health care. But *why* has such inequality developed in human societies? And how much differentiation among people, if any, is actually essential?

Functionalist and conflict theorists offer contrasting explanations for the existence and necessity of social stratification. Functionalists maintain that a differential system of rewards and punishments is necessary for the efficient operation of society. Conflict theorists argue that competition for scarce resources results in significant political, economic, and social inequality.

FUNCTIONALIST VIEW

Would people go to school for many years to become physicians if they could make as much money and gain as much respect working as street cleaners? Functionalists say no, which is partly why they believe that a stratified society is universal.

In the view of Kingsley Davis and Wilbert Moore (1945), society must distribute its members among a variety of social positions. It must not only make sure that these positions are filled but also see that they are staffed by people with the appropriate talents and abilities. Rewards, including money and prestige, are based on the importance of a position and the relative scarcity of qualified personnel. Yet this assessment often devalues work performed by certain segments of society, such as women's work as homemakers or in occupations traditionally filled by women, as well as low-status work such as fast-food jobs.

Davis and Moore argue that stratification is universal and that social inequality is necessary so that people will be motivated to fill functionally important positions. But unequal rewards are not the only means of encouraging people to fill critical positions and occupations. Personal pleasure, intrinsic satisfaction, and value orientations also motivate people to enter particular careers. Functionalists agree but note that society must use some type of reward to motivate people to enter unpleasant or dangerous jobs and jobs that require a long training period. This response does not justify stratification systems in which status is largely inherited, such as slave, caste, or estate systems. Similarly, it is difficult to explain the high salaries our society offers to professional athletes or entertainers on the basis of how critical those jobs are to society's survival (R. Collins 1975; Kerbo 2009; Tumin 1953, 1985).

Even if stratification is inevitable, the functionalist explanation for differential rewards does not explain the wide disparity between the rich and the poor. Critics of the functionalist approach point out that the richest 10 percent of households account for 22 percent of the nation's income in Sweden, 25 percent in France, and 30 percent in the United States. In their view, the level of income inequality found in contemporary industrial societies cannot be defended—even though those societies have a legitimate need to fill certain key occupations (World Bank 2008:68–70).

In your view, is the extent of social inequality in the United States helpful or harmful to society as a whole? Explain.

CONFLICT VIEW

The writings of Karl Marx lie at the heart of conflict theory. Marx viewed history as a continuous struggle between the oppressors and the oppressed—one that would ultimately culminate in an egalitarian, classless society. In terms of stratification, he argued that the dominant class under capitalism—the bourgeoisie—manipulated the economic and political systems in order to maintain control over the exploited proletariat. Marx did not believe that stratification was inevitable, but he did see inequality and oppression as inherent in capitalism (Wright et al. 1982).

Like Marx, contemporary conflict theorists believe that human beings are prone to conflict over such scarce resources as wealth, status, and power. However, while Marx focused primarily on class conflict, more recent theorists have extended the analysis to include conflicts based on gender, race, age, and other dimensions. The British sociologist Ralf Dahrendorf has been one of the most influential contributors to the conflict approach.

Dahrendorf (1959) modified Marx's analysis of capitalist society to apply to *modern* capitalist societies. For Dahrendorf, social classes are groups of people who share common interests resulting from their authority relationships. In identifying the most powerful groups in society, he includes not only the bourgeoisie—the owners of the means of production—but also industrial managers, legislators, the judiciary, heads of the government bureaucracy, and others. In that respect, Dahrendorf has merged Marx's emphasis on class conflict with Weber's recognition that power is an important element of stratification (Cuff et al. 1990).

Conflict theorists, including Dahrendorf, contend that the powerful of today, like the bourgeoisie of Marx's time, want society to run smoothly so that they can enjoy their privileged positions. Because the status quo suits those with wealth, status, and power, they have a clear interest in preventing, minimizing, or controlling societal conflict. One way for the powerful to maintain the status quo is to define society's dominant ideology—the set of cultural beliefs and practices that supports powerful social, economic, and political interests. From a conflict perspective, society's most powerful groups and institutions control not only wealth and property but the means of influencing people's cultural beliefs through religion, education, and the media (Abercrombie et al. 1980, 1990; Robertson 1988).

The powerful, such as leaders of government, also use limited social reforms to buy off the oppressed and reduce the danger of challenges to their dominance. For example, minimum wage laws and unemployment compensation unquestionably give some valuable assistance to needy men and women. Yet these reforms also serve to pacify those who might otherwise rebel. Of course, in the view of conflict theorists, such maneuvers can never entirely eliminate conflict, since workers will continue to demand equality, and the powerful will not give up their control of society.

Table 5–1 Three Major Perspectives on Social Stratification

	Functionalist	Conflict	Interactionist
Purpose of social stratification	Facilitates filling of social positions	Facilitates exploitation	Influences people's lifestyles
Attitude toward social inequality	Necessary to some extent	Excessive and growing	Influences intergroup relations
Analysis of the wealthy	Talented and skilled, creating opportunities for others	Use the dominant ideology to further their own interests	Exhibit conspicuous consumption and conspicuous leisure

summingUP

Conflict theorists see stratification as a major source of societal tension and conflict. They do not agree with Davis and Moore that stratification is functional for a society or that it serves as a source of stability. Rather, conflict sociologists argue that stratification will inevitably lead to instability and social change. Table 5–1 summarizes the three major sociological perspectives on social stratification (R. Collins 1975; Coser 1977).

LENSKI'S VIEWPOINT

Let's return to the question posed earlier—Is stratification universal?—and consider the sociological response. Some form of differentiation is found in every culture, from the most primitive to the most advanced industrial societies of our time. Sociologist Gerhard Lenski, in his sociocultural evolution approach, described how economic systems change as their level of technology becomes more complex, beginning with hunting and gathering and culminating eventually with industrial society. In subsistence-based hunting-and-gathering societies, people focus on survival. While some inequality and differentiation is evident, a stratification system based on social class does not emerge because there is no real wealth to be claimed.

As a society advances in technology, it becomes capable of producing a considerable surplus of goods. The emergence of surplus resources greatly expands the possibilities for inequality in status, influence, and power and allows a well-defined, rigid social class system to develop. In order to minimize strikes, slowdowns, and industrial sabotage, the elites may share a portion of the economic surplus with the lower classes, but not enough to reduce their own power and privilege.

As Lenski argued, the allocation of surplus goods and services controlled by those with wealth, status, and power reinforces the social inequality that accompanies stratification systems. While this reward system may once have served the overall purposes of society, as functionalists contend, the same cannot be said for the large disparities separating the haves from the have-nots in current societies. In contemporary industrial society, the degree of social and economic inequality far exceeds the need to provide for goods and services (Lenski 1966; Nolan and Lenski 2009).

Stratification by Social Class

MEASURING SOCIAL CLASS

We assess how wealthy people are by looking at the cars they drive, the houses they live in, the clothes they wear, and so on. Yet it is not so easy to locate an individual within our social hierarchies as it would be in slavery, caste, or estate systems of stratification. To determine someone's class position, sociologists generally rely on the objective method.

Objective Method   The *objective method* of measuring social class views class largely as a statistical category. Researchers assign individuals to social classes on the basis of criteria such as occupation, education, income, and place of residence. The key to the objective method is that the *researcher*, rather than the person being classified, identifies an individual's class position.

The first step in using this method is to decide what indicators or causal factors will be measured objectively, whether wealth, income, education, or occupation. The prestige ranking of occupations has proved to be a useful indicator of a person's class position. For one thing, it is much easier to determine accurately than income or wealth. The term *prestige* refers to the respect and admiration that an occupation holds in a society. "My daughter, the physicist" connotes something very different from "my daughter, the waitress." Prestige is independent of the particular individual who occupies a job, a characteristic that distinguishes it from esteem. *Esteem* refers to the reputation that a specific person has earned within an occupation. Therefore, one can say that the position of president of the United States has high prestige, even though it has been occupied by people with varying degrees of esteem. A hairdresser may have the esteem of his clients, but he lacks the prestige of a corporate president.

Table 5–2 shows the prestige rankings of a number of occupations. In a series of national surveys, sociologists assigned prestige rankings to about 500 occupations, ranging from physician to newspaper vendor. The highest possible prestige score was 100; the lowest was 0. Physician, lawyer, dentist, and college professor were the most highly regarded occupations. Sociologists have used such data to assign prestige rankings to virtually all jobs and have found stability in rankings from 1925 to 1991. Similar studies in other countries have also developed useful prestige rankings for occupations.

Table 5-2 Prestige Rankings of Occupations

Occupation	Score	Occupation	Score
Surgeon	87	Farm manager	48
Physician	86	Mail carrier	47
Lawyer	75	Secretary	46
Dentist	74	Insurance agent	45
College professor	74	Bank teller	43
Architect	73	Nurse's aide	42
Psychiatrist	72	Farmer	40
Clergy	69	Correctional officer	40
Pharmacist	68	Receptionist	39
Registered nurse	66	Carpenter	39
High school teacher	66	Barber	36
Accountant	65	Child care worker	35
Optician	65	Hotel clerk	32
Elementary school teacher	64	Bus driver	32
Banker	63	Auto body repairer	31
Veterinarian	62	Truck driver	30
Legislator	61	Salesworker (shoes)	28
Airline pilot	60	Garbage collector	28
Police officer or detective	60	Waiter and waitress	28
Prekindergarten teacher	55	Cook in a pizza shop	27
Librarian	54	Bartender	25
Firefighter	53	Farmworker	23
Social worker	52	Janitor	22
Dental hygienist	52	Newspaper vendor	19
Electrician	51	Prostitute	14
Funeral director	49	Panhandler	11

NOTE: 100 is the highest and 0 the lowest possible prestige score.

SOURCE: J. Davis et al. 2009. See also Nakao and Treas 1994.

Think About It
Can you name what you think are two more high-prestige occupations?
Two more low-prestige occupations?

Multiple Measures   Another complication in measuring social class is that advances in statistical methods and computer technology have multiplied the factors used to define class under the objective method. No longer are sociologists limited to annual income and education in evaluating a person's class position. Today, studies use as criteria the value of homes, sources of income, assets, years in present occupation, neighborhoods, and considerations regarding dual careers. Adding these variables will not necessarily paint a different picture of class differentiation in the United States, but it does allow sociologists to measure class in a more complex and multidimensional way. When researchers use multiple measures, they typically speak of ***socioeconomic status (SES),*** a measure of social class that is based on income, education, and occupation. To determine the socioeconomic status of a young person, such as a college student under the age of 25, they use *parental* income, education, and occupation.

Whatever the technique used to measure class, the sociologist is interested in real and often dramatic differences in power, privilege, and opportunity in a society. The study of stratification is a study of inequality. Nowhere is this more evident than in the distribution of wealth and income.

INCOME AND WEALTH

By all measures, income in the United States is distributed unevenly. Nobel Prize–winning economist Paul Samuelson has described the situation in the following words: "If we made an income pyramid out of building blocks, with each layer portraying $500 of income, the peak would be far higher than Mount Everest, but most people would be within a few feet of the ground" (Samuelson and Nordhaus 2010:324).

Recent data support Samuelson's analogy. In 2008 the median household income in the United States was $50,303. In other words, half of all households had higher incomes that year and half had lower incomes. However, this fact does not fully convey the income disparities in our society. We can get some sense of income inequality by contrasting this median (middle) income with the mean arithmetic average, which in 2008 was $68,424. The mean is so much higher than the median because some people make a lot more money than others, which draws the mean up. Thus, the mean is a less useful statistic than the median for describing the "average," or typical, income (DeNavas-Walt et al. 2009:29).

We can gain additional insight into income inequality in the United States by looking at the relative placement of households within the income distribution. One of the most common ways of doing so is to line up all income-earning households from low to high and then break them into quintiles, or fifths. Because there are approximately 117 million households in the United States, each quintile includes an equal number of about 23.4 million households. This method gives us a sense of the average income within each quintile, along with the percentage of the nation's total income earned in each quintile.

As Figure 5–1 shows, looking at the population in this way reveals a significant degree of income inequality. The mean income for households in the lowest quintile is $11,656; in the top quintile, it is $171,057. Those households in the top 5 percent—the ones most responsible for bringing up the arithmetic mean—average a staggering $294,709 in annual income. If we were to move up even higher in the income distribution, we would find that the top 0.01 percent of taxpayers—about 15,000 households—make incomes of at least $11.5 million a year. Collectively, they control 6 percent of the nation's total income (Sloan 2009:27).

There has been a modest redistribution of income in the United States over the past 80 years, but not always to the benefit of the poor or even the middle class. From 1929 through 1970, the government's economic and tax policies shifted some income to the poor. However, in the past four decades—especially in the 1980s and in the decade from 2001 through 2010—federal tax policies have favored the affluent. Moreover, while the salaries of highly skilled workers and professionals have continued to rise, the wages of less skilled workers have *decreased* when controlled for inflation.

Just how dramatic has this growth in inequality been? Consider the period between 1984 and 2008. In just 25 years, the following changes occurred in real household income (adjusted for inflation):

- For the lowest 20 percent of the population, income rose 9 percent.

- For the next lowest 20 percent of the population, income rose 10 percent.

- For the middle 20 percent of the population, income rose 13 percent.

- For the next highest 20 percent of the population, income rose 20 percent.

- For the top 20 percent of the population, income rose a whopping 40 percent.

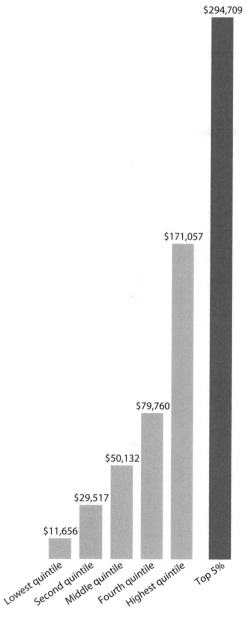

Figure 5–1
Mean Household Income by Quintile
SOURCE: Data for 2008 in DeNavas-Walt et al.2009:38; Bureau of the Census 2009e: Table H-3.

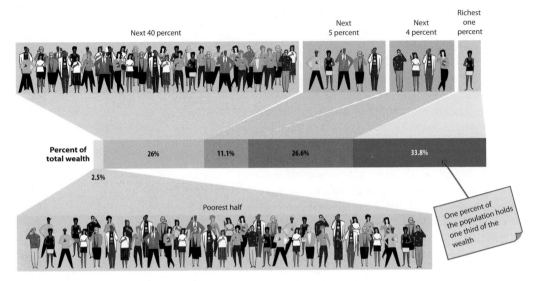

Figure 5–2
Distribution of Wealth in the United States
SOURCE: Data for 2007, as reported in a 2009 Federal Reserve Bank study. See Kennickell 2009:35.

The pattern is clear. Though everyone has done better, by far the biggest winners have been the affluent.

Has the recent economic slowdown reduced income inequality? Not really. A comparison of household incomes in 1999 (the peak before the 2001 recession) with the most recent income data shows that lower-income households' earnings have declined, while the higher-income households' earnings have held steady. By one measure, inequality between the top 10th and the bottom 10th of the income distribution has increased 9 percent (DeNavas-Walt et al. 2009:38–39).

Wealth is distributed much more unevenly than income in the United States. A 2009 Federal Reserve Bank study showed that half the population controls 2.5 percent of the nation's wealth; the other half controls over 97 percent (see Figure 5–2). Put another way, the wealth of the top 1 percent exceeds the collective wealth of the bottom 90 percent. Researchers have also found a dramatic disparity in wealth between African Americans and Whites. This disparity is evident even when educational backgrounds are held constant: the households of college-educated Whites have about three times as much wealth as the households of college-educated Blacks (Conley 2010; Kennickell 2009; Oliver and Shapiro 2006, 2008).

POVERTY

Approximately one out of every nine people in the United States lives below the poverty line established by the federal government. In 2007, no fewer than 37.2 million people were living in poverty. The economic boom of the 1990s passed these people by. A Bureau of the Census report shows that one in five households has trouble meeting basic needs, from paying the utility bills to buying dinner (Bauman 1999; DeNavas-Walt et al. 2009).

One contributor to the United States' high poverty rate has been the large number of workers employed at minimum wage. The federal government has raised the minimum wage over the past half century from 75 cents in 1950 to $6.55 in 2008 and $7.25 in 2009. But in terms of its real value adjusted for inflation, the minimum wage has frequently failed to keep pace with the cost of living.

Studying Poverty The efforts of sociologists and other social scientists to better understand poverty are complicated by the difficulty of defining it. This problem is evident even in government programs that conceive of poverty in either absolute or relative terms. *Absolute poverty* refers to a minimum level of subsistence that no family should be expected to live below. Policies concerning minimum wages, housing standards, or school lunch programs for the poor imply a need to bring citizens up to some predetermined level of existence.

One commonly used measure of absolute poverty is the federal government's *poverty line,* a money income figure that is adjusted annually to reflect the consumption requirements of families based on their size and composition. The poverty line serves as an official definition of which people are poor. In 2008, for example, any family of four (two adults and two children) with a combined income of $21,834 or less fell below the poverty line. This definition determines which individuals and families will be eligible for certain government benefits (DeNavas-Walt et al. 2009:43).

Although by absolute standards, poverty has declined in the United States, it remains higher than in many other industrial nations. A comparatively large proportion of U.S. households are poor, meaning that members are unable to purchase basic consumer goods. If anything, this cross-national comparison understates the extent of poverty in the United States, since U.S. residents are likely to pay more for housing, health care, child care, and education than do residents of other countries, where such expenses are often subsidized.

By contrast, *relative poverty* is a floating standard of deprivation by which people at the bottom of a society, whatever their lifestyles, are judged to be disadvantaged *in comparison with the nation as a whole.* Therefore, even if the poor of the 1990s are better off in absolute terms than the poor of the 1930s or 1960s, they are still seen as deserving special assistance.

Debate has been growing over the accuracy of the federal government's measure of poverty, which has remained largely unchanged since 1963. If noncash benefits such as Medicare, Medicaid, tax credits, food stamps, public housing, and health care and other employer-provided fringe benefits were included, the reported poverty rate would be lower. On the other hand, if out-of-pocket medical expenses and mandatory work expenses for transportation and child care were included, the poverty rate would be higher. Although the current poverty measure does consider family size, it does not consider a household's location, whether in a relatively expensive city like New York or in a less expensive rural area. Nor does it consider whether a householder pays rent or a mortgage installment, lives at home or with someone else.

To address some of these shortcomings, in 2010 the federal government launched a second statistic called the Supplemental Poverty Measure (SPM), which will be used to estimate economic hardship. The SPM is a relative poverty measure that is based on a broad range of changing household resources and expenses. It will be calculated beginning in late 2011, but will not replace the poverty line in determining a household's eligibility for benefits (Blank 2008; Department of Commerce 2010).

Who Are the Poor?   Not only does the category of the poor defy any simple definition, but it counters common stereotypes about poor people. For example, many people in the United States believe that the vast majority of the poor are able to work but will not. Yet many poor adults do work outside the home, although only a small proportion work full-time throughout the year. In 2008, about 27 percent of all poor working adults worked full-time, compared to 66 percent of all adults. Of those poor adults who do not work, most are ill or disabled, or are occupied in maintaining a home (DeNavas-Walt et al. 2009:14).

A sizable number of the poor live in urban slums, but a majority live outside those areas. Poverty is no stranger to rural areas, from Appalachia to hard-hit farming regions and Native American reservations. Table 5–3 provides additional statistical information regarding these low-income people.

Since World War II, women have constituted an increasing proportion of the poor people of the United States. Many of them are divorced or never-married mothers. In 1959 female householders accounted for 26 percent of the nation's poor; by 2008 that figure had risen to 51 percent (see Table 5–3). This alarming trend, known as the *feminization of poverty,* is evident not just in the United States but around the world.

About half of all women in the United States who are living in poverty are "in transition," coping with an economic crisis caused by the departure, disability, or death of a husband. The other half tend to be economically dependent either on the welfare system or on friends and relatives living nearby. A major factor in the feminization of poverty has been the increase in families with women as single heads of the household. Conflict theorists and other observers trace the higher rates of poverty among women to three distinct factors: the difficulty in finding affordable child care, sexual harassment, and sex discrimination in the labor market (see Chapter 7).

Analyses of the poor in general reveal that they are not a static social class. The overall composition of the poor changes continually, because

Table 5–3 Who Are the Poor in the United States?

Group	Percentage of the Population of the United States	Percentage of the Poor of the United States
Age		
Under 18 years old	25%	35%
18 to 64 years old	62	56
65 years and older	13	9
Race-Ethnicity		
Whites (non-Hispanic)	65	43
Blacks	13	24
Hispanics	16	28
Asians and Pacific Islanders	4	4
Family Composition		
Married couples with male householders	75	40
Female householders	18	51

SOURCE: Data for 2008, as reported by the Bureau of the Census; DeNavas-Walt et al. 2009:14.

some individuals and families near the top edge of poverty move above the poverty level after a year or two, while others slip below it. Still, hundreds of thousands of people remain in poverty for many years at a time. Blacks and Latinos are more likely than Whites to be persistently poor. Both Latinos and Blacks are less likely than Whites to leave the welfare rolls as a result of welfare reform (Jäntii 2009).

Explaining Poverty   Why does poverty pervade a nation of such vast wealth? Sociologist Herbert Gans (1995) has applied functionalist analysis to this question; he argues that various segments of society actually *benefit* from the existence of the poor. Gans has identified a number of social, economic, and political functions that the poor perform for society:

- The presence of poor people means that society's dirty work—physically dirty or dangerous, underpaid and undignified, dead-end and menial jobs—will be performed at low cost.
- Poverty creates jobs for occupations and professions that "service" the poor. It creates both legal employment (public health experts, welfare caseworkers) and illegal jobs (drug dealers, numbers runners).
- The identification and punishment of the poor as deviants uphold the legitimacy of conventional social norms and mainstream values regarding hard work, thrift, and honesty.

- Within a relatively hierarchical society, the existence of poor people guarantees the higher status of the affluent. As psychologist William Ryan (1976) has noted, affluent people may justify inequality (and gain a measure of satisfaction) by "blaming the victims" of poverty for their disadvantaged condition.

- Because of their lack of political power, the poor often absorb the costs of social change. Under the policy of deinstitutionalization, mental patients released from long-term hospitals have been "dumped" primarily into low-income communities and neighborhoods. Similarly, halfway houses for rehabilitated drug abusers, often rejected by more affluent communities, tend to end up in poorer neighborhoods.

In Gans's view, then, poverty and the poor actually perform positive functions for many nonpoor groups in the United States.

LIFE CHANCES

Max Weber thought that class was closely related to one's *life chances*—that is, the opportunities people have to provide themselves with material goods, positive living conditions, and favorable life experiences (Gerth and Mills 1958). Life chances are reflected in such measures as housing, education, and health. Occupying a higher position in society improves a person's life chances and brings greater access to social rewards. Occupying a lower position forces a person to devote more energy and resources to the necessities of life.

Class position also affects people's vulnerability to natural disasters. When Hurricane Katrina hit the Gulf Coast of the United States in 2005, affluent and poor people alike became its victims. However, poor people who did not own automobiles (100,000 of them in New Orleans alone) were less able than others to evacuate in advance of the storm. Those who survived its fury had no nest egg to draw on and thus were more likely than others to accept relocation wherever social service agencies could place them—sometimes hundreds or thousands of miles from home (Department of Homeland Security 2006).

Some people have hoped that the Internet revolution would help to level the playing field by making information and markets uniformly available. Unfortunately, however, not everyone can get onto the information superhighway, so yet another aspect of social inequality has emerged—the *digital divide.* The poor, minorities, and those who live in rural communities and inner cities are not getting connected at home or at work. A recent government study found that despite falling computer prices, the Internet gap between the haves and have-nots has not narrowed.

For example, although 70 percent of all people in the United States used the Internet in 2007, that group included 93 percent of people with incomes over $75,000 but fewer than 49 percent of people with incomes less than $30,000. As wealthier people switch to high-speed Internet connections, they will be able to take advantage of even more sophisticated interactive services, and the digital divide will grow even wider (Pew Internet Project 2008).

Wealth, status, and power may not ensure happiness, but they certainly provide additional ways of coping with problems and disappointments. For this reason, the opportunity for advancement—for social mobility—is of special significance to those on the bottom of society. These people want the rewards and privileges that are granted to high-ranking members of a culture. What can society do to increase their social mobility? One strategy is to offer financial aid to college students from low-income families, on the theory that education lifts people out of poverty. Yet such programs are not having as great an effect as their authors once hoped, because many of today's graduates will be paying off their college loans for years to come.

Imagine a society in which there are no social classes—no differences in people's wealth, income, and life chances. What would such a society be like? Would it be stable, or would its social structure change over time?

Social Mobility

In the movie *Maid in Manhattan,* Jennifer Lopez plays the lead in a modern-day Cinderella story, rising from the lowly status of chambermaid in a big-city hotel to become a company supervisor and the girlfriend of a well-to-do politician. The ascent of a person from a poor background to a position of prestige, power, or financial reward is an example of social mobility. Formally defined, the term *social mobility* refers to the movement of individuals or groups from one position in a society's stratification system to another. But how significant—how frequent, how dramatic—is mobility in a class society such as the United States?

OPEN VERSUS CLOSED STRATIFICATION SYSTEMS

Sociologists use the terms *open stratification system* and *closed stratification system* to indicate the degree of social mobility in a society. An *open system* implies that the position of each individual is influenced by his or her *achieved* status. Such a system encourages competition among members of society. The United States is moving toward this ideal type as the nation attempts to reduce the barriers facing women, racial and ethnic minorities, and people born in the lower social classes.

At the other extreme of social mobility is the *closed system,* which allows little or no possibility of moving up. The slavery, caste, and estate systems of stratification are examples of closed systems. In such societies, social placement is based on *ascribed* statuses that cannot be changed, such as race or family background.

TYPES OF SOCIAL MOBILITY

An airline pilot who becomes a police officer moves from one social position to another of the same rank. Each occupation has the same prestige ranking: 60 on a scale ranging from a low of 0 to a high of 100 (see Table 5–2 on page 141). Sociologists call this kind of movement *horizontal mobility*. However, if the pilot were to become a lawyer (prestige ranking of 75), he or she would experience *vertical mobility,* the movement of a person from one social position to another of a different rank. Vertical mobility can also involve moving *downward* in a society's stratification system, as would be the case if the airline pilot became a bank teller (prestige ranking of 43). Pitirim Sorokin ([1927] 1959) was the first sociologist to distinguish between horizontal and vertical mobility.

Most sociological analysis focuses on vertical social mobility. One way of examining vertical mobility is to contrast intergenerational and intragenerational mobility. *Intergenerational mobility* involves changes in the social position of children relative to their parents. Thus, a plumber whose father was a physician provides an example of downward intergenerational mobility. A film star whose parents were both factory workers illustrates upward intergenerational mobility. Because education contributes significantly to upward mobility, any barrier to the pursuit of advanced degrees can definitely limit intergenerational mobility (Isaacs 2007a; Sawhill and Morton 2007).

Intragenerational mobility involves changes in a person's social position within his or her adult life. A woman who enters the paid labor force as a teacher's aide and eventually becomes superintendent of the school district experiences upward intragenerational mobility. A man who becomes a taxicab driver after his accounting firm goes bankrupt undergoes downward intragenerational mobility.

SOCIAL MOBILITY IN THE UNITED STATES

The belief in upward mobility is an important value in our society. Does that mean the United States is indeed the land of opportunity? Not unless such ascriptive characteristics as race, gender, and family background have ceased to be significant in determining one's future prospects. We can see the impact of these factors in the occupational structure.

Occupational Mobility   Two sociological studies conducted a decade apart offer insight into the degree of social mobility in the nation's occupational structure (Blau and Duncan 1967; Featherman and Hauser 1978). Taken together, these investigations lead to several noteworthy conclusions. First, occupational mobility (both intergenerational and intragenerational) has been common among males. Approximately 60 to 70 percent of sons are employed in higher-ranked occupations than their fathers.

Second, although there is a great deal of social mobility in the United States, much of it covers a very short distance. That is, people who reach an occupational level different from that of their parents usually advance or fall back only one or two out of a possible eight occupational levels. Thus, the child of a laborer may become an artisan or a technician, but he or she is less likely to become a manager or professional. The odds against reaching the top are extremely high unless one begins from a relatively privileged position.

The Impact of Education   Another conclusion of both studies is that education plays a critical role in social mobility. The impact of formal schooling on adult status is even greater than that of family background (although as we have seen, family background influences the likelihood that one will receive higher education). Furthermore, education represents an important means of intergenerational mobility. A person who was born into a poor family but who graduates from college has a 1 in 5 chance of entering the top fifth of all income earners as an adult (Isaacs et al. 2008).

Education's impact on social mobility has diminished somewhat in the last decade, however. An undergraduate degree—a B.A. or a B.S.— serves less as a guarantee of upward mobility today than it did in the past simply because more and more entrants into the job market now hold such a degree. Moreover, intergenerational mobility is declining, since there is no longer such a stark difference between generations. In earlier decades many high school–educated parents successfully sent their children to college, but today's college students are increasingly likely to have college-educated parents (Sawhill and Morton 2007).

The Impact of Race and Ethnicity   Sociologists have long documented the fact that the class system is more rigid for African Americans than it is for members of other racial groups. Black men who have good jobs, for example, are less likely than White men to see their adult children attain the same status. The cumulative disadvantage of discrimination plays a significant role in the disparity between the two groups' experience. Compared to White households, the relatively modest wealth of African American households means that adult Black children are less likely than adult White children to receive financial support from their parents. Indeed, young Black couples are much more likely than young White couples to be assisting their parents—a sacrifice that hampers their social mobility (Favreault 2008).

The African American middle class has grown over the last few decades, due to economic expansion and the benefits of the civil rights movement of the 1960s. Yet many of these middle-class households have little savings, a fact that puts them in danger during times of crisis. Studies stretching back several decades show that downward mobility is significantly higher for Blacks than it is for Whites (Oliver and Shapiro 2006, 2008; Sernau 2001; W. J. Wilson 1996).

The Latino population is not doing much better. The typical Hispanic has less than 10 percent of the wealth that a White person enjoys. A 2004 study suggests that in recent years, Latinos have even lost ground. Their continuing immigration accounts for part of the disparity: most of the new arrivals are destitute. But even the wealthiest 5 percent of Latino households have only a third as much net worth as the top 5 percent of White households (Kochhar 2008).

The Impact of Gender   Studies of mobility, even more than those of class, have traditionally ignored the significance of gender, but some research findings are now available that explore the relationship between gender and mobility.

Women's employment opportunities are much more limited than men's (as Chapter 7 will show). Moreover, according to recent research, women whose skills far exceed the jobs offered them are more likely than men to withdraw entirely from the paid labor force. Their withdrawal violates an assumption common to traditional mobility studies: that most people will aspire to upward mobility and seek to make the most of their opportunities.

In contrast to men, women have a rather large range of clerical occupations open to them. But modest salary ranges and small prospects for advancement limit their chance of upward mobility. Moreover, self-employment as shopkeepers, entrepreneurs, independent professionals, and the like—an important road to upward mobility for men—is more difficult for women, who find it harder to secure the necessary financing. Although sons commonly follow in the footsteps of their fathers, women are unlikely to move into their fathers' positions. Consequently, gender remains an important factor in shaping social mobility within the United States. Women in the United States (and in other parts of the world) are

Use Your Sociological Imagination

Which factor— occupation, education, race and ethnicity, or gender—do you expect will have the greatest impact on your own social mobility? Explain.

especially likely to be trapped in poverty, unable to rise out of their low-income status (Beller 2009; Heilman 2001).

On the positive side, though today's women lag behind men in employment, their earnings have increased faster than their mothers' did at a comparable age, so that their incomes are substantially higher. The one glaring exception to this trend is the daughters of low-income parents. Because these women typically care for children—many as single parents—and sometimes for other relatives as well, their mobility is severely restricted (Isaacs 2007b).

The Global Divide

In some parts of the world, the people who have dedicated their lives to fighting starvation refer to what they call "coping mechanisms"—ways in which the desperately poor attempt to control their hunger. Eritrean women will strap flat stones to their stomachs to lessen their hunger pangs. In Mozambique, people eat the grasshoppers that have destroyed their crops, calling them "flying shrimp." Though dirt eating is considered a pathological condition (called *pica*) among the well fed, the world's poor eat dirt to add minerals to their diet. And in many countries, mothers have been known to boil stones in water, to convince their hungry children that supper is almost ready. As they hover over the pot, these women hope that their malnourished children will fall asleep (McNeil 2004).

Around the world, inequality is a significant determinant of human behavior, opening doors of opportunity to some and closing them to others. Indeed, disparities in life chances are so extreme that in some places, the poorest of the poor may not be aware of them. Western media images may have circled the globe, but in extremely depressed rural areas, those at the bottom of society are not likely to see them.

A few centuries ago, such vast divides in global wealth did not exist. Except for a very few rulers and landowners, everyone in the world was poor. In much of Europe, life was as difficult as it was in Asia or South America. This was true until the Industrial Revolution and rising agricultural productivity produced explosive economic growth. The resulting rise in living standards was not evenly distributed across the world.

The divide between industrial and developing nations is sharp, but sociologists recognize a continuum of nations, from the richest of the rich to the poorest of the poor. For example, in 2009, the average value of goods and services produced per citizen (or per capita gross national income) in the industrialized countries of the United States, Japan, Switzerland, Belgium, and Norway was more than $34,000. In at least 12 poorer countries, the value was just $900 or less. Most countries fell somewhere between those extremes (Haub and Kent 2009).

Still, the contrasts are stark. Three forces discussed here are particularly responsible for the domination of the world marketplace by a few nations: the legacy of colonialism, the advent of multinational corporations, and modernization.

LEGACY OF COLONIALISM

Colonialism occurs when a foreign power maintains political, social, economic, and cultural domination over a people for an extended period. In simple terms, it is rule by outsiders. The long reign of the British Empire over much of North America, parts of Africa, and India is an example of colonial domination. The same can be said of French rule over Algeria, Tunisia, and other parts of North Africa. Relations between the colonial nation and colonized people are similar to those between the dominant capitalist class and the proletariat, as described by Karl Marx.

By the 1980s, colonialism had largely disappeared. Most of the nations that were colonies before World War I had achieved political independence and established their own governments. However, for many of these countries, the transition to genuine self-rule was not yet complete. Colonial domination had established patterns of economic exploitation that continued even after the colonies achieved their nationhood—in part because they were unable to develop their own industry and technology. Their dependence on more industrialized nations, including their former colonial masters, for managerial and technical expertise, investment capital, and manufactured goods kept former colonies in a subservient position. Such continuing dependence and foreign domination constitute ***neocolonialism.*** Today neocolonialism can be seen in the factories and assembly plants that serve more industrialized nations, including Mexico's *maquiladoras* and China's electronics plants.

The economic and political consequences of colonialism and neocolonialism are readily apparent. Drawing on the conflict perspective, sociologist Immanuel Wallerstein (1974, 1979a, 2004) views the global economic system as one divided between nations that control wealth and nations from which resources are taken. Neocolonialism, he believes, allows industrialized societies to accumulate even more capital.

Wallerstein has advanced a ***world-systems analysis*** to describe the unequal economic and political relationships in which certain industrialized nations (among them the United States, Japan, and Germany) and their global corporations dominate the *core* of the world's economic system (see Figure 5–3). At the *semiperiphery* of the system are countries with marginal economic status, such as Israel, Ireland, and South Korea. Wallerstein suggests that the poor developing countries of Asia, Africa, and Latin America are on the *periphery* of the world's economic system. Core nations and their corporations control and exploit these nations' economies, much as the old colonial empires ruled their colonies (Chase-Dunn and Grimes 1995).

Use Your Sociological Imagination

You are traveling through a developing country. What evidence do you see of neocolonialism?

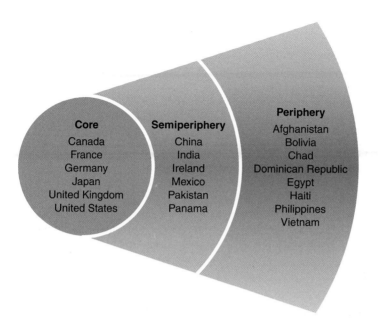

Figure 5–3
World-Systems Analysis at the Beginning of the 21st Century

NOTE: *Figure shows only a partial listing of countries selected by author.*

The division between core and periphery nations is significant and remarkably stable. A study by the International Monetary Fund (2000) found little change over the course of the *last 100 years* for the 42 economies studied. The only changes were Japan's movement up into the group of core nations and China's movement down toward the margins of the semiperiphery nations. Yet Wallerstein (2000) speculates that the world system as we currently understand it may soon undergo unpredictable changes. The world is becoming increasingly urbanized, a trend that is gradually eliminating the large pools of low-cost workers in rural areas. In the future, core nations will have to find other ways to reduce their labor costs. The exhaustion of land and water resources through clear-cutting and other forms of pollution is also driving up the costs of production worldwide.

Wallerstein's world-systems analysis is the most widely used version of *dependency theory.* According to this theory, even as developing countries make economic advances, they remain weak and subservient to core nations and corporations in an increasingly intertwined global economy. Their weakness allows industrialized nations to continue to exploit them. In a sense, dependency theory applies the conflict perspective on a global scale.

According to world-systems analysis and dependency theory, a growing share of the human and natural resources of developing countries is being redistributed to the core industrialized nations. In part, this redistribution occurs because developing countries owe huge sums of money to industrialized nations as a result of foreign aid, loans, and

When you see a developing country on television or in the movies, does the film or program emphasize the country's progress or its problems?

trade deficits. Thus, the global debt crisis has intensified the Third World dependency begun under colonialism, neocolonialism, and multinational investment (see page 157). International financial institutions are now pressuring indebted countries to take severe measures to meet their interest payments. The result is that developing nations may be forced to devalue their currencies, freeze workers' wages, increase the privatization of industry, and reduce government services and employment.

GLOBALIZATION

Closely related to these problems is *globalization,* or the worldwide integration of government policies, cultures, social movements, and financial markets through trade and the exchange of ideas. While public discussion of globalization is relatively recent, intellectuals have been pondering its social consequences for a long time. Karl Marx and Friedrich Engels warned in the *Communist Manifesto* (written in 1848) of a world market that would lead to production in distant lands, sweeping away existing working relationships.

Today, developments outside a country are as likely to influence people's lives as changes at home. For example, though much of the world was already in recession by September 2001, within weeks the economic repercussions of the terrorist attacks on New York and Washington, D.C., had begun to affect African game wardens and Asian taxi drivers. The impact of globalization appears to be most problematic in developing countries in Latin America and Africa. In Asia developing nations seem to do better, because foreign investment there involves the high-tech sector, which produces more sustainable economic growth.

Some observers see globalization and its effects as the natural result of advances in communications technology, particularly the Internet and satellite transmission of the mass media. Others view it more critically, as a process that allows multinational corporations to expand unchecked. We will examine this issue more fully in the next section (Chase-Dunn et al. 2000; Kerbo 2006).

MULTINATIONAL CORPORATIONS

Worldwide corporate giants play a key role in neocolonialism. The term *multinational corporations* refers to commercial organizations that are headquartered in one country but do business throughout the world. Such private trade and lending relationships are not new; merchants have conducted business abroad for hundreds of years, trading gems, spices, garments, and other goods. However, today's multinational giants are not merely buying and selling overseas; they are also *producing* goods all over the world, from sneakers to sewing machines (Wallerstein 1974).

Moreover, today's "global factories" (factories throughout the developing world that are run by multinational corporations) now sit alongside the "global office." Multinationals based in core countries are beginning to establish reservations services, claims adjustment offices, and data processing centers in periphery nations. As service industries become more important in the international marketplace, many companies are concluding that the low costs of overseas operations more than offset the expense of transmitting information around the world.

Do not underestimate the size of these global corporations. As Figure 5–4 shows, the total revenues of many multinational businesses are equivalent to the total value of goods and services exchanged in *entire nations.* Foreign sales represent an important source of profit for multinational corporations, a fact that encourages them to expand into other countries (in many cases, the developing nations). The economy of the United States is heavily dependent on foreign commerce, much of which is conducted by multinationals. Over 10 percent of all goods and services produced in the United States relates to the export of goods to foreign countries, which accounts for 20 percent of the nation's annual growth (U.S. Trade Representative 2007).

Sociologists differ in their appraisal of the economic and social effects of these behemoth organizations. We'll examine two perspectives on multinational corporations, the functionalist view and the conflict view.

Functionalist View   Functionalists believe that multinational corporations can actually help the developing nations of the world. They bring jobs and industry to areas where subsistence agriculture previously served as the only means of survival. Multinationals promote rapid development through the diffusion of inventions and innovations from industrial nations. Viewed from a functionalist perspective, the combination of skilled technology and management provided by multinationals and the relatively cheap labor available in developing nations is ideal for a global enterprise. Multinationals can take maximum advantage of technology while reducing costs and boosting profits.

The international ties of multinational corporations also facilitate the global exchange of ideas and technology, making the nations of the world more interdependent. These ties may prevent certain disputes from reaching the point of serious conflict. A country cannot afford to sever diplomatic relations, or engage in warfare, with a nation that is the head-quarters for its main business suppliers or a key outlet for its exports.

Conflict View   Conflict theorists challenge this favorable evaluation of the impact of multinational corporations. They emphasize that multi-nationals exploit local workers to maximize profits. Starbucks—the international coffee retailer based in Seattle—gets some of its coffee from farms in Guatemala. But to earn enough money to buy a pound of Starbucks coffee, a Guatemalan farmworker would have to pick 500 pounds of beans, an amount that represents five days of work (Entine and Nichols 1996).

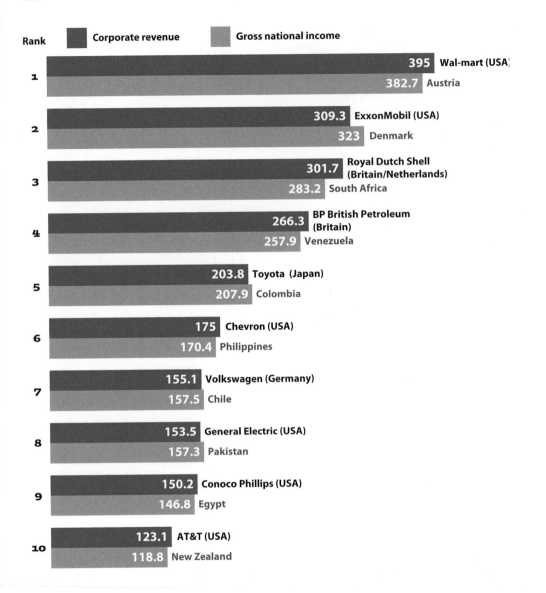

Figure 5–4
*Multinational
Corporations Compared
to Nations*
Sources: Ranking prepared
by author. Revenue from
corporate quarterly
report statements (Q2
2009 through Q1 2010).
GNI from World Bank
2010a:32–34.

Think About It
What happens to society when corporations grow richer than countries
and spill across international borders?

The pool of cheap labor in the developing world prompts multinationals to move their factories out of core countries. An added bonus
for the multinationals is the fact that the developing world discourages
strong trade unions. In industrialized countries, organized labor insists
on decent wages and humane working conditions, but governments

seeking to attract or keep multinationals may develop a "climate for investment" that includes repressive antilabor laws—laws that restrict union activity and collective bargaining. These governments know that if labor's demands become too threatening, the multinational firm will simply move its plant elsewhere. Nike, for example, moved its factories from the United States to Korea to Indonesia to Vietnam in search of the lowest labor costs. Conflict theorists conclude that on the whole, multinational corporations have a negative social impact on workers in both industrialized and developing nations.

Several sociologists who have surveyed the effects of foreign investment conclude that although it may initially contribute to a host nation's wealth, it eventually increases economic inequality within developing nations. In both income and ownership of land, the upper and middle classes benefit most from economic expansion; the lower classes are less likely to benefit. Multinationals invest in limited industries and restricted regions. Although certain sectors of the host nation's economy, such as hotels and expensive restaurants, expand, their very expansion appears to retard growth in agriculture and other economic sectors. Moreover, multinational corporations often buy out or force out local entrepreneurs and companies, increasing a nation's economic and cultural dependence (Chase-Dunn and Grimes 1995; Kerbo 2009; Wallerstein 1979b).

MODERNIZATION

Around the world, millions of people are witnessing a revolutionary transformation of their day-to-day life. Contemporary social scientists use the term **modernization** to describe the far-reaching process through which developing nations move from traditional or less developed institutions to those characteristic of more developed societies.

Wendell Bell (1981), whose definition of modernization we are using, notes that modern societies tend to be urban, literate, and industrial. They have sophisticated transportation and media systems. Their families tend to be organized on the nuclear-family rather than the extended-family model. Members of societies that have undergone modernization shift their allegiance from traditional sources of authority, such as parents and priests, to newer authorities, such as government officials.

Many sociologists are quick to note that terms such as *modernization* and even *development* contain an ethnocentric bias. The unstated assumption behind these terms is that "they" (people living in developing countries) are struggling to become more like "us" (in the core industrialized nations). Viewed from a conflict perspective, these terms perpetuate the dominant ideology of capitalist societies.

The term *modernization* also suggests positive change. Yet change, if it comes, often comes slowly, and when it does it tends to serve the affluent segments of industrial nations. This truism seems to apply to the spread of the latest electronic technologies to the developing world.

A similar criticism has been made of *modernization theory,* the functionalist view that modernization and development will gradually improve the lives of people in developing nations. According to this theory, though countries develop at uneven rates, the development of peripheral countries is assisted by innovations transferred from the industrialized world. Critics of modernization theory, including dependency theorists, counter that any such technology transfer only increases the dominance of core nations over developing countries and facilitates further exploitation. Table 5–4 summarizes the sociological perspectives on global inequality.

When we see all the Coca-Cola and Dunkin' Donuts signs going up in developing countries, it is easy to assume that globalization and economic change are effecting cultural change. But that is not always the case, researchers note. Distinctive cultural traditions, such as a particular religious orientation or a nationalistic identity, often persist in developing nations and can soften the impact of modernization. Some contemporary sociologists emphasize that both industrialized and developing countries are "modern." Increasingly, researchers are viewing modernization as movement along a series of social indicators—among them degree of urbanization, energy use, literacy, political democracy, and use of birth control. Clearly, these are subjective indicators; even in industrialized nations, not everyone would agree that wider use of birth control represents "progress" (Armer and Katsillis 1992; Hedley 1992; Inglehart and Baker 2000).

Current modernization studies generally take a convergence perspective. Using the indicators just noted, researchers focus on how societies are moving closer together, despite their traditional differences. From a conflict perspective, however, the modernization of developing countries often perpetuates their dependence on—and continued exploitation by—more industrialized nations. Conflict theorists view such continuing dependence on foreign powers as a form of contemporary neocolonialism.

Table 5–4 Sociological Perspectives on Global Inequality

Approach	Sociological Perspective	Explanation
World systems analysis	Functionalist and conflict	Unequal economic and political relationships maintain sharp divisions between nations
Dependency theory	Conflict	Industrial nations exploit developing countries through colonialism and multinational corporations
Modernization theory	Functionalist	Developing countries are moving away from traditional cultures and toward the cultures of industrialized nations

summing**UP**

Sociology Matters

Sociology matters because it defines your social class, an important part of your place in the social system.

- Do wide differences in family wealth and income separate students on your campus? What about the people in your hometown? How do sociologists explain these differences?

- What is your family's social class, and what measures of social class do you base your answer on? How does your family's social class affect your life chances?

- Where do you fit in the global stratification system? How many of the products you use were made by workers in developing nations? Would your social standing be different if you couldn't afford to buy those products?

CHAPTER RESOURCES

Summary

Stratification is the structured ranking of entire groups of people in a society, so as to perpetuate **social inequality.** Worldwide, stratification can be seen in the unequal distribution of **income** and **wealth** within countries, as well as in the gap between rich and poor nations. This chapter examined four systems of stratification, including the **class system** that prevails in the United States. It considered two theoretical explanations for the existence of social inequality, as well as the relationship between stratification and **social mobility.** It closed with a discussion of stratification in developing countries.

1. All cultures manifest some degree of **social inequality** through stratification systems such as **slavery, castes, estates,** and **classes.**

2. Karl Marx wrote that **capitalism** created two distinct social classes, the **bourgeoisie** (owners of the means of production) and the **proletariat** (workers).

3. Max Weber identified three analytically distinct components of **stratification: class, status group,** and **power.**

4. Functionalists assert that stratification benefits society by motivating people to fill demanding positions. Conflict theorists, however, see stratification as a major source of societal tension. Interactionists stress the way in which stratification shapes an individual's lifestyle.

5. Sociologists distinguish between **absolute poverty,** which is defined as a minimum level of subsistence, and **relative poverty,** a floating standard of deprivation that is based on comparison with society as a whole.

6. One's **life chances**—opportunities to obtain material goods, positive living conditions, and favorable life experiences—are related to one's social class. The higher a person's social class, the better one's life chances.

7. **Social mobility** is more likely to be found in an **open system** that emphasizes a person's **achieved status** than in a **closed system** that focuses on a person's **ascribed status.**

8. In 2006 the per capita gross national income of several developing countries was $900 or less. Many such countries, former colonies of developed nations, are still subject to foreign domination through the process of **neocolonialism.**

9. According to sociologist Immanuel Wallerstein, the global economic system is divided between industrialized nations that control the world's wealth, called *core nations,* and the developing nations they exploit, called *periphery nations.* Wallerstein's teaching, a version of **dependency theory,** is referred to as **world-systems analysis.**

www.mhhe.com/schaefersm5e
Visit the Online Learning Center for *Sociology Matters* to access quizzes, review activities, and other learning tools.

10. Critics blame the process of **globalization**—the worldwide integration of government policies, cultures, social movements, and financial markets through trade and the exchange of ideas—for contributing to the cultural domination of periphery nations by core nations. They also charge that **multinational corporations** exploit workers in developing countries in order to maximize their profits.

Key Terms

absolute poverty, 145

achieved status, 130

ascribed status, 130

bourgeoisie, 133

capitalism, 133

caste, 131

class, 135

class consciousness, 134

class system, 131

closed system, 150

colonialism, 154

dependency theory, 155

estate system, 131

esteem, 140

false consciousness, 134

feminization of poverty, 146

globalization, 156

horizontal mobility, 150

income, 130

intergenerational mobility, 150

intragenerational mobility, 150

life chances, 148

modernization, 159

modernization theory, 160

multinational corporation, 156

neocolonialism, 154

objective method, 140

open system, 150

power, 135

prestige, 140

proletariat, 133

relative poverty, 145

slavery, 130

social inequality, 130

social mobility, 149

socioeconomic status (SES), 142

status group, 135

stratification, 130

vertical mobility, 150

wealth, 130

world-systems analysis, 154

Inequality by Race and Ethnicity

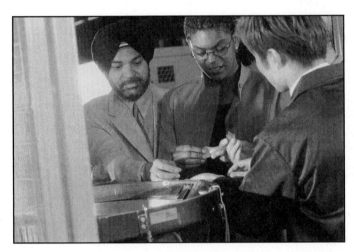

The Privileges of the Dominant

The Social Construction of Race and Ethnicity

Immigration and New Ethnic Groups

Sociological Perspectives on Race and Ethnicity

Patterns of Prejudice and Discrimination

In 1900, in an address to the Anti-Slavery Union in London, scholar William E. B. DuBois predicted that "the color line" would become the foremost problem of the 20th century. DuBois, born a free Black man in 1868, had witnessed prejudice and discrimination throughout the United States. His comment was prophetic. Today, over a century later, race and ethnicity still carry enormous weight in the United States (DuBois [1900] 1969).

The color line has blurred significantly since 1900, however. Interracial marriage is no longer forbidden by law and custom. Thus, Geetha Lakshmi-narayanan, a native of Ann Arbor, Michigan, is both White and Asian Indian. Often mistaken for a Filipina or Latina, she has grown accustomed to the blunt question "What are you?" (Navarro 2005). Public figures, rather than hide their mixed ancestry, now flaunt it. Singer Mariah Carey celebrates her Irish American background, and Barack Obama speaks of being born in Hawaii to a Kenyan father and a White mother from Kansas.

Today, the color line is drawn more clearly between the native born and recent immigrants. In July 2010, hundreds of students who are illegal aliens held a mock graduation ceremony near the U.S. Capital.

Wearing caps and gowns, they were lobbying for passage of the proposed Development, Relief, and Education for Alien Minors (DREAM) Act. The legislation, first advanced in 2001, would provide a path to citizenship for undocumented youths aged 15 and younger who have lived in the United States for at least five consecutive years. They must have no criminal record, and must graduate from high school or be accepted into college. After completing either a college degree or two years of military service, they would become eligible to begin a six-year citizenship process.

An estimated 65,000 young people would benefit from the legislation. Although for them, U.S. citizenship represents a dream, many native-born citizens regard it as a nightmare—an inappropriate reward for parents who violate immigration law. The legislation, they claim, would increase competition for the limited number of seats in college classrooms. Although DuBois could not have envisioned this 21st century policy debate, he was certainly right about the overriding significance of the color line in U.S. society (DAP 2010; FAIR 2010).

Clearly, race and ethnicity still matter in the United States. On a collective level, our racial biases underlie the societal prejudice that members of some ethnic and racial groups encounter every day. In this chapter we will see how the ascribed characteristics of race and ethnicity create social privilege for some and discrimination for others. We will see that race and ethnicity are socially constructed concepts rather than genetically determined traits. Though functionalists, conflict theorists, labeling theorists, and interactionists have offered different explanations for the unequal treatment of Whites and Blacks, all agree that prejudice and discrimination are real, on both an individual and an institutional level.

The Privileges of the Dominant

One aspect of discrimination that is often overlooked is the privileges that dominant groups enjoy at the expense of others. For instance, we tend to focus more on the difficulty women have getting ahead at work and getting a hand at home than on the ease with which men avoid household chores and manage to make their way in the world. Similarly, we concentrate more on discrimination against racial and ethnic minorities than on the advantages members of the White majority enjoy. Indeed, most White people rarely think about their "Whiteness," taking their status for granted.

Sociologists and other social scientists are becoming increasingly interested in what it means to be "White," for White privilege is the other side of the proverbial coin of racial discrimination. In this context, **White privilege** refers to rights or immunities granted to people as a particular benefit or favor simply because they are White

(Ferber and Kimmel 2008). This view of Whiteness as a privilege echoes an observation by W. E. B. DuBois, that rather than wanting fair working conditions for all laborers, White workers had accepted the "public and psychological wage" of Whiteness ([1935] 1962:700).

The feminist scholar Peggy McIntosh (1988) became interested in White privilege after noticing that most men would not acknowledge that there were privileges attached to being male—even if they would agree that being female had its disadvantages. Did White people suffer from a similar blind spot regarding their own racial privilege? she wondered. Intrigued, McIntosh began to list all the ways in which she benefited from her Whiteness. She soon realized that the list of unspoken advantages was long and significant.

McIntosh found that as a White person, she rarely needed to step out of her comfort zone, no matter where she went. If she wished to, she could spend most of her time with people of her own race. She could find a good place to live in a pleasant neighborhood and get the foods she liked to eat in almost any grocery store. She could attend a public meeting without feeling that she did not belong, that she was different from everyone else.

McIntosh discovered, too, that her skin color opened doors for her. She could cash checks and use credit cards without suspicion, browse through stores without being shadowed by security guards. She could be seated without difficulty in a restaurant. If she asked to see the manager, she could assume he or she would be of her own race. If she needed help from a doctor or a lawyer, she could get it.

McIntosh also realized that her Whiteness made the job of parenting easier. She did not need to worry about protecting her children from people who did not like them. She could be sure that their textbooks would show pictures of people who looked like them, and that their history texts would describe White people's achievements. She knew that the television programs they watched would include White characters.

Finally, McIntosh had to admit that others did not constantly evaluate her in racial terms. When she appeared in public, she didn't need to worry that her clothing or behavior might reflect poorly on White people. If she was recognized for an achievement, it was seen as her achievement, not that of an entire race. And no one ever assumed that the personal opinions she voiced should be those of all White people. Because McIntosh blended in with the people around her, she wasn't always onstage.

These are only some of the privileges McIntosh found she took for granted as a result of her membership in the dominant racial group in the United States. Whiteness *does* carry privileges—to a much greater extent than most White people realize. In the following section we will examine the social construction of race and ethnicity—abstract concepts that have enormous practical consequences for millions of people throughout the world (Fitzgerald 2008; Picca and Feagin 2007).

Use Your Sociological Imagination

How often do you think people are privileged because of their race or ethnicity? How about yourself—how often are you privileged?

The Social Construction of Race and Ethnicity

Racial definitions are crystallized through what Michael Omi and Howard Winant (1994) have called *racial formation,* a sociohistorical process in which racial categories are created, inhibited, transformed, and destroyed. In this process, those who have power define groups of people according to a racist social structure. The creation of a reservation system for Native Americans in the late 1800s is one example of racial formation. Federal officials combined what were distinctive tribes into a single racial group, which we refer to today as Native Americans. The extent and frequency to which peoples are subject to racial formation is such that no one escapes it.

Another example of racial formation from the 1800s was known as the "one-drop rule." If a person had even a single drop of "Black blood," that person was defined and viewed as Black, even if he or she appeared to be White. Clearly, race had social significance, enough so that White legislators established official standards about who was "Black" and who was "White."

The one-drop rule was a vivid example of the *social construction of race*—the process by which people come to define a group as a race based in part on physical characteristics, but also on historical, cultural, and economic factors. For example, in the 1800s, immigrant groups such as Italian and Irish Americans were not at first seen as being "White," but as foreigners who were not necessarily trustworthy. The social construction of race is an ongoing process that is subject to debate, especially in a diverse society such as the United States, where each year increasing numbers of children are born to parents of different racial backgrounds.

In the late 20th century, with immigration from Latin America rising, the fluid nature of racial formation became evident. Suddenly, people were speaking about the "Latin Americanization" of the United States, or about a biracial, Black–White society being replaced by a triracial one. In the 2000 census, over 7 million people in the United States (or about 2.6 percent of the population) reported that they were of two or more races. Half the people classified as multiracial were under age 18, suggesting that this segment of the population will grow in the years to come. People who claimed both White and American Indian ancestry were the largest group of multiracial residents (Bonilla-Silva 2004; N. Jones 2005).

This statistical finding of millions of multiracial people obscures how individuals handle their identity. The prevailing social construction of race pushes people to choose just one race, even if they acknowledge a broader cultural background. Still, many individuals, especially young adults, struggle against social pressure to choose a single identity and instead openly embrace multiple heritages. Tiger Woods, the world's best-known professional golfer, considers himself both Asian and African American.

Ethnicity, too, is subject to social construction. Which ethnic groups are White, for instance? Do we consider Turkish and Arab Americans to be White? We have seen that in the 1800s, Irish and Italian Americans were viewed as non-White and treated as such. But gradually, as other ethnic groups came to see them as White, Irish and Italian Americans became accepted members of mainstream society.

Social construction of race and ethnicity occurs throughout the world, as people in virtually all societies define their positions in the social hierarchy in terms of race, ethnicity, and nationality. Thus, a dominant or majority group has the power not only to define itself legally but to define a society's values. Sociologist William I. Thomas (1923), an early critic of theories of racial and gender differences, wrote that the "definition of the situation" could even mold the individual personality. To put it another way, people respond not only to the objective features of a situation or person but also to the *meaning* that situation or person has for them. In this way, we can create false images or stereotypes that become real in their consequences. **Stereotypes** are unreliable generalizations about all members of a group that do not recognize individual differences within the group.

How do sociologists today conceive of race and ethnicity? Sociologists frequently distinguish between racial and ethnic groups. The term ***racial group*** is used to describe a group that is set apart from others because of obvious physical differences. Whites, African Americans, and Asian Americans are all considered racial groups in the United States. While race does turn on physical differences, it is the culture of a particular society that constructs and attaches social significance to those differences, as we will see later. Unlike racial groups, an ***ethnic group*** is set apart from others primarily because of its national origin or distinctive cultural patterns. In the United States, Puerto Ricans, Jews, and Polish Americans are all categorized as ethnic groups (see Table 6–1).

Using a TV remote control, how quickly do you think you could find a television show in which all the characters share your own racial or ethnic background? What about a show in which all the characters share a different racial or ethnic background from your own—how quickly could you find one?

RACE

The term *racial group* refers to those minorities (and the corresponding dominant groups) set apart from others by obvious physical differences. But what is an "obvious" physical difference? Each society determines which differences are important, while ignoring other characteristics that could serve as a basis for social differentiation. In the United States, we see differences in both skin color and hair color. Yet people learn informally that differences in skin color have a dramatic social and political meaning, while differences in hair color do not.

When observing skin color, people in the United States tend to lump others rather casually into such categories as "Black," "White," and "Asian." More subtle differences in skin color often go unnoticed. However, such is not the case in other societies. In many nations of Central America and South America, people distinguish among color gradients

Table 6–1 Racial and Ethnic Groups in the United States, 2008

Classification	Number in Thousands	Percentage of Total Population
Racial groups		
Whites (non-Hispanic)	198,943	65.4%
Blacks/African Americans	37,586	12.4
Native Americans, Alaskan Natives	2,443	0.8
Asian Americans	13,414	4.4
Chinese	3,078	1.0
Asian Indians	2,496	0.8
Filipinos	2,426	0.8
Vietnamese	1,432	0.5
Koreans	1,344	0.4
Japanese	710	0.2
Pacific Islanders and other	2,356	0.8
Ethnic groups		
White ancestry (single or mixed, non-Hispanic)		
Germans	50,272	16.5
Irish	36,278	11.9
English	27,517	9.0
Italians	17,749	5.8
Poles	9,887	3.3
French	9,447	3.1
Scottish and Scotch-Irish	9,365	3.1
Jews	6,489	2.1
Hispanics (or Latinos)	46,891	15.4
Mexican Americans	30,739	10.1
Puerto Ricans	4,217	1.4
Cubans	1,617	0.5
Salvadorans	1,592	0.5
Dominicans	1,328	0.4
Other Hispanics	7,398	2.4
Total (All groups)	**304,060**	

NOTE: Percentages do not total 100 and subtotals do not add up to totals in major categories because of overlap between groups (e.g., Polish American Jews or people of mixed ancestry, such as Irish and Italian).

SOURCE: 2008 data from American Community Survey 2009:Tables B02003, B02005, B02006, B03001, B03002, C0207, and Bureau of the Census 2009a:Table 77.

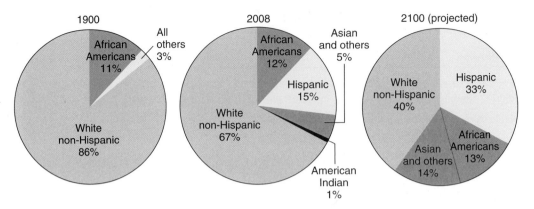

Figure 6–1
Racial and Ethnic Groups in the United States, 1900–2100 (Projected)

The racial and ethnic composition of what is today the United States is undergoing rapid change.

SOURCES: Author's estimate; American Community Survey 2009; Bureau of the Census 2004a. Data for 2008 and 2100, African American and Asian and others are for non-Hispanics.

on a continuum from light to dark skin. Brazil has approximately 40 color groupings, while in other countries people may be described as "Mestizo Hondurans," "Mulatto Colombians," or "African Panamanians." What we see as "obvious" differences, then, is subject to each society's social definitions.

The largest racial minorities in the United States are African Americans (or Blacks), Native Americans (or American Indians), and Asian Americans (Japanese Americans, Chinese Americans, and other Asian peoples). Figure 6–1 provides information about the changing population of racial and ethnic groups in the United States over the past century. It suggests that the racial and ethnic composition of the U.S. population will change as much in the next 50 years as it has in the last 100.

ETHNICITY

An ethnic group, unlike a racial group, is set apart from others because of its national origin or distinctive cultural patterns. Among the ethnic groups in the United States are peoples with a Spanish-speaking background, referred to collectively as *Latinos* or *Hispanics,* such as Puerto Ricans, Mexican Americans, Cuban Americans, and other Latin Americans. Other ethnic groups in this country include Jewish, Irish, Italian, and Norwegian Americans. While these groupings are convenient, they serve to obscure differences *within* these ethnic categories (as in the case of Hispanics) as well as to overlook the mixed ancestry of so many ethnic people in the United States.

The distinction between racial and ethnic groups is not always clear-cut. Some members of racial groups, such as Asian Americans, may have significant cultural differences from other groups. At the same time, certain ethnic groups, such as Latinos, may have obvious physical differences that set them apart from other residents of the United States.

Despite categorization problems, sociologists continue to feel that the distinction between racial groups and ethnic groups is socially significant. In most societies, including the United States, socially constructed physical differences tend to be more visible than ethnic differences. Partly as a result of this fact, stratification along racial lines is more resistant to change than stratification along ethnic lines. Over time, members of an ethnic minority can sometimes become indistinguishable from the majority—although the process may take generations and may never include all members of the group. In contrast, members of a racial minority find it much more difficult to blend in with the larger society and gain acceptance from the majority.

Immigration and New Ethnic Groups

A significant segment of the population of the United States is made up of White ethnics whose ancestors arrived from Europe within the last 100 years. The nation's White ethnic population includes about 50 million people who claim at least partial German ancestry, 36 million Irish Americans, 18 million Italian Americans, and 10 million Polish Americans, as well as immigrants from other European nations (see Table 6–1 on page 169). Some of these people continue to live in close-knit ethnic neighborhoods, while others have largely assimilated and left the "old ways" behind.

Many White ethnics today identify only sporadically with their heritage. *Symbolic ethnicity* refers to an emphasis on such concerns as ethnic food or political issues rather than on deeper ties to one's ethnic heritage. This identity is reflected in the occasional family trip to an ethnic bakery, in the celebration of a ceremonial event such as St. Joseph's Day among Italian Americans, or among Irish Americans in particular, concern about the future of Northern Ireland. Except in cases in which new immigration reinforces old traditions, symbolic ethnicity tends to decline with each passing generation (Alba 1990; Gans 1979).

HISTORY OF IMMIGRATION

The contemporary diversity of the United States is not accidental, but reflects centuries of immigration. The United States has long had policies to determine who has preference to enter the country. Often, clear racial and ethnic biases are built into these policies. In the 1920s, U.S. policy gave preference to people from western Europe, while making it difficult for residents of southern and eastern Europe, Asia, and Africa to enter the country. During the late 1930s and early 1940s, the federal government refused to lift or loosen restrictive immigration quotas to allow Jewish refugees to escape the terror of the Nazi regime. In line with this policy, the *S.S. St. Louis,* with more than 900 Jewish refugees on board, was denied permission to land in the United States in 1939. The ship was forced to sail back to Europe, where at least a few hundred of its passengers later died at the hands of the Nazis (Morse 1967; G. Thomas and Witts 1974).

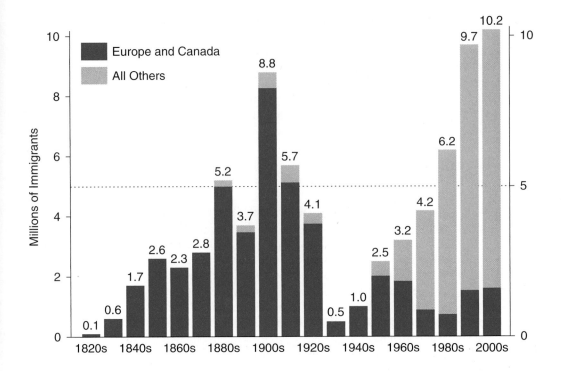

Figure 6–2

*Legal Immigration
in the United States,
1820–2010*

SOURCES: Author's
estimates for the period
2000–2010; Office of
Immigration Statistics
2008:8–11.

Since the 1960s, policies in the United States have encouraged the immigration of people who have relatives here as well as of those who have needed skills. This change has significantly altered the pattern of sending nations. Previously, Europeans dominated, but for the last 40 years, immigrants have come primarily from Latin America and Asia (see Figure 6–2). This means that in the future, an ever-growing proportion of the United States will be Asian or Hispanic. To a large degree, fear and resentment of this growing racial and ethnic diversity is a key factor in opposition to immigration. Many people are very concerned that the new arrivals do not reflect the nation's cultural and racial heritage.

The long border with Mexico provides ample opportunity for illegal immigration into the United States. Throughout the 1980s, the public perception that the United States had lost control of its borders grew. Feeling pressure for immigration control, Congress ended a decade of debate by approving the Immigration Reform and Control Act of 1986. The act marked a historic change in the nation's immigration policy. For the first time, the hiring of illegal aliens was outlawed, and employers caught violating the law became subject to fines and even prison sentences. Just as significant a change was the extension of amnesty and legal status to many illegal immigrants already living in the United States.

More than 20 years later, the act appears to have had mixed results. Substantial numbers of illegal immigrants continue to enter the country each year; an estimated 11 million are present at any given time. Increased border surveillance since September 11, 2001, has reduced their freedom to move back and forth across the border, however. Illegal immigrants to the United States are employed disproportionately in low-income jobs, making them an important part of the workfore (D. Wood 2010).

FUNCTIONS OF IMMIGRATION

Despite people's fears about it, immigration performs many valuable functions. For the receiving society, it alleviates labor shortages, such as exist in the fields of health care and technology in the United States. In 1998 Congress debated not whether individuals with technological skills should be allowed into the country, but just how much to increase the annual quota. For the sending nation, migration can relieve economies unable to support large numbers of people. Often overlooked is the large amount of money immigrants send *back* to their home nations. According to the World Bank's estimate, globally, immigrants from developing nations send more than $300 billion back to their home countries (DeParle 2007).

Immigration can be dysfunctional as well. Although studies generally show that immigration has a positive impact on the receiving nation's economy, areas that accept high concentrations of immigrants may find it difficult to meet short-term social service needs. Furthermore, when migrants with skills or educational potential leave developing countries, it can be dysfunctional for those nations as well. No amount of money sent back home can make up for the loss of valuable human resources from poor nations (Borjas et al. 2006; Kochhar 2006; Sum et al. 2006).

THE CONFLICT APPROACH TO IMMIGRATION

White ethnics and racial minorities have often been antagonistic toward one another because of economic competition—an interpretation rooted in the conflict approach to sociology. As Blacks, Latinos, and Native Americans emerge from the lower class, they compete with working-class Whites for jobs, housing, and educational opportunities. In times of high unemployment or inflation, any such competition can easily generate intense intergroup conflict.

Conflict theorists have noted how much of the debate over immigration is phrased in economic terms. The debate intensifies when the arrivals are of different racial and ethnic backgrounds from the host population. For example, Europeans often refer to "foreigners," but the term does not necessarily mean one of foreign birth. In Germany, "foreigners" refers to people of non-German ancestry, even if they were *born* in Germany; it does not refer to people of German ancestry born in another country, who may choose to immigrate to their "mother country." Fear and dislike of "new" ethnic groups divide countries throughout the world.

You have immigrated to another country with a very different culture. What steps might you take to assimilate?

Sociological Perspectives on Race and Ethnicity

To understand how and why people make social distinctions based on race and ethnicity, we must turn to theory. All the major theoretical perspectives presume that culture, rather than biology, is the major determinant of racial-ethnic distinctions, yet they offer quite different explanations for discrimination. Viewing race from the macro level, functionalists observe that prejudice and discrimination based on race and ethnicity serve positive functions for dominant groups. In contrast, feminists and conflict theorists see the economic structure as a central factor in the exploitation of minorities. Interactionists stress the myriad ways in which everyday contact between people of different racial and ethnic backgrounds contributes to tolerance or hostility.

THE FUNCTIONALIST VIEW

What possible use could racial bigotry have for society? Functionalist theorists, while agreeing that racial hostility is hardly to be admired, point out that it indeed serves positive functions for those practicing discrimination.

Anthropologist Manning Nash (1962) has identified three functions that racially prejudiced beliefs have for the dominant group:

1. Racist views provide a moral justification for maintaining an unequal society that routinely deprives a subordinate group of its rights and privileges. For example, southern Whites justified slavery by believing that Africans were physically and spiritually subhuman and devoid of souls.

2. Racist beliefs discourage members of the subordinate group from attempting to question their lowly status, which would be to question the very foundations of society.

3. Racial myths encourage support for the existing order by introducing the argument that any major societal change (such as an end to discrimination) would only bring greater poverty to the subordinate group and lower the dominant group's standard of living. As a result, Nash suggests, racial prejudice grows when a society's value system (for example, one underlying a colonial empire or a regime that perpetuates slavery) is being threatened.

Although racial prejudice and discrimination may serve the interests of the powerful, such unequal treatment can also be dysfunctional for a society, and even for its dominant group. Sociologist Arnold Rose (1951) outlined four dysfunctions associated with racism:

1. A society that practices discrimination fails to use the resources of all individuals. Discrimination limits the search for talent and leadership to the dominant group.

2. Discrimination aggravates social problems such as poverty, delinquency, and crime and places the financial burden to alleviate those problems on the dominant group.

3. Society must invest a good deal of time and money to defend the barriers to full participation of all members.

4. Racial prejudice and discrimination often undercut goodwill and friendly diplomatic relations between nations.

THE CONFLICT RESPONSE

Conflict theorists would certainly agree with Arnold Rose that racial prejudice and discrimination have many harmful consequences for society. Sociologists such as Oliver Cox (1948), Robert Blauner (1972), and Herbert M. Hunter (2000) have used **exploitation theory** (also called *Marxist class theory*) to explain the basis of racial subordination in the United States. As we saw in Chapter 5, Karl Marx viewed the exploitation of the lower class as a basic part of the capitalist economic system. From a Marxist point of view, racism keeps members of subordinate groups in low-paying jobs, thereby supplying the capitalist ruling class with a pool of cheap labor. Moreover, by forcing these workers to accept low wages, capitalists can restrict the wages of *all* members of the proletariat. Workers from the dominant group who demand higher wages can always be replaced by those from the subordinate group, who have no choice but to accept low-paying jobs.

The conflict view of race relations seems persuasive in a number of instances. Japanese Americans were the object of little prejudice until they began to enter jobs that brought them into competition with

Whites. The movement to keep Chinese immigrants out of the United States became most fervent during the latter half of the 19th century, when Chinese and Whites fought over dwindling work opportunities. Both the enslavement of Blacks and the extermination and removal westward of Native Americans were, to a significant extent, economically motivated.

THE LABELING PERSPECTIVE

The practice of racial profiling fits both the conflict perspective and labeling theory. **Racial profiling** may be defined as any arbitrary action initiated by an authority based on race, ethnicity, or national origin rather than on a person's behavior. Generally, racial profiling occurs when law enforcement officers—customs officials, airport security personnel, and police—assume that people who fit certain descriptions are likely to be engaged in illegal activities. Skin color became a key characteristic of criminal profiles beginning in the 1980s, with the emergence of the crack cocaine market. But profiling can also involve a much more explicit use of stereotypes. For example, the federal antidrug initiative Operation Pipeline encouraged officers to look specifically for people wearing dreadlocks and for Latino men traveling together.

Today, authorities continue to rely on racial profiling, despite overwhelming evidence that it is misleading. A recent study showed that African Americans are still more likely than Whites to be frisked and handled with force when they are stopped. Yet Whites are more likely than Blacks to possess weapons, illegal drugs, or stolen property (Farrell and McDevitt 2010).

Use Your Sociological Imagination

Describe an example of labeling that you are personally familiar with.

THE INTERACTIONIST APPROACH

A Hispanic woman is transferred from a job on an assembly line to a similar position working next to a White man. At first, the White man is patronizing, assuming that she must be incompetent. She is cold and resentful; even when she needs assistance, she refuses to admit it. After a week, the growing tension between the two leads to a bitter quarrel. Yet over time, each slowly comes to appreciate the other's strengths and talents. A year after they begin working together, these two workers become respectful friends. This story is an example of what interactionists call the *contact hypothesis* in action.

The **contact hypothesis** states that interracial contact between people of equal status who are engaged in a cooperative task will cause them to become less prejudiced and to abandon previous stereotypes. People will begin to see one another as individuals and discard the broad generalizations characteristic of stereotyping. Note the phrases *equal status* and *cooperative task*. In the example just given, if the two workers

summingUP

Table 6–2 Sociological Perspectives on Race

Perspective	Emphasis
Functionalist	The dominant majority benefits from the subordination of racial minorities
Conflict	Vested interests perpetuate racial inequality through economic exploitation
Labeling	People are profiled and stereotyped based on their racial and ethnic identities
Interactionist	Cooperative interracial contacts can reduce hostility

had been competing for one vacancy as a supervisor, the racial hostility between them might have worsened (Allport 1979; Fine 2008).

In the United States, as Latinos and other subordinate groups slowly gain access to better-paying, more responsible jobs, the contact hypothesis may take on even greater significance. The trend in our society is toward increasing contact between individuals from dominant and subordinate groups. This may be one way of eliminating—or at least reducing—racial and ethnic stereotyping and prejudice. Another may be the establishment of interracial coalitions, an idea suggested by sociologist William Julius Wilson (1999). To work, such coalitions would obviously need to be built on an equal role for all members.

Table 6–2 summarizes the four major sociological perspectives on race. No matter what the explanation for racial and ethnic distinctions—functionalist, conflict, labeling, or interactionist—these socially constructed inequalities can have powerful consequences in the form of prejudice and discrimination. In the next section we will see how inequality based on the ascribed characteristics of race and ethnicity can poison people's interpersonal relations, depriving whole groups of opportunities others take for granted.

Patterns of Prejudice and Discrimination

In recent years, college campuses across the United States have been the scene of bias-related incidents. Student-run newspapers and radio stations have ridiculed subordinate racial and ethnic groups; threatening literature has been stuffed under students' doors; graffiti endorsing the views of White supremacist organizations such as the Ku Klux Klan have been scrawled on university walls. In some cases, violent clashes have occurred between groups of White and Black students (Southern Poverty Law Center 2009). What causes such ugly incidents?

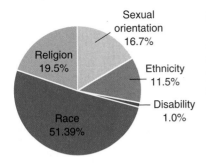

Figure 6–3
*Categorization of
Reported Hate Crimes*

SOURCE: Department of
Justice 2009.

PREJUDICE

Prejudice is a negative attitude toward an entire category of people, often an ethnic or racial group. If you resent your roommate because he or she is sloppy, you are not necessarily guilty of prejudice. However, if you immediately stereotype your roommate on the basis of such characteristics as race, ethnicity, or religion, that is a form of prejudice. Prejudice tends to perpetuate false definitions of individuals and groups.

Sometimes prejudice results from ***ethnocentrism***—the tendency to assume that one's own culture and way of life represent the norm or are superior to all others. Ethnocentric people judge other cultures by the standards of their own group, which leads quite easily to prejudice against other cultures.

One important and widespread form of prejudice is ***racism,*** the belief that one race is supreme and all others are innately inferior. When racism prevails in a society, members of subordinate groups generally experience prejudice, discrimination, and exploitation. Racism can be subtle and deep-seated. Though many Americans both White and Black condemn racism, research results suggest that racist stereotypes—such as that of the violent Black male—may be rooted in our subconscious thought processes.

In 1990, as concern mounted about racist attacks in the United States, Congress passed the Hate Crimes Statistics Act. A ***hate crime*** is a criminal offense committed because of the offender's bias against a race, religion, ethnic group, national origin, or sexual orientation. In 2008 alone, more than 7,700 hate crimes were reported to authorities. As Figure 6–3 shows, more than half those crimes involved racial bias. Most were carried out by individuals acting alone or with a few friends.

COLOR-BLIND RACISM

Over the last three generations, nationwide surveys have consistently shown growing support among Whites for integration, interracial dating, and the election of minority group members to public office—including even the presidency of the United States. How can this trend be explained, given the persistence of residential segregation and the commission of thousands of hate crimes every year? The answer, to some extent, is that prejudice and discriminatory attitudes are no longer expressed as freely as they once were. Often, they are couched in terms of equal opportunity.

Color-blind racism is the use of the principle of race neutrality to defend a racially unequal status quo. Proponents of race neutrality claim they believe that everyone should be treated equally. However, the way in which they apply the principle to government policy is anything but neutral. Proponents of this approach oppose affirmative action (see page 181), public welfare assistance, and to a large extent, government-funded health insurance, all of which they see largely as favors to minority groups. Yet they do not object to practices that privilege Whites, such as college admissions criteria that give preference to the relatives of alumni. Nor do they oppose tax breaks for homeowners, most of whom are White, or government financial aid to college students, who are also disproportionately White. Though race neutrality is not based on theories of racial superiority or inferiority, then, the idea that society should be color-blind only perpetuates racial inequality.

Color-blind racism has also been referred to as "laissez-faire racism," "aversive racism," or "covert racism." Although its proponents rarely speak of racism, other indicators of social status, such as social class or citizenship, tend to become proxies for race. Thus, many White people can convince themselves that they are not racist—nor do they know anyone who is—and yet remain prejudiced against "welfare mothers" and "immigrants." They can conclude, mistakenly, that racial tolerance, or even racial and ethnic equality, has been achieved.

Researchers who have surveyed White attitudes toward African Americans over the past several decades have come to two inescapable conclusions. First, people's attitudes do change. In periods of social upheaval, dramatic attitudinal shifts can occur within a single generation. Second, less racial progress was made in the late twentieth and early twenty-first centuries than in the relatively brief period of the 1950s and 1960s. Today, economically disadvantaged groups such as African Americans and Latinos have become so closely associated with urban decay, homelessness, welfare, and crime that those problems are now viewed as racial issues, even if they are not labeled as such. The tendency to *blame the victims* of these social ills complicates their resolution, especially at a time when government's ability to address social problems is limited by anti-tax initiatives and concern over terrorism. In short, the color line is still in place, even if more and more people refuse to acknowledge its existence (Ansell 2008; Bonilla-Silva 2006; Coates 2008; Dovidio 2001; Meredith King 2007:3–4; Quillian 2006; Winant 1994:106–108).

DISCRIMINATORY BEHAVIOR

Prejudice often leads to **discrimination,** the denial of opportunities and equal rights to individuals and groups based on some type of arbitrary bias. Say that a White corporate president with a prejudice against Asian Americans has to fill an executive position. The most qualified candidate for the job is a Vietnamese American. If the president refuses to hire this candidate and instead selects an inferior White candidate, he or she is engaging in an act of racial discrimination.

Prejudiced *attitudes* should not be equated with discriminatory *behavior*. Although the two are generally related, they are not identical; either condition can be present without the other. A prejudiced person does not always act on his or her biases. The White president, for example, might choose—despite his or her stereotypes—to hire the Vietnamese American. That would be prejudice without discrimination. On the other hand, a White corporate president with a completely respectful view of Vietnamese Americans might refuse to hire them for executive posts, out of fear that biased clients would take their business elsewhere. In that case, the president's action would constitute discrimination without prejudice.

Discrimination persists even for the most educated and qualified people from the best family backgrounds. Despite their talents and experiences, they sometimes encounter attitudinal or organizational bias that prevents them from reaching their full potential. The term *glass ceiling* refers to an invisible barrier that blocks the promotion of a qualified individual in a work environment because of the individual's gender, race, or ethnicity (Schaefer 2011; Yamagata et al. 1997).

In early 1995, the federal Glass Ceiling Commission issued the first comprehensive study of barriers to promotion in the United States. The commission found that glass ceilings continued to block women and men from subordinate racial and ethnic groups from top management positions in the nation's industries. Although White men constitute 45 percent of the labor force today, they hold down a much higher proportion of the top positions. Even in the most diverse corporations, as listed in *Fortune* magazine in 2002, White men held over 80 percent of both the board of directors seats and the top 50 paid positions. According to the commission, the existence of this glass ceiling results principally from the fears and prejudices of many middle- and upper-level White male managers, who believe that the inclusion of women and men from subordinate groups in management circles will threaten their own prospects for advancement (Bureau of the Census 2009a; Department of Labor 1995a, 1995b; Hickman 2002).

INSTITUTIONAL DISCRIMINATION

Which would be more socially significant, the elimination of prejudice or the elimination of discrimination?

Discrimination is practiced not only by individuals in one-to-one encounters but also by institutions. Social scientists are particularly concerned with the ways in which structural factors such as employment, housing, health care, and government administration maintain the social significance of race and ethnicity. *Institutional discrimination* refers to the denial of opportunities and equal rights to individuals and groups that results from the normal operations of a society. This kind of discrimination consistently affects certain racial and ethnic groups more than others.

The U.S. Commission on Civil Rights (1981:9–10) has identified various forms of institutional discrimination, including:

• Rules requiring that only English be spoken at a place of work, even when it is not a business necessity to restrict the use of other languages.

- Preferences shown by law and medical schools in the admission of children of wealthy and influential alumni, nearly all of whom are White.

- Restrictive employment-leave policies, coupled with prohibitions on part-time work, that make it difficult for the heads of single-parent families (most of whom are women) to obtain and keep jobs.

Institutional discrimination occurred in the wake of the September 11, 2001, terrorist attack on the United States. In the heat of demands to prevent terrorist takeovers of commercial airplanes, Congress passed the Aviation and Transportation Security Act, which was intended to strengthen airport screening procedures. The law stipulated that all airport screeners must be U.S. citizens. Nationally, 28 percent of all airport screeners are legal residents but not citizens of the United States; as a group, they are disproportionately Latino, Black, and Asian. Many observers noted that other airport and airline workers, including pilots, cabin attendants, and even armed National Guardsmen stationed at airports, need not be citizens. Efforts are now being made to test the constitutionality of the act. At the least, the debate over its fairness shows that even well-meant legal measures can have disastrous consequences for some racial and ethnic groups.

In some cases, even seemingly neutral institutional standards can turn out to have discriminatory effects. African American students at a midwestern state university protested a policy under which fraternities and sororities that wished to use campus facilities for a dance were required to post $150 security deposits to cover possible damages. The Black students complained that the policy had a discriminatory impact on their organizations. Campus police countered that the university's policy applied to all student groups interested in using campus facilities. However, since the overwhelmingly White fraternities and sororities at the school used their own houses for dances, the policy indeed affected only African Americans and other subordinate groups.

Attempts have been made to eradicate or compensate for discrimination in the United States. The 1960s saw the passage of many pioneering civil rights laws, including the landmark 1964 Civil Rights Act (which prohibits discrimination in public accommodations and publicly owned facilities on the basis of race, color, creed, national origin, and gender). In two important rulings in 1987, the Supreme Court held that federal prohibitions against racial discrimination protect members of all ethnic minorities—including Hispanics, Jews, and Arab Americans—even though they may be considered White.

For more than 20 years, affirmative action programs have been instituted to overcome past discrimination. *Affirmative action* refers to positive efforts to recruit members of subordinate groups or women for jobs, promotions, and educational opportunities. Many people resent these programs, arguing that advancing one group's cause merely shifts the discrimination to another group. By giving priority to African Americans in admissions, for example, a school may overlook more qualified White candidates. In many parts of the country and many sectors of the economy, affirmative action is being rolled back, even though it was never fully implemented.

Discriminatory practices continue to pervade nearly all aspects of life in the United States today, in part because various individuals and groups actually *benefit* from them in terms of money, status, and influence. Even ex-convicts who are White are privileged in comparison to non-Whites.

A study by sociologist Devah Pager (2003) documents this kind of racial discrimination. Pager sent four young men out to look for an entry-level job in Milwaukee, Wisconsin. All four were 23-year-old college students, but they presented themselves as high school graduates with similar job histories. Two of the men were Black and two were White. One Black applicant and one White applicant claimed to have served 18 months in jail for a felony conviction (possession of cocaine with intent to distribute).

As one might expect, the four men's experiences with 350 potential employers were vastly different. Predictably, the White applicant with a purported prison record received only half as many callbacks as the other White applicant—17 percent compared to 34 percent. But as dramatic as the effect of his criminal record was, the effect of his race was more significant. Despite his prison record, he received slightly more callbacks than the Black applicant *with no criminal record* (17 percent compared to 14 percent). Race, it seems, was more of a concern to potential employers than a criminal background. The implications of this research are not limited to any one city, such as Milwaukee. Pager and fellow sociologist Bruce Western replicated (that is, repeated) her study in New York City, with similar results. Other studies have confirmed discriminatory handling of job applications in Chicago, San Diego, and Washington, D.C. Over time, the cumulative effect of such differential behavior by employers contributes to significant differences in income (Pager 2007; Pager et al. 2009).

MEASURING DISCRIMINATION

Can discrimination be measured in terms of lost income or opportunities? Doing so is a complicated process. Researchers must first confirm that prejudice exists by assessing people's attitudes toward a racial or ethnic group and showing that its members are treated differently from others. Then they must find a way to assign a cost to the discrimination.

Researchers have managed to draw some tentative conclusions, however, by comparing income data for African Americans versus Whites and for men versus women. As Figure 6–4 shows, with a median income of $52,228, White men earned 30 percent more money than Black men

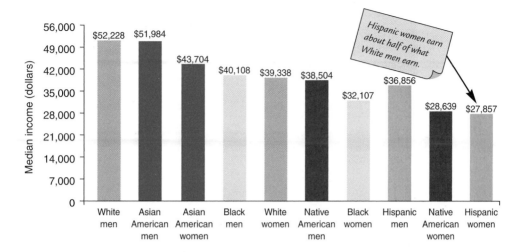

Figure 6–4

U.S. Median Income by Race, Ethnicity, and Gender

NOTE: Data released in 2009 for income earned in 2008. Includes only people working full-time, year-round, 25 years old and older. "White" refers to non-Hispanic Whites.

SOURCE: DeNavas-Walt et al. 2009; for Native Americans, author's estimate based on Bureau of the Census data in Ogunwole 2006.

in 2008 and nearly twice what Hispanic women earned. Black women earned significantly less than White women ($32,107 compared to $39,338), indicating that they bore a double burden because of their race and gender. The strong disparity between Black women's and White men's incomes has remained unchanged over more than 60 years. As great as this apparent inequality of income is, studies show that inequality in wealth among racial and ethnic groups is even greater.

These differences are not entirely the result of discrimination in employment, for members of these groups are not equally prepared to obtain high-paying jobs. Past discrimination is a significant factor in the poor educational backgrounds of some groups. Historically, taxpayers, who are predominantly White, have been unwilling to subsidize the public education of African Americans and Hispanics at the same level as that of White pupils. Test results in today's inner-city schools show the continuing effect of such discriminatory spending patterns.

To address this problem, researchers have compared the median incomes of Blacks, Whites, and Hispanics, as well as men and women, with approximately the same educational level. As Table 6–3 shows, even though workers with higher educational levels generally earn more money than others, the disparity between the races and the sexes remains. The gap between the races does narrow a bit as educational levels rise; still, both African Americans and women lag behind. In some cases, the contrast is dramatic: women with a master's degree earn about $8,300 less than men who have only a baccalaureate degree ($57,512 compared to $65,800).

Note, too, what happens to Asian American households. Though highly educated Asian Americans earn high incomes, they too trail behind their White counterparts. With a doctorate holder in the family, the typical Asian American household earns an estimated $126,894 a year—more than $5,000 less than a White household.

Table 6–3 Median Income by Race and Sex, Holding Education Constant

Even at the very highest levels of schooling, the income gap remains between Whites and Blacks. Education also has little apparent effect on the income gap between male and female workers.

	Race				Sex	
	White Families	Black Families	Asian Families	Hispanic Families	Male	Female
Total	71,273	41,064	75,751	41,488	49,000	36,679
HIGH SCHOOL						
Nongraduate	36,683	22,209	40,300	30,838	29,678	20,405
Graduate	53,813	35,000	42,970	41,767	39,009	28,382
COLLEGE						
Associate degree	73,113	50,801	66,069	61,106	50,417	36,760
Bachelor's degree	97,332	67,125	91,296	70,915	65,800	47,026
Master's degree	108,455	99,117	116,648	Not available	80,962	57,512
Doctorate degree	132,332	112,702	126,894	Not available	101,255	74,025

NOTES: Data released in 2009 for income earned in 2008. Figures are median income from all sources except capital gains. Included are public assistance payments, dividends, pensions, unemployment compensation, and so on. Incomes are for all workers over 25 years of age. High school graduates include those with GEDs. Data for Whites are for White non-Hispanics. "Some college" excludes associate degree holders. Family data above bachelor's degree are average (not median) incomes and data for doctorate-holders' families are author's estimate.

SOURCE: DeNavas-Walt et al. 2009.

The income gap shown in Table 6–3 may not be caused entirely by employment discrimination. The table shows only the level of schooling obtained by workers, not the quality. Though in recent years, efforts have been made to eliminate geographical disparities in school funding, subordinate racial groups are still more likely than Whites to attend inadequately financed schools. Inequality of educational opportunity may also affect women, since educational institutions often shepherd women into low-paid sex-segregated occupations, such as nursing and elementary education.

What is the collective effect of discrimination in employment? Economist Andrew Brimmer (1995), citing numerous government studies, estimates that if employers used African Americans' talents and abilities, based on their formal schooling, to the fullest, the nation's gross domestic product (GDP) would be about 3 or 4 percent higher each year. Estimates of the economic cost of discrimination have not changed much since the mid-1960s. The percentage of GDP lost would be even higher, of course, if economists were to include losses from the underutilization of women's and other subordinate groups' talents. The widespread practice of steering women toward low-paid, low-level jobs, even if they are qualified for more challenging and rewarding work, has a hidden cost to society.

Sociology Matters

Sociology matters because it makes us think about why some people in our society are treated better than others.

- Do you hold any prejudices against subordinate racial or ethnic groups? If so, has your reading of this chapter helped you to see those groups from a different perspective? How would your life change if you yourself were a member of one of those groups?

- Are you White? If so, what privileges, perhaps because of your race or citizenship, do you enjoy that you have always taken for granted? Can you think of a way to reduce one or more of those privileges so that others can be more equal—and would you cooperate with such an effort?

  Sociology matters because it makes us more aware of prejudice and discrimination against members of certain racial and ethnic groups.

- Are you non-White? If so, what kinds of stereotyping and discrimination have you seen non-Whites experience? Do you think racial discrimination can be reduced through cooperative contact among people of different races?

- Are you or your parents recent immigrants to the United States? If so, what is the primary basis on which others react to you— your ethnic group, race, or country of origin? Do you think you or your children will someday blend into mainstream society in the United States, and if so, what might hasten that process?

CHAPTER RESOURCES

Summary

The social dimensions of race and ethnicity are important factors in shaping people's lives. In this chapter, we defined the meaning of race and ethnicity and examined the social construction of those ascribed statuses. We discussed four theoretical perspectives on the unequal treatment of individuals based on their **racial** and **ethnic groups.** We noted some patterns of **prejudice** and **discrimination** against members of those groups, many of whom are recent immigrants.

And we studied the economic effects of the unequal treatment of subordinate groups.

1. In the United States, people who are White enjoy numerous rights and immunities simply because they are White. Yet they rarely acknowledge their **White privilege,** to themselves or to people of other races.

2. Race and ethnicity are socially constructed. The meaning people attach to the physical characteristics of certain groups, which are often expressed in **stereotypes,** gives race and ethnicity their social significance.

3. A **racial group** is set apart from others by obvious physical differences, whereas an **ethnic group** is set apart primarily because of national origin or distinctive cultural patterns.

4. Over the last century, the racial and ethnic composition of immigrants to the United States has changed as the major sending nations changed. One hundred years ago, White ethnics from Europe predominated; today's immigrants come mainly from Latin America and Asia.

5. Functionalists point out that to the dominant groups in a society, discrimination against subordinate groups may seem to be functional. But for society as a whole, discrimination can be dysfunctional.

6. Conflict theorists stress the harmful consequences of racial subordination. They see the unequal treatment of subordinate groups as an integral part of capitalism, a view known as **exploitation theory.**

7. Interactionists focus on the micro level of race relations, pointing out the ways in which Whites dominate members of other racial and ethnic groups in everyday social interactions. According to their **contact hypothesis,** racial prejudice and discrimination can be reduced through cooperative contact between the races.

8. **Prejudice** is a negative attitude toward an entire group, often an ethnic or racial minority. Prejudice is often based on **ethnocentrism**—the belief that one's own culture is superior to all others—or on **racism**—the belief that one race is supreme and all others are inferior.

9. Prejudice often leads to **discrimination** against members of certain racial and ethnic groups. In the workplace, members of these groups may encounter a **glass ceiling,** an invisible barrier that blocks their promotion.

10. Discrimination that results from the normal operations of a society is known as **institutional discrimination.** To remedy this kind of discrimination, governments, businesses, and schools have developed **affirmative action** programs.

www.mhhe.com/schaefersm5e
Visit the Online Learning Center for *Sociology Matters* to access quizzes, review activities, and other learning tools.

Key Terms

Inequality by Gender

The Social Construction of Gender

Sociological Perspectives on Gender

Women: The Oppressed Majority

Women in the Workforce of the United States

He works. She works. Both are family practice physicians—a high-status occupation with considerable financial rewards. He makes $165,000. She makes $145,000.

These median earnings for physicians in the United States were released in 2005. They are typical of the results of the Census Bureau's detailed study of occupations and income. Take air traffic controllers. He makes $67,000; she earns $56,000. Or housekeepers: he makes $19,000; she earns $15,000. What about teacher's assistants? He makes $20,000; she earns $15,000.

Statisticians at the bureau looked at the median earnings for no fewer than 821 occupations ranging from dishwasher to chief executive. After adjusting for workers' age, education, and work experience, they came to an unmistakable conclusion: Across the board, there is a substantial gender gap in the median earnings of full-time workers.

Men do not always earn more than women for doing the same work. Researchers at the Census Bureau found 2 occupations out of 821 in which women typically earn about 1 percent more income than men: hazardous materials recovery and telecommunications line installation. These two occupations, however, employed less than

1 out of every 1,000 workers the bureau studied. Forecasting analyses show no convincing evidence that the wage gap is narrowing.

What accounts for these yawning wage gaps between men and women in the same occupation? Scholars at the Census Bureau studied the following characteristics of men and women in the same occupation:

- Age and degree of formal education
- Marital status and the presence of children at home
- Specialization within the occupation (for example, family practice versus surgical practice)
- Years of work experience
- Hours worked per year

Taking all these factors into consideration reduced the pay gap between men and women by only three cents. Women still earned only 80 cents for every dollar earned by men. In sum, the disparity in pay between men and women cannot be explained by pointing to women's career choices (Government Accountability Office 2003; Weinberg 2004, 2007).

In this chapter we will see how the ascribed characteristic of gender creates privilege for men and discrimination for women. Like differences in race, differences in gender are visible. And like race and ethnicity, gender is socially constructed. Though functionalists, conflict theorists, feminists, and interactionists take different views of this subject, all agree that our society treats women and men unequally. Women may be a majority in terms of their numbers, but they are treated more like a subordinate racial or ethnic group. For some women, the intersection of gender, race, and class creates a degree of discrimination that no other subordinate group faces.

The Social Construction of Gender

How do airline passengers react when the captain's voice belongs to a female? What do we make of a father who announces that he will be late for work because his son has a routine medical checkup? Consciously or unconsciously, we are likely to assume that flying a commercial plane is a *man's* job, and that most parental duties are, in fact, *maternal* duties. Gender is such a routine part of our everyday activities that we typically take it for granted, noticing only when someone deviates from conventional behavior and expectations.

Although a few people begin life with an unclear sexual identity, the overwhelming majority begin with a definite sex and quickly receive societal messages about how to behave. Many societies have established social distinctions between females and males that do not inevitably result from biological differences between the sexes (such as women's reproductive capabilities).

In studying gender, sociologists are interested in the gender-role socialization that leads females and males to behave differently. In Chapter 2, *gender roles* were defined as expectations regarding the proper behavior, attitudes, and activities of males and females. The application of traditional gender roles leads to many forms of differentiation between women and men. Both sexes are physically capable of learning to cook and sew, yet most Western societies determine that women should perform these tasks. Both men and women are capable of learning to weld and fly airplanes, but these functions are generally assigned to men.

Gender roles are evident not only in our work and behavior but in how we react to others. We are constantly "doing gender" without realizing it. If the father just mentioned sits in the doctor's office with his son in the middle of a workday, he will probably receive approving glances from the receptionist and from other patients. "Isn't he a wonderful father?" runs through their minds. But if the boy's mother leaves *her* job and sits with the son in the doctor's office, she will not receive such silent applause.

We socially construct our behavior to create or exaggerate male–female differences. For example, men and women come in a variety of heights, sizes, and ages. Yet traditional norms regarding marriage and even casual dating tell us that in heterosexual couples, the man should be older, taller, and wiser than the woman. As we will see throughout this chapter, such social norms help to reinforce and legitimize patterns of male dominance.

In recent decades, women have entered occupations and professions that were once dominated by men. Yet our society still focuses on "masculine" and "feminine" qualities, as if men and women must be evaluated in those terms. Clearly, we continue to "do gender," and the social construction of gender continues to define significantly different expectations for females and males.

GENDER-ROLE SOCIALIZATION

Male babies get blue blankets; females get pink ones. Boys are expected to play with trucks, blocks, and toy soldiers; girls receive dolls and kitchen goods. Boys must be masculine—active, aggressive, tough, daring, and dominant—but girls must be feminine—soft, emotional, sweet, and submissive. These traditional gender-role patterns have been influential in the socialization of children in the United States.

An important element in traditional views of proper "masculine" and "feminine" behavior is *homophobia,* or fear of and prejudice against homosexuality. Homophobia contributes significantly to rigid gender-role socialization, since many people stereotypically associate male homosexuality with femininity and lesbianism with masculinity. Consequently, men and women who deviate from traditional expectations about gender roles are often presumed to be gay. Despite the advances made by the gay liberation movement, the continuing stigma attached to homosexuality in our culture places pressure on all males (whether gay or not) to exhibit only narrow "masculine" behavior and on all females (whether lesbian or not) to exhibit only narrow "feminine" behavior (Lindsey 2005; Seidman 2002).

It is *adults,* of course, who play a critical role in guiding children into those gender roles deemed appropriate by society. Parents are normally the first and most crucial agents of socialization. But other adults, older siblings, the mass media, and religious and educational institutions also exert an important influence on gender-role socialization, in the United States and elsewhere.

It is not hard to test how rigid gender-role socialization can be. Just try transgressing some gender norm—say, by smoking a cigar in public if you are female, or by carrying a purse if you are male. That was exactly the assignment given to sociology students at the University of Colorado and Luther College in Iowa. Professors asked students to behave in ways that they thought violated the norms of how a man or woman should act. The students had no trouble coming up with gender-norm transgressions (see Table 7–1), and they kept careful notes on others' reactions to their behavior, ranging from amusement to disgust (Nielsen et al. 2000).

WOMEN'S AND MEN'S GENDER ROLES

How does a girl come to develop a feminine self-image, while a boy develops one that is masculine? In part, they do so by identifying with females and males in their families and neighborhoods and in the media.

Table 7–1 An Experiment in Gender Norm Violation by College Students

Norm Violations by Women	Norm Violations by Men
Send men flowers	Wear fingernail polish
Spit in public	Needlepoint in public
Use men's bathroom	Throw Tupperware party
Buy jock strap	Cry in public
Buy/chew tobacco	Have pedicure
Talk knowledgeably about cars	Apply to babysit
Open doors for men	Shave body hair

Source: Nielsen et al. 2000:287.

In an experiment testing gender-role stereotypes, sociology students were asked to behave in ways that might be regarded as violations of gender norms, and to keep notes on how others reacted. This is a sample of their choices of behavior over a seven-year period. Do you agree that these actions test the boundaries of conventional gender behavior?

If a young girl regularly sees female characters on television working as defense attorneys and judges, she may believe that she herself can become a lawyer. It will not hurt if the women that she knows—her mother, sister, parents' friends, or neighbors—are lawyers. But if she sees women portrayed in the media only as models, nurses, and secretaries, her identification and self-image will be quite different. Even if she does become a professional, she may secretly regret falling short of the media stereotypes—a shapely, sexy young woman in a bathing suit, or the perfect wife and mother.

Television is far from alone in stereotyping women. Studies of children's books published in the United States in the 1940s, 1950s, and 1960s found that females were significantly underrepresented in central roles and illustrations. Virtually all female characters were portrayed as helpless, passive, incompetent, and in need of a strong male caretaker. Studies of picture books published from the 1970s through the 1990s found some improvement, but males still dominated the central roles. While males were portrayed as a variety of characters, females tended to be shown mostly in traditional roles, such as mother, grandmother, or volunteer, even if they also held nontraditional roles, such as working professional (Etaugh 2003).

Social research on gender roles reveals some persistent differences between men and women in North America and Europe. Women experience a mandate to marry and become mothers. Often, marriage is viewed as their true entry into adulthood. And they are expected not only to become mothers but to *want* to be mothers. Though marriage and parenthood play a role in men's lives, they do not appear to be as critical in a man's life course. Rather, society defines men's roles in terms of economic success. While women may achieve recognition in the labor force, it is not as important to their identity as it is for men (Brettell and Sargent 2005).

Men's roles are socially constructed in much the same way as women's roles. Family, peers, and the media all influence how a boy or a man comes to view his appropriate role in society. Robert Brannon (1976) and James Doyle (1995) have identified five aspects of the male gender role:

- Antifeminine element—show no "sissy stuff," including any expression of openness or vulnerability.
- Success element—prove one's masculinity at work and in sports.
- Aggressive element—use force in dealing with others.
- Sexual element—initiate and control all sexual relations.
- Self-reliant element—keep cool and unflappable.

No systematic research has established all these elements as necessarily common to all males, but specific studies have confirmed individual elements.

Males who do not conform to the socially constructed gender role face constant criticism and even humiliation, both from children when they are boys and from adults as men. It can be agonizing to be treated as a "chicken" or a "sissy" as a youth—particularly if such remarks come from one's father or brothers. And grown men who pursue non-traditional occupations, such as preschool teaching or nursing, must constantly deal with others' misgivings and strange looks. In one study, interviewers found that such men frequently had to alter their behavior in order to minimize others' negative reactions. One 35-year-old nurse reported that he had to claim he was "a carpenter or something like that" when he "went clubbing," because women weren't interested in getting to know a male nurse. The subjects made similar accommodations in casual exchanges with other men (Cross and Bagilhole 2002:215).

In the last 40 years, inspired in good part by the contemporary feminist movement (examined later in the chapter), increasing numbers of men in the United States have criticized the restrictive aspects of the traditional male gender role. Some men have taken strong public positions in support of women's struggle for full equality, and have even organized voluntary associations for the purpose. However, their actions have been countered by other men who feel they are unfairly penalized by laws related to alimony, child support and custody, family violence, and affirmative action (Kimmel 2008; National Organization for Men Against Sexism 2008).

Recent research on gender roles has shown that in fact there is no single, simple characterization of the male gender role. Australian sociologist R. W. Connell (1987, 2002, 2005) has spoken of *multiple masculinities,* meaning that men play a variety of gender roles, including a nurturing-caring role and an effeminate-gay role, in addition to their traditional gender role of dominating women. Nevertheless, society reinforces their traditional, dominating role more than any other role.

One example of multiple masculinities is the difference between the roles of extremely advantaged men with high-status positions and those of working-class men, whose roles are not necessarily devalued, but afford fewer opportunities for advancement. For example, an analysis of the attack on the World Trade Center on September 11, 2001, contrasts the roles of men from different social classes. Consider the relatively modest status of first responders to the disaster, compared with the high status of the affluent managerial professionals who worked at the trade center. Many of the first responders lost their lives to rescue the high-status men in upper-echelon positions in finance and investment banking. One can only imagine the firefighters climbing up the stairwells as the financiers made their way down (Langewiesche 2002).

A CROSS-CULTURAL PERSPECTIVE

To what extent do actual biological differences between the sexes contribute to these cultural differences associated with gender? This question brings us back to the debate over nature versus nurture (see Chapter 2).

In assessing the alleged and real differences between men and women, it is useful to examine cross-cultural data.

Around the world, anthropologists have documented highly diverse constructions of gender that do not always conform to our own ideals of masculinity and femininity. Beginning with the path-breaking work of Margaret Mead ([1935] 2001) and continuing through contemporary fieldwork, these scholars have shown that gender roles can vary greatly from one physical environment, economy, and political system to the next. Peggy Reeves Sanday's (2002, 2008) work in West Sumatra, Indonesia, for example, describes the 4 million–member Minangkabau society as one in which men and women are not competitors, but partners for the common good. This society is based on a nurturing approach to the environment, blended with Islamic religious ethics. Women control the land through inheritance; in the event of a divorce, the ex-husband leaves with only his clothes. The larger community may be governed by men, women, or both men and women working together. Sanday's findings, together with Mead's, confirm the influential role of culture and socialization in gender-role differentiation. There appear to be no innate or biologically determined gender roles for men and women.

We can see the social construction of gender roles in process in societies strained by war and social upheaval. By summer 2004, a year after the war in Iraq began, young girls in Baghdad seldom ventured out to the park or swimming pool. When they did, their parents made sure they were dressed conservatively, in loose clothing and perhaps a headscarf. The overthrow of Saddam Hussein's secular regime had emboldened Islamic fundamentalists, who had begun visiting schools, urging young women to wear long sleeves and cover their heads. Though school officials resisted, many girls dropped out, some out of fear for their safety and others because of financial hardship. In the atmosphere of violence and lawlessness that followed the 2003 invasion, young women wondered what the future would hold for them and whether they would ever have the opportunity to become educated professionals, as their mothers had (Sengupta 2004).

Use Your Sociological Imagination

You are living in a society in which there are no gender roles. What is your life like?

Sociological Perspectives on Gender

THE FUNCTIONALIST VIEW

Cross-cultural studies have shown that societies dominated by men are much more common than those in which women play the decisive role. Functionalists maintain that this type of gender differentiation contributes to overall social stability. Sociologists Talcott Parsons and Robert Bales (1955), for instance, argued that to function most effectively, the family requires adults who will specialize in particular roles. They viewed the traditional arrangement of gender roles as arising out of the need to establish a division of labor between marital partners.

Parsons and Bales contended that women take the expressive, emotionally supportive role and men the instrumental, practical role, with the two complementing each other. ***Instrumentality*** refers to an emphasis on tasks, a focus on more distant goals, and a concern for the external relationship between one's family and other social institutions. ***Expressiveness*** denotes a concern for the maintenance of harmony and the internal emotional affairs of the family. According to this theory, women's interest in expressive goals frees men for instrumental tasks, and vice versa. Women become "anchored" in the family as wives, mothers, and household managers; men become anchored in the occupational world outside the home. Of course, Parsons and Bales offered this framework in the 1950s, when many more women were full-time homemakers than is true today. Though they did not explicitly endorse traditional gender roles, they implied that dividing tasks between spouses was functional for the family unit.

Given the typical socialization of women and men in the United States, the functionalist view may seem persuasive. However, it would lead us to expect girls and women with no interest in children to become babysitters and mothers. Similarly, males who love spending time with children might be "programmed" into careers in the business world. Such differentiation might harm the individual who does not fit into prescribed roles, while depriving society of the contributions of many talented people who are confined by gender stereotyping. Moreover, the functionalist approach does not convincingly explain why men should be categorically assigned to the instrumental role and women to the expressive role.

THE CONFLICT RESPONSE

Viewed from a conflict perspective, the functionalist approach to explaining gender distinctions masks the underlying power relations between men and women. Parsons and Bales never explicitly presented the expressive and instrumental tasks as being of unequal value to society, yet their inequality is quite evident. Although social institutions may pay lip service to women's expressive skills, men's instrumental skills are more highly rewarded, whether in terms of money or prestige. Consequently, any division of labor by gender into instrumental and expressive tasks is far from neutral in its impact on women.

Conflict theorists contend that the relationship between females and males has traditionally been one of unequal power, with men occupying the dominant position. Men may originally have become powerful in preindustrial times because their size, physical strength, and freedom from childbearing duties allowed them to dominate women physically. In contemporary societies, such considerations are not so important, yet cultural beliefs about the sexes are long established. Such beliefs support a social structure that places males in controlling positions.

Thus, conflict theorists see gender differences as a reflection of the subjugation of one group (women) by another group (men). If we use an analogy to Marx's analysis of class conflict (see Chapter 5), we can say that males are like the bourgeoisie, or capitalists; they control most of society's wealth, prestige, and power. Females are like the proletariat, or workers; they can acquire valuable resources only by following the dictates of their "bosses." Men's work is uniformly valued; women's work (whether unpaid labor in the home or wage labor outside the home) is devalued.

THE FEMINIST PERSPECTIVE

A significant component of the conflict approach to gender stratification draws on feminist theory. Although use of the term *feminist theory* is comparatively recent, the critique of women's position in society and culture goes back to some of the earliest influences on sociology. Among the most important are Mary Wollstonecraft's *A Vindication of the Rights of Women* (originally published in 1792), John Stuart Mill's *The Subjection of Women* (originally published in 1869), and Friedrich Engels's *The Origin of the Family, Private Property, and the State* (originally published in 1884).

Engels, a close associate of Karl Marx's, argued that women's subjugation coincided with the rise of private property during the Industrial Revolution. Only when people moved beyond an agrarian economy could males enjoy the luxury of leisure and withhold rewards and privileges from women. Drawing on the work of Marx and Engels, contemporary feminist theorists often view women's subordination as part of the overall exploitation and injustice they see as inherent in capitalist societies. Some radical feminist theorists, however, view the oppression of women as inevitable in *all* male-dominated societies, whether they are labeled "capitalist," "socialist," or "communist" (Feuer 1959; Tuchman 1992).

Feminist sociologists would find little to disagree with in the conflict theorists' perspective, but they are more likely to embrace a political action agenda. Feminists would also argue that the very discussion of women and society, however well meaning, has been distorted by the exclusion of women from academic thought, including sociology. In Chapter 1 we noted the many accomplishments of Jane Addams and Ida Wells-Barnett, but they generally worked outside the discipline, focusing on what we would now call *applied sociology* and social work. At the time, their efforts, while valued as humanitarian, were seen as unrelated to the research and conclusions being reached in academic circles, which of course were male academic circles (Andersen 2007; Howard 1999).

Contemporary feminists recognize the differential treatment of some women not just because of their gender, but because of their race, ethnicity, and socioeconomic status. Simply put, Whites dominate these poor, non-White women because they are non-White; men dominate them because they are women; and the affluent dominate them because they are poor. The African American feminist theorist Patricia Hill Collins (2000) has termed the convergence of social forces that contributes to the subordinate status of these low-status women the ***matrix of domination*** (see Figure 7–1).

Gender, race, and social class are not the only sources of oppression in the United States, though they do profoundly affect women and people of color. Other forms of categorization and stigmatization that might be included in the matrix are sexual orientation, religion, disability, and age. If we apply the matrix to the world as a whole, we might add citizenship status or perceived colonial or neocolonial status to the list (Winant 2006).

Though feminists have addressed themselves to the needs of minority women, these women are oppressed much more by their race and ethnicity than by their gender. The question for Latinas (Hispanic women), African American women, Asian American women, and Native American women appears to be whether they should unite with their brothers against racism or challenge them for their sexism. The answer is that our society must eradicate both sexism and racism (Beisel and Kay 2004; Breines 2007; Epstein 1999).

The discussion of gender roles among African Americans has always provoked controversy. Advocates of Black nationalism contend that feminism only distracts women from participating fully in the African American struggle. The existence of feminist groups among Blacks, in their view, simply divides the Black community, thereby serving the dominant White majority. In contrast, Black feminists such as bell hooks (1994) argue that little is to be gained by accepting the gender-role divisions of the dominant society, which place women in a separate, subservient position. Though the media commonly portray Black women in a negative light—as illiterates, welfare queens, or prostitutes—Black feminists emphasize that it is not solely Whites and the White-dominated media who focus on such negative images. Black men (most recently, Black male rap artists) have also portrayed African American women in a negative way (Raybon 1989; Threadcraft 2008).

Historically, Native Americans stand out as an exception to the patriarchal tradition in North America. At the time of the European settlers' arrival, Native American gender roles varied greatly from tribe to tribe. Southern tribes, for reasons unclear to today's scholars, were usually matriarchal and traced their descent through the mother. European missionaries, who sought to make the native peoples more like Europeans, set out to transform this arrangement, which was not entirely universal. Like members of other groups, some Native American women have resisted gender stereotypes (Marubbio 2006).

Latinas are usually considered as part of either the Hispanic or feminist movements, and their distinctive experience ignored. In the past, they have been excluded from decision making in the two social

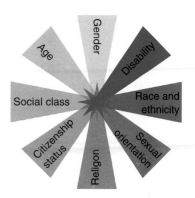

Figure 7–1
Matrix of Domination
The matrix of domination illustrates how several social factors, including gender, social class, and race and ethnicity, regularly converge to create a cumulative impact on a person's social standing.
Source: Developed by author.

Which elements of the matrix of domination privilege you? Which place you at a disadvantage?

institutions that most affect their daily lives: the family and the church. Particularly in the lower class, the Hispanic family suffers from the pervasive tradition of male domination. And the Catholic Church relegates women to supportive roles, while reserving the leadership positions for men (Browne 2001; De Anda 2004).

Prior to this chapter, much of our discussion has focused on the social effects of race and ethnicity, coupled with poverty, low incomes, and meager wealth. The matrix of domination highlights the confluence of these factors with gender discrimination, which we must include to fully understand the plight of women of color.

THE INTERACTIONIST PERSPECTIVE

While functionalists and conflict theorists who study gender distinctions typically focus on macro-level social forces and institutions, interactionist researchers tend to examine gender stratification on the micro level of everyday behavior. The key to this approach is the way gender is socially constructed in everyday interactions. We "do gender" by reinforcing traditionally masculine and feminine actions. For example, a man "does masculinity" by opening a door for his girlfriend; she "does femininity" by consenting to his assistance. Obviously, the social construction of gender goes beyond these relatively trivial rituals. Interactionists recognize, too, that people can challenge traditional gender roles. A female golfer who uses the "men's tees" and a man who actively arranges a birthday luncheon at work are redoing gender (Deutsch 2007; West and Zimmerman 1987).

One continuing subject of investigation is the role of gender in crosssex conversations (sometimes referred to as "crosstalk"), specifically the idea that men interrupt women more than women interrupt men. Interestingly, empirical research does not clearly support this assertion. True, people in positions of authority or status—who are much more likely to be male than female—do dominate interpersonal conversations. That does not necessarily mean that women per se cannot be heard, however. Future research results may de-emphasize the clichéd advice that women must speak up in favor of a focus on the situational structures that cast men in dominant positions (Cameron 2007; Hyde 2005; Tannen 1990).

Table 7–2 summarizes the major sociological perspectives on gender.

Women: The Oppressed Majority

Many people, both male and female, find it difficult to conceive of women as a subordinate and oppressed group. Yet take a look at the political structure of the United States: women remain noticeably underrepresented. As of mid-2009, for example, only 6 of the nation's 50 states had a female governor (Arizona, Connecticut, Hawaii, Michigan, North Carolina, and Washington).

summingUP

Table 7–2 Sociological Perspectives on Gender

Theoretical Perspective	Emphasis
Functionalist	Gender differentiation contributes to social stability
Conflict	Gender inequality is rooted in the female–male power relationship
Feminist	Women's subjugation is integral to society and social structure
Interactionist	Gender distinctions and doing gender are reflected in people's everyday behavior

Women have made slow but steady progress in certain political arenas. In 1981, out of 535 members of Congress, there were only 21 women: 19 in the House of Representatives and 2 in the Senate. In contrast, the Congress that held office in mid-2010 had 90 women: 73 in the House and 17 in the Senate. Yet the membership and leadership of Congress remain overwhelmingly male (Center for American Women and Politics 2010).

SEXISM AND SEX DISCRIMINATION

Just as African Americans are victimized by racism, women suffer from sexism in our society. *Sexism* is the ideology that one sex is superior to the other. The term is generally used to refer to male prejudice and discrimination against women. In Chapter 6 we noted that Blacks can suffer from both individual acts of racism and institutional discrimination. *Institutional discrimination* was defined as the denial of opportunities and equal rights to individuals or groups that results from the normal operations of a society. In the same sense, women suffer from both individual acts of sexism (such as sexist remarks or acts of violence) and institutional sexism.

It is not simply that particular men in the United States are biased in their treatment of women. All the major institutions of our society— the government, the armed forces, large corporations, the media, universities, and the medical establishment—are controlled by men. In their "normal," day-to-day operations, these institutions often discriminate against women, perpetuating sexism. For example, if the central office of a nationwide bank sets a policy that single women are a bad risk for loans—regardless of their incomes and investments—the bank will discriminate against women in state after state. It will do so even at branches in which loan officers hold no personal biases concerning women but are merely "following orders."

Our society is run by male-dominated institutions, yet with the power that flows to men come responsibility and stress. Men have higher

Think of organizations or institutions you belong to whose leadership positions are customarily held by men. What would those organizations be like if they were led by women?

reported rates of certain types of mental illness than women do and a greater likelihood of death from heart attack or stroke. The pressure on men to succeed, and then to remain on top in the competitive world of work, can be especially intense. That is not to suggest that gender stratification is as damaging to men as it is to women. But the power and privilege men enjoy are no guarantee of well-being.

SEXUAL HARASSMENT

U.S. courts recognize two kinds of sexual harassment. Legally, *sexual harassment* is defined as behavior that occurs when work benefits are made contingent on sexual favors (as a quid pro quo) or when touching, lewd comments, or the appearance of pornographic material creates a hostile environment in the workplace. In 1998 the Supreme Court ruled that harassment applies to people of the same sex as well as the opposite sex. The quid pro quo type of harassment is fairly easy to identify in a court of law. But the issue of a hostile environment has become the subject of considerable debate, both in court and among the general public (Greenhouse 1998; Lewin 1998).

Sexual harassment must be understood in the context of continuing prejudice and discrimination against women. Whether it occurs in the federal bureaucracy, in the corporate world, or in universities, sexual harassment generally takes place in organizations in which White males are at the top of the hierarchy of authority and women's work is valued less than men's. One survey of the private sector found that African American women were three times more likely than White women to experience sexual harassment. From a conflict perspective, it is not surprising that women—and especially women of color—are most likely to become victims of sexual harassment. In terms of job security, these groups are typically an organization's most vulnerable employees (J. Jones 1988).

THE STATUS OF WOMEN WORLDWIDE

A detailed overview of the status of the world's women, issued by the United Nations in 2001, noted that women and men live in two different worlds. In too many nations women are denied equal pay, sexually harassed at work, or dismissed from their jobs because they are pregnant. These abuses happen even in places where such treatment is prohibited by law. Women who assert their rights are routinely ignored or even punished for their protests. To achieve gender equality, the report concludes, society must hold the powerful accountable to women (United Nations Development Fund for Women 2009).

This critique applies to Western as well as non-Western countries. Although Westerners tend to view some societies—for example, Muslim countries—as being particularly harsh toward women, that perception is actually an overgeneralization. Muslim countries are exceedingly varied and complex and do not often fit the stereotypes created by the Western media.

Regardless of culture, however, women everywhere suffer from second-class status. It is estimated that women grow half the world's food, but they rarely own land. They constitute one-third of the world's paid labor force, but are generally found in the lowest-paying jobs. Single-parent households headed by women, which appear to be on the rise in many nations, are typically found in the poorest sections of the population. The feminization of poverty has become a global phenomenon. As in the United States, women around the world are underrepresented politically.

Despite these challenges, women are not responding passively; they are mobilizing, individually and collectively. Given the significant underrepresentation of women in government offices and national legislatures, however, the task is difficult.

In industrial countries, women's unequal status can be seen in the division of housework, as well as in the jobs they hold and the pay they earn. Sociologist Makiko Fuwa (2004) analyzed gender inequality in 22 industrial countries using data from the International Social Survey Programme. Fuwa looked first at how couples divided up their housework. Then she compared that data to society-wide measures of women's presence in high-status occupations, as well as to their wages relative to men's. She found that while gender differences in empowerment vary widely from one country to the next, equality between the sexes is rare.

Women in the Workforce of the United States

More than 30 years ago, the Commission on Civil Rights (1976:1) concluded that the passage in the Declaration of Independence proclaiming that "all men are created equal" had been taken too literally for too long. That is especially true with respect to opportunities for employment. In this section we will see how gender bias has limited women's opportunities for employment outside the home, at the same time that it forces them to carry a disproportionate burden inside the home.

LABOR FORCE PARTICIPATION

Women's participation in the paid labor force of the United States increased steadily throughout the 20th century and into the 21st century (see Figure 7–2). Today, millions of women—married or single, with or without children, pregnant or recently having given birth—are working in the labor force. Overall, 57 percent of adult women in the United States were in the labor force in 2006, compared to 41 percent in 1970. (The comparable data for men were 70 percent in 2006 and 76 percent in

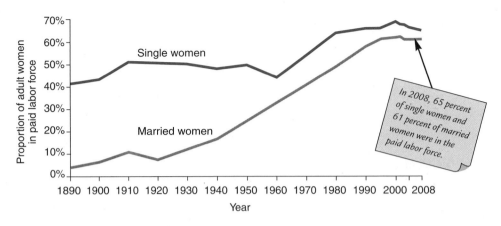

Figure 7–2

Trends in U.S. Women's Participation in the Paid Labor Force, 1890–2008

SOURCES: Bureau of the Census 1975, 2009a:377.

Think About It

In the 1960s, married women's participation in the labor force rose to a rate that approached single women's participation. At the same time, single women's participation dropped slightly—why?

1970.) Presently, 57 percent of women who are pregnant with their first child work full time, compared to less than 40 percent in the early 1960s. Among married mothers, 41 percent of those with children under age 6 were in the labor force in 2006, compared to 30 percent in 1970 (Bureau of the Census 2007a:Tables 571, 580; T. Johnson 2008).

Yet women entering the job market find their options restricted in important ways. Particularly damaging is occupational segregation, or confinement to sex-typed "women's jobs." For example, in 2008, women accounted for 98 percent of all dental hygienists and 84 percent of all librarians. Entering such sex-typed occupations places women in "service" roles that parallel the traditional gender-role standard under which housewives "serve" their husbands.

Women are *underrepresented* in occupations historically defined as "men's jobs," which often carry much greater financial rewards and prestige than women's jobs. For example, in 2008, women accounted for approximately 46 percent of the paid labor force of the United States, yet they constituted only 10 percent of civil engineers, 28 percent of all computer systems analysts, and 31 percent of all physicians (see Table 7–3).

Such occupational segregation is not unique to the United States but typical of industrial countries. In Great Britain, for example, only 29 percent of computer analysts are women, while 81 percent of cashiers and 90 percent of nurses are women (Cross and Bagilhole 2002).

Women from all groups and men from minority groups sometimes encounter attitudinal or organizational bias that prevents them from

Table 7–3 U.S. Women in Selected Occupations: Women as a Percentage of All Workers in the Occupation

Underrepresented		Overrepresented	
Aircraft pilots	3%	High school teachers	56%
Firefighters	5	Cashiers	76
Civil engineers	10	Social workers	79
Police officers	15	Elementary teachers	81
Clergy	15	File clerks	84
Photographers	16	Librarians	84
Chefs and head cooks	17	Tellers	85
Dentists	27	Registered nurses	92
Computer systems analysts	28	Word processors and typists	93
Physicians	31	Receptionists	94
Mail carriers	33	Child care workers	96
Lawyers	34	Dental hygienists	98

NOTE: Women constituted 45 percent of the entire labor force.

SOURCE: Data for 2008 reported in Bureau of the Census 2009a:387–389.

reaching their full potential. As we saw in Chapter 6, the term **glass ceiling** refers to an invisible barrier that blocks the promotion of a qualified individual in a work environment because of the individual's gender, race, or ethnicity. A study of the *Fortune* 500 largest corporations in the United States showed that in 2008, less than 15 percent of the seats on their boards of directors were held by women. Furthermore, less than 7 percent of their top earners were female (Catalyst 2009a, 2009b; Kalev 2009).

When women do gain entry to corporate boards of directors, the response in the financial world is not entirely positive. Despite objective tests showing that gender diversity in leadership is associated with strong financial performance, some investors tend to balk. Research by Frank Dobbin and Jiwook Jung (2010) shows that small investors tend to sell their shares when women become corporate leaders. These investors seem to subscribe to the stereotype that associates males with success. Their sell pattern is not characteristic of large institutional investors, who have long argued that diversification is good for business.

Worldwide, women hold less than 1 percent of corporate managerial positions. In recognition of the underrepresentation of women on boards of directors, the Norwegian legislature established minimum quotas for the number of female board members. As the architects of the plan put it, "instead of assuming what people *can't* do at work, provide opportunities for employees to prove what they can do." The goal was not complete equity for women, but 40 percent representation by 2008. The percentage in Norway now stands at 36—much higher than Europe's average of 9 percent. About 1 in 6 of Norway's biggest companies have failed to meet the quota, however, and a handful still have no women on their boards (Center for Corporate Diversity 2008; Fouché 2008; Goering 2008).

THE SOCIAL CONSEQUENCES OF WOMEN'S EMPLOYMENT

Today, many women face the challenge of trying to juggle work and family. Their situation has many social consequences. For one thing, it puts pressure on child care facilities, public financing of day care, and even the fast-food industry, which provides many of the meals women used to prepare themselves. For another, it raises questions about what responsibility male wage earners have in the household.

Who does the housework when women become productive wage earners? Studies indicate that there is a clear gender gap in the performance of housework, although the differences are narrowing. Women do more housework and spend more time on child care than men, whether on a workday or a nonworkday. Taken together, then, a woman's workday on and off the job is much longer than a man's (Sayer et al. 2004).

Sociologist Arlie Hochschild (1989, 1990, 2005) has used the phrase *second shift* to describe the double burden—work outside the home followed by child care and housework—that many women face and few men share equitably. On the basis of interviews with and observations of

In your opinion, how important is it for a couple to share the housework?

52 couples over an eight-year period, Hochschild reports that wives (but not their husbands) drive home from the office while planning domestic schedules and play dates for their children—and then begin their second shift. Drawing on national studies, she concludes that women spend 15 fewer hours in leisure activities each week than their husbands. In a year, these women work an extra month of 24-hour days because of the "second shift"; over a dozen years, they work an extra year of 24-hour days. Hochschild found that the women she studied were fraying at the edges, and so were their careers and their marriages. With such reports in mind, many feminists have advocated greater governmental and corporate support for child care, more flexible family leave policies, and other reforms designed to ease the burden on the nation's families (Moen and Roehling 2005).

The greater amounts of time women put into caring for their children, and to a lesser degree into housework, take a special toll on women who are pursuing careers. In a 2005 survey published in the *Harvard Business Review,* about 40 percent of women indicated that they had voluntarily left work for months or years, compared to only 24 percent of men. As Figure 7–3 shows, women were much more likely than men to take time off for family reasons.

Though women in the United States have a long way to go toward equality in housework, they are doing as well as or better than women in most other countries, including industrial nations. By one measure, 30 percent of the couples in U.S. households share most of the housework, compared to 4 percent in Japan, 25 percent in Great Britain, 27 percent in Sweden, and 32 percent in Canada (Geist 2005).

Figure 7–3
Why Leave Work?
*Not one of top 5 reasons

NOTE: *Based on a representative Harris Interactive survey of "highly qualified" workers, defined as those with a graduate degree, a professional degree, or a high honors undergraduate degree.* SOURCE: Figure adapted from Sylvia Ann Hewlett and Carolyn Burk Luce, 2005. "Off-Ramps and On-Ramps: Keeping Talented Women on the Road to Success," *Harvard Business Review,* March 2005. Copyright © 2005 by the Harvard Business School Publishing Corporation, all rights reserved. Reprinted by permission of Harvard Business Review.

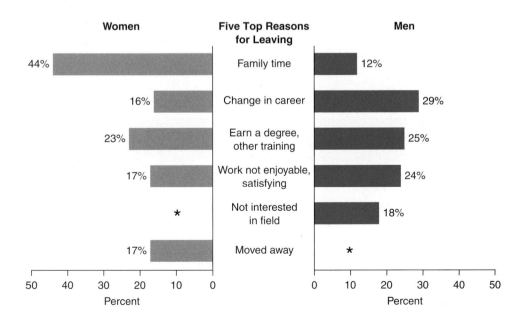

Sociology Matters

Sociology matters because it explains how we come to be feminine or masculine.

- What was your childhood idea of how a person of your gender should behave, and where did you get it? Did you ever feel confined by the gender roles you learned as a child?

- Has your concept of your gender role changed over time? If so, who or what influenced you to change your thinking and behavior? Will your children learn the same gender roles as you? Why or why not?

Sociology matters because it raises our awareness of the unequal treatment of women and men.

- Have you and a friend ever been treated differently because one of you was male and the other was female? If so, did you resent the unequal treatment? Can you think of a way to change it?

- Do you believe men and women will ever be equal? Why or why not?

Sociology matters because it highlights the many different social statuses that affect men's and women's lives.

- Have you begun to pay more attention to the ways in which gender, social class, and even citizenship status affect people's lives?

- Which statuses have the biggest effect on those who are closest to you?

CHAPTER RESOURCES

Summary

Like race and ethnicity, gender has an enormous influence on people's lives. In this chapter we explained the cultural basis for gender and examined the ways in which gender defines a person's social roles. We discussed four theoretical perspectives on gender and studied the economic and social effects of prejudice and discrimination on women around the world.

1. Like race, gender is an ascribed status that is socially constructed. **Gender roles** show up in our work and behavior and in how we react to others. Throughout history, these roles have restricted women much more than they have men.

2. In the United States, **homophobia**—fear of and prejudice against homosexuality—contributes to rigid gender-role socialization. Family, peers, and the media reinforce gender-role stereotypes for both sexes.

3. Though men may exhibit a variety of different gender roles, called **multiple masculinities,** society reinforces their traditional role of dominating women.

4. Anthropological research points to the importance of cultural conditioning in defining the social roles of males and females.

5. Functionalists maintain that well-defined gender roles contribute to a society's stability. They stress the **instrumentality,** or emphasis on tasks, of the male role and the **expressiveness,** or emphasis on harmony, of the female role.

6. Conflict theorists stress men's dominance over women. They see women's inequality of income, wealth, prestige, and power as the result of men's deliberate subjugation of women.

7. Like conflict theorists, feminists stress the power struggle between the sexes. More than conflict theorists, they tend to see women's inequality as part of the exploitation inherent in capitalist societies.

8. Interactionists stress that gender is socially constructed through people's everyday interactions. People "do gender" by reinforcing traditionally masculine and feminine behavior.

9. Women experience a special kind of prejudice known as **sexism.** They suffer institutional discrimination in the form of lower pay and restricted opportunities as well as **sexual harassment** in school and on the job.

10. Worldwide, women are undereducated, underpaid, and overworked. In the United States, women who work in the paid labor force are restricted by a **glass ceiling** that blocks their promotion to higher-paying jobs. These women commonly work a **second shift** when they get home.

www.mhhe.com/schaefersm5e
Visit the Online Learning Center for *Sociology Matters* to access quizzes, review activities, and other learning tools.

Key Terms

expressiveness, 195

gender role, 190

glass ceiling, 203

homophobia, 190

instrumentality, 195

matrix of
    domination, 197

multiple
    masculinities, 193

second shift, 204

sexism, 199

sexual
    harassment, 200

Social Institutions: Family and Religion

CHAPTER 8

**Sociological Perspectives
on Social Institutions**

The Family: A Global View

**Sociological Perspectives
on the Family**

**Religion as a Social
Institution**

Components of Religion

Among the Nyinba people of
Nepal and Tibet, a woman
may be married to more than
one man at a time, usually
brothers. This system allows sons to share the limited amount of good
land they may inherit. Among the Betsileo of Madagascar, a man has
multiple wives, each one living in a different village where he cultivates
rice. Wherever he has the best rice field, that wife is considered his first
or senior wife. Among the Yanomami of Brazil and Venezuela, it is considered proper to have sexual relations with your opposite-sex cousins
if they are the children of your mother's brother or your father's sister. But if your opposite-sex cousins are the children of your mother's
sister or your father's brother, the same practice is considered to be
incest. What can we learn from such varied patterns of family life?
Though they may seem to defy generalization, sociologists have discovered that the stunning diversity of families around the world masks
similarities in their social function (Haviland et al. 2011; Kottak 2011;
Levine 1988; Stockard 2002).

Similar observations may be made about the diversity of religion
around the world. When we in the United States think of religion, a
variety of images may spring to mind. We may picture a solemn prayer
service in a small New England town, a passionate revival meeting in
the Deep South, or a Hare Krishna group chanting on the streets of

209

San Francisco. If we think of worldwide religious observances, we may imagine Islamic travelers on pilgrimage to Mecca, Orthodox Jews praying at Jerusalem's Western Wall, or an African tribe marking the birth of a child through ritual. Around the world, we find an amazing diversity in religion. Yet sociologists would stress the social functions that all religions perform.

Religion and the family are both **social institutions**—organized patterns of beliefs and behavior that are centered on basic social needs, such as replacing personnel (the family) and preserving order (the government). All societies have social institutions; they may be thought of as *cultural universals*—general practices found in every culture, such as sports, food preparation, and funeral ceremonies (see Chapter 2). The fact that all societies have these cultural universals is not surprising, for they meet our needs for food, clothing, and shelter as well as for support and reassurance, occupational training, and social order. In this chapter we will begin by considering social institutions from the three major sociological perspectives: functionalist, conflict, and interactionist. Then we will apply those perspectives to two major social institutions, the family and religion. In Chapter 9 we will extend the analysis to three more social institutions: education, government, and the economy (Murdock 1945).

Sociological Perspectives on Social Institutions

Though social institutions are fundamental to the well-being of any society, not all sociologists see them in the same way. Functionalists, as we will see, stress the basic needs that social institutions fulfill. But conflict theorists see social institutions such as the family and religion as mixed blessings—as sources of inequality and oppression as well as of nurturing and reassurance. Interactionists stress the ways in which social institutions help to define individuals' social roles and statuses.

FUNCTIONALIST VIEW

One way to study social institutions is to examine how they fulfill essential functions. To survive, any society or relatively permanent group must accomplish five major tasks, or functional prerequisites (see Table 8–1).

1. *Replacing personnel.* Any group or society must replace personnel when they die, leave, or become incapacitated. This function is accomplished through such means as immigration, annexation of neighboring groups, acquisition of slaves, or sexual reproduction. The Shakers, a religious sect that came to the United States in 1774, are a conspicuous example of a group that has *failed* to replace personnel. Their religious beliefs commit the Shakers to celibacy;

Table 8–1 Five Major Functions of Institutions

Functional Prerequisite	Related Social Institutions
Replacing personnel	Family Government (immigration)
Teaching new recruits	Family (basic skills) Economy (occupations) Education (schools) Mass media Religion (sacred teachings)
Producing and distributing goods and services	Family (food preparation) Economy Government (regulations regarding labor and commerce) Health care system
Preserving order	Family (child rearing, regulation of sexual behavior) Government Religion (morals)
Providing and maintaining a sense of purpose	Government (patriotism) Religion

to survive, the group must recruit new members. At first, the Shakers proved quite successful in attracting members, reaching a peak of about 6,000 in the 1840s. As of 2010, however, the only Shaker community left in this country was a farm in Maine with three members—one man and two women (Schaefer and Zellner 2011).

2. *Teaching new recruits.* No group or society can survive if many of its members reject the established behavior and responsibilities. Thus, finding or producing new members is not sufficient. The group or society must encourage recruits to learn and accept its values and customs. Such learning can take place formally in schools (where learning is a manifest function) or informally, through interaction and negotiation in peer groups (where instruction is a latent function).

3. *Producing and distributing goods and services.* Any relatively permanent group or society must provide and distribute desired goods and services to its members. Each society establishes a set of rules for the allocation of financial and other resources. These rules must satisfy the needs of most members to some extent, or the society will risk the possibility of discontent and ultimately disorder.

4. *Preserving order.* Throughout the world, indigenous and aboriginal peoples have struggled to protect themselves from outside invaders, with varying degrees of success. Failure to preserve order and defend against conquest leads to the death not only of a people but of a culture as well.

5. *Providing and maintaining a sense of purpose.* People must feel motivated to continue as members of a group or society in order to fulfill the first four requirements. On January 20, 2009, in the midst of what would prove the worst economic crisis since the Great Depression, some 2 million Americans crowded the National Mall to witness the inauguration of President Barack Obama, the first African American to be elected to the nation's highest office. The celebration, an expression of both patriotism and Black pride, convinced people of all races that change was possible and better times lay ahead. Faced with huge layoffs and massive home foreclosures, Americans heard the new president's call to serve their nation. Patriotism and racial pride, then, can help people to develop and maintain a sense of purpose. For others, tribal identities, religious values, or personal moral codes are especially meaningful. Whatever the motivator, in any society there remains one common and critical reality: if an individual does not have a sense of purpose, he or she has little reason to contribute to a society's survival.

This list of functional prerequisites does not specify *how* a society and its corresponding social institutions should perform each task. For example, one society may protect itself from external attack by amassing a frightening arsenal of weaponry, while another may make a determined effort to remain neutral in world politics and to promote cooperative relationships with its neighbors. No matter what the strategy, any society or relatively permanent group must attempt to satisfy all these functional prerequisites for survival. If a society fails on even one condition, it runs the risk of extinction (Aberle et al. 1950; Mack and Bradford 1979).

CONFLICT VIEW

Conflict theorists do not concur with the functionalist approach to social institutions. Although theorists of both perspectives agree that institutions are organized to meet basic social needs, conflict theorists object to the implication that the outcome is necessarily efficient and socially desirable.

From a conflict perspective, the present organization of social institutions is no accident. Major institutions, such as education, help to maintain the privileges of the most powerful individuals and groups in a society, while contributing to the powerlessness of others. To give one example, public schools in the United States are financed largely through property taxes, an arrangement that allows people from more affluent areas to provide their children with better-equipped schools and better-paid teachers than people from low-income areas can provide. As a result, children from prosperous communities are better prepared to compete academically than children from impoverished communities. The structure of the nation's educational system permits and even promotes such unequal treatment of schoolchildren.

Conflict theorists argue that social institutions such as education are inherently conservative. Without question, it has been difficult to implement educational reforms that promote equal opportunity—whether bilingual education, school desegregation, or mainstreaming of students with disabilities. From a functionalist perspective, social change can be dysfunctional, since it often leads to instability. But from a conflict view, why should we preserve the existing social structure if it is unfair and discriminatory?

Social institutions also operate in gendered and racist environments, as conflict theorists, as well as feminists and interactionists, have pointed out. In schools, offices, and government institutions, assumptions about what people can do reflect the sexism and racism of the larger society. For instance, many people assume that women cannot make tough decisions—even those in the top echelons of corporate management. Others assume that all Black students at elite colleges represent affirmative action admissions. Inequality based on gender, economic status, race, and ethnicity thrives in such an environment—to which we might add discrimination based on age, physical disability, and sexual orientation. The truth of this assertion can be seen in routine decisions by employers on how to advertise jobs as well as whether to provide fringe benefits such as child care and parental leave.

INTERACTIONIST VIEW

Social institutions affect our everyday behavior, whether we are driving down the street or waiting in a long shopping line. Sociologist Mitchell Duneier (1994a, 1994b) studied the social behavior of the word processors, all women, who work in the service center of a large Chicago law firm. Duneier was interested in the informal social norms that emerged in this work environment and the rich social network that the female employees had created.

The Network Center, as it is called, is a single, windowless room in a large office building where the law firm occupies seven floors. The center is staffed by two shifts of word processors, who work either from 4:00 P.M. to midnight or from midnight to 8:00 A.M. Each word processor works in a cubicle with just enough room for her keyboard, terminal, printer, and telephone. Work assignments for the word processors are placed in a central basket and completed according to precise procedures.

At first glance, we might think that these women labor with little social contact, apart from limited work breaks and occasional conversations with their supervisor. However, drawing on the interactionist perspective, Duneier learned that despite working in a large office, these women found private moments to talk (often in the halls or outside the washroom) and share a critical view of the law firm's attorneys and daytime secretaries. Indeed, the word processors routinely suggested that

Table 8–2 Sociological Perspectives on Social Institutions

Perspective	Role of Social Institutions	Focus
Functionalist	Meeting basic social needs	Essential functions
Conflict	Meeting basic social needs	Maintenance of privileges and inequality
Interactionist	Fostering everyday behavior	Influence of the roles and statuses we accept

Do you think that social networks might be more important to a migrant worker in California than to someone with political and social clout? Why or why not?

their assignments represented work that the "lazy" secretaries should have completed during the normal workday. One word processor in particular resented the lawyers' superior attitude and pointedly refused to recognize or speak with any attorney who would not address her by name (Duneier 1994b).

Interactionist theorists emphasize that our social behavior is conditioned by the roles and statuses we accept, the groups we belong to, and the institutions within which we function. For example, the social roles associated with being a judge occur within the larger context of the criminal justice system. The status of "judge" stands in relation to other statuses, such as attorney, plaintiff, defendant, and witness as well as to the social institution of government. Although courts and jails have great symbolic importance, the judicial system derives its continued significance from the roles people carry out in their social interactions (Berger and Luckmann 1966).

Table 8–2 summarizes the three major sociological perspectives on social institutions.

The Family: A Global View

As we saw at the beginning of this chapter, there are many variations in "the family" from one culture to the next. Yet the family as a social institution exists in all cultures. Moreover, certain general principles concerning its composition, kinship patterns, and authority patterns are universal.

COMPOSITION: WHAT IS THE FAMILY?

A *family* may be defined as a set of people who are related by blood, marriage (or some other agreed-upon relationship), or adoption who share the primary responsibility for reproduction and caring for members of society. If we were to take our information on what a family is from what we see on television, we might come up with some strange scenarios. The media don't always present a realistic view of the family. Moreover, many people still think of the family in very narrow terms—as a married couple and their unmarried children living together.

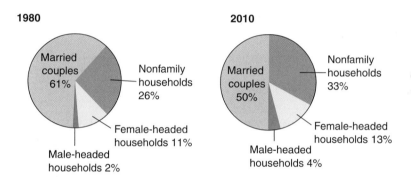

Figure 8–1
U.S. Households by Family Type, 1940–2010

NOTE: *Nonfamily households include women and men living alone.*

SOURCE: Author's estimate based on Bureau of the Census 1996; Jason Fields 2004; see also McFalls 2003:23.

However, that is but one type of family, what sociologists refer to as a **nuclear family.** The term *nuclear family* is well chosen, since this type of family serves as the nucleus, or core, on which larger family groups are built.

Most people in the United States see the nuclear family as the preferred family arrangement. Yet by 2000, only about a third of the nation's family households fit this model. The proportion of households in the United States composed of married couples with children at home has decreased steadily over the last 30 years and is expected to continue shrinking. At the same time, the number of female-headed households has increased (see Figure 8–1). Similar trends are evident in other industrialized nations, including Canada, Great Britain, and Japan.

A family in which relatives—such as grandparents, aunts, or uncles—live in the same home as parents and their children is known as an **extended family.** Although not common, such living arrangements do exist in the United States. The structure of the extended family offers certain advantages over that of the nuclear family. Crises such as death, divorce, and illness put less strain on family members, since there are more people who can provide assistance and emotional support. In addition, the extended family constitutes a larger economic unit than the nuclear family. If the family is engaged in a common enterprise—a farm or small business—the additional family members may represent the difference between prosperity and failure.

In considering these differing family types, we have limited ourselves to the form of marriage that is characteristic of the United States— monogamy. The term *monogamy* describes a form of marriage in which one woman and one man are married only to each other. Some observers, noting the high rate of divorce in the United States, have suggested that "serial monogamy" is a more accurate description of the form that monogamy takes in the United States. In *serial monogamy,* a person may have several spouses in his or her life, but only one spouse at a time.

Serial monogamy is certainly more common today than it was a century ago due to a greater incidence and acceptance of divorce. In the United States and many other countries, divorce began to increase in the late 1960s but then leveled off; since the late 1980s, it has declined by 30 percent. This trend is due partly to the aging of the baby boomer population and the corresponding decline in the proportion of people of marriageable age. However, it also indicates an increase in marital stability in recent years (Coontz 2006).

Some cultures allow an individual to have several husbands or wives simultaneously. This form of marriage is known as *polygamy.* In fact, most societies throughout the world, past and present, have preferred polygamy to monogamy. Anthropologist George Murdock (1949, 1957) sampled 565 societies and found that some type of polygamy was the preferred form in more than 80 percent. While polygamy declined steadily through most of the 20th century and into the 21st, in at least 5 African nations 20 percent or more of the men are still living in polygamous unions (Population Reference Bureau 1996).

There are two basic types of polygamy. According to Murdock, the most common—endorsed by the majority of cultures he sampled—was *polygyny,* in which a husband may have several wives at the same time. The wives are often sisters, who are expected to hold similar values and to have experience sharing a household. In polygynous societies, relatively few men have multiple spouses. Most individuals live in monogamous families; having multiple wives is viewed as a mark of status.

The other principal variation of polygamy is *polyandry,* in which a woman may have several husbands at the same time. Such is the case in Tibet, as we saw in the chapter opening. Polyandry, however, is exceedingly rare. It is accepted in some extremely poor societies that practice female infanticide (the killing of baby girls) and thus have a relatively small number of women. Like many other societies, polyandrous cultures devalue the social worth of women.

Today, recognized family patterns have expanded to include single-parent families and households headed by same-sex couples. The lifestyles of lesbians and gay men are varied. Some live in long-term, monogamous relationships; others live alone or with roommates.

Use Your Sociological Imagination

In a society that maximizes the welfare of all family members, how easy should it be for couples to divorce? How easy should it be to get married?

Some remain in "empty-shell" heterosexual marriages and do not publicly acknowledge their homosexuality. Others live with children from a former marriage or with adopted children. Based on election exit polls, researchers for the National Health and Social Life Survey and the Voter News Service estimate that 2 to 5 percent of the adult population identify themselves as either gay or lesbian. An analysis of the 2000 Census shows a minimum of at least 600,000 gay households, and a gay and lesbian adult population approaching 10 million (Laumann et al. 1994b:293; David M. Smith and Gates 2001).

KINSHIP PATTERNS: TO WHOM ARE WE RELATED?

Many of us can trace our roots by looking at a family tree or listening to our elders talk about their lives—and the lives of ancestors who died long before we were born. Yet a person's lineage is more than a personal history; it reflects societal patterns that govern descent. In every culture, children encounter relatives to whom they are expected to show an emotional attachment. This state of being related to others is called *kinship.* Kinship is culturally learned, rather than being totally determined by biological or marital ties. For example, adoption creates a kinship tie that is legally acknowledged and socially accepted.

The family and the kin group are not necessarily one and the same. The family is a household unit, but kin do not always live together or function as a collective body on a daily basis. Kin groups include aunts, uncles, cousins, in-laws, and so forth. In a society such as the United States, the kinship group may come together only rarely, usually for a wedding or funeral. However, kinship ties frequently create obligations and responsibilities. We may feel compelled to assist our kin, and we feel free to call upon relatives for many types of aid, including loans and babysitting.

How do we identify kinship groups? The principle of descent assigns people to kinship groups according to their relationship to their mother or father. There are three primary ways of determining descent. The United States follows the system of *bilateral descent,* in which both sides of a person's family are regarded as equally important. For example, no higher value is given to the brothers of one's father than to the brothers of one's mother.

Most societies—according to George Murdock, 64 percent—favor one side of the family or the other in tracing descent. *Patrilineal* (from Latin *pater,* "father") *descent* favors the father's relatives in terms of property, inheritance, and emotional ties. *Matrilineal* (from Latin *mater,* "mother") *descent* favors the mother's relatives.

New forms of reproductive technology will soon force a new way of looking at kinship. Today, a combination of biological and social processes can "create" a family member, requiring that more distinctions be made about who is related to whom.

In your own family, which relatives do you have a significant relationship with? Which do you hardly ever see?

AUTHORITY PATTERNS: WHO RULES?

Imagine that you have recently married and must begin to make decisions about the future of your new family. You and your spouse face many questions. Where will you live? How will you furnish your home? Who will do the cooking, the shopping, the cleaning? Whose friends will be invited to dinner? Each time a decision must be made, an issue is raised: Who has the power to make the decision? In simple terms, who rules the family? Conflict theorists examine these questions in the context of traditional gender distinctions, which have given men a dominant position over women.

Societies vary in the way that power is distributed within the family. If a society expects men to dominate in family decision making, it is termed a *patriarchy.* In patriarchal societies such as Iran, the eldest male frequently wields the greatest power, although wives are expected to be treated with respect and kindness. An Iranian woman's status is typically defined by her relationship to a male relative, usually as a wife or daughter. In many patriarchal societies, women find it more difficult to obtain a divorce than a man does. By contrast, in a *matriarchy,* women dominate in family decision making. Matriarchies are rare; they emerged among Native American tribal societies and in nations where men were absent for long periods, for warfare or food gathering expeditions (Farr 1999).

In a third type of authority pattern, the *egalitarian family,* spouses are regarded as equals. This pattern does not mean that each decision is shared, however. Wives may hold authority in some spheres, husbands in others. Many sociologists believe the egalitarian family has begun to replace the patriarchal family as the social norm in the United States.

Clearly, there is great variation in the composition, kinship patterns, and authority patterns of families around the world. Yet as we have seen, the family fulfills certain universal social functions. In the next section we will examine those functions from three different sociological perspectives.

Sociological Perspectives on the Family

Do we really need the family? A century ago, Friedrich Engels ([1884] 1959), a colleague of Karl Marx's, described the family as the ultimate source of social inequality because of its role in the transfer of power, property, and privilege. More recently, conflict theorists have argued that the family contributes to societal injustice, denies women opportunities that are extended to men, and limits freedom in sexual expression and mate selection. In contrast, the functionalist perspective focuses on the ways in which the family gratifies the needs of its members and contributes to social stability. The interactionist view considers the intimate, face-to-face relationships that occur in the family. And the feminist approach examines the role of the wife and mother, especially in the absence of an adult male.

FUNCTIONALIST VIEW

The family performs six major functions, first outlined nearly 80 years ago by sociologist William F. Ogburn (Ogburn and Tibbits 1934):

1. *Reproduction.* For a society to maintain itself, it must replace dying members. In this sense, the family contributes to human survival through its function of reproduction.

2. *Protection.* Unlike the young of other animal species, human infants need constant care and economic security. In all cultures, the family assumes the ultimate responsibility for the protection and upbringing of children.

3. *Socialization.* Parents and other kin monitor a child's behavior and transmit the norms, values, and language of their culture to the child.

4. *Regulation of sexual behavior.* Sexual norms are subject to change both over time (for instance, in the customs for dating) and across cultures (compare strict Saudi Arabia to the more permissive Denmark). Whatever the period or cultural values of a society, however, standards of sexual behavior are most clearly defined within the family circle.

5. *Affection and companionship.* Ideally, the family provides members with warm and intimate relationships, helping them to feel satisfied

and secure. Of course, a family member may find such rewards outside the family—from peers, in school, at work—and may even perceive the home as an unpleasant or abusive setting. Nevertheless, we expect our relatives to understand us, to care for us, and to be there for us when we need them.

6. *Provision of social status.* We inherit a social position because of the family background and reputation of our parents and siblings. The family presents the newborn child with an ascribed status based on race and ethnicity that helps to determine his or her place within society's stratification system. Moreover, family resources affect children's ability to pursue certain opportunities, such as higher education and special lessons.

Traditionally, the family has fulfilled a number of other functions, such as providing religious training, education, and recreation. But Ogburn argued that other social institutions have gradually assumed many of those functions. Education once took place by the family fireside; now it is the responsibility of professionals working in schools and colleges. Even the family's traditional recreational function has been transferred to outside groups such as Little Leagues, athletic clubs, and online groups.

CONFLICT VIEW

Conflict theorists view the family not as a contributor to social stability but as a reflection of the inequality in wealth and power that is found within the larger society. Feminist and conflict theorists note that the family has traditionally legitimized and perpetuated male dominance. Throughout most of human history—and in a wide range of societies—husbands have exercised overwhelming power and authority in the family. Not until the first wave of contemporary feminism in the United States during the mid-1800s was a substantial challenge made to the historic status of wives and children as the legal property of husbands.

While the egalitarian family has become a more common pattern in the United States in recent decades—owing in good part to the activism of feminists beginning in the late 1960s and early 1970s—male dominance over the family has hardly disappeared. Sociologists have found that while married men are increasing their involvement in child care, their wives still perform a disproportionate amount of it. Furthermore, for every stay-at-home dad there are 38 stay-at-home moms. And unfortunately, many husbands reinforce their power and control over wives and children through acts of domestic violence (Jason Fields 2004:11–12; Sayer et al. 2004).

Conflict theorists also view the family as an economic unit that contributes to societal injustice. The family is the basis for transferring power, property, and privilege from one generation to the next. Although the United States is viewed widely as a land of opportunity, social mobility is restricted in important ways. Children inherit the privileged or less-than-privileged social and economic status of their parents (and in some cases, of earlier generations as well). As conflict theorists point out, the social class of parents significantly influences children's socialization experiences and the degree of protection they receive. Thus, the socioeconomic status of a child's family will have a marked influence on his or her nutrition, health care, housing, educational opportunities, and, in many respects, life chances as an adult.

INTERACTIONIST VIEW

Interactionists focus on the micro level of family and other intimate relationships. They are interested in how individuals interact with one another, whether they are cohabiting partners or longtime married couples. For example, in a study of both Black and White two-parent households, researchers found that when fathers are more involved with their children (reading to them, helping them with homework, or restricting their television viewing), children have fewer behavior problems, get along better with others, and are more responsible (Mosley and Thomson 1995).

Another interactionist study might examine the role of the stepparent. The increased number of single parents who remarry has sparked interest in those who are helping to raise other people's children. Studies have found that stepmothers are more likely than stepfathers to accept the blame for bad relations with their stepchildren. Interactionists theorize that stepfathers (like most fathers) may simply be unaccustomed to interacting directly with children when the mother isn't there (Bray and Kelly 1999; Furstenberg and Cherlin 1991).

FEMINIST VIEW

Because "women's work" has traditionally focused on family life, feminist sociologists have taken a strong interest in the family as a social institution. As we saw in Chapter 7, research on gender roles in child care and household chores has been extensive. Sociologists have looked particularly closely at how women's work outside the home impacts their child care and housework—duties Arlie Hochschild (1989, 1990) has referred to as the "second shift." Today, researchers recognize that for many women, the second shift includes the care of aging parents as well.

Feminist theorists have urged social scientists and social agencies to rethink the notion that families in which no adult male is present are automatically a cause for concern, or even dysfunctional. They have also contributed to research on single women, single-parent households, and lesbian couples. In the case of single mothers, researchers have focused on the resiliency of many such households, despite economic stress. According to Velma McBride Murray and her colleagues (2001) at the

summingUP

Table 8–3 Sociological Perspectives on the Family

Theoretical Perspective	Emphasis
Functionalist	The family as a contributor to social stability Roles of family members
Conflict	The family as a perpetuator of inequality Transmission of poverty or wealth across generations
Interactionist	Relationships among family members
Feminist	The family as a perpetuator of gender roles Female-headed households

University of Georgia, such studies show that among African Americans, single mothers draw heavily on kinfolk for material resources, parenting advice, and social support. Considering feminist research on the family as a whole, one researcher concluded that the family is the "source of women's strength" (V. Taylor et al. 2007).

Finally, feminists stress the need to investigate neglected topics in family studies. For instance, in a small but significant number of dual income households, the wife earns a higher income than the husband. Researchers estimate that in 11 percent of marriages, the wife earns at least 60 percent of the family's income. Yet beyond individual case studies, little research has been done on how these families may differ from those in which the husband is the major breadwinner (Wills and Risman 2006).

Table 8–3 summarizes the four major theoretical perspectives on the family.

Religion as a Social Institution

According to Émile Durkheim ([1912] 2001), *religion* is a unified system of beliefs and practices relative to sacred things. As a cultural universal, religion plays a basic role that includes both manifest and latent social functions. Among its *manifest* (open and stated) functions, religion defines the spiritual world and gives meaning to the divine. Religion also provides an explanation for events that seem difficult to understand, such as what lies beyond the grave. In contrast, the *latent* functions of religion are unintended, covert, or hidden. Even though the manifest function of church services is to offer a forum for religious worship, they might at the same time fulfill a latent function as a meeting ground for unmarried members.

In this section we'll consider four functions that sociologists have stressed in their study of religion. We'll see that religion helps to integrate society and provides people with social support in time of need.

We'll discuss Max Weber's view of religion as a source of social change. Finally, we'll examine the conflict perspective on religion as a means of social control. Note that for the most part, religion's impact is best understood from a macro-level viewpoint, oriented toward the larger society. The social support function is an exception: it is best viewed on the micro level, directed toward the individual.

THE INTEGRATIVE FUNCTION OF RELIGION

Émile Durkheim viewed religion as an integrative power in human society—a perspective that is reflected in functionalist thought today. Durkheim sought to answer a perplexing question: "How can human societies be held together when they are composed of individuals and social groups with diverse interests and aspirations?" In his view, religious bonds often transcend these personal and divisive forces. Durkheim acknowledged that religion is not the only integrative force; nationalism or patriotism may serve the same end.

How does religion provide this "societal glue"? Religion, whether it be Buddhism, Islam, Christianity, or Judaism (see Table 8–4), offers people meaning and purpose. It gives them certain ultimate values and ends to hold in common. Although those values and ends are subjective and not always fully accepted, they help society to function as an integrated social system. For example, funerals, weddings, bar and bat mitzvahs,

summingUP

Table 8–4 Major World Religions

Faith	Current Following, in Millions (and Percent of World Population)	Primary Location of Followers Today	Founder (and Approximate Birth Date)	Important Texts (and Holy Sites)
Buddhism	463 (6.8%)	Southeast Asia, Mongolia, Tibet	Gautama Siddhartha (563 B.C.)	Triptaka (areas in Nepal)
Christianity	2,264 (33.2%)	Europe, North America, South America	Jesus (6 B.C.)	Bible (Jerusalem, Rome)
Hinduism	935 (13.7%)	India, Indian communities overseas	No specific founder (1500 B.C.)	Sruti and Smrti texts (seven sacred cities, including Vavansi)
Islam	1,523 (22.3%)	Middle East, Central Asia, North Africa, Indonesia	Muhammad (A.D. 570)	Qur'an or Koran (Mecca, Medina, Jerusalem)
Judaism	15 (0.2%)	Israel, United States, France, Russia	Abraham (2000 B.C.)	Torah, Talmud (Jerusalem)

SOURCES: Author based on Brittanica Online 2010; Swatos 1998.

What evidence do you see of different religions in the area surrounding your college or university? What about on campus?

and confirmations serve to integrate people into larger communities through shared beliefs and values about the ultimate questions of life.

Religion also serves to bind people together in times of crisis and confusion. Immediately after the terrorist attacks of September 11, 2001, on New York City and Washington, D.C., attendance at worship services in the United States increased dramatically. Muslim, Jewish, and Christian clerics made joint appearances to honor the dead and urge citizens not to retaliate against those who looked, dressed, or sounded different from others. The integrative power of religion can be seen, too, in the role that churches, synagogues, and mosques have traditionally played and continue to play for immigrant groups in the United States. For example, Roman Catholic immigrants may settle near a parish church that offers services in their native language, such as Polish or Spanish. Similarly, Korean immigrants may join a Presbyterian church with many Korean American members and with religious practices like those of churches in Korea. Like other religious organizations, these Roman Catholic and Presbyterian churches help to integrate immigrants into their new homeland.

Religious conflict is evident in the United States as well; sociologist James Davison Hunter (1991) refers to it as a "culture war." In many communities, Christian fundamentalists, conservative Catholics, and Orthodox Jews have joined forces in a battle against their liberal counterparts for control of the secular culture. The battlefield is an array of familiar social issues, among them multiculturalism, child care, abortion, home schooling, gay rights, media censorship, and government funding for the arts.

RELIGION AND SOCIAL SUPPORT

Most of us find it difficult to accept the stressful events of life—the death of a loved one, a serious injury, bankruptcy, divorce, and so forth. Our difficulty is especially pronounced when something "senseless" happens. How can family and friends come to terms with the death of a talented college student, not even 20 years old?

Through its emphasis on the divine and the supernatural, religion allows us to "do something" about the calamities we face. In some faiths, adherents can offer sacrifices or pray to a deity in the belief that such acts will change their earthly condition. At a more basic level, religion encourages us to view our personal misfortunes as relatively unimportant in the broader perspective of human history—or even as part of an undisclosed divine purpose. Friends and relatives of the deceased college student may see his death as being "God's will," as having some ultimate benefit that we cannot understand now. This perspective may be much more comforting than the terrifying feeling that any of us can die senselessly at any moment—that there is no divine "answer" to why one person lives a long and full life, while another dies tragically at a relatively early age.

RELIGION AND SOCIAL CHANGE

When a person seems driven to work and succeed, we often attribute his or her ambition to the "Protestant work ethic." The term comes from the writings of Max Weber, who carefully examined the connection between religious allegiance and capitalist development. Weber's findings appeared in his pioneering work *The Protestant Ethic and the Spirit of Capitalism* ([1904] 2009).

Weber noted that in European nations with both Protestant and Catholic citizens, an overwhelming number of business leaders, owners of capital, and skilled workers were Protestant. In his view, this pattern was no mere coincidence. Weber pointed out that the followers of John Calvin (1509–1564), a leader of the Protestant Reformation, emphasized a disciplined work ethic, this-worldly concerns, and a rational orientation to life that he termed the **Protestant ethic.** One byproduct of the Protestant ethic was a drive to accumulate savings that could be used for future investment. This "spirit of capitalism," to use Weber's phrase, contrasted with the moderate work hours, leisurely work habits, and lack of ambition that he saw as typical of the times.

Few books on the sociology of religion have aroused as much commentary and criticism as Weber's work. It has been hailed as one of the most important theoretical works in the field and an excellent example of macro-level analysis. Like Durkheim, Weber demonstrated that religion is not solely a matter of intimate personal belief. Rather, the collective nature of religion has social consequences for society as a whole.

Weber provided a convincing description of the origins of European capitalism. But the capitalist economic system has since been adopted by non-Calvinists in many parts of the world. Contemporary studies done in the United States show little or no difference in achievement orientation between Roman Catholics and Protestants. Apparently, the "spirit of capitalism" has become a generalized cultural trait (Greeley 1989).

Conflict theorists caution that Weber's theory—even if it is accepted—should not be regarded as applicable to mature capitalism, as reflected in the rise of multinational corporations. Marxists would disagree with Weber, not on the origins of capitalism, but on its future. Unlike Marx, Weber believed that capitalism could endure indefinitely as an economic system. He added, however, that the decline of religion as an overriding force in society opened the way for workers to express their discontent more vocally (R. Collins 1980).

The social support that religious groups provide is suddenly withdrawn from your community. How will your life or the lives of others change? What will happen if religious groups stop pushing for social change?

RELIGION AND SOCIAL CONTROL: A CONFLICT VIEW

Karl Marx ([1844] 1964) thought that religion *impeded* social change by encouraging oppressed people to focus on otherworldly concerns rather than on their immediate poverty or exploitation. Marx described religion as an "opiate" that was particularly harmful to oppressed peoples.

He felt that religion often drugged the masses into submission by offering a consolation for their harsh lives on earth: the hope of salvation in an ideal afterlife. For example, during the period of slavery in the United States, White masters forbade Blacks to practice native African religions. Instead, they encouraged them to adopt Christianity, which taught that obedience would lead to salvation and eternal happiness. Viewed from a conflict perspective, Christianity may have pacified certain slaves and blunted the rage that often fuels rebellion.

Marx acknowledged that religion plays an important role in propping up the existing social structure. Religious values, as already noted, reinforce other social institutions and the social order as a whole. From Marx's perspective, however, religion's promotion of social stability only helps to perpetuate patterns of social inequality. According to Marx, the dominant religion reinforces the interests of those in power.

Consider, for example, India's traditional caste system. Castes define the social structure of that society, at least among the Hindu majority. The caste system was almost certainly the creation of the priesthood, but it also serves the interests of India's political rulers by granting a certain religious legitimacy to social inequality.

Like the Hindu faith, contemporary Christianity reinforces traditional patterns of behavior that call for the subordination of the less powerful. The role of women in the church is an example of uneven distribution of power. Assumptions about gender roles leave women in a subservient position both within Christian churches and at home. In fact, women find it as difficult to achieve leadership positions in many churches as they do in large corporations. Like Marx, conflict theorists argue that to whatever extent religion actually does influence social behavior, it reinforces existing patterns of dominance and inequality.

From the Marxist perspective, religion functions as an "agent of depoliticization" (J. Wilson 1978). In simpler terms, religion keeps people from seeing their lives and societal conditions in political terms—for example, by obscuring the overriding significance of conflicting economic interests. Marxists suggest that by inducing a "false consciousness" among the disadvantaged, religion lessens the possibility of collective political action, which can end capitalist oppression and transform society.

Religion is not the only social institution whose functions have been the subject of controversy among theorists. Conflict theorists charge that schools, too, discriminate in favor of the powerful and against the disadvantaged, as we will see in Chapter 9.

FEMINIST PERSPECTIVE ON RELIGION

Drawing on the feminist approach, researchers and theorists have stressed the fundamental role women play in religious socialization. Most people develop their allegiance to a particular faith in their

Table 8–5 Sociological Perspectives on Religion

Theoretical Perspective	Emphasis
Functionalist	Religion as a source of social integration and unification
	Religion as a source of social support for individuals
Conflict	Religion as a potential obstacle to structural social change
Interactionist	Individual religious expression through belief, ritual, and experience
Feminist	Religion as an instrument of women's subordination, except for their role in religious socialization

childhood, with their mothers playing a critical role in the process. Significantly, nonworshiping mothers tend to influence their children to be highly skeptical of organized religion.

On the other hand, women generally take a subordinate role in religious governance. Indeed, most faiths have a long tradition of exclusively male spiritual leadership. Furthermore, because most religions are patriarchal, they tend to reinforce men's dominance in secular as well as spiritual matters. Women do play a vital role as volunteers, staff, and religious educators, but even today, religious decision making and leadership typically fall to the men. Exceptions to this rule, such as the Shakers and Christian Scientists, as well as Hinduism with its long goddess heritage, are rare (Schaefer and Zellner 2011).

Nationally, women compose 14.8 percent of U.S. clergy, though they account for 39 percent of students enrolled in theological institutions. Women clerics typically have shorter careers than men, often in related fields that do not involve congregational leadership, such as counseling. In faiths that restrict leadership positions to men, women still serve unofficially. For example, about 4 percent of Roman Catholic congregations are led by women who hold nonordained pastoral positions—a necessity in a church that faces a shortage of male priests (Association of Theological Schools 2010; Bureau of the Census 2009a:368).

Table 8–5 summarizes the major sociological perspectives on religion.

Components of Religion

All religions have certain elements in common, yet those elements are expressed in the distinctive manner of each faith. These patterns of religious behavior, like other patterns of social behavior, are of great interest to sociologists—especially interactionists—since they underscore the relationship between religion and society.

Religious beliefs, religious rituals, and religious experience all help to define what is sacred and to differentiate the sacred from the profane. Let's examine these three dimensions of religious behavior, as seen through the eyes of interactionists.

BELIEF

Some people believe in life after death, in supreme beings with unlimited powers, or in supernatural forces. *Religious beliefs* are statements to which members of a particular religion adhere. These views can vary dramatically from one religion to another.

In the late 1960s, something rather remarkable took place in the expression of religious beliefs in the United States. Denominations that held to relatively liberal interpretations of religious scripture (such as the Presbyterians, Methodists, and Lutherans) declined in membership, while those that held to more conservative interpretations grew in numbers. Furthermore, in most faiths, those members who held strict views of scripture became more outspoken, questioning those who remained open to a variety of newer interpretations. The term *fundamentalism* refers to a rigid adherence to fundamental religious doctrines. Often, fundamentalism is accompanied by a literal application of scripture or historical beliefs to today's world.

The phrase "religious fundamentalism" was first applied to Protestant believers in the United States who took a literal interpretation of the Bible, but fundamentalism is found worldwide among most major religious groups, including Roman Catholicism, Islam, and Judaism. Fundamentalists vary immensely in their behavior. Some stress the need to be strict in their own personal faith but take little interest in broad social issues. Others are watchful of societal actions, such as government policies, that they see as conflicting with fundamentalist doctrine.

The Adam and Eve account of creation found in Genesis, the first book of the Old Testament, is an example of a religious belief. Many people in the United States strongly adhere to this biblical explanation of creation and even insist that it be taught in public schools. These people, known as *creationists,* are worried by the secularization of society and oppose teaching that directly or indirectly questions biblical scripture.

In general, spirituality is not as strong in industrialized nations as in developing nations. The United States is an exception to the trend toward secularization, in part because the government encourages religious expression (without explicitly supporting it) by allowing religious groups to claim charitable status and even to receive federal aid for activities such as educational services. And although belief in God is relatively weak in formerly communist states such as Russia, surveys show a growth in spirituality in communist countries over the last 10 years (Norris and Inglehart 2004).

RITUAL

Religious rituals are practices required or expected of members of a faith. Rituals usually honor the divine power (or powers) worshiped by believers; they also remind adherents of their religious duties and responsibilities. Rituals and beliefs can be interdependent; rituals generally affirm beliefs, as in a public or private statement confessing a sin. Like any social institution, religion develops distinctive norms to structure people's behavior. Moreover, sanctions are attached to religious rituals, whether rewards (bar mitzvah gifts) or penalties (expulsion from a religious institution for violation of norms).

In the United States, rituals may be very simple, such as saying grace at a meal or observing a moment of silence to commemorate someone's death. Yet certain rituals, such as the process of canonizing a saint, are quite elaborate. Most religious rituals in our culture focus on services conducted at houses of worship. Attendance at a service, silent and spoken prayers, communion, and singing of spiritual hymns and chants are common forms of ritual behavior that generally take place in group settings. From an interactionist perspective, these rituals serve as important face-to-face encounters in which people reinforce their religious beliefs and their commitment to their faith.

For Muslims, a very important ritual is the *hajj,* a pilgrimage to the Grand Mosque in Mecca, Saudi Arabia. Every Muslim who is physically and financially able is expected to make this trip at least once. Each year 2 million pilgrims go to Mecca during the one-week period indicated by the Islamic lunar calendar. Muslims from all over the world make the *hajj,* including those in the United States, where many tours are arranged to facilitate the trip.

In recent decades, participation in religious rituals has tended to hold steady or decline in most countries. Figure 8–2 shows rates of religious participation in selected countries in 2006.

Use Your Sociological Imagination

Choose a religious tradition other than your own. How would your religious beliefs, rituals, and experience differ if you had been raised in that tradition?

EXPERIENCE

In the sociological study of religion, the term *religious experience* refers to the feeling or perception of being in direct contact with the ultimate reality, such as a divine being, or of being overcome with religious emotion. A religious experience may be rather slight, such as the feeling of exaltation a person receives from hearing a choir sing Handel's "Hallelujah Chorus." But many religious experiences are more profound, such as a Muslim's experience on *hajj.* In his autobiography, the late African American activist Malcolm X (1964:338) wrote of his *hajj* and how deeply moved he was by the way Muslims in Mecca came together across race and color lines. For Malcolm X, the color blindness of the Muslim world "proved to me the power of the One God."

Another profound religious experience, for many Christians, is being "born again"—that is, at a turning point in one's life, making a personal

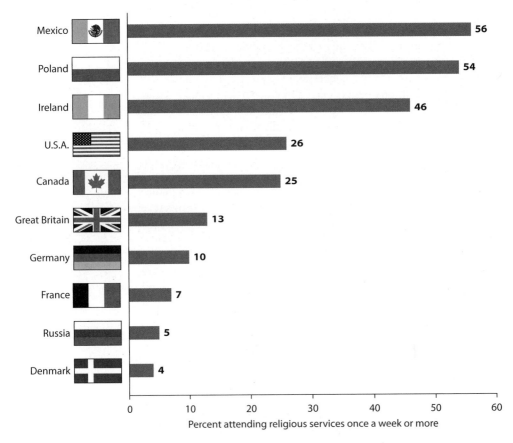

Figure 8–2

Religious Participation in Selected Countries, 2006

NOTE: Data are for 2006, except for Canada and Mexico, which are for 2004.
SOURCE: Tom W. Smith 2009:28, 60, 72.

Think About It
Are you surprised by the variation in religious participation from one nation to another? Why or why not?

commitment to Jesus. According to a 2006 national survey, 43 percent of people in the United States claim they have had a born-again Christian experience at some time in their lives. An earlier survey found that Southern Baptists (75 percent) were the most likely to report such experiences; in contrast, only 21 percent of Catholics and 24 percent of Episcopalians stated that they had been born again. The collective nature of religion, as emphasized by Durkheim, is evident in these statistics. The beliefs and rituals of a particular faith can create an atmosphere either friendly or indifferent to this type of religious experience. Thus, a Baptist would be encouraged to come forward and share such experiences with others, whereas an Episcopalian who claims to have been born again would receive much less interest (Gallup 2009c; Gallup Opinion Index 1978).

Table 8–6 summarizes the three elements of religious behavior.

summingUP

Table 8–6 Elements of Religious Behavior

Element	Definition	Examples
Belief	Statement to which members of a particular religion adhere	Creation account Sacred characters or people
Ritual	Practice required or expected of members of a faith	Worship Prayer Singing or chanting
Experience	Feeling or perception of being in direct contact with the ultimate reality (such as a divine being) or of being overcome with religious emotion	Born-again experience Communion with holy spirit

Sociology Matters

Sociology matters because it explains the purposes and functions of our most basic social institutions.

• Do you see the institutions of the family and religion differently now that you have read this chapter? Did anything you learned surprise you?

• The family and religion are two social institutions whose authority has declined over the last century. Why do you think they have lost some of their importance? Do you think our society is weaker or stronger as a result?

   Sociology matters because it helps us to look at familiar social institutions from new and different perspectives.

• Which of the four major perspectives on the family strikes you as the most meaningful? Why?

• Which of the four major perspectives would be most helpful to you in studying religion?

CHAPTER RESOURCES

Summary

The **social institutions** of the **family** and **religion** are cultural universals, found in various forms in all human cultures. Functionalists stress the essential tasks social institutions perform, but conflict theorists charge that social institutions strengthen the powerful at the expense of the powerless. This chapter examined **kinship** and the family around the world; four sociological perspectives on the family; the social functions of religion; and three components of religion.

1. To survive, a society must perform five essential functions: it must replace its personnel, teach new recruits, produce and distribute goods and services, preserve order, and provide people with a sense of purpose. **Social institutions** perform these essential functions.

2. The **extended family,** common in the past, offers certain advantages over today's **nuclear family.** Some sociologists think that in the United States, the **egalitarian family** has become the norm, replacing the older **patriarchal family.**

3. All cultures determine **kinship** in one of three ways: by descent from both parents, a method called **bilateral descent;** by descent from the father only, called **patrilineal descent;** or by descent from the mother only, called **matrilineal descent.**

4. William F. Ogburn outlined six basic functions of the **family:** reproduction, protection, socialization, regulation of sexual behavior, companionship, and the provision of social status.

5. Conflict theorists charge that male dominance of the family contributes to social injustice and denies women opportunities that are extended to men. Like feminists, they see the family's role in socializing children as the primary source of sexism.

6. Émile Durkheim stressed the social impact of **religion** in attempting to understand individual religious behavior within the context of the larger society.

7. Religion helps to integrate a diverse society and provides social support in time of need. It can serve as a source of social change and a means of social control.

8. Max Weber saw a connection between capitalism and religious allegiance, which he termed the **Protestant ethic.**

9. Karl Marx charged that religion reinforces the control of those in power, discouraging collective political action to end capitalist oppression.

10. Religious behavior is expressed through **religious belief, ritual,** and **experience.** These three components of religion help to define the sacred and differentiate it from the profane.

www.mhhe.com/schaefersm5e
Visit the Online Learning Center for *Sociology Matters* to access quizzes, review activities, and other learning tools.

Key Terms

bilateral descent, 218

egalitarian family, 218

extended family, 215

family, 214

fundamentalism, 228

kinship, 217

matriarchy, 218

matrilineal descent, 218

monogamy, 216

nuclear family, 215

patriarchy, 218

patrilineal descent, 218

polyandry, 216

polygamy, 216

polygyny, 216

Protestant ethic, 225

religion, 222

religious belief, 228

religious experience, 229

religious ritual, 229

serial monogamy, 216

social institution, 210

Social Institutions: Education, Government, and the Economy

Sociological Perspectives on Education

Education: Schools as Formal Organizations

Government: Power and Authority

Economic Systems

Capitalism in China

Changing Economies

In the United States today, nearly 6 out of 10 people ages 3 to 34 are in school. Seven out of 10 adults are in the labor force. Of those who are employed, 2.7 million work for the national government, whose combined payroll is over $167 billion. Clearly, the three social institutions of education, government, and the economy have a profound impact on our daily lives. These institutions also have a significant effect on one another. For example, government data released in 2008 show that the typical college graduate earns over $41,000 a year, compared to about $25,000 a year for a high school graduate. Higher education confers significant economic benefits (Bureau of the Census 2009a:145, 320, 321; DeNavas-Walt et al. 2009).

In the last chapter we learned that a *social institution* is an organized pattern of beliefs and behavior centered on basic social needs. We saw that two institutions, the family and religion, meet our need for support and a sense of purpose. In this chapter we will concentrate on the three institutions of education, government, and the economy, which are devoted to fulfilling our need for learning, social order, and the goods and services that sustain life. We will begin with a discussion of four sociological perspectives on education, followed by a consideration of schools as formal organizations. Then we will examine government as the source of legitimate authority and power. We'll look at three different models of the power structure in the United States. Next, we'll compare two major economic systems, capitalism and socialism. The chapter will close with a discussion of the economic transformations our own society and those of developing countries are currently undergoing.

Sociological Perspectives on Education

Education is a formal process of learning in which some people consciously teach while others adopt the social role of learner. Besides being a major industry in the United States, education is the social institution that formally socializes members of our society. In the last few decades, increasing proportions of people have obtained high school diplomas, college degrees, and advanced professional degrees. For example, the proportion of people 25 years of age or over with a high school diploma increased from 41 percent in 1960 to more than 86 percent in 2008. Those with a college degree rose from 8 percent in 1960 to about 29 percent in 2008. The functionalist, conflict, and interactionist perspectives offer distinctive views of this increasingly important social institution (Bureau of the Census 2009a:149).

FUNCTIONALIST VIEW

Like other social institutions, education has both manifest (open, stated) and latent (hidden) functions. The most basic *manifest* function of education is the transmission of knowledge. Schools teach students how to read, speak foreign languages, and repair automobiles. Another important manifest function is the bestowal of status. Because many believe this function is performed inequitably, we will consider it later, in the section on the conflict view of education.

In addition to these manifest functions, schools perform a number of *latent* functions: transmitting culture, promoting social and political integration, maintaining social control, and serving as an agent of change.

Transmitting Culture   As a social institution, education performs the function of—transmitting the dominant culture. Schooling exposes each generation of young people to the existing beliefs, norms, and values of their culture. In our society, we learn respect for social control and reverence for established institutions, such as religion, the family, and the presidency. Of course, this statement is true of many other cultures as well. While schoolchildren in the United States are hearing about the accomplishments of George Washington and Abraham Lincoln, British children are hearing about the distinctive contributions of Queen Elizabeth I and Winston Churchill.

In retrospect, what do you think of the version of U.S. history that you learned in high school?

Sometimes nations may reassess the ways in which they transmit culture. Recently, the Chinese government revised the nation's history curriculum. Students are now taught that the Chinese Communist Party, not the United States, played a central role in defeating Japan in World War II. No mention is made of the estimated 30 million Chinese who died from famine because of party founder Mao Zedong's Great Leap Forward (1958–1962), a failed effort to transform China's agrarian economy into an industrial powerhouse. In the urban, Western-oriented areas of Shanghai, textbooks acknowledge the technological advances made in Western industrial countries but avoid any criticism of past policies of the Chinese government (French 2004; Kahn 2006).

Promoting Social and Political Integration   Many institutions require students in their first year or two of college to live on campus, to foster a sense of community among diverse groups. Education serves the latent function of promoting social and political integration by transforming a population composed of diverse racial, ethnic, and religious groups into a society whose members share—to some extent—a common identity. Historically, schools in the United States have played an important role in socializing the children of immigrants into the norms, values, and beliefs of the dominant culture. From a functionalist perspective, the common identity and social integration fostered by education contribute to societal stability and consensus (Touraine 1974).

In the past, the integrative function of education was most obvious in its emphasis on promoting a common language. Immigrant children were expected to learn English. In some instances, they were even forbidden to speak their native languages on school grounds. More recently, bilingualism has been defended both for its educational value and as a means of encouraging cultural diversity. However, critics argue that bilingualism undermines the social and political integration that education has traditionally promoted.

Maintaining Social Control   In performing the manifest function of transmitting knowledge, schools go far beyond teaching skills like reading, writing, and mathematics. Like other social institutions, such as the family and religion, education prepares young people to lead productive and orderly lives as adults by introducing them to the norms, values, and sanctions of the larger society.

Through the exercise of social control, schools teach students various skills and values essential to their future positions in the labor force. They learn punctuality, discipline, scheduling, and responsible work habits as well as how to negotiate the complexities of a bureaucratic organization. As a social institution, education reflects the interests of both the family and another social institution, the economy. Students are trained for what is ahead, whether it be the assembly line or a physician's office. In effect, then, schools serve as a transitional agent of social control, bridging the gap between parents and employers in the life cycle of most individuals (Bowles and Gintis 1976; Cole 1988).

Serving as an Agent of Change   So far, we have focused on the conservative functions of education—on its role in transmitting the existing culture, promoting social and political integration, and maintaining social control. Yet education can also stimulate or bring about desired social change. Sex education classes were introduced in public schools in response to a soaring pregnancy rate among teenagers. Affirmative action in admissions—giving priority to females or minorities—has been endorsed as a means of countering racial and sexual discrimination. Project Head Start, an early childhood program that serves more than 908,000 children annually, has sought to compensate for the disadvantages in school readiness experienced by children from low-income families (Bureau of the Census 2009a:362).

These educational programs can and have transformed people's lives. For example, continued formal education has had a positive effect on the income people earn; median earnings rise significantly with each step up the educational ladder (Figure 9–1). Consider the difference that these substantial annual increases can make when they are multiplied by the number of years a person works.

CONFLICT VIEW

Conflict theorists view education as an instrument of elite domination. They point to the sharp inequalities that exist in the educational opportunities available to different racial and ethnic groups. The year 2004

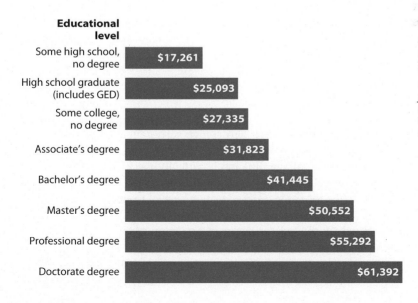

Educational level

Some high school, no degree	$17,261
High school graduate (includes GED)	$25,093
Some college, no degree	$27,335
Associate's degree	$31,823
Bachelor's degree	$41,445
Master's degree	$50,552
Professional degree	$55,292
Doctorate degree	$61,392

Figure 9–1
Annual Median Earnings by Educational Level

NOTE: *Includes full-time, full-year wage and salary for workers ages 25–34 in 2008.*
SOURCE: DeNavas-Walt et al. 2009: PINC-03.

marked the 50th anniversary of the Supreme Court's landmark decision *Brown v. Board of Education,* which declared unconstitutional the segregation of public schools. Yet today, our schools are still characterized by racial isolation. Nationwide, White students are the most isolated; only 23 percent of their classmates came from minority groups in the 2005–2006 school year. In comparison, Black and Latino students have more classmates from different racial and ethnic backgrounds, though they typically do not include Whites (Orfield and Lee 2007).

Conflict theorists also argue that the educational system socializes students into values dictated by the powerful, that schools stifle individualism and creativity in the name of maintaining order, and that the level of change they promote is relatively insignificant. From a conflict perspective, the inhibiting effects of education are particularly apparent in the "hidden curriculum" and the differential way in which status is bestowed on students.

The Hidden Curriculum   Schools are highly bureaucratic organizations, as we will see later. Many teachers rely on rules and regulations to maintain order. Unfortunately, the need for control and discipline can take precedence over the learning process. Teachers may focus on obedience to the rules as an end in itself, in which case students and teachers alike become victims of what Philip Jackson (1968) has called the *hidden curriculum.*

The term ***hidden curriculum*** refers to standards of behavior that are deemed proper by society and are taught subtly in schools. According to this curriculum, children must not speak until the teacher calls on them and must regulate their activities according to the clock or bells. In addition, they are expected to concentrate on their own work rather than assist other students who learn more slowly. A hidden curriculum is evident in schools around the world. For example, Japanese schools offer guidance sessions that seek to improve the classroom experience and develop healthy living skills. In effect, these sessions instill values and encourage behavior useful in the Japanese business world, such as self-discipline and openness to group problem solving and decision making (Okano and Tsuchiya 1999).

Credentialism   Fifty years ago, a high school diploma was the minimum requirement for entry into the paid labor force of the United States. Today, a college diploma is virtually the bare minimum. This change reflects the process of ***credentialism***—a term used to describe an increase in the lowest level of education needed to enter a field.

In recent decades, the number of occupations that are viewed as professions has risen. Credentialism is one symptom of this trend. Employers and occupational associations typically contend that such changes are a logical response to the increasing complexity of many jobs. However, in many cases, employers raise the degree requirements for a position simply because all applicants have achieved the existing minimum credential (Brown 2001; Hurn 1985).

Conflict theorists observe that credentialism may reinforce social inequality. Applicants from poor and minority backgrounds are especially likely to suffer from the escalation of qualifications, they lack the financial resources needed to obtain degree after degree. In addition, upgrading of credentials serves the self-interest of the two groups most responsible for this trend. Educational institutions profit from prolonging the investment of time and money that people make by staying in school. Moreover, current jobholders have a stake in raising occupational requirements, since credentialism can increase the status of an occupation and lead to demands for higher pay. Max Weber anticipated this possibility as early as 1916, concluding that the "universal clamor for the creation of educational certificates in all fields makes for the formation of a privileged stratum in businesses and in offices" (Gerth and Mills 1958:240–241).

Bestowal of Status Conflict theorists are far more critical of the *differential* way in which education bestows status. They stress that schools sort pupils according to their social class backgrounds. Although the educational system helps certain poor children to move into middle-class professional positions, it denies most disadvantaged children the same educational opportunities afforded to children of the affluent. In this way, schools tend to preserve social class inequalities in each new generation (Giroux 1988; Pinkerton 2003).

Even a single school can reinforce class differences by putting students in tracks. The term *tracking* refers to the practice of placing students in specific curriculum groups on the basis of their test scores and other criteria. Tracking begins very early, often in reading groups during first grade. The practice can reinforce the disadvantages that children from less affluent families may face if they haven't been exposed to reading materials, computers, and other forms of educational stimulation during their early childhood years. To ignore this connection between tracking and students' race and social class is to fundamentally misunderstand how schools perpetuate the existing social structure.

Not surprisingly, most recent research on tracking raises questions about its effectiveness, especially for low-ability students. In one study of low-income schools in California, researchers discovered a staggering difference between students who were tracked and those who were not. At one school, all interested students were allowed to enroll in advanced placement (AP) courses, not just those who were selected by the administration. Half the open enrollment students scored high enough to qualify for college credit—a much higher proportion than in selective programs, in which only 17 percent of students qualified for college credit. Tracking programs do not necessarily identify those students with the potential to succeed (Ellison 2008; Sacks 2007).

Use Your Sociological Imagination

How would you react if the job you have or plan to pursue suddenly required a higher-level degree? If suddenly the requirements were lowered?

FEMINIST VIEW

The educational system of the United States, like many other social institutions, has long been characterized by discriminatory treatment of women. In 1833 Oberlin College became the first institution of higher learning to admit female students—some 200 years after the first men's college was established. But Oberlin's administrators believed that women should aspire to become wives and mothers, not lawyers and intellectuals. In addition to attending classes, female students washed men's clothing, cared for their rooms, and served them at meals. In the 1840s, Lucy Stone, then an Oberlin undergraduate and later one of the nation's most outspoken feminist leaders, refused to write a commencement address because it would have been read to the audience by a male student.

In the 20th century, sexism in education showed up in many ways—in textbooks with negative stereotypes of women, counselors' pressure on female students to prepare for "women's work," and unequal funding for women's and men's athletic programs. But perhaps nowhere was educational discrimination more evident than in the employment of teachers. The positions of university professor and college administrator, which hold relatively high status in the United States, were generally filled by men. Public school teachers, who earn much lower salaries, were largely female.

Women have made great strides in one area: the proportion of women who continue their schooling. Women's access to graduate education and to medical, dental, and law schools has increased dramatically in the last few decades as a result of the Education Act of 1972, which forbade discrimination against women in education.

Much has been made of the superior academic achievement of girls and women. Today, researchers are beginning to examine the reasons for their comparatively strong performance in school—or to put it another way, for men's lackluster performance. Some studies suggest that men's aggressiveness, together with the fact that they do better in the workplace than women, even with less schooling, predisposes them to undervalue higher education. While the "absence of men" on many college campuses has captured headlines, it has also created a false crisis in public discourse. Few students realize their potential exclusively through formal education; other factors, such as ambition and personal talent, contribute to their success. And many students, including low-income and immigrant children, face much greater challenges than the so-called gender gap in education (Buchmann et al. 2008; Corbett et al. 2008; Kimmel 2006).

In cultures in which traditional gender roles remain the social norm, women's education suffers appreciably. Since September 11, 2001, the growing awareness of the Taliban's repression of Afghan women has dramatized the gender disparities in education in developing nations. Research has demonstrated that women are critical to economic development and good governance, and that education is instrumental in preparing them for those roles. Educating women, especially young girls, yields high social returns by lowering birthrates and improving agricultural productivity through better management (Coleman 2004).

INTERACTIONIST VIEW

The labeling approach suggests that if we treat people in particular ways, they may fulfill our expectations. Children who are labeled as "trouble-makers" may come to view themselves as delinquents. Similarly, a dominant group's stereotyping of subordinate racial groups may limit their opportunities to break away from expected roles.

Can the labeling process operate in the classroom? Psychologist Robert Rosenthal and school principal Lenore Jacobson (1968, 1992) documented what they referred to as a *teacher-expectancy effect*—the impact that a teacher's expectations about a student's performance may have on the student's actual achievements. This effect is especially evident in the lower grades (through grade three).

In their experiment, children in a San Francisco elementary school were administered a verbal and reasoning pretest. Rosenthal and Jacobson then *randomly* selected 20 percent of the sample and designated them as "spurters"—children of whom teachers could expect superior performance. On a later verbal and reasoning test, the spurters scored significantly higher than before. Moreover, teachers evaluated them as more interesting, more curious, and better adjusted than their classmates. These results were striking. Apparently, teachers' perceptions that the students were exceptional led to noticeable improvements in their performance.

Studies in the United States have revealed that teachers wait longer for an answer from a student they believe to be a high achiever and are more likely to give such children a second chance. In one experiment, teachers' expectations were even shown to have an impact on students' athletic achievements. Teachers obtained better athletic performance—as measured by the number of sit-ups or push-ups performed—from those students of whom they *expected* higher numbers (Babad and Taylor 1992; Rosenthal and Jacobson 1992: 247–262).

Table 9–1 summarizes the four major theoretical perspectives on education.

What kinds of labels do school authorities apply to students? What is the outcome of those labels?

Education: Schools as Formal Organizations

Mid-20th-century educators would be amazed at the scale of schools in the United States as we head into the 21st century. California's public school system, the largest in the nation, currently enrolls as many children as there were in the entire country's secondary schools in 1950 (Bureau of the Census 1975:368; 2003a).

summingUP

Table 9–1 Sociological Perspectives on Education

Theoretical Perspective	Emphasis
Functionalist	Transmission of the dominant culture Social and political integration Maintenance of social control Promotion of desirable social change
Conflict	Domination by the elite through unequal access to schooling Hidden curriculum Credentialism Differential bestowal of status
Feminist	Treatment of female students Role of women's education in economic development
Interactionist	Teacher-expectancy effect

In many respects, today's schools are similar to factories, hospitals, and business firms when viewed as formal organizations. Like those other organizations, schools do not operate autonomously; they are influenced by the market of potential students. This market orientation is especially true of private schools but could have broader impact if acceptance of voucher plans and other school choice programs increases. The parallels between schools and other formal organizations will become more apparent as we examine the bureaucratic nature of schools, teaching as an occupational role, and student subcultures (Dougherty and Hammack 1992).

BUREAUCRATIZATION OF SCHOOLS

A single teacher simply cannot transmit culture and skills to children of varying ages or prepare them for many diverse occupations. The growing number of students being served by individual schools and school systems, as well as the greater degree of specialization required by a technologically complex society, have combined to bureaucratize schools.

Max Weber noted five basic characteristics of bureaucracy, all of which are evident in the vast majority of schools, whether at the elementary, secondary, or college level.

1. *Division of labor.* Specialized experts teach particular age levels and specific subjects. For example, public elementary and secondary schools now employ instructors whose sole responsibility is to work with children with learning disabilities or physical impairments.

2. *Hierarchy of authority.* Each employee of a school system is responsible to a higher authority. Teachers must report to principals

and assistant principals and may also be supervised by department heads. Principals are answerable to a superintendent of schools, and the superintendent is hired and fired by a board of education.

3. *Written rules and regulations.* Teachers and administrators must conform to numerous rules and regulations in the performance of their duties. This bureaucratic requirement can become dysfunctional; the time invested in completing forms could instead be spent on preparing lessons or conferring with students.

4. *Impersonality.* The university has been portrayed as a giant, faceless bureaucracy that cares little for the uniqueness of the individual. As class sizes have swelled at schools and universities, it has become more difficult for teachers to give personal attention to each student. In fact, bureaucratic norms may actually encourage teachers to treat all students in the same way, despite the fact that students have distinctive personalities and learning needs.

5. *Employment based on technical qualifications.* At least in theory, the hiring of teachers and college professors is based on professional competence and expertise. Promotions are normally dictated by written personnel policies; people who excel may be granted lifelong job security through tenure.

Functionalists take a generally positive view of the bureaucratization of education. Teachers can master the skills needed to work with a specialized clientele, since they no longer are expected to cover a broad range of instruction. The chain of command within schools is clear. Students are presumably treated in an unbiased fashion because of uniformly applied rules. Finally, security of position protects teachers from unjustified dismissal. In general, then, functionalists maintain that bureaucratization of education increases the likelihood that students, teachers, and administrators will be dealt with fairly—that is, on the basis of rational, equitable criteria.

In contrast, conflict theorists argue that the trend toward more centralized education has had harmful consequences for disadvantaged people. The standardization of educational curricula, including textbooks, generally reflects the values, interests, and lifestyles of the most powerful groups in our society and may ignore those of racial and ethnic minorities. In addition, the disadvantaged, more so than the affluent, will find it difficult to sort through complex educational bureaucracies and to organize effective lobbying groups. In the view of conflict theorists, then, low-income and minority parents are likely to have even less influence over citywide and statewide educational administrators than they have over local school officials (Bowles and Gintis 1976; Katz 1971).

Finally, some schools can seem overwhelmingly bureaucratic, with the effect of stifling rather than nourishing intellectual curiosity in students.

How would you make your school less bureaucratic? What would it be like?

This problem has led many parents and policymakers to push for school choice programs—that is, allowing parents to choose the school that suits their children's needs, forcing schools to compete for their "customers."

TEACHERS: EMPLOYEES AND INSTRUCTORS

Whether they instruct preschoolers or graduate students, teachers are employees of formal organizations with bureaucratic structures. There is an inherent conflict in serving as a professional within a bureaucracy. The organization follows a hierarchy of authority and expects adherence to its rules, but professionalism demands individual responsibility of the practitioner. This conflict is very real for teachers, who experience all the positive and negative consequences of working in bureaucracies.

A teacher undergoes many perplexing stresses every day. While teachers' academic assignments have become more specialized, the demands on their time remain diverse and contradictory. Conflicts arise from serving as an instructor, a disciplinarian, and an employee of a school district at the same time. In too many schools, discipline means dealing with violence. Burnout is one result of these stresses: between a quarter and a third of new teachers quit within their first three years, and as many as half leave poor urban schools in their first five years (Wallis 2008).

Given these difficulties, does teaching remain an attractive profession in the United States? In 2009, 4.1 percent of first-year college students indicated that they were interested in becoming elementary school teachers, and 4.4 percent, high school teachers. These figures are dramatically lower than the 11 percent of first-year male students and 37 percent of first-year female students who held those occupational aspirations in 1966 (Pryor et al. 2007a:76, 122; 2009:30).

Undoubtedly, economic considerations enter into students' feelings about the attractiveness of teaching. In 2008 the average salary for all public elementary and secondary school teachers in the United States was reported at $51,009, placing teachers somewhere near the average of all the nation's wage earners. In most other industrial countries, teachers' salaries are higher in relation to the general standard of living. Of course, teachers' salaries vary considerably from state to state (see Figure 9–2), and even from one school district to another. Nevertheless, the economic reward for teaching is miniscule compared to some career options: The CEO of a major corporation makes more money in a day than the average teacher makes in a year (American Federation of Teachers 2007; Herring 2006).

The status of any job reflects several factors, including the level of education required, financial compensation, and the respect given the occupation by society. The teaching profession (see Table 5–2, page 141) is feeling pressure in all three of these areas. First, the level of formal schooling required for teaching remains high, and the public has

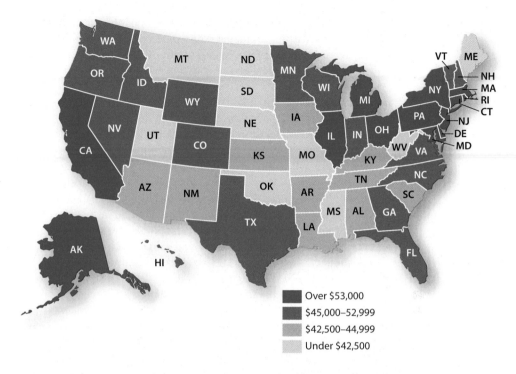

Over $53,000
$45,000–52,999
$42,500–44,999
Under $42,500

Figure 9–2

Average Salary for Teachers

State averages for teacher salaries range from a low of $35,378 in South Dakota to a high of $63,640 in Massachusetts.

NOTE: *Data released in 2008 for 2006–2007.*
SOURCE: Di Carlo and Johnson 2008.

Think About It

Why are salaries high in the dark blue states? Why are they low in the lightest blue states?

begun to call for new competency examinations. Second, the statistics just cited demonstrate that teachers' salaries are significantly lower than those of many professionals and skilled workers. Finally, the overall prestige of the teaching profession has declined in the last decade. Many teachers have become disappointed and frustrated and have left the educational world for careers in other professions.

Government: Power and Authority

A society does not exist in a vacuum. Someone or some group makes important decisions about how to use resources and how to allocate goods, whether it be a tribal chief, a parliament, or a dictator. A cultural universal common to all societies, then, is the exercise of authority and power. The struggle for authority and power inevitably involves *politics,* which political scientist Harold Lasswell (1936) tersely defined as "who gets what, when, and how." In their study of politics and government, sociologists are concerned with social interactions among individuals and groups and their impact on the larger political and economic order.

Power lies at the heart of a political system. According to Max Weber, *power* is the ability to exercise one's will over others. To put it another way, whoever can control the behavior of others is exercising power. Power relations can involve large organizations, small groups, or even people in an intimate association.

There are three basic sources of power in any political system—force, influence, and authority. *Force* is the actual or threatened use of coercion to impose one's will on others. When leaders imprison or even execute political dissidents, they are applying force; so, too, are terrorists when they seize or bomb an embassy or assassinate a political leader.

In the 21st century, force has taken on new meaning as nations clamp down on use of the Internet to oppose the central government or assert freedom of expression, human rights, and minority or religious views. When a military coup overthrew the democratically elected government of Thailand in September 2006, for example, citizens lost access to websites that criticized the takeover. As of 2008, 18 nations had placed political controls on Internet content. Censorship of online content is just as much a use of force as closing down a newspaper or arresting dissidents (Deibert et al. 2008; OpenNet Initiative 2008; Zittrain and Palfrey 2008).

Influence, on the other hand, refers to the exercise of power through a process of persuasion. A citizen may change his or her position regarding a Supreme Court nominee because of a newspaper editorial, the expert testimony of a law school dean before the Senate Judiciary Committee, or a stirring speech at a rally by a political activist. In each case, sociologists would view such efforts to persuade people as examples of influence. Now let's take a look at the third source of power, *authority*.

TYPES OF AUTHORITY

The term *authority* refers to power that has been institutionalized and is recognized by the people over whom it is exercised. Sociologists commonly use the term in connection with those who hold legitimate power through elected or publicly acknowledged positions. A person's authority is limited by the constraints of a particular social position. Thus, a referee has the authority to decide whether a penalty should be called during a football game but has no authority over the price of tickets to the game.

Max Weber ([1913] 1947) developed a system for classifying authority that has become one of the most useful and frequently cited contributions of early sociology. Weber identified three ideal types of authority: traditional, rational-legal, and charismatic. He did not insist that only one type characterizes a given society or organization. All can be present in a single society, but their relative importance will vary. Sociologists have found Weber's typology valuable in understanding different manifestations of legitimate power.

Traditional Authority   Until the middle of the last century, Japan was ruled by a revered emperor, whose absolute power was passed down from generation to generation. In a political system based on *traditional authority,* legitimate power is conferred by custom and accepted practice. A king or queen is accepted as ruler of a nation simply by virtue of inheriting the crown; a tribal chief rules because that is the accepted practice. The ruler may be loved or hated, competent or destructive; in terms of legitimacy, that does not matter. For the traditional leader, authority rests in custom, not in personal characteristics, technical competence, or even written law. People accept such authority because "this is how things have always been done." Traditional authority is absolute when the ruler has the ability to determine a society's laws and policies.

Rational-Legal Authority   The U.S. Constitution gives Congress and our president the authority to make and enforce laws and policies. Power made legitimate by law—by the written rules and regulations of a political system—is known as *rational-legal authority.* Generally, in societies based on rational-legal authority, leaders are thought to have specific fields of competence and authority but are not thought to be endowed with divine inspiration, as in certain societies with traditional forms of authority.

Charismatic Authority   Joan of Arc was a simple peasant girl in medieval France, yet she was able to rally the French people and lead them into battle against English invaders. How was this possible? As Weber observed, power can be legitimized by an individual's *charisma.* The term *charismatic authority* refers to power made legitimate by a leader's exceptional personal or emotional appeal to his or her followers. Charisma lets a person lead or inspire without relying on set rules or traditions. In fact, charismatic authority is derived more from the beliefs of followers than from the actual qualities of leaders. So long as people *perceive* a leader to have qualities that set him or her apart from ordinary citizens, that leader's authority will remain secure and often unquestioned.

Unlike traditional rulers, charismatic leaders often become well known by breaking with established institutions and advocating dramatic changes in the social structure and economic system. Their strong hold over their followers enables them to build protest movements that challenge the dominant norms and values of a society. Thus, charismatic leaders such as Jesus, Joan of Arc, Mahatma Gandhi, Malcolm X, and Martin Luther King Jr. all used their power to press for changes in accepted social behavior. But so did Adolf Hitler, whose charismatic appeal turned people toward violent and destructive ends in Nazi Germany.

Observing from an interactionist perspective, sociologist Carl Couch (1996) points out that the growth of the electronic media has facilitated the development of charismatic authority. During the 1930s and 1940s, the heads of state of the United States, Great Britain, and Germany all

What would our government be like if it were founded on traditional rather than rational-legal authority? What difference would it make to the average citizen?

used radio to issue direct appeals to citizens. In recent decades, television has allowed leaders to "visit" people's homes and communicate with them. Time and again, Saddam Hussein rallied the Iraqi people through shrewd use of television appearances. In both Taiwan and South Korea in 1996, troubled political leaders facing reelection campaigns spoke frequently to national audiences and exaggerated military threats from neighboring China and North Korea, respectively. And in 2004, during his successful reelection campaign, President George W. Bush would land before camera crews in the *Marine One* helicopter, dramatically reinforcing his image as commander in chief.

Though Weber distinguished between traditional, rational-legal, and charismatic authority as ideal types, in reality, individual leaders and political systems often combine two or more of these forms. Presidents Franklin D. Roosevelt, John F. Kennedy, and Ronald Reagan wielded power largely through rational-legal authority. At the same time, they were unusually charismatic leaders who commanded the personal loyalty of large numbers of citizens.

WHO RULES IN THE UNITED STATES?

Who really holds power in the United States? Do "we the people" genuinely run the country through our elected representatives? Or is it true that behind the scenes, a small elite controls both our government and our economic system? It is difficult to determine the location of power in a society as complex as the United States. In exploring this critical question, social scientists have developed two basic views of our nation's power structure: the power elite and the pluralist models.

Power Elite Models   Karl Marx believed that 19th-century representative democracy was essentially a sham. He argued that industrial societies were dominated by relatively small numbers of people who owned factories and controlled natural resources. In Marx's view, government officials and military leaders were servants of this capitalist class and followed their wishes. Therefore, any key decisions made by politicians inevitably reflected the interests of the dominant bourgeoisie. Like others who hold to an *elite model* of power relations, Marx believed that society is ruled by a small group of individuals who share a common set of political and economic interests.

Mills's Model   Sociologist C. Wright Mills took this model a step further in his pioneering work *The Power Elite* ([1956] 2000b). Mills described a small group of military, industrial, and government leaders who controlled the fate of the United States. Power rested in the hands of a few, both inside and outside government, called the ***power elite.***

A pyramid illustrates the United States' power structure in Mills's model (see Figure 9–3a). At the top are the corporate rich, leaders of the

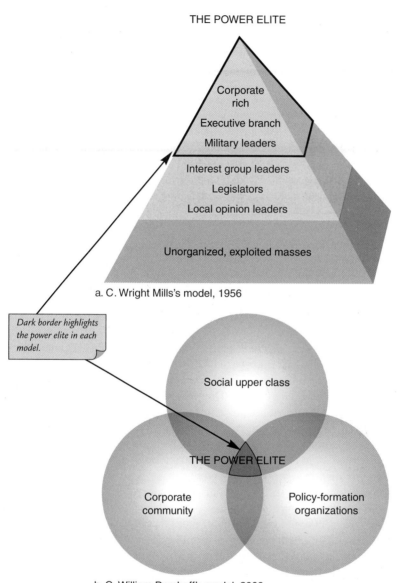

THE POWER ELITE

Corporate rich

Executive branch

Military leaders

Interest group leaders

Legislators

Local opinion leaders

Unorganized, exploited masses

a. C. Wright Mills's model, 1956

Dark border highlights the power elite in each model.

Social upper class

THE POWER ELITE

Corporate community

Policy-formation organizations

b. G. William Domhoff's model, 2009

Figure 9–3
Power Elite Models
SOURCE: Top, author based on C. W. Mills [1956] 2000b; bottom, Domhoff 2009:116.

executive branch of government, and heads of the military (whom Mills called the "warlords"). These are the power elite. Directly below are local opinion leaders, members of the legislative branch of government, and leaders of special interest groups. Mills thought these individuals and groups would basically follow the wishes of the dominant power elite. At the bottom of the pyramid are the unorganized, exploited masses.

This power elite model is similar to the work of Karl Marx in many respects. The most striking difference is that Mills believed that the economically powerful coordinate their maneuvers with the military and political establishments, to serve their common interests. Yet, reminiscent of Marx, Mills argued that the corporate rich were perhaps the most powerful element of the power elite (first among "equals"). And of course, the powerless masses at the bottom of Mills's power elite model certainly bring to mind Marx's portrait of the oppressed workers of the world, who have "nothing to lose but their chains."

A fundamental element in Mills's thesis is that the power elite operates as a self-conscious, cohesive unit. Although not necessarily diabolical or ruthless, the elite comprises similar types of people who interact with one another regularly and have essentially the same political and economic interests. Mills's power elite is not a conspiracy, but rather a community of interest and sentiment among a small number of influential people (Hacker 1964).

Admittedly, Mills failed to clarify when the elite opposes protests and when it tolerates them; he also failed to provide detailed case studies to substantiate the interrelationship among members of the power elite. Nevertheless, his challenging theory forced scholars to look more critically at the democratic political system of the United States.

Domhoff's Model   More recently, sociologist G. William Domhoff has agreed with Mills that a powerful elite runs the United States. He finds that it is still largely White, male, and upper class, as he wrote in his book with Richard L. Zweigenhaft (1998), *Diversity in the Power Elite.* But Domhoff stresses the role played both by elites of the corporate community and by leaders of policy-formation organizations, such as chambers of commerce and labor unions. Many of the people in both groups belong to the social upper class. And he notes the presence of a small number of women and minority men in key positions—groups that were excluded from Mills's top echelon and are still underrepresented today.

While these groups overlap (see Figure 9–3b), they do not necessarily agree on specific policies. Domhoff notes that in the electoral arena, two different coalitions have exercised influence. A *corporate-conservative coalition* has played a large role in both political parties and has generated support for particular candidates through direct-mail appeals. It is opposed by a *liberal-labor coalition* based in unions, local environmental organizations, a segment of the minority group community, liberal churches, and the university and arts communities (Zweigenhaft and Domhoff 1998).

The Pluralist Model   Several social scientists insist that in the United States, power is more widely shared than the elite models indicate. In their view, a *pluralist model* more accurately describes the nation's political system. According to the **pluralist model,** many competing groups within the community have access to government officials, so that no single group is dominant.

The pluralist model suggests that a variety of groups play a significant role in decision making. Typically, pluralists make use of intensive case studies or community studies based on observation research. One of the most famous—an investigation of decision making in New Haven, Connecticut—was reported by Robert Dahl in his book *Who Governs?* (1961). Dahl found that although the number of people involved in any important decision was rather small, community power was nonetheless diffuse. Few political actors exercised decision-making power on all issues. One individual or group might be influential in a battle over urban renewal but at the same time have little impact over educational policy. Several other studies of local politics in such communities as Chicago and Oberlin, Ohio, further document the absence of monolithic power structures on the local level of government.

The pluralist model, however, has not escaped serious questioning. Domhoff (1978, 2006) reexamined Dahl's study of decision making in New Haven and argued that Dahl and other pluralists had failed to show that elites prominent in local decision making belonged to a larger national ruling class. In addition, studies of community power, such as Dahl's work in New Haven, can examine decision making only on issues that become part of the political agenda. They fail to address the possible power of elites to keep certain matters that threaten their dominance entirely *out* of the realm of government debate.

Dianne Pinderhughes (1987) has criticized the pluralist model for failing to account for the exclusion of African Americans from the political process. Drawing on her studies of Chicago politics, Pinderhughes points out that the residential and occupational segregation of Blacks and their long political disenfranchisement violate the logic of pluralism—which would hold that such a substantial minority should always have been influential in community decision making. This critique applies to many cities across the United States where other large racial and ethnic minorities, among them Asian Americans, Puerto Ricans, and Mexican Americans, are relatively powerless.

Historically, pluralists have stressed ways in which large numbers of people can participate in or influence governmental decision making. New communications technologies like the Internet are increasing the opportunity to be heard, not just in countries such as the United States but in developing countries the world over. One common point of the elite and pluralist perspectives stands out, however: in the political system of the United States, power is unequally distributed. All citizens may be equal in theory, yet those who are high in the nation's power structure are "more equal." New communications technologies may or may not change that distribution power.

The power struggles that underlie government and politics, no matter what model a social scientist uses to analyze them, have a great deal to do with the distribution of a society's economic resources. In the next sections of this chapter we will study the economy, both in theory and in its practical implications for tomorrow's workforce.

Use Your Sociological Imagination

Which is a better model of the power structure in the United States, the power elite model or the pluralist model? Justify your answer.

Economic Systems

The economy fulfills the basic social function of producing and distributing goods and services (see Table 8–1 on page 211). But how is this seemingly amorphous social institution organized? A society's *economic system* for producing, distributing, and consuming goods and services will depend on both its level of development and its political ideology. In this section we will consider the two basic economic systems associated with contemporary industrial societies: capitalism and socialism. In theory, these two economic systems conform perfectly to certain ideals, such as private or collective ownership. However, real economic systems rarely measure up to the ideal types on which they are based. To a greater or lesser extent, most economic systems today incorporate some elements of both capitalism and socialism.

CAPITALISM

In preindustrial societies, land was the source of virtually all wealth. The Industrial Revolution changed all that. It required that certain individuals and institutions be willing to take substantial risks in order to finance new inventions, machinery, and business enterprises. Eventually, bankers, industrialists, and other holders of large sums of money replaced landowners as the most powerful economic force. These people invested their funds in the hope of realizing even greater profits in factories and business firms.

The transition to private ownership of business was accompanied by the emergence of the capitalist economic system. *Capitalism* is an economic system in which the means of production are held largely in private hands, and the main incentive for economic activity is the accumulation of profits. In practice, capitalist systems vary in the degree to which the government regulates private ownership and economic activity (Rosenberg 1991).

Immediately following the Industrial Revolution, the prevailing form of capitalism was what is termed *laissez-faire* ("let them do"). Under the principle of laissez-faire, as expounded and endorsed by British economist Adam Smith (1723–1790), businesses could compete freely, with minimal government intervention. They retained the right to regulate themselves, operating essentially without fear of government interference (Smelser 1963).

Two centuries later, capitalism has taken on a somewhat different form. Private ownership and maximization of profits still remain the most significant characteristics of capitalist economic systems. However, in contrast to the era of laissez-faire, today's form of capitalism features extensive government regulation of economic relations. Without restrictions, business firms can mislead consumers, endanger their workers, and even defraud investors—all in the pursuit of greater profits.

That is why the government of a capitalist nation often monitors prices, sets safety standards for industries, protects the rights of consumers, and regulates collective bargaining between labor unions and management. Yet in a capitalist system, government rarely takes over ownership of an entire industry.

Contemporary capitalism also differs from laissez-faire in another important respect: it tolerates monopolistic practices. A ***monopoly*** exists when a single business firm controls the market. Domination of an industry allows the firm to effectively control a commodity by dictating pricing, standards of quality, and availability. Buyers have little choice but to yield to the firm's decisions; there is no other place to purchase the product or service. Monopolistic practices violate the ideal of free competition cherished by Adam Smith and other supporters of laissez-faire capitalism.

Some capitalistic nations, such as the United States, attempt to outlaw monopolies through antitrust legislation. Such laws are meant to prevent any business from taking over so much of an industry that it gains control of the market. The U.S. government approves of monopolies only in certain exceptional cases, such as the utility and transportation industries. Even then, regulatory agencies scrutinize these officially approved monopolies to protect the public. The protracted legal battle between the Justice Department and Microsoft, owner of the dominant operating system for personal computers, illustrates the uneasy relationship between government and virtual private monopolies in capitalistic countries.

Conflict theorists point out that although *pure* monopolies are not a basic element of the U.S. economy, competition is much more restricted than one might expect in what is called a *free enterprise system.* In numerous industries, a few companies dominate the field and prevent new enterprises from entering the marketplace.

SOCIALISM

Socialist theory was refined in the writings of Karl Marx and Friedrich Engels. These European radicals were disturbed by the exploitation of the working class that emerged during the Industrial Revolution. In their view, capitalism forced large numbers of people to exchange their labor for low wages. The owners of industry profited from workers' labor primarily because they paid workers less than the value of the goods produced.

As an ideal type, a socialist economic system attempts to eliminate such economic exploitation. Under ***socialism,*** the means of production and distribution in a society are collectively rather than privately owned. The basic objective of the economic system is to meet people's needs rather than to maximize profits. Socialists reject the laissez-faire philosophy that free competition benefits the general public. Instead, they believe that the central government, acting on behalf of the people, should make basic economic decisions. Therefore, government ownership of all major industries—including steel production, automobile manufacturing, and agriculture—is a major feature of socialism as an ideal type.

In practice, socialist economic systems vary in the extent to which they tolerate private ownership. For example, in Great Britain, a nation with some aspects of both a socialist and a capitalist economy, passenger airline service is concentrated in the government-owned corporation British Airways. Yet private airline companies are allowed to compete with British Airways.

Socialist societies differ from capitalist nations in their commitment to social service programs. For example, the U.S. government provides health care and health insurance to the elderly and poor through the Medicare and Medicaid programs. In contrast, socialist countries typically offer government-financed medical care to *all* citizens. In theory, the wealth of the people as a collectivity is used to provide health care, housing, education, and other key services to each individual and family.

Marx believed that the socialist state would eventually "wither away" and evolve into a *communist* society. As an ideal type, **communism** refers to an economic system in which all property is communally owned and no social distinctions are made on the basis of people's ability to produce. In recent decades, the Soviet Union, the People's Republic of China, Vietnam, Cuba, and the nations of Eastern Europe were popularly thought of as communist economic systems. However, this viewpoint represents an incorrect usage of a term with sensitive political connotations. All nations known as communist actually fall far short of the ideal type.

By the early 1990s, Communist parties were no longer ruling the nations of Eastern Europe. The first major challenge to Communist rule came in 1980, when Poland's Solidarity movement—led by Lech Walesa and backed by many workers—questioned the injustices of that society. Though martial law forced Solidarity underground, the movement eventually negotiated the end of Communist party rule, in 1989. Over the next two years, Communist parties were overthrown by popular uprisings in the Soviet Union and throughout Eastern Europe. The former Soviet Union, Czechoslovakia, and Yugoslavia were then subdivided to accommodate ethnic, linguistic, and religious differences within those areas.

As we have seen, capitalism and socialism serve as ideal types. In reality, the economy of each industrial society—including the United States, the European Union, and Japan—contains certain elements of both capitalism and socialism (see Table 9–2). Whatever the differences—whether a country more closely fits the ideal type of capitalism or socialism—all industrial societies rely chiefly on mechanization in the production of goods and services. And all economies, whether capitalist or socialist, change as a result of social and technological advances. In the next section we will examine some of the economic trends that are transforming the United States and the world at the beginning of the 21st century.

Use Your Sociological Imagination

The U.S. economy has become predominantly socialistic rather than capitalistic. What do you as a worker have now that you did not have before? What do you lack?

Table 9–2 Characteristics of the Three Major Economic Systems

Economic System	Characteristics	Contemporary Examples
Capitalism	Private ownership of the means of production Accumulation of profits the main incentive	Canada Mexico United States
Socialism	Collective ownership of the means of production Meeting people's needs the basic objective	Germany Russia Sweden
Communism	Communal ownership of all property No social distinctions made on basis of people's ability to produce	Cuba North Korea Vietnam

NOTE: Countries listed in column 3 are typical of one of the three economic systems, but not perfectly so. In practice, the economies of most countries include a mix of elements from the three major systems.

Capitalism in China

Today's China is not the China of past generations; it is expected to become the world's largest economy by 2020. In this country where the Communist Party once dominated people's lives, few now bother to follow party proceedings. Instead, after a decade of rapid economic growth, most Chinese are more interested in acquiring the latest consumer goods.

Ironically, it was party officials' decision to transform China's economy by opening it up to capitalism that reduced the once omnipotent institution's influence (*The Economist* 2006a).

Today, the entrepreneurs who weathered government harassment during the Communist Party's early years are among the nation's wealthiest capitalists. Some even hold positions on government advisory boards. The growing free-market economy they spawned has brought significant inequality to Chinese workers, however, especially between urban and rural workers. Though the move toward market-driven development has been slowing, questions are still being raised about the accumulation of wealth by a few (Sicular et al. 2006).

For Chinese workers, the loosening of state control over the economy has meant a rise in occupational mobility, which was severely limited in the early days of Communist Party rule. The new markets created by private entrepreneurs are allowing ambitious workers to advance their careers by changing jobs or even cities. On the other hand, many middle-aged urban workers have lost their jobs to rural migrants seeking higher wages. Moreover, the privately owned factories that churn out lawn chairs and power tools for multinational corporations offer limited opportunities and very long hours. Wages average $120 to $200 a month for a six-day workweek.

Serious social problems have accompanied China's massive economic growth. Because safety is not a priority in many businesses, workers suffer from high injury rates. Harsh working conditions contribute to rapid turnover in the labor force. There is no pension system in China, so retirees must struggle to find other ways to support themselves. Pollution is common in urban areas, and environmental problems are extraordinary (Barboza 2008; French 2008).

For the average worker, party membership is less important now than in the past. Instead, managerial skill and experience are much in demand. Hong Kong sociologist Xiaowei Zang (2002) surveyed 900 workers in a key industrial city and found that party members still had an advantage in government and state-owned companies, where they earned higher salaries than other workers. But in private businesses, seniority and either managerial or entrepreneurial experience were what counted. As might be expected, being male and well educated also helped.

Women have been slower to advance in the workplace than men. Traditionally, Chinese women have been relegated to subservient roles in the patriarchal family structure. Communist Party rule has allowed them to make significant gains in employment, income, and education, although not as quickly as promised. For rural women in China, the growth of a market economy has meant a choice between working in a factory or on a farm. Still, despite recent economic changes, emerging research shows that Chinese women receive lower wages than men who work in the same job sectors (Wang and Cai 2006).

Use Your Sociological Imagination

Why do you think China's economy has grown as fast as it has?

Changing Economies

As advocates of the power elite model point out, the trend in capitalist societies has been toward concentration of ownership by giant corporations, especially multinational ones. The U.S. economy is changing in important ways, in part because it is increasingly intertwined with and dependent on the global economy. In the following sections, we will examine two outgrowths of this trend in the United States, deindustrialization and the changing face of the workforce, as well as a countertrend: the rise of microfinancing in developing countries. As these trends show, any change in the economy has social and political implications.

MICROFINANCING

In some respects it offers a small solution to a big problem. *Microfinancing* is lending small sums of money to the poor so they can work their way out of poverty. Borrowers use the money to get small businesses off the ground—to buy the tools, equipment, and bamboo to make stools, yarn to weave into cloth, or cows to produce milk. The products they produce are then sold in the local shops. Typically, microloans are less than $100, often as little as $12. The recipients are people who ordinarily would not be able to qualify for banking services.

Sometimes referred to as "banking the unbanked," microfinancing was the brainchild of Bangladeshi economist Muhammad Yunus. In 1976, in the midst of a devastating famine in Bangladesh, Yunus founded the Grameen (meaning "Village") Bank. The idea came to him when he reached into his pocket to lend $27 to a group of villagers who had asked him for help. Working through local halls or meeting places, the Grameen Bank has now extended credit to nearly 7 million people. The idea has spread, and has even been underwritten by a thousand for-profit banks and multinational organizations. According to estimates, in 2009 microfinancing was reaching 75 million people in 100 countries. The success of microfinancing to date indicates that it is all too easy to underestimate poor people's ability to improve their circumstances, given even modest assistance (Microfinance Information Exchange 2008, 2009).

Because an estimated 90 percent of the recipients of microcredit are women, feminist theorists are especially interested in the growth of microfinancing. Women's economic status has been found to be critical to the well-being of their children, and the key to a healthy household environment. In developing countries, where women often are not treated as well as men, being entrusted with credit is particularly empowering to them. Research indicates that women recipients are more likely than men to participate in networks and collective action groups, perhaps because they must overcome resistance to women as economic decision makers (Sanyal 2009).

THE CHANGING FACE OF THE WORKFORCE

In the United States the workforce is constantly changing. During World War II, when men were mobilized to fight abroad, women entered the workforce in large numbers. And with the rise of the civil rights movement, minorities found numerous job opportunities open to them. The active recruitment of women and minorities into the workplace, known as *affirmative action,* has helped minorities to climb the occupational ladder. More recently, immigrants have entered the U.S. labor force in increasing numbers.

While predictions are not always reliable, sociologists and labor specialists foresee a workforce increasingly composed of women and racial and ethnic minorities. Today, the number of Black, Latino, and Asian American workers is increasing at a rate faster than the number of White workers. Moreover, most of today's immigrants come from Asia and Latin America rather than from northern Europe, the source of the dominant culture in the United States (see Figure 9–4). More and more, the workforce reflects this diversity, as ethnic minorities enter the labor force and immigrants and their children move from marginal jobs or employment to positions of greater visibility and responsibility.

The impact of this changing labor force is not merely statistical. A more diverse workforce means that relationships between workers are more likely to cross gender, racial, and ethnic lines. Interactionists note that people will find themselves supervising and being supervised by people very different from themselves. In response to these changes, 75 percent of businesses have instituted some type of cultural diversity training program (Melia 2000).

DEINDUSTRIALIZATION

What happens when a company decides it is more profitable to move its operations out of a long-established community to another part of

Figure 9–4
Origins of the Foreign-Born Working-Age Population of the United States
SOURCE: 2004 Bureau of Labor Statistics data in Mosisa 2006:48.

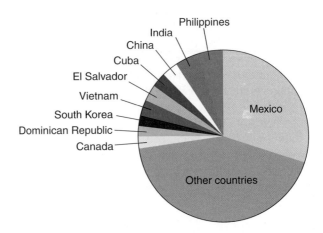

the country, or out of the country altogether? People lose jobs; stores lose customers; the local government's tax base declines and it cuts services. This devastating process has occurred again and again over the last decade or so.

The term *deindustrialization* refers to the systematic, widespread withdrawal of investment in basic aspects of productivity, such as factories and plants. Giant corporations that deindustrialize are not necessarily refusing to invest in new economic opportunities. Rather, the targets and locations of investment change, and the need for labor decreases as technology continues to automate production. First, plants may relocate from the central city to the suburbs. The next step may be a move from suburban areas of the Northeast and Midwest to southern states, where labor laws place more restrictions on unions. Finally, a corporation may simply relocate *outside* the United States to a country with lower wages. General Motors, for example, decided to build a multibillion-dollar plant in China rather than in Kansas City or even in Mexico (Lynn 2003).

Although deindustrialization often involves relocation, in some instances it takes the form of corporate restructuring, as companies seek to reduce costs in the face of growing worldwide competition. When a restructuring occurs, the impact on the bureaucratic hierarchy of formal organizations can be significant. A large corporation may choose to sell off or entirely abandon less productive divisions and eliminate layers of management viewed as unnecessary. Wages and salaries may be frozen and fringe benefits cut—all in the name of "restructuring." Increasing reliance on automation also spells the end of work as we have known it.

The term *downsizing* was introduced in 1987 to refer to reductions taken in a company's workforce as part of deindustrialization. Viewed from a conflict perspective, the unprecedented attention given to downsizing in the mid-1990s reflected the continuing importance of social class in the United States. Conflict theorists note that job loss has long been a feature of deindustrialization among blue-collar workers. But when large numbers of middle-class managers and other white-collar employees with substantial incomes began to be laid off, suddenly the media began expressing great concern over downsizing.

What evidence of deindustrialization or downsizing do you see, specifically, in your community? What broad economic shifts brought about those changes?

The extended economic downturn that began in 2008 accelerated the processes of deindustrialization and downsizing. As the recession deepened, many plants shut down either temporarily or permanently, leaving more and more workers without jobs. With those jobs and shuttered plants went any hope of restoring or expanding heavy industry.

The social costs of deindustrialization and downsizing cannot be overemphasized. Plant closings lead to substantial unemployment in a community, which can have a devastating impact on both the micro and macro levels. On the micro level, the unemployed person and his or her family must adjust to a loss of spending power. Painting or re-siding the house, buying health insurance or saving for retirement, even thinking about having another child must be put aside. Both marital happiness and family cohesion may suffer as a result. Although many dismissed workers eventually reenter the paid labor force, they must often accept less desirable positions with lower salaries and fewer benefits.

Sociology Matters

Sociology matters because it prompts us to look critically at the social institutions that shape our lives.

- What was the hidden curriculum in the primary and secondary schools you attended? Were students assigned to tracks? Do you think the teachers' expectations had an effect on students' academic achievement?

- Do you know anyone who has lost a job because a factory closed, an office was downsized, or jobs were sent to a foreign country? Do the cost savings U.S. consumers get when jobs are sent overseas make up for the losses to U.S. workers?

Sociology matters because it highlights the struggle between the powerful and the powerless.

- Analyze your school or workplace in terms of power and authority. Who governs it, and by what kind of authority? Which model (power elite or pluralist) better fits its power structure?

- Do you consider the division of power and authority in the United States to be fair and just? If not, which social institution do you think is most in need of reform? How would you work to change it?

CHAPTER RESOURCES

Summary

Like the family and religion, the social institutions of **education,** government, and the economy are cultural universals, found in various forms in all human cultures. This chapter examined three sociological perspectives on education; schools as formal organizations; forms of

authority and **power** in government; two basic **economic systems;** and several trends that are transforming the U.S. and world economies.

1. Functionalists stress that schools perform *latent* as well as *manifest functions.* Their latent (hidden) functions include the transmission of culture, the promotion of social and political integration, the maintenance of social control, and the advancement of social change.

2. Conflict theorists note that schools have a **hidden curriculum** that supports conventional social standards. They charge that schools **track** students according to their social class and perpetuate the unequal treatment of women.

3. Interactionists have noted a **teacher-expectancy effect,** in which teachers' assumptions about students' abilities may affect students' academic performance.

4. Today, most schools in the United States are organized in a bureaucratic fashion. Max Weber's five basic characteristics of bureaucracy are all evident in schools.

5. Schools are complex social organizations. Teachers suffer from the stress of role conflict—that of being both an educator and a disciplinarian—that is inherent in their job.

6. There are three basic sources of **power** in any political system: **force, influence,** and **authority.** Max Weber identified three ideal types of authority: **traditional, rational-legal,** and **charismatic.**

7. Advocates of the **elite model** of the nation's power structure see the United States as being ruled by a small group of individuals, called the **power elite,** who share common political and economic interests. Advocates of the **pluralist model** believe that power is shared more widely among conflicting groups.

8. Though capitalist **economic systems** vary in the degree to which government regulates economic activity, all emphasize the two fundamental principles of **capitalism,** private ownership and the profit motive. In recent years, the government of China has begun to encourage capitalist activity.

9. Socialist economic systems, in contrast, aim to eliminate economic exploitation and meet people's needs through government regulation and even ownership. Marx believed that **communism** would evolve naturally out of **socialism.**

10. The world's economies are changing, both in the United States and abroad. In developing countries, **microfinancing** is improving the lives of millions of poor people. In the United States, workers are coping with **deindustrialization** and employers are training an increasingly diverse workforce.

www.mhhe.com/schaefersm5e
Visit the Online Learning Center for *Sociology Matters* to access quizzes, review activities, and other learning tools.

Key Terms

authority, 246

capitalism, 252

charismatic authority, 247

communism, 254

credentialism, 238

deindustrialization, 259

downsizing, 259

economic system, 252

education, 235

elite model, 248

force, 246

hidden curriculum, 238

influence, 246

laissez-faire, 252

microfinancing, 257

monopoly, 253

pluralist model, 250

politics, 245

power, 246

power elite, 248

rational-legal authority, 247

socialism, 253

teacher-expectancy effect, 241

tracking, 239

traditional authority, 247

Population, Community, Health, and the Environment

Imagine that on January 1, 2000, explorers discovered a new mini-continent, about the size of California, in the Pacific Ocean. We can use this imaginary landmass, which we will call Populandia, to illustrate the world's population growth. What would happen if from January 1 onward, we transplanted the natural increase in the world's population—that is, all those babies born above and beyond the number needed to replace those people who have died—to Populandia?

According to the best estimates, a jumbo jet carrying at least 280 newborns would arrive at Populandia International Airport every 2 minutes. By the end of the first day (January 1, 2000), 204,224 people would reside in Populandia—about as many as currently live in Mobile, Alabama. Eleven years later, at the beginning of the year 2011, the population would have climbed to over 803 million, making Populandia the world's third-largest nation—more populous than either the United States or Indonesia (*Intercom* 1978; Bureau of the Census 2010d).

The striking growth of our hypothetical continent of Populandia suggests the pressure that the natural increase in population is placing on our planet. Population growth has a direct impact on the quality of life in our communities, both rural and urban. It threatens our health and strains the capacity of our environment to support us. Anyone who is concerned about these issues must be concerned about population growth. This chapter begins with the debate about the threat of overpopulation, a subject that has occupied some of the world's best minds since the end of the 18th century. To better understand this debate, we will learn some basic concepts that researchers have developed in their study of population. Then we will look at communities, health, and the environment from a sociological perspective, noting their interdependence and their connection to population issues.

Demography: The Study of Population

Population issues engage the attention of both natural and social scientists. The biologist explores the nature of reproduction and casts light on factors that affect *fertility,* the level of reproduction in a society. The medical pathologist examines and analyzes trends in the causes of death. Geographers, historians, and psychologists also have distinctive contributions to make to our understanding of population. Sociologists, more than these other researchers, focus on the *social* factors that influence population rates and trends.

Sociologists are keenly aware that various elements of population—such as fertility and *mortality* (the number of deaths)—are profoundly affected by the norms, values, and social patterns of a society. Fertility is influenced by people's age of entry into sexual unions and by their use of contraception—both of which, in turn, reflect the social and religious values that guide a particular culture. Mortality is shaped by a nation's level of nutrition, acceptance of immunization, and provisions for sanitation, as well as its general commitment to health care and health education.

The formal term for the scientific study of population is *demography.* Demographers draw on several components of population, including size, composition, and territorial distribution, to understand the social consequences of population change. They study geographical variations and historical trends in their effort to develop population forecasts. They also analyze the structure of a population—the age, gender, race, and ethnicity of its members. This type of analysis was popularized by Thomas Malthus.

MALTHUS'S THESIS AND MARX'S RESPONSE

The Reverend Thomas Robert Malthus (1766–1834) was educated at Cambridge University and spent his life teaching history and political economy. He strongly criticized two major institutions of his time—the church and slavery—yet his most significant legacy for contemporary scholars is his still-controversial *Essays on the Principle of Population,* published in 1798.

Essentially, Malthus held that the world's population was growing more rapidly than the available food supply. He argued that food supply increases in an arithmetic progression (1, 2, 3, 4, and so on), whereas population expands by a geometric progression (1, 2, 4, 8, and so on). According to his analysis, the gap between food supply and population will continue to grow over time. Even though the food supply will increase, it will not increase nearly enough to meet the needs of an expanding world population.

Malthus advocated population control to close the gap between rising population and food supply, yet he explicitly denounced artificial means of birth control because they were not sanctioned by religion. For Malthus, one appropriate way to control population was to postpone marriage. He argued that couples must take responsibility for the number of children they choose to bear; without such restraint, the world would face widespread hunger, poverty, and misery (Malthus et al. [1824] 1960; Petersen 1979).

Karl Marx strongly criticized Malthus's views on population. Marx pointed to the nature of economic relations in Europe's industrial societies as the central problem. He could not accept the Malthusian notion that rising world population, rather than capitalism, was the cause of social ills. In Marx's opinion, there was no special relationship between world population and the supply of resources (including food). If society is well ordered, he reasoned, increases in population should lead to greater wealth, not to hunger and misery.

Of course, Marx did not believe that capitalism operated under these ideal conditions. He maintained that capitalism devoted resources to the financing of buildings and tools rather than to more equitable distribution of food, housing, and other necessities of life. Marx's work is important to the study of population because he linked overpopulation to the unequal distribution of resources. His concern with the writings of Malthus also testifies to the importance of population in political and economic affairs.

The insights of Malthus and Marx regarding population issues have since been incorporated in what is termed the *neo-Malthusian view.* Paul Ehrlich (1968; Ehrlich and Ehrlich 1990), author of *The Population Bomb,* and other neo-Malthusians agree with Malthus that world population growth is outstretching natural resources. However, in contrast to the British theorist, they insist that birth control measures are needed to regulate population increases. Their condemnation of developed nations, which despite their low birthrates consume a disproportionately large share of world resources, is founded on Marxist thought. While they are rather pessimistic about the future, these theorists stress that birth control and sensible use of resources are essential responses to rising world population (Tierney 1990; Weeks 2008).

Use Your Sociological Imagination

You are living in a country that is so heavily populated, basic resources such as food, water, and living space are running short. What will you do? How will you respond to the crisis if you are a government social planner? A politician?

STUDYING POPULATION TODAY

The relative balance of births and deaths is no less important today than it was during the lifetimes of Malthus and Marx. The suffering that Malthus spoke of is certainly a reality for many people of the world, who are chronically hungry and poor. Malnutrition remains the largest contributing factor to illness and death among children in developing countries. Almost 18 percent of these children will die before age five—a rate over 11 times higher than in developed nations. Warfare and large-scale migration intensify problems of population and food supply. For example, recent strife in Bosnia, Iraq, and Sudan caused very uneven distribution of food supplies, leading to regional concerns about malnutrition and even starvation. Combating world hunger may require reducing human births, dramatically increasing the world's food supply, or perhaps both at the same time (World Bank 2000:277).

In the United States and most other countries, the census is the primary mechanism for collecting population information. A ***census*** is an enumeration, or counting, of a population. The Constitution of the United States requires that a census be held every 10 years to determine congressional representation. This periodic investigation is supplemented by ***vital statistics,*** or records of births, deaths, marriages, and divorces that are gathered through a registration system maintained by governmental units. In addition, other governmental surveys provide up-to-date information on commercial developments, educational trends, industrial expansion, agricultural practices, and the status of such groups as children, the elderly, racial minorities, and single parents.

In administering a nationwide census and conducting other types of research, demographers employ many of the skills and techniques described in Chapter 1, including questionnaires, interviews, and sampling. The precision of population projections depends on the accuracy of a series of estimates that demographers must make. First, they must determine past population trends and establish a base population as of the date for which the forecast begins. Next, birthrates and death rates must be established, along with estimates of future fluctuations. In projecting a nation's population trends, demographers must consider migration as well, since a significant number of individuals may enter and leave a country.

ELEMENTS OF DEMOGRAPHY

Demographers communicate population facts with a language derived from the basic elements of human life—birth and death. The ***birthrate*** (or more specifically, the *crude birthrate*) is the number of live births per 1,000 population in a given year. In 2010, for example, there were 14 live births per 1,000 people in the United States. The birthrate provides information on the actual reproductive patterns of a society.

One way demographers can project future growth in a society is to make use of the ***total fertility rate (TFR).*** The TFR is the average number of children born alive to any woman, assuming that she conforms to current fertility rates. The TFR reported for the United States in 2010 was 2.0 live births per woman—not high compared to over 7.4 births per woman in a developing country such as Niger.

Mortality, like fertility, is measured in several different ways. The ***death rate*** (also known as the *crude death rate*) is the number of deaths per 1,000 population in a given year. In 2010, the United States had a death rate of 8.0 per 1,000 population. The ***infant mortality rate*** is the number of deaths of infants under one year of age per 1,000 live births in a given year. This particular measure serves as an important indicator of a society's level of health care; it reflects prenatal nutrition, delivery procedures, and infant screening measures. The infant mortality rate also functions as a useful indicator of future population growth, since those infants who survive to adulthood will contribute to further population increases. Figure 10–1 compares the infant mortality rates in selected countries.

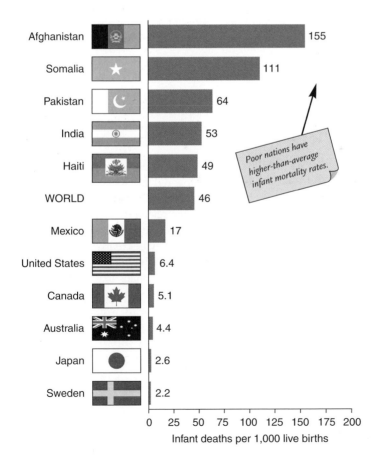

Figure 10–1
Infant mortality rates in selected countries
Source: Haub 2010.

Another general measure of health used by demographers is *life expectancy*, or the median number of years a person can be expected to live under current mortality conditions. This figure is usually reported as life expectancy *at birth*. At present, Japan reports a life expectancy at birth of 83 years—slightly higher than the United States' figure of 78 years. By contrast, life expectancy at birth is less than 45 in several developing nations, including Zimbabwe.

The *growth rate* of a society is the difference between births and deaths, plus the difference between *immigrants* (those who enter a country to establish permanent residence) and *emigrants* (those who leave a country permanently) per 1,000 population. For the world as a whole, the growth rate is simply the difference between births and deaths per 1,000 population, since worldwide immigration and emigration must of necessity be equal. In 2010, the United States had a growth rate of 0.6 percent—half the estimated growth rate for the entire world (Haub 2010).

What do these growth rates suggest about the world's future? Was Malthus right when he wrote that the world's population will inevitably outstrip our ability to feed ourselves? Before we attempt to answer this question, let's take a look at how agricultural production has changed over time. The next section will present a brief history of communities, including their methods of production, from the early days of civilization to the present.

How Did Communities Originate?

EARLY COMMUNITIES

A *community* is a unit of social organization, either spatial or political, that gives people a sense of belonging. How did this social arrangement come into being? For most of human history, people used very basic tools and knowledge to survive. They satisfied their need for an adequate food supply through hunting, foraging for fruits or vegetables, fishing, and herding. In comparison with later industrial societies, early civilizations were much more dependent on the physical environment and much less able to alter that environment to their advantage. Perhaps that is why early peoples banded together in nomadic groups in the first known communities.

The emergence of horticultural societies, in which people actually cultivated food rather than merely gathering fruits and vegetables, led to many dramatic changes in human social organization. It was no longer necessary to move from place to place in search of food. Because people had to remain in specific locations to cultivate crops, more stable and enduring communities began to develop. As agricultural techniques became more and more sophisticated, a cooperative division of labor involving both family members and others developed. It gradually became possible for people to produce more food than they actually needed for themselves. They could give food, perhaps as part of an exchange, to others who might be involved in nonagricultural labor.

This transition from subsistence to surplus represented a critical step in the emergence of cities. Eventually, people produced enough goods to cover both their own needs and those of people not engaged in agricultural tasks. The surplus was limited to agricultural products at first, but gradually it evolved to include all types of goods and services. Residents of a city came to rely on community members who provided craft products and means of transportation, gathered information, and so forth (Nolan and Lenski 2009).

With these social changes came an even more elaborate division of labor as well as greater opportunity for differential rewards and privileges. So long as everyone was engaged in the same tasks, stratification was limited to such factors as gender, age, and perhaps the ability to perform the task (a skillful hunter could win unusual respect from the community). However, the surplus allowed for expansion of goods and services, leading to greater differentiation, a hierarchy of occupations, and social inequality. Therefore, surplus was a precondition not only for the establishment of cities but for the division of members of a community into social classes (see Chapter 5). The ability to produce goods for other communities, then, marked a fundamental shift in human social organization.

PREINDUSTRIAL CITIES

It is estimated that beginning about 10,000 B.C., permanent settlements free from dependence on crop cultivation emerged. By today's standards, these early communities would barely qualify as cities. The *preindustrial city,* as it is termed, generally had only a few thousand people living within its borders, and was characterized by a relatively closed class system and limited mobility. In these early cities, status was usually based on ascribed characteristics such as family background, and education was limited to members of the elite. All the residents relied on perhaps 100,000 farmers and their own part-time farming to provide the needed agricultural surplus. The Mesopotamian city of Ur had a population of about 10,000 and was limited to roughly 220 acres of land, including the canals, the temple, and the harbor.

Why were these early cities so small and relatively few in number? Several key factors restricted urbanization:

- *Reliance on animal power (both humans and beasts of burden) as a source of energy for economic production.* This factor limited the ability of humans to make use of and alter the physical environment.

- *Modest levels of surplus produced by the agricultural sector.* Between 50 and 90 farmers may have been required to support one city resident (K. Davis [1949] 1995).

- *Problems in transportation and the storage of food and other goods.* Even an excellent crop could easily be lost as a result of such difficulties.

- *Hardships of migration to the city.* For many peasants, migration was both physically and economically impossible. A few weeks of travel was out of the question without more sophisticated food storage techniques.

- *Dangers of city life.* Concentrating a society's population in a small area left it open to attack from outsiders as well as more susceptible to extreme damage from plagues and fires.

Gideon Sjoberg (1960) examined the available information on early urban settlements in medieval Europe, India, and China. He identified three preconditions of city life: advanced technology in both agricultural and nonagricultural areas, a favorable physical environment, and a well-developed social organization. For Sjoberg, the criteria for defining a "favorable" physical environment were variable. Proximity to coal and iron helps only if a society knows how to *use* those natural resources. Similarly, proximity to a river is particularly beneficial only if a culture has the means to transport water efficiently to the fields for irrigation and to the cities for consumption. Specialized social roles were important because cities brought people together in new ways through the exchange of goods and services. A well-developed social organization ensured that these relationships were clearly defined and acceptable to all.

INDUSTRIAL AND POSTINDUSTRIAL CITIES

Imagine how harnessing the energy in air, water, and other natural resources could change society. Just as advances in agricultural technology once led to dramatic changes in community life, so did the process of industrialization. The *Industrial Revolution,* which began in the middle of the 18th century, focused on the application of nonanimal sources of power to labor tasks. Industrialization had a wide range of effects on people's lifestyles as well as on the structure of communities. Emerging urban settlements became centers not only of industry but of banking, finance, and industrial management as well.

The factory system that developed during the Industrial Revolution led to a much more refined division of labor than existed in early preindustrial cities. In turn, the many new jobs it created produced a complex set of relationships among workers. Thus, the **industrial city** was not merely more populous than its preindustrial predecessors; it was based on very different principles of social organization. Sjoberg outlined the contrasts between preindustrial and industrial cities (see Table 10–1).

In comparison with preindustrial cities, industrial cities had a more open class system and more mobility. After initiatives in industrial cities by women's rights groups, labor unions, and other political activists,

summingUP

Table 10-1   Comparing Types of Cities

Preindustrial Cities (through 18th century)	Industrial Cities (18th through mid-20th century)	Postindustrial Cities (beginning late 20th century)
Closed class system—pervasive influence of social class at birth	Open class system—mobility based on achieved characteristics	Wealth based on ability to obtain and use information
Economic realm controlled by guilds and a few families	Relatively open competition	Corporate power dominates
Beginnings of division of labor in creation of goods	Elaborate specialization in manufacturing of goods	Sense of place fades, transnational networks emerge
Pervasive influence of religion on social norms	Influence of religion limited to certain areas as society becomes more secularized	Religion becomes more fragmented; greater openness to new religious faiths
Little standardization of prices, weights, and measures	Standardization enforced by custom and law	Conflicting views of prevailing standards
Population largely illiterate, communication by word of mouth	Emergence of communication through posters, bulletins, and newspapers	Emergence of extended electronic networks
Schools limited to elites and designed to perpetuate their privileged status	Formal schooling open to the masses and viewed as a means of advancing the social order	Professional, scientific, and technical personnel become increasingly important

SOURCE: Based on E. Phillips 1996:132–135; Sjoberg 1960:323–328.

formal education gradually became available to children from poor and working-class families. While ascribed characteristics such as gender, race, and ethnicity remained important, a talented or skilled individual had more opportunity to better his or her social position than in the past. In these and other respects, the industrial city was genuinely a different world from the preindustrial urban community.

In the latter part of the 20th century, a new type of urban community emerged. The ***postindustrial city*** is a city in which global finance and the electronic flow of information dominate the economy. Production is decentralized and often takes place outside urban centers, but control is centralized in multinational corporations whose influence transcends urban and even national boundaries. Social change is a constant feature of the postindustrial city. Economic and spatial restructuring seems to occur each decade, if not more frequently. In the postindustrial world, cities are forced into increasing competition with one another for economic opportunities, which deepens the plight of the urban poor (E. Phillips 1996; D. Smith and Timberlake 1993).

Sociologist Louis Wirth (1928, 1938) argued that a relatively large and permanent settlement leads to distinctive patterns of social behavior, which he called ***urbanism.*** He identified three critical factors that contribute to urbanism: the size of the population, population density, and the heterogeneity (variety) of the population. A frequent result of

What would the ideal city of the future look like? Describe its architecture, public transportation, neighborhoods, schools, and workplaces. What kinds of people would live and work there?

urbanism, according to Wirth, is that residents become insensitive to events around them and restrict their attention to the primary groups to which they are emotionally attached.

In most parts of the world today, populations are concentrating more and more in urban areas. What are the effects of urbanization on the people who congregate in cities? In the following section we will see how urbanization shapes both the neighborhoods Americans live or do not live in and the economic well-being of people in developing countries.

Urbanization and Its Consequences

The 1990 census was the first to demonstrate that more than half the U.S. population lives in urban areas of 1 million or more residents. In only four states (Maine, Mississippi, Vermont, and West Virginia) do more than half the residents live in rural areas. Clearly, urbanization has become a central aspect of life in the United States (Bureau of the Census 2009a).

Urbanization can be seen throughout the rest of the world, too. In 1900 only 10 percent of the world's people lived in urban areas, but by 2005 that proportion had risen to around 50 percent. By the year 2025, the number of city dwellers could reach 5 billion (Koolhaas et al. 2001:3; United Nations Population Division 2004b).

During the 19th and early 20th centuries, rapid urbanization occurred primarily in European and North American cities. Since World War II, however, an urban "explosion" has hit the world's developing countries. Such rapid growth is evident in the rising number of "squatter settlements," outlying areas occupied by the very poor.

The trend toward urbanization is so important, some sociologists have devoted their careers to the study of its effects. In the following sections we will examine two contrasting perspectives on urbanization, a functionalist view called *urban ecology* and a conflict view called the *new urban sociology.*

FUNCTIONALIST VIEW: URBAN ECOLOGY

Human ecology is an area of study that is concerned with the interrelationships between people and their spatial setting and physical environment. Human ecologists have long been interested in how the physical environment shapes people's lives (for example, rivers can serve as a barrier to residential expansion) as well as in how people influence the surrounding environment (for example, air-conditioning has accelerated the growth of major metropolitan areas in the Southwest). ***Urban ecology*** focuses on such relationships as they emerge in urban areas. Although the urban ecological approach examines social change in cities, it is nevertheless functionalist in its orientation because it emphasizes that different elements in urban areas contribute to social stability.

Early urban ecologists such as Robert Park (1916, 1936) and Ernest Burgess (1925) concentrated on city life but drew on the approaches used by ecologists in studying plant and animal communities. With few exceptions, today's urban ecologists trace their work back to the ***concentric-zone theory*** Burgess devised in the 1920s (see Figure 10–2a). Using Chicago as an example, Burgess proposed a theory for describing land use in industrial cities. At the center, or nucleus, of such a city is the central business district. Large department stores, hotels, theaters, and financial institutions occupy this highly valued land. Surrounding this urban center are other zones that contain other types of land use. According to this theory, the city grows over time by spreading outward from the center.

Note that the creation of zones is a *social* process, not the result of nature alone. Families and business firms compete for the most valuable land; those possessing the most wealth and power generally win. Thus, the concentric-zone theory is a dynamic model of urban growth. As urban growth proceeds, each zone moves even farther from the central business district. Yet while the theory allows for outward growth of cities, it does not provide for major restructuring, as happens when a dying central business district gives way to the pull of outlying centers of commerce and technology. In such cases, the theory assumes a greater degree of stability than actually exists.

Because of its functionalist orientation and its emphasis on stability, the concentric-zone theory tended to understate or ignore certain tensions apparent in metropolitan areas. For example, urban ecologists viewed uncritically the growing use by the affluent of land in a city's peripheral areas. Some described the arrival of African Americans in White neighborhoods in the 1930s with terms such as "invasion" and "succession." Moreover, urban ecologists gave little thought to gender inequities, such as the establishment of men's softball and golf leagues in city parks without any programs for women. Consequently, the urban ecological approach has been criticized for its failure to address issues of gender, race, and class.

Use Your Sociological Imagination

Consider the spatial arrangements in your everyday life from the point of view of urban ecology. How do man-made constructions and barriers affect your travel patterns?

Figure 10–2
Ecological Theories of Urban Growth
Source: Harris and Ullman 1945:13.

1. Central business district
2. Wholesale light manufacturing
3. Low-class residential
4. Medium-class residential
5. High-class residential
6. Heavy manufacturing
7. Outlying business district
8. Residential suburb
9. Industrial suburb
10. Commuters' zone

a. Concentric-zone theory   b. Multiple-nuclei theory

By the middle of the 20th century, urban populations had spread beyond traditional city limits. No longer could urban ecologists focus exclusively on *growth* in the central city, for large numbers of urban residents were abandoning the cities to live in suburban areas. In response to the emergence of more than one focal point in some metropolitan areas, Chauncy D. Harris and Edward Ullman (1945) presented the **multiple-nuclei theory** (see Figure 10–2b). In their view, all urban growth does not radiate outward from a central business district. Instead, a metropolitan area may have many centers of development, each of which reflects a particular urban need or activity. Thus, a city may have a financial district, a manufacturing zone, a waterfront area, an entertainment center, and so forth. Certain types of business firms and certain types of housing will naturally cluster around each distinctive nucleus (Squires 2002).

The rise of suburban shopping malls is a vivid example of the phenomenon of multiple nuclei within metropolitan areas. Initially, all major retailing was located in the city's central business district. Each residential neighborhood had its own grocers, bakers, and butchers, but people traveled to the center of the city to make major purchases at department stores. However, as metropolitan areas expanded and the suburbs became more populous, an increasing number of people began to shop nearer their homes. Today, the suburban mall is a significant retailing and social center in communities across the United States.

In a refinement of the multiple-nuclei theory, contemporary urban ecologists have begun to study what journalist Joel Garreau (1991) has called "edge cities." These communities, which have grown up on the outskirts of major metropolitan areas, are economic and social centers with identities of their own. By any standard of measurement—height of buildings, amount of office space, presence of medical or leisure-time facilities, or of course, population—edge cities qualify as independent cities rather than as large suburbs (R. Lang and LeFurgy 2007).

Whether metropolitan areas include edge cities or multiple nuclei, more and more of them are characterized by spread-out development and unchecked growth. In recent years, Las Vegas has been the most dramatic example. By 2010 the city had grown to nine times its size in 1950, and its population had exploded from less than 25,000 to about 600,000. The social consequences of such rapid growth are equally dramatic, from a shortage of affordable housing and an inadequate number of food pantries to an overstretched water supply, poor health care delivery, and impossible traffic. Today's cities are very different from the preindustrial cities of a thousand years ago.

Use Your Sociological Imagination

You have fast-forwarded to a future in which there are no central cities—just sprawling suburbs and isolated rural communities. What are the economic and social effects of the disappearance of the downtown area?

CONFLICT VIEW: NEW URBAN SOCIOLOGY

Contemporary sociologists point out that metropolitan growth is not governed by waterways and rail lines, as a purely ecological interpretation might suggest. From a conflict perspective, communities are human creations that reflect people's needs, choices, and decisions—though some people have more influence than others over those decisions. Drawing on conflict theory, proponents of an approach that has come to be called the **new urban sociology** consider the interplay of local, national, and worldwide forces and their effect on local space, with special emphasis on the impact of global economic activity (Gottdiener and Hutchison 2010).

New urban sociologists note that urban ecologists typically have avoided examining the social forces, largely economic in nature, that have guided urban growth. For example, central business districts may be upgraded or abandoned, depending on whether urban policy makers grant substantial tax exemptions to developers. The suburban boom in the post–World War II era was fueled by federal housing policies that channeled investment capital into the construction of single-family homes rather than affordable rental housing in the cities. Similarly, while some observers suggest that the growth of sun-belt cities results from a "good business climate," new urban sociologists counter that the term is a euphemism for hefty state and local government subsidies and antilabor policies (Gottdiener and Feagin 1988; M. Smith 1988).

The new urban sociology draws generally on the conflict perspective and more specifically on sociologist Immanuel Wallerstein's **world-systems analysis** (see Chapter 5). Wallerstein argues that certain industrialized nations (among them the United States, Japan, and Germany) hold a dominant position at the *core* of the global economic system. The poor developing countries of Asia, Africa, and Latin America occupy the *periphery* of the global economy, where they are controlled and exploited by core industrialized nations. Through world-systems analysis, new urban sociologists consider urbanization from a global perspective. They view cities not as independent and autonomous entities but rather as the outcome of decision-making processes directed or influenced by a society's dominant classes and by core industrialized nations. New urban sociologists note that the rapidly growing cities of the world's developing countries were shaped first by colonialism and then by a global economy controlled by core nations and multinational corporations (Gottdiener and Feagin 1988; D. Smith 1995).

The urban ecologists of the 1920s and 1930s were not ignorant of the role that the larger economy played in urbanization, but their theories emphasized the impact of local rather than national or global forces. In contrast, through a broad, global emphasis on social inequality and social conflict, new urban sociologists concentrate on such topics as the existence of an underclass, the power of multinational corporations, deindustrialization, homelessness, and residential segregation. Developers, builders, and investment bankers, they suggest, are not especially interested in urban growth when it means providing housing for middle- or low-income people. This lack of interest contributes to the problem of homelessness. Urban elites counter that the nation's housing shortage and

summing UP

Table 10–2 Sociological Perspectives on Urbanization

	Urban Ecology	New Urban Sociology
Theoretical perspective	Functionalist	Conflict
Primary focus	Relationship of urban areas to their spatial setting and physical environment	Relationship of urban areas to global, national, and local forces
Key source of change	Technological innovations such as new methods of transportation	Economic competition and monopolization of power
Initiator of actions	Individuals, neighborhoods, communities	Real estate developers, banks and other financial institutions, and multinational corporations
Allied disciplines	Geography, architecture	Political science, economics

the plight of the homeless are not their fault—and insist that they do not have the capital needed to construct and support such housing. But affluent people *are* interested in growth and *can* somehow find capital to build new shopping centers, office towers, and ballparks. Why, then, can't they provide the capital for affordable housing, ask new urban sociologists?

Part of the answer is that developers, bankers, and other powerful real estate interests view housing in quite a different manner from tenants and most homeowners. For a tenant, an apartment is shelter, housing, a home. But for developers and investors—many of them large (and sometimes multinational) corporations—an apartment is simply a housing investment. These financiers and owners are concerned primarily with maximizing profit, not with solving social problems (Feagin 1983; Gottdiener and Hutchison 2010).

As we have seen throughout this textbook in studying such varied issues as deviance, race, and ethnicity, no single theoretical approach necessarily offers the only valuable perspective. As Table 10–2 shows, urban ecology and the new urban sociology offer significantly different ways of viewing urbanization, both of which enrich our understanding of this complex phenomenon. Clearly, however, urbanization does affect the well-being of those who live in our cities, including their health and quality of life. In the following two sections we will discuss the concepts of health and illness from a sociological perspective, as well as the distribution of health care and the relative health of different social groups.

Health and Illness: Sociological Perspectives

In the preamble to its 1946 constitution, the World Health Organization defined **health** as a "state of complete physical, mental, and social well-being, and not merely the absence of disease and infirmity" (Leavell and Clark 1965:14). Imagine a continuum with health on one end and death on the other. In this definition, the "healthy" end of our continuum represents an ideal rather than a precise condition. Along the continuum, people define themselves as "healthy" or "sick" on the basis of criteria established by themselves, relatives, friends, co-workers, and medical practitioners. Because health is relative, we can view it in a social context and consider how it varies in different situations or cultures.

Who controls definitions of health and illness in our society, and for what ends? Why is it that you may consider yourself sick or well when others do not agree? What are the consequences of viewing yourself (or of being viewed) as ill or disabled? In this section, by drawing on four sociological perspectives—functionalism, conflict theory, interactionism, and labeling theory—we will gain insight into the social context that shapes definitions of health and the treatment of illness.

FUNCTIONALIST APPROACH

Illness entails breaks in our social interactions both at work and at home. From a functionalist perspective, then, "being sick" must be controlled so that not too many people are released from their societal responsibilities at any one time. Functionalists contend that an overly broad definition of illness would disrupt the workings of a society.

"Sickness" requires that one take on a social role, even if temporarily. The *sick role* refers to societal expectations about the attitudes and behavior of a person viewed as being ill. Sociologist Talcott Parsons (1951, 1975), well known for his contributions to functionalist theory, has outlined the behavior required of people considered "sick." They are exempted from their normal, day-to-day responsibilities and generally do not suffer blame for their condition. Yet they are obligated to try to get well, which includes seeking competent professional care. This obligation arises from the common view that illness is dysfunctional, because it can undermine social stability. Attempting to get well is particularly important in the world's developing countries. Modern, automated industrial societies can absorb a greater degree of illness or disability than horticultural or agrarian societies, where the availability of workers is far more critical (Conrad 2009b).

According to Parsons's theory, physicians function as "gatekeepers" for the sick role. They either verify a patient's condition as "illness" or designate the patient as "recovered." The ill person becomes dependent on the doctor, who can control valuable rewards (not only treatment of illness but excused absences from work and school). Parsons suggests that the doctor–patient relationship is somewhat like that between parent and child. Like a parent, the physician helps the patient to enter society as a full and functioning adult (Weitz 2007).

The concept of the sick role is not without criticism. First, patients' judgments regarding their own state of health may be related to their gender, age, social class, and ethnic group. For example, younger people may fail to detect warning signs of a dangerous illness, while the elderly may focus too much on the slightest physical malady. Second, the sick role

Describe some situations you have witnessed that illustrate different definitions of the "sick role."

may be more applicable to people experiencing short-term illnesses than to those with recurring, long-term illnesses. Finally, even simple factors, such as whether or not a person is employed, seem to affect the willingness to assume the sick role—as does the impact of socialization into a particular occupation or activity. For example, beginning in childhood, athletes learn to define certain ailments as "sports injuries" and therefore do not regard themselves as "sick." Nonetheless, sociologists continue to rely on Parsons's model for functionalist analysis of the relationship between illness and societal expectations of the sick (Curry 1993).

CONFLICT APPROACH

Conflict theorists observe that the medical profession has assumed a preeminence that extends well beyond whether to excuse a student from school or an employee from work. Sociologist Eliot Freidson (1970:5) has likened the position of medicine today to that of state religions yesterday—it has an officially approved monopoly of the right to define health and illness and to treat illness. Conflict theorists use the term *medicalization of society* to refer to the growing role of medicine as a major institution of social control (Conrad 2007; McKinlay and McKinlay 1977; Zola 1972, 1983).

The Medicalization of Society   Social control involves techniques and strategies for regulating behavior in order to enforce the distinctive norms and values of a culture. Typically, we think of informal social control as occurring within families and peer groups, and of formal social control as being carried out by authorized agents such as police officers, judges, school administrators, and employers. However, viewed from a conflict perspective, medicine is not simply a "healing profession"; it is a regulating mechanism as well.

How does medicine manifest its social control? First, the field has greatly expanded its domain of expertise in recent decades. Physicians now examine a wide range of issues, among them sexuality (including homosexuality), old age, anxiety, obesity, child development, alcoholism, and drug addiction. Society tolerates such expansion of the boundaries of medicine in the hope that these experts can bring new "miracle cures" to complex human problems, just as they have to the control of certain infectious diseases.

The social significance of this expanding medicalization is that once a problem is viewed using a *medical model*—once medical experts become influential in proposing and assessing relevant public policies—it becomes more difficult for "common people" to join the discussion and exert influence on decision making. It also becomes more difficult to view these issues as being shaped by social, cultural, or psychological factors rather than simply by physical or medical factors (Caplan 1989; Conrad 2007; Starr 1982).

Second, medicine serves as an agent of social control by retaining absolute jurisdiction over many health care procedures. It has even attempted to guard its jurisdiction by placing health care professionals such as chiropractors and nurse-midwives outside the realm of acceptable medicine. Despite the fact that midwives first brought professionalism to child delivery, they have been portrayed as having invaded the "legitimate" field of obstetrics in both the United States and Mexico. Nurse-midwives have sought licensing as a way to achieve professional respectability, but physicians continue to exert power to ensure that midwifery remains a subordinate occupation (Scharnberg 2007).

Inequities in Health Care The medicalization of society is but one concern of conflict theorists. As we have seen throughout this textbook, when analyzing any issue, conflict theorists seek to determine who benefits, who suffers, and who dominates at the expense of others. From a conflict perspective, glaring inequities exist in health care delivery in the United States. For example, poor and rural areas tend to be underserved, because medical services concentrate where people are numerous and/or wealthy.

Similarly, from a global perspective, we can see obvious inequities in health care delivery. Today, the United States has about 27 times the number of physicians per 1,000 people that most African and Asian nations have. This situation is only worsened by the ***brain drain***—the immigration to the United States and other industrialized nations of skilled workers, professionals, and technicians who are desperately needed in their home countries. As part of the brain drain, physicians, nurses, and other health care professionals have come to the United States from developing countries such as India, Pakistan, and various African states. Conflict theorists view such emigration out of the Third World as yet another way in which the world's core industrialized nations enhance their quality of life at the expense of developing countries. One way that developing countries suffer is in lower life expectancy. In Africa and much of Latin America and Asia, life expectancy is far lower than in industrialized nations (Bureau of the Census 2009a; World Bank 2009).

Conflict theorists emphasize that inequities in health care have clear life-and-death consequences. From a conflict perspective, the dramatic differences in infant mortality rates around the world (see Figure 10–1, page 267) reflect, at least in part, unequal distribution of health care resources based on the wealth or poverty of various nations. This measure is an important indicator of a society's level of health care; it reflects prenatal nutrition, delivery procedures, and infant screening measures. Still, despite the wealth of the United States, at least 44 nations have *lower* infant mortality rates, among them Canada, Great Britain, and Japan. Conflict theorists point out that unlike the United States, these countries offer some form of government-supported health care for all citizens, which typically leads to greater availability and use of prenatal care (Haub 2010).

Use Your Sociological Imagination

From a sociological point of view, what might be the greatest challenge to reducing inequities in health care?

INTERACTIONIST APPROACH

From an interactionist point of view, patients are not passive; often, they actively seek the services of a health care practitioner. In examining health, illness, and medicine as a social institution, then, interactionists engage in micro-level study of the roles played by health care professionals and patients. Interactionists are particularly interested in how physicians learn to play their occupational role. According to Brenda L. Beagan (2001), the technical language students learn in medical school becomes the basis for the script they follow as novice physicians. The familiar white coat is their costume—one that helps them to appear confident and professional at the same time that it identifies them as doctors to patients and other staff members. Beagan found that many medical students struggle to project the appearance of competence they think their role demands.

Sometimes patients play an active role in health care by *failing* to follow a physician's advice. For example, some patients stop taking medications long before they should. Some take an incorrect dosage on purpose, and others never even fill their prescriptions. Such noncompliance results in part from the prevalence of self-medication in our society; many people are accustomed to self-diagnosis and self-treatment. On the other hand, patients' active involvement in their health care can sometimes have very *positive* consequences. Some patients read books about preventive health care techniques, attempt to maintain a healthful and nutritious diet, carefully monitor any side effects of medication, and adjust the dosage based on perceived side effects. Finally, physicians may *change* their approach to a patient at the patient's request.

LABELING APPROACH

Labeling theory helps us to understand why certain people are *viewed* as deviants, "bad kids," or criminals, whereas others whose behavior is similar are not. Labeling theorists also suggest that the designation "healthy" or "ill" generally involves social definition by others. Just as police officers, judges, and other regulators of social control have the power to define certain people as criminals, health care professionals (especially physicians) have the power to define certain people as "sick." Moreover, like labels that suggest nonconformity or criminality, labels associated with illness commonly reshape how others treat us and how we see ourselves. Our society attaches serious consequences to labels that suggest less-than-perfect physical or mental health (Becker 1963; C. Clark 1983; H. Schwartz 1987).

A historical example illustrates perhaps the ultimate extreme in labeling social behavior as a sickness. In the 19th century, as enslavement of Africans in the United States came under increasing attack, medical authorities provided new rationalizations for the oppressive practice. Noted physicians published articles stating that the skin color of Africans deviated from "healthy" white skin coloring because Africans suffered from congenital leprosy. Moreover, the continuing efforts of enslaved Africans to escape from their White masters were classified as an example of the "disease" of drapetomania (or "crazy runaways"). The prestigious *New Orleans Medical and Surgical Journal* suggested that the remedy for this "disease" was to treat slaves kindly, as one might treat children. Apparently, medical authorities would not entertain the view that it was healthy and sane to flee slavery or join in a slave revolt (T. Szasz 2010).

By the late 1980s, the power of another label—"person with AIDS"— had become quite evident. This label often functions as a master status that overshadows all other aspects of a person's life. Once someone is told that he or she has tested positive for HIV, the virus associated with AIDS, that person is forced to confront immediate and difficult questions: Should I tell my family members, my sexual partner(s), my friends, my co-workers, my employer? How will these people respond? The public's intense fear of this disease has led to prejudice and discrimination—even social ostracism—against those who have (or are suspected of having) AIDS. A person who has AIDS must deal not only with the serious medical consequences of the disease but also with the distressing social consequences associated with the label.

According to labeling theorists, we can view a variety of life experiences as illnesses or not. Recently, premenstrual syndrome, posttraumatic disorders, and hyperactivity have been "labeled" medically recognized disorders. In addition, disagreements have arisen in the medical community over whether chronic fatigue syndrome constitutes a medical illness.

Probably the most noteworthy medical example of labeling is the case of homosexuality. For years, psychiatrists classified being gay or lesbian not as a lifestyle but as a mental disorder subject to treatment. This official sanction by the psychiatric profession became an early target of the growing gay and lesbian rights movement in the United States. In 1974 members of the American Psychiatric Association voted to drop homosexuality from the standard manual on mental disorders (Conrad 2009a).

Table 10–3 summarizes the four sociological approaches to health and illness just described. They share certain common themes. First, any person's health or illness is more than an organic condition, since it is subject to the interpretation of others. The impact of culture, family and friends, and the medical profession means that health and illness are not purely biological occurrences but sociological occurrences as well. Second, since members of a society (especially industrial societies) share the same health care delivery system, health is a group and societal concern. Although health may be defined as the complete well-being of an individual, it is also the result of the social environment, as the next section will show (Cockerham 2009).

Use Your Sociological Imagination

Describe an occasion on which people you know disagreed about a socially applied medical label. What was the label, and why did people disagree?

summingUP

Table 10–3 Sociological Perspectives on Health and Illness

	Functionalist	Conflict	Interactionist	Labeling
Major emphasis	Control of the number of people who are considered sick	Overmedicalization Gross inequities in health care	Doctor–patient relationship Interaction of medical staff	Definition of illness and health
Controlling factors	Physician as gatekeeper	Medical profession Social inequities	Medical profession	Medical profession
Proponents	Talcott Parsons	Paul Starr Thomas Szasz Irving Zola	Doug Maynard	Thomas Szasz

Social Epidemiology

Social epidemiology is the study of the distribution of disease, impairment, and general health status across a population. The first epidemiologists concentrated on the scientific study of epidemics, focusing on how the diseases started and spread. Contemporary social epidemiology is much broader in scope, concerned not only with epidemics but with nonepidemic diseases, injuries, drug addiction and alcoholism, suicide, and mental illness. The field draws on the work of a wide variety of scientists and researchers, among them physicians, sociologists, public health officials, biologists, veterinarians, demographers, anthropologists, psychologists, and meteorologists. Recently, epidemiologists at the federal government's Centers for Disease Control and Prevention took on the new role of tracking bioterrorism. In 2001 they mobilized to trace the anthrax outbreak and prepare for any terrorist use of smallpox or other lethal microbes that could start an epidemic.

Researchers in social epidemiology commonly use two concepts: *incidence* and *prevalence*. **Incidence** refers to the number of new cases of a specific disorder occurring within a given population during a stated period, usually a year. For example, the incidence of AIDS in the United States in 2007 was 42,655 cases. In contrast, *prevalence* refers to the total number of cases of a specific disorder that exist at a given time. The prevalence of HIV/AIDS in the United States through 2009 was about one million cases (Centers for Disease Control 2009).

When incidence figures are presented as rates, or as the number of reports of a disorder per 100,000 people, they are called **morbidity rates.** (The term **mortality rate** refers to the incidence of *death* in a given population.) Sociologists find morbidity rates useful because they reveal that a specific disease occurs more frequently among one segment of a population than another. As we shall see, social class, race, ethnicity, gender, and age can all affect a population's morbidity rates.

SOCIAL CLASS

Social class is clearly associated with differences in morbidity and mortality rates. Studies in the United States and other countries have consistently shown that people in the lower classes have higher rates of mortality and disability than others.

Why is class linked to health? Crowded living conditions, substandard housing, poor diet, and stress all contribute to the ill health of many low-income people in the United States. In certain instances, poor education may lead to a lack of awareness of measures necessary to maintain good health. Financial strains are certainly a major factor in the health problems of less affluent people.

Another reason for the link between class and health is that the poor—many of whom belong to racial and ethnic minorities—are less able than others to afford quality medical care. As Figure 10–3 shows, the affluent are more likely than the poor to have health insurance, either because they can afford it or because they have jobs that provide it. This situation has been deteriorating over time, as employer-provided coverage (the most common form of health insurance) declined steadily from 2000 through 2009. In 2009, as a deep recession took hold, more and more people reported going without health care because they could not pay for it. And increasingly, pharmacists reported that people were purchasing only those medications they "needed the most," or were buying in small quantities, such as four pills at a time. Not surprisingly, these problems were most common among those with low incomes and among the growing numbers of unemployed.

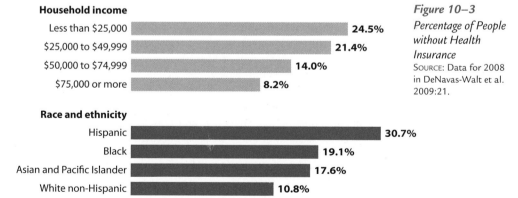

Household income

Less than $25,000	24.5%
$25,000 to $49,999	21.4%
$50,000 to $74,999	14.0%
$75,000 or more	8.2%

Race and ethnicity

Hispanic	30.7%
Black	19.1%
Asian and Pacific Islander	17.6%
White non-Hispanic	10.8%

Figure 10–3
Percentage of People without Health Insurance
SOURCE: Data for 2008 in DeNavas-Walt et al. 2009:21.

Think About It
Do you know people who don't have health insurance? If so, how has the lack of insurance affected their decisions about medical treatment?

In 2010, largely in response to the millions of people who do not have health insurance, Congress enacted the Patient Protection and Affordable Care Act. Beginning in 2014, this legislation—the most significant health care reform since passage of Medicare in 1965—will help people who are sick or have lost a job to afford medical care. In the meantime, certain high-risk people will receive immediate coverage. By 2019, about 95 percent of citizens and legal residents who are not covered by Medicare should have health insurance. In the next few years, researchers will be busy assessing the effect of the legislation on health care inequities.

Finally, in the view of Karl Marx and contemporary conflict theorists, capitalist societies such as the United States care more about maximizing profits than they do about the health and safety of industrial workers. As a result, government agencies do not take forceful action to regulate conditions in the workplace, and workers suffer many preventable job-related injuries and illnesses. As we will see later in this chapter, research also shows that the lower classes are more vulnerable to environmental pollution than are the affluent, not only where they work but where they live.

Does the cost of health care affect the way you receive medical services?

RACE AND ETHNICITY

Health profiles of many racial and ethnic minorities reflect the social inequality evident in the United States. Research shows that the lower classes and members of racial and ethnic minorities are more vulnerable than affluent citizens to environmental pollution. Class plays a role, but race is more oppressive: though upwardly mobile Whites can generally escape from pollution centers, even well-off Blacks tend to be restricted in their residential mobility. The poor economic and environmental conditions of groups such as African Americans, Hispanics, and Native Americans are manifested in high morbidity and mortality rates. It is true that some afflictions, such as sickle-cell anemia among Blacks, have a clear genetic basis, but in most instances, environmental factors contribute to the differential rates of disease and death.

In many respects, the mortality rates for African Americans are distressing. Compared with Whites, Blacks have higher death rates from heart disease, pneumonia, diabetes, and cancer. The death rate from stroke is twice as high among African Americans. Such epidemiological findings reflect in part the fact that a higher proportion of Blacks are found among the nation's lower classes. According to the National Center for Health Statistics, Whites can expect to live 77.7 years. In contrast, life expectancy for Blacks is 72.3 years (Arias 2004).

As noted earlier, infant mortality is regarded as a primary indicator of health care. There is a significant gap in the United States between the infant mortality rates of African Americans and Whites. Generally, the rate of infant death is more than twice as high among Blacks. African Americans account for 15 percent of all live births in the nation but

29 percent of infant deaths. Puerto Ricans and Native Americans have infant mortality rates that are lower than African Americans' but higher than Whites' (MacDorman et al. 2005).

The medical establishment is not exempt from racism. Unfortunately, the media often focus on obvious forms of racism, such as hate crimes, while overlooking more insidious forms in social institutions like the medical establishment. Minorities receive inferior medical care even when they are insured. Despite having access to care, Blacks, Latinos, and American Indians are treated unequally as a result of racial prejudice and differences in the quality of various health care plans. Furthermore, national clinical studies have shown that even allowing for differences in income and insurance coverage, racial and ethnic minorities are less likely than other groups to receive both standard health care and life-saving treatment for conditions such as HIV infection (Common Wealth Fund 2008; Long and Masi 2009; Mays et al. 2007; Weden 2007).

Drawing on the conflict perspective, sociologist Howard Waitzkin (1986) suggests that racial tensions contribute to the medical problems of Blacks. In his view, the stress resulting from racial prejudice and discrimination helps to explain the higher rates of hypertension found among African Americans (and Hispanics) compared with Whites. Hypertension—twice as common in Blacks as in Whites—is believed to be a critical factor in Blacks' high mortality rates from heart disease, kidney disease, and stroke (Morehouse Medical Treatment Effectiveness Center 1999).

Some Mexican Americans, as well as many other Latinos, adhere to cultural beliefs that make them less likely to use the established medical system. Most Hispanics probably use folk healers, or *curanderos,* infrequently, but perhaps 20 percent rely on home remedies. They may interpret their illnesses according to traditional Latino folk practices, or **curanderismo**—a form of holistic health care and healing. *Curanderismo* influences how one approaches health care and even how one defines illness. Some illnesses are defined according to folk beliefs, such as *susto* (fright sickness) and *atague* (or fighting attack). Because these complaints often have biological bases, sensitive medical practitioners need to deal with them carefully and diagnose and treat illnesses accurately (Council on Scientific Affairs 1999; Durden and Hummer 2006; Trotter and Chavira 1997).

GENDER

A large body of research indicates that in comparison with men, women experience a higher prevalence of many illnesses, though they tend to live longer. There are variations—for example, men are more likely to have parasitic diseases, whereas women are more likely to become diabetic—but as a group, women appear to be in poorer health than men.

The apparent inconsistency between the ill health of women and their greater longevity deserves an explanation, and researchers have advanced a theory. Women's lower rate of cigarette smoking (reducing their risk of heart disease, lung cancer, and emphysema), lower consumption of alcohol (reducing their risk of auto accidents and cirrhosis of the liver), and lower rate of employment in dangerous occupations explain about one-third of their greater longevity. Moreover, some clinical studies suggest that the differences in morbidity may actually be less pronounced than the data show. Researchers argue that women are much more likely than men to seek treatment, to be diagnosed as having a disease, and thus to have their illness reflected in the data examined by epidemiologists.

From a conflict perspective, women have been particularly vulnerable to the medicalization of society, with everything from birth to beauty being treated in an increasingly medical context. Such medicalization may contribute to women's higher morbidity rates compared to those of men. Ironically, even though women have been especially affected by medicalization, medical researchers have often excluded women from clinical studies. Female physicians and researchers charge that sexism lies at the heart of such research practices and insist there is a desperate need for studies of female subjects (Rieker and Bird 2000).

Use Your Sociological Imagination

Which is a more important factor in the adequate delivery of health care, race, or gender?

AGE

Health is the overriding concern of the elderly. Most older people in the United States report having at least one chronic illness, but only some of those conditions are potentially life threatening or require medical care. At the same time, health problems can affect the quality of life of older people in important ways. Almost half of older people in the United States are troubled by arthritis, and many have visual or hearing impairments that can interfere with the performance of everyday tasks.

Older people are also especially vulnerable to certain types of mental health problems. Alzheimer's disease, the leading cause of dementia in the United States, afflicts an estimated 5.1 million older people. While some individuals with Alzheimer's exhibit only mild symptoms, the risk of severe problems resulting from the disease rises substantially with age. Only 13 percent of people age 65 and over have symptoms of Alzheimer's, but the figure rises to 48 percent for people age 85 and over (Alzheimer's Association 2010:10).

Not surprisingly, older people in the United States (age 75 and older) are five times more likely to use health services than younger people (ages 15–24). The disproportionate use of the U.S. health care system by older people is a critical factor in all discussions about the cost of health care and possible reforms of the health care system (Bureau of the Census 2009a).

In sum, to achieve greater access and reduce health disparities, federal health officials must overcome inequities that are rooted not just in age, but in social class, race and ethnicity, and gender. If that were not enough, they must also deal with a geographical disparity in health care resources. Dramatic differences in the availability of physicians, hospitals, and nursing homes exist from one state to another and between urban and rural areas within the same state.

The disparity in health resources that exists from one place to another, both within the United States and throughout the globe, is only one way in which our environment can affect our well-being. Our quality of life, whether in the cities, the suburbs, or rural areas, is closely related to the environment. In the final section of this chapter we will see how burgeoning population levels and consumption patterns can have a negative effect on our natural surroundings and on the health of whole communities.

The Environment: The World and Our Place in It

Urban sprawl has been encroaching on the fields and forests that surround U.S. cities, replacing them with residential developments and malls. The new construction disturbs wildlife and threatens the water supply, and the cars residents drive to work every day choke the highways, contributing to air pollution and global warming.

In recent years, public attention has turned increasingly to global warming, manifested in the shrinking of the polar ice caps and the increasing ferociousness of tropical storms as they cross warmer-than-normal ocean waters. Human activities have contributed to the documented warming of the planet over the last half century, through the altered chemical composition of the atmosphere and the buildup of greenhouse gases such as carbon dioxide, methane, and nitrous oxide. While environmental problems may be easy to identify scientifically, however, devising socially and politically acceptable solutions is much more difficult. In the following sections we will survey some identifiable environmental problems and see what sociologists have to say about them.

ENVIRONMENTAL PROBLEMS: AN OVERVIEW

Unfortunately, the environmental problems caused by unbridled development have effects far beyond the places where they are created. Witness Muhammad Ali, a Bangladeshi man who has had to flee flood waters five times in the last decade. Scientists believe that global warming is to blame, both for worsening monsoons and for the raging waters of the Jamuna River, swollen by abnormally high glacier melt from the Himalayas. Every time the river floods, Ali tears down his house, made of tin and bamboo, and moves to higher ground. But he is running out of land to move to. "Where we are standing, in five days it will be gone," he says. "Our future thinking is that if this problem is not taken care of, we will be swept away" (Goering 2007).

Increasingly, people are recognizing the need to address such challenges to the environment. Yet in the United States, survey respondents do not see environmental issues as the most pressing of problems, and they often balk at proposed solutions. Little wonder, given that, in a 2010 national survey, nearly half the respondents were unsure of the evidence presented by scientists, and 48 percent thought the seriousness of global warming was exaggerated. Only 10 percent of those surveyed expected that they would see the effects of global warming in their lifetime (Newport 2010).

We will discuss the enormous challenge of global warming later in this section. First, we will discuss air and water pollution, which are thought to contribute to global warming. We will close the section with a discussion of the impact of globalization.

Air Pollution   Worldwide, more than 1 billion people are exposed to potentially health-damaging levels of air pollution. Unfortunately, in cities around the world, residents have come to accept smog and polluted air as normal. Urban air pollution is caused primarily by emissions from automobiles and secondarily by emissions from electric power plants and heavy industries. Smog not only limits visibility; it can lead to health problems as uncomfortable as eye irritation and as deadly as lung cancer. Such problems are especially severe in developing countries. The World Health Organization estimates that up to 700,000 premature deaths per year could be prevented if pollutants were brought down to safer levels (Carty 1999; World Resources Institute 1998).

People are capable of changing their behavior, but they are also unwilling to make such changes permanent. During the 1984 Olympics in Los Angeles, residents were asked to carpool and stagger their work hours to relieve traffic congestion and improve the quality of the air athletes would breathe. These changes resulted in a remarkable 12 percent drop in ozone levels. But when the Olympians left, people reverted to their normal behavior and the ozone levels climbed back up. Similarly, in the 2008 Olympics, China took drastic action to ensure that Beijing's high levels of air pollution did not mar the games. Construction work in the city ceased, polluting factories and power plants closed down, and roads were swept and sprayed with water several times a day. However, this temporary solution hardly solved China's ongoing problem (*The Economist* 2008).

Water Pollution   Throughout the United States, dumping of waste materials by industries and local governments has polluted streams, rivers, and lakes. Consequently, many bodies of water have become unsafe for drinking, fishing, and swimming. Around the world, pollution of the oceans is an issue of growing concern. Such pollution results regularly from waste dumping and is made worse by fuel leaks from shipping and occasional oil spills. When the oil tanker *Exxon Valdez* ran aground in

Prince William Sound, Alaska, in 1989, its cargo of 11 million gallons of crude oil spilled into the sound and washed onto the shore, contaminating 1,285 miles of shoreline. All together, about 11,000 people joined in a massive cleanup effort that cost over $2 billion. Globally, oil tanker spills occur regularly. In 2010 a much more dramatic spill occurred at BP's Deepwater Horizon drilling platform in the Gulf of Mexico. The size of the huge spill was estimated at *16 times or more* that of the *Exxon Valdez* (ITOPF 2006; Shapley 2010).

Less dramatic than large-scale accidents or disasters, but more common in many parts of the world, are problems with the basic water supply. Worldwide, over 1.1 billion people lack safe and adequate drinking water, and 2.6 billion have no acceptable means of sanitation—a problem that further threatens the quality of water supplies. The health costs of unsafe water are enormous (United Nations Development Programme 2007).

Water scarcity in and of itself is another critical issue. For centuries, competition for limited supplies of water has led to conflict. Today, for example, the continuing war over the Darfur region of the Sudan is fueled by a growing population and a shrinking water supply. In many of the world's poorest regions, particularly in Africa, millions of people spend much of their day simply searching for water. Obviously, their time and labor could be better used in creating a self-sustaining environment (Pacific Institute 2010a, 2010b; Velasquez-Manoff 2009).

Global Warming Based primarily on complex computer models, scientists have made hundreds of projections of global warming. The term ***global warming*** refers to the significant rise in the earth's surface temperatures that occurs when industrial gases like carbon dioxide turn the planet's atmosphere into a virtual greenhouse. These so-called *greenhouse gas emissions,* which also include methane, nitrous oxide, and ozone, trap heat in the lower atmosphere. Even one additional degree of warmth in the globe's average surface temperature can increase the likelihood of wildfires, shrinkage of rivers and lakes, expansion of deserts, and torrential downpours, including typhoons and hurricanes. Scientists now track and project carbon dioxide emissions around the world (Lynas 2008).

Although scientific concern over global warming has heated up, climate change remains low on policy makers' list of concerns. The problem seems abstract, and in many countries, officials think that the real impact of any action they may take depends on decisive action by other nations. The Kyoto Protocol was intended to reduce global emissions of heat-trapped gases, which can contribute to global warming and climate change. To date, 190 countries have signed the accord, but the United States has failed to ratify it. Opponents of the protocol argue that doing so would place the nation at a disadvantage in the global marketplace.

In 2009, shortly after Barack Obama became president, the United States pledged to become involved in negotiating a new, broader agreement. Besides reducing greenhouse emissions, the proposed agreement would

To combat global warming, increasing numbers of people are seeking to achieve net-zero carbon emissions, both by avoiding emissions when possible—for example, by walking rather than driving—and through offsets (such as planting trees).

"Two can live as carbon-neutral as one."

give technical assistance to developing countries struggling to cope with climate change. However, the 2009 summit, held in Copenhagen, served only to reinforce the global divide over how to address climate change. Europeans were unhappy that their countries seemed to be the only ones with binding objectives to reduce carbon emissions. Poorer nations objected to being left out of many of the critical negotiations. Environmental groups gave a cautious nod of approval, but with goals stretching to 2050, the summit's lasting impact will be difficult to assess (Broder 2009; E. Rosenthal 2009; United Nations Framework Convention on Climate Change 2010).

In writing about the global environment, activists often assert, "We're all in this together." Though we are all in this together, the reality is that globally, the most vulnerable countries tend to be the poorest. Developing nations are more likely than others to have economies that are built on limited resources or on a small number of crops vulnerable to drought, flood, and fluctuations in worldwide demand (Nordhaus and Shellenberger 2007; Revkin 2007).

We can view global warming from the point of view of world-systems analysis. Historically, core nations have been the major emitters of greenhouse gases. Today, however, manufacturing has moved to semiperiphery and periphery nations, where greenhouse gas emissions are escalating. Ironically, many of the forces that are now

Table 10–4 Estimated Time for Each Successive Increase of 1 Billion People in World Population

Population Level	Time Taken to Reach New Population Level	Year of Attainment
First billion	Human history before 1800	1804
Second billion	123 years	1927
Third billion	32 years	1959
Fourth billion	15 years	1974
Fifth billion	12 years	1986
Sixth billion	13 years	1999
Seventh billion	13 years	2012
Eighth billion	15 years	2027
Ninth billion	18 years	2045

SOURCE: Bureau of the Census 2008b.

calling for a reduction in the human activity that contributes to global warming are located in core nations, which have contributed disproportionately to the problem. We want our hamburgers, but we decry the destruction of the rain forests to create grazing land for cattle. We want inexpensive clothes and toys, but we condemn developing countries for depending on coal-fired power plants, which are expected to increase 46 percent by 2030. The challenge of global warming, then, is closely tied to global inequality (M. Jenkins 2008; J. Roberts et al. 2003).

As you think about all the problems facing our society, how often do you consider global warming? How often do your friends give it much thought?

What are the causes of this global environmental crisis? Some observers, such as Paul Ehrlich and Anne Ehrlich, see the pressure of world population growth as the central factor in environmental deterioration. They argue that population control is essential in preventing widespread starvation and environmental decay. Table 10–4 shows the dramatic escalation of population growth over the last two centuries.

Barry Commoner, a biologist, counters that the primary cause of environmental ills is the increasing use of technological innovations that are destructive to the environment—among them plastics, detergents, synthetic fibers, pesticides, herbicides, and chemical fertilizers. Conflict theorists see the despoliation of the environment through the lens of world-systems analysis. And interactionists stress efforts by informed individuals and groups to reduce their carbon footprint—that is, their daily or even lifetime production of greenhouse gases—through careful selection of the goods they consume (Carbon Trust 2010; Commoner 1990, 2007; Ehrlich and Ellison 2002).

The Impact of Globalization Globalization can be both good and bad for the environment. On the negative side, it can create a race to the bottom, as polluting companies relocate to countries with less stringent environmental standards. Similarly, globalization allows multinationals to reap the resources of developing countries for short-term profit. From Mexico to China, the industrialization that often accompanies globalization has increased pollution of all types.

Yet globalization can have a positive impact, as well. As barriers to the international movement of goods, services, and people fall, multinational corporations have an incentive to carefully consider the cost of natural resources. Overusing or wasting resources makes little sense, especially when they are in danger of depletion (Kwong 2005).

One reflection of the interplay between globalization and the environment is the emergence of so-called *environmental refugees*. Europe in particular is beginning to see an influx of such immigrants from developing nations. According to a European Union report, global warming can be viewed as a "threat multiplier" that exacerbates prolonged droughts and a shortage of arable land, and along with them, poverty, poor health, and poor living conditions. Viewed through the lens of world-systems analysis, periphery countries may become overburdened by environmental problems, precipitating migrations to industrial nations or conflicts that cause mass displacements of their populations. "Europe must expect substantially increased migratory pressure" from these environmental refugees, the report concludes (Traynor 2008).

Against these potentially negative effects of globalization we must note the potential for new jobs in what are called green industries. Installing solar panels, weatherizing homes, brewing biofuels, building hybrid cars, growing organic foods, manufacturing organic garments, and erecting giant wind turbines are all classified as *green-collar jobs*. However, skeptics question how many such jobs will be created, and to what degree they will offset job losses in pollution-prone industries like oil, gas, and coal mining (S. Greenhouse 2008b; R. Pinderhughes 2008).

HUMAN ECOLOGY

Earlier, we noted that human ecology is concerned with interrelationships between people and their environment. As Barry Commoner (1971:39) has stated, "Everything is connected to everything else." Human ecologists focus both on how the physical environment shapes people's lives and on how people influence the surrounding environment.

In an application of the human ecological perspective, sociologist Riley Dunlap suggests that the natural environment serves three basic functions for humans, as it does for the many animal species (Dunlap 1993; Dunlap and Catton 1983):

1. *The environment provides the resources essential for life.* They include air, water, and materials used to create shelter, transportation, and other necessities. If human societies exhaust these resources—for example, by polluting the water supply or cutting down rain forests—the consequences can be dire.

2. *The environment serves as a waste repository.* More so than other living species, humans produce a huge quantity and variety of waste products—bottles, boxes, papers, sewage, and garbage, to name just a few. Various types of pollution have become more common because human societies are generating more wastes than the environment can safely absorb.

3. *The environment "houses" our species.* It is our home, our living space, the place where we reside, work, and play. At times we take this home for granted, but not when day-to-day living conditions become unpleasant and difficult. If our air is "heavy," if our tap water turns brown, if toxic chemicals seep into our neighborhoods, we remember why it is vital to live in a healthful environment.

There is no shortage of illustrations of the interconnectedness of people and their environment. For example, scientific research has linked pollutants in the physical environment to people's health and behavior. The increasing prevalence of asthma, lead poisoning, and cancer has been tied to human alterations to the environment. Similarly, the rise in melanoma (skin cancer) diagnoses has been linked to global warming. And ecological changes in our food and diet have been related to early obesity and diabetes.

With its view that "everything is connected to everything else," human ecology stresses the trade-offs inherent in every decision that alters the environment. In facing the environmental challenges of the 21st century, government policy makers and environmentalists must determine how they can fulfill humans' pressing needs for food, clothing, and shelter while preserving the environment as a source of resources, a waste repository, and our home.

A CONFLICT VIEW OF ENVIRONMENTAL ISSUES

In Chapter 5 we drew on world-systems analysis to show how a growing share of the human and natural resources of developing countries is being redistributed to the core industrialized nations. This process only intensifies the destruction of natural resources in poorer regions of the world. From a conflict perspective, less affluent nations are being forced to exploit their mineral deposits, forests, and fisheries in order to meet their debt obligations to industrialized nations. The poor turn to the only means of survival available to them: They plow mountain slopes, burn tropical forests, and overgraze grasslands (World Bank 2010b).

Brazil exemplifies this interplay between economic troubles and environmental destruction. Each year more than 5.7 million acres of forest are cleared for crops and livestock. The elimination of the rain forest affects worldwide weather patterns, heightening the gradual warming of the earth. These socioeconomic patterns, with their harmful environmental consequences, are evident not only in Latin America but in many regions of Africa and Asia as well.

Although deforestation of the rain forest has long been a concern, only in the last few years have policy makers begun to listen to the indigenous peoples who live in these areas. In 2008, native peoples from Brazil to the Congo to Indonesia convened to make the case that wealthier countries should compensate them for conservation of the tropical rain forests. Preservation of the rain forests may make sense at the global level, but for many local peoples, it limits their efforts to cultivate crops or graze cattle (Barrionuevo 2008).

Conflict theorists are well aware of the environmental implications of land use policies in the Third World, but they contend that focusing on the developing countries is ethnocentric. Who, they ask, is more to blame for environmental deterioration: the poverty-stricken and "food-hungry" populations of the world or the "energy-hungry" industrialized nations? These theorists point out that the industrialized nations of North America and Europe account for only 12 percent of the world's population but are responsible for 60 percent of worldwide consumption. The money their residents spend on ocean cruises each year could provide clean drinking water for everyone on the planet. Ice cream expenditures in Europe alone could be used to immunize every child in the world. Thus, conflict theorists charge, the most serious threat to the environment comes from the global consumer class (Gardner et al. 2004; Shah 2009).

Allan Schnaiberg (1994) further refines this analysis by shifting the focus from affluent consumers as the cause of environmental troubles. In his view, a capitalist system creates a "treadmill of production" because of its inherent need to build ever-expanding profits. This treadmill necessitates creating an increasing demand for products, obtaining natural resources at minimal cost, and manufacturing products as quickly and cheaply as possible—no matter what the long-term environmental consequences.

From the perspective of developing nations, many calls for the reduction of greenhouse gases unfairly target countries that are just beginning to industrialize.

ENVIRONMENTAL JUSTICE

In autumn 1982, nearly 500 African Americans participated in a six-week protest against a hazardous waste landfill in North Carolina. Their protests and legal actions against the dangerous cancer-causing chemicals continued until 2002, when decontamination of the site finally began. This 20 year battle could be seen as yet another "not in my backyard" (NIMBY) event. But today, the Warren County struggle is viewed as a transformative moment in contemporary environmentalism: the beginning of the environmental justice movement (Bullard 1993; McGurty 2000; North Carolina Department of Environment and Natural Resources 2008).

Environmental justice is a legal strategy based on claims that racial minorities and the lower classes are subjected disproportionately to environmental hazards. Some observers have heralded environmental justice as the "new civil rights of the 21st century" (Kokmen 2008:42). Since the start of the environmental justice movement, activists and scholars have discovered other environmental disparities that break along racial and social class lines. In general, poor people and people of color are much more likely than others to be victimized by the everyday consequences of our built environment, including the air pollution from expressways and incinerators.

Following reports from the Environmental Protection Agency (EPA) and other organizations documenting the discriminatory location of hazardous waste sites, President Bill Clinton issued an executive order in 1994 that requires all federal agencies to ensure that low-income and minority communities have access to better information about their environment and an opportunity to participate in shaping government policies that affect their health. Initial efforts to implement the policy, along with increased activity by the environmental justice movement, aroused widespread opposition because of the delays it imposes in establishing new industrial sites. Some observers question the wisdom of an order that slows economic development in areas that are in dire need of employment opportunities. Others point out that such businesses employ few unskilled or less skilled workers, and only make the environment less livable (Laszewski 2008; A. Szasz 1994; D. Taylor 2000).

Sociology Matters

Sociology matters because it explains the connection between population patterns and the community in which you live.

- What kind of community—urban, suburban, or rural—do you live in? Is your community growing, or has its population been declining? What is responsible for the growth or decline of your community?

- Examine the city nearest you from the point of view of an urban sociologist. Is its economy industrial or postindustrial? Which theory describes its growth better, the concentric-zone theory or the multiple-nuclei theory? Does the city have any global economic ties?

Sociology matters because it highlights the relationship between your race, ethnicity, and social class and your quality of life.

- Evaluate the health of the people in your community: Do you think it is better than average, average, or worse than average? How many people in your community have low incomes or are members of minority groups? How many lack health care or health insurance?

- Describe your community's environment. Does it present any health hazards? If so, could some of the health problems in your community be related to those hazards?

CHAPTER RESOURCES

Summary

The size, composition, and distribution of the world's population have an important influence on our **communities,** our **health,** and our environment. This chapter introduced **demography,** the scientific study of population. We followed the growth of communities from prehistory through the present and considered urbanization from both the functionalist and conflict perspectives. We studied the relationship between people's health, their geographic distribution, and the social groups to which they belong. And we acknowledged the connection between our health and the environment we live in.

1. Thomas Robert Malthus suggested that the world's population was growing more rapidly than the available food supply and that the gap between the two would increase over time. But Karl Marx saw capitalism, rather than rising population, as the main cause of the world's social ills.

2. The primary tool for obtaining **vital statistics** on the population of the United States and most other countries is the **census.**

3. Stable **communities** first developed when humans became farmers, and their surplus production allowed others to live in **preindustrial cities.** Thousands of years later, the mechanization of production ushered in the era of the **industrial city,** a large population center dominated by factories. In the 20th century, globalization and the electronic flow of information gave rise to the **postindustrial city,** characterized by corporate offices rather than factories.

4. **Urban ecology** is a functionalist view of urbanization that focuses on the interrelationships between city dwellers and their environment. Urban ecologists developed two theories of urban growth, the **concentric-zone theory** and the **multiple-nuclei theory.**

5. **New urban sociology,** a conflict view of urbanization, focuses on the interplay of local, national, and global economic forces and their effect on cities throughout the world. This school of thought draws on Immanuel Wallerstein's **world-systems analysis.**

6. Functionalists, conflict theorists, and labeling theorists all see medicine as an institution of social definition and control. Functionalists see doctors as gatekeepers to the **sick role;** conflict theorists see them as proponents of the medicalization of society.

7. **Social epidemiology** is the study of the distribution of disease, disability, and **health** across a population. Epidemiological studies have shown that lower-class people have higher rates of **mortality** and disability than upper-class people. Similarly, racial and ethnic minorities have higher rates of **morbidity** and mortality than Whites.

8. From the perspective of **human ecology,** the natural environment serves three basic functions: It provides essential resources, serves as a waste repository, and houses our species. Thus, air and water pollution, as well as global warming, threaten our health and well-being.

9. Conflict theorists charge that the most serious threat to the environment comes from Western industrialized nations, which consume a disproportionate amount of the world's resources.

10. Racial minorities and the lower classes tend to be exposed more than other groups to environmental hazards, a social pattern that has prompted calls for **environmental justice.**

Key Terms

birthrate, 266

brain drain, 279

census, 266

community, 268

concentric-zone
    theory, 273

curanderismo, 285

death rate, 267

demography, 264

environmental
    justice, 295

fertility, 264

global
    warming, 289

growth rate, 268

health, 276

human ecology, 272

incidence, 282

industrial city, 270

infant mortality
    rate, 267

life expectancy, 268

morbidity rates, 282

mortality rates, 282

multiple-nuclei
    theory, 274

new urban
    sociology, 275

postindustrial
    city, 271

preindustrial city, 269

prevalence, 282

sick role, 277

social
    epidemiology, 282

total fertility rate
    (TFR), 267

urban ecology, 272

urbanism, 271

vital statistics, 266

world-systems
    analysis, 275

Social Movements, Social Change, and Technology

Social Movements

Theories of Social Change

Resistance to Social Change

Technology and the Future

On Eighth Avenue in New York City, an electronic billboard plays a trailer for an upcoming television miniseries. As you watch the giant screen, it watches you. A tiny camera photographs you, while a computer determines your gender, estimates your age, and measures your attention span. Science fiction? No, this scenario is real. In just months, millions of people have been "caught" by watchful billboards installed throughout Europe and North America. Similar applications are scanning shoppers' habits in stores.

Virtual reality has penetrated the family, as well. Forget "Over the hills and through the woods, to Grandmother's house we go." Today, virtual family reunions are beginning to replace traditional get-togethers. Propelled by the frustrations and high costs of travel, families are turning to webcams and online reunion sites. Will these new technologies unite only far-flung relatives, who could never "see" one another in person, or will they replace even short car trips? Maybe you're thinking you don't want to share your family with the world. That problem has been solved by the creation of restricted websites that allow families to schedule private get-togethers.

Even society is being redefined by electronic networking. As Figure 11–1 shows, social networking sites are beginning to rival the largest nations in terms of the number of people who "reside" there. Like shoppers and families, society experiences *social change* as a result of the introduction of new technologies.

Population/registered users, 2010

13	7	6	5	4	3	2	1
Twitter: 124m	Brazil: 193m	Indonesia: 235m	MySpace: 300m	United States: 318m	Facebook: 500m	India: 1.19bn	China: 1.34bn

Figure 11–1

Largest Societies, Real and Virtual

NOTE: *Pakistan, Bangladesh, Nigeria, Russia, and Japan rank 8–12.*
SOURCES: Author, data drawing upon Haub 2010; McGrath 2010; and Figure adapted from *The Economist,* "The future is another country." © *The Economist Newspaper* Limited, London, July 24, 2010.

Social change may be defined as significant alteration over time in behavior patterns and culture (Moore 1967). Eventually, the existence of surveillance cameras in public places, of virtual family get-togethers on the World Wide Web, and of social networking sites may greatly influence the way people behave. In this chapter we will examine the process of social change, with special emphasis on the impact of technological advances. We will begin with social movements, which often spearhead social change. Then we will consider different socio-logical perspectives on change and note how vested interests attempt to block it. Finally, we will look at the role of technology in spurring social change, from Web surfing and the offshoring of service jobs to censorship and genetic engineering.

Social Movements

Social movements are the most powerful source of social change. Although such factors as the physical environment, population, technology, and social inequality also serve as sources of change, it is the *collective* effort of individuals organized into social movements that ultimately leads to change.

Sociologists use the term **social movements** to refer to organized collective activities to bring about or resist fundamental change in an existing group or society (Benford 1992). Herbert Blumer (1955:19) recognized the special importance of social movements when he defined them as "collective enterprises to establish a new order of life."

In many nations, including the United States, social movements have had a dramatic impact on the course of history and the evolution of social structure. Consider the actions of abolitionists, suffragists, civil rights workers, and activists opposed to the war in Vietnam. Members of each social movement stepped outside traditional channels for bringing about social change and yet had a noticeable influence on public policy. In Eastern Europe, equally dramatic collective efforts helped to topple

Communist regimes in a largely peaceful manner, in nations that many observers had felt were "immune" to such change (Ramet 1991).

Though social movements imply the existence of conflict, we can also analyze their activities from a functionalist perspective. Even when unsuccessful, social movements contribute to the formation of public opinion. Initially, the ideas of Margaret Sanger and other early advocates of birth control were viewed as "radical," yet contraceptives are now widely available in the United States. Moreover, functionalists view social movements as training grounds for leaders of the political establishment. Such heads of state as Cuba's Fidel Castro and South Africa's Nelson Mandela came to power after serving as leaders of revolutionary movements. Poland's Lech Walesa, Russia's Boris Yeltsin, and Czech playwright Václav Havel led protest movements against Communist rule and later became leaders of their countries' governments.

How and why do social movements emerge? Obviously, people are often discontented with current conditions. But what causes them to organize at a particular moment in a collective effort to work for change? In this section we will examine two different explanations for why people mobilize: the relative deprivation approach and the resource mobilization approach. We will also acknowledge the often underestimated role of gender in social movements and study recent changes in the character of social movements.

Use Your Sociological Imagination

What social movements are most visible on your campus? In the community where you live?

THE RELATIVE DEPRIVATION APPROACH

Those members of a society who feel most frustrated and disgruntled by the social and economic conditions of their lives are not necessarily "worst off" in an objective sense. Social scientists have long recognized that what is most significant is how people *perceive* their situation. Karl Marx pointed out that although the misery of the workers was important to their perception of their oppressed state, so was their position *relative* to the capitalist ruling class (Marx and Engels [1847] 1955).

The term **relative deprivation** is defined as the conscious feeling of a negative discrepancy between legitimate expectations and present actualities (J. Wilson 1973). In other words, life isn't as good as you hoped it would be. Such a state may be characterized by scarcity rather than complete lack of necessities (as we saw in the distinction between absolute and relative poverty in Chapter 5). A relatively deprived person is dissatisfied because he or she feels downtrodden relative to some appropriate reference group. Thus, blue-collar workers who live in two-family houses with little lawn space—though they are hardly at the bottom of the economic ladder—may nevertheless feel deprived in comparison with corporate managers and professionals who live in lavish and exclusive suburbs.

In addition to the feeling of relative deprivation, two other elements must be present before discontent will be channeled into a social movement. First, people must feel that they have a *right* to their goals, that they deserve better than what they have. Sociologists at Oxford University gathered data on 404 militant extremists from 31 nations. Among them the researchers found many highly educated individuals, including engineers and other high-level achievers. Yet these relatively fortunate people still felt disadvantaged by what they perceived as corrupt or misguided governments. Second, the disadvantaged people must perceive that they cannot attain their goals through conventional means. This belief may or may not be correct. Whichever is the case, the group will not mobilize into a social movement unless members share the perception that they can end their relative deprivation *only* through collective action (*The Atlantic* 2008; Gambetta and Hertog 2007).

Critics of this approach have noted that an increase in feelings of deprivation is not always necessary before people are moved to act. In addition, this approach fails to explain why certain feelings of deprivation are transformed into social movements, whereas in other similar situations, no collective effort is made to reshape society. Consequently, in recent years, sociologists have given increasing attention to the forces needed to bring about the emergence of social movements (Alain 1985; Finkel and Rule 1987; Orum and Date 2009).

THE RESOURCE MOBILIZATION APPROACH

It takes more than desire to start a social movement. Money, political influence, access to the media, and personnel all help. The term ***resource mobilization*** refers to the ways in which a social movement utilizes such resources. The success of a movement for change will depend in good part on what resources it has and how effectively it mobilizes them (Gamson 1989; Tilly 1964, 2003; Walder 2007).

Sociologist Anthony Oberschall (1973:199) has argued that to sustain social protest or resistance, there must be an "organizational base and continuity of leadership." As people become part of a social movement, norms develop to guide their behavior. Members of the movement may be expected to attend regular meetings of organizations, pay dues, recruit new adherents, and boycott "enemy" products or speakers. They may be expected to adopt special language or new words for familiar terms. In recent years, social movements have been responsible for such new terms of self-reference as *Blacks* and *African Americans* (used to replace *Negroes*), *senior citizens* (used to replace *old folks*), *gays* (used to replace *homosexuals*), and *people with disabilities* (used to replace *the handicapped*).

Leadership is a central factor in the mobilization of the discontented into social movements. Often, a movement will be led by a charismatic figure, such as Dr. Martin Luther King Jr. As Max Weber described it in 1904, *charisma* is that quality of an individual that sets him or her apart from ordinary people. Of course, charisma can fade abruptly, which accounts for the fragility of certain social movements (Morris 2000).

Yet many social movements do persist over long periods because their leadership is well organized and ongoing. Ironically, as Robert Michels (1915) noted, political movements that fight for social change eventually take on bureaucratic forms of organization. Leaders tend to dominate the decision-making process without directly consulting followers. The bureaucratization of social movements is not inevitable, however. More radical movements that advocate major structural change in society and embrace mass actions tend not to be hierarchical or bureaucratic (Fitzgerald and Rodgers 2000).

Why do certain individuals join a social movement, whereas others in similar situations do not? Some people are recruited to join. Karl Marx recognized the importance of recruitment when he called on workers to become *aware* of their oppressed status and develop a shared class consciousness. Marx held that the development of a social movement (specifically, the revolt of the proletariat) would require leaders to sharpen the awareness of the oppressed. They would need to help workers to overcome *false consciousness,* or attitudes that did not reflect workers' objective position, in order to organize a revolutionary movement. Similarly, sociologists who take the resource mobilization approach point out that one of the challenges women's liberation activists of the late 1960s and early 1970s faced was to convince women that they were being deprived of their rights and of socially valued resources.

Unlike the relative deprivation approach, the resource mobilization perspective focuses on the strategic difficulties facing social movements. Moreover, any movement for fundamental change will almost certainly arouse opposition. Effective mobilization will depend in part, then, on how the movement deals with resistance to its activities.

Today, through global text-messaging and the Internet, social activists can reach a large number of people around the world almost instantaneously, with relatively little effort and expense. The Internet's listservs and chat rooms allow organizers of social movements to enlist like-minded people without face-to-face contact, or even simultaneous interaction (Calhoun 1998).

GENDER AND SOCIAL MOVEMENTS

Sociologists point out that gender is an important element in understanding the development of social movements. In our male-dominated society, women find it difficult to assume leadership positions in social movement organizations. While women often serve disproportionately as volunteers in these movements, their work is not always recognized, nor are their voices as easily heard as men's. Moreover, gender bias causes the real extent of women's influence to be overlooked. Traditional examinations of the sociopolitical system tend to focus on such male-dominated corridors of power as legislatures and corporate boardrooms, to the neglect of more female-dominated domains, such as households, community-based groups, or faith-based networks. But efforts to influence family values, child rearing, relationships between parents and schools, and spiritual values are clearly significant to a culture and society (Ferree and Merrill 2000; Noonan 1995).

Scholars of social movements now realize that gender can affect even the way we view organized efforts to bring about or resist change. For example, an emphasis on using rationality and cold logic to achieve goals helps to obscure the importance of passion and emotion in successful social movements. Calls for a more serious study of the role of emotion are frequently seen as applying only to the women's movement, because emotion is traditionally thought of as feminine. Yet it would be difficult to find any movement, from labor battles to voting rights to animal rights, in which passion was not part of the consensus-building force (Ferree and Merrill 2000; V. Taylor 1999, 2004).

Use Your Sociological Imagination

What aspects of traditional gender roles explain the roles that women and men typically play in social movements?

NEW SOCIAL MOVEMENTS

Beginning in the late 1960s, European social scientists observed a change in both the composition and the targets of emerging social movements. In the past, traditional social movements had focused on economic issues, often led by labor unions or by people who shared the same occupation. However, many social movements that have become active in recent decades—including the contemporary women's movement, the peace movement, and the environmental movement—do not have the social class roots typical of the labor protests in the United States and Europe over the past century (Tilly 1993, 2004).

The term *new social movements* refers to organized collective activities that address values and social identities as well as improvements in the quality of life. These movements may be involved in developing collective identities. Many have complex agendas that go beyond a single issue and even cross national boundaries. Educated, middle-class people are significantly represented in some of these new social movements, such as the women's movement and the movement for lesbian and gay rights.

New social movements generally do not view government as their ally in the struggle for a better society. While they typically do not seek to overthrow the government, they may criticize, protest, or harass public officials. Researchers have found that members of new social movements show little inclination to accept established authority, even scientific or technical authority. This characteristic is especially evident in the environmental and anti–nuclear power movements, whose activists present their own experts to counter those of government or big business (Garner 1996; Polletta and Jasper 2001; A. Scott 1990).

The environmental movement is one of many new movements that have adopted a worldwide focus. In their efforts to reduce air and water pollution, curtail global warming, and protect endangered animal species,

Table 11–1 Contributions to Social Movement Theory

Approach	Emphasis
Relative deprivation approach	Social movements are especially likely to arise when rising expectations are frustrated.
Resource mobilization approach	The success of social movements depends on which resources are available and how effectively they are used.
New social movement theory	Social movements arise when people are motivated by value issues and social identity questions.

environmental activists have realized that establishing strong regulatory measures within a single country is not sufficient. Similarly, labor union leaders and human rights advocates cannot adequately address exploitative sweatshop conditions in a developing country if a multinational corporation can simply move the factory to another country where workers are paid even less. Whereas traditional social movements tend to emphasize resource mobilization on a local level, new social movements take a broader, global perspective on social and political activism.

Table 11–1 summarizes the three sociological approaches that have contributed to social movement theory. Each approach has added to our understanding of the development of social movements. But in a larger sense, what causes social change? In the next section we will see how sociologists have used some of the major theoretical perspectives to analyze and interpret the process of social change.

Use Your Sociological Imagination

Try to imagine a society without any social movements. Under what conditions could such a society exist? Would you want to live in it?

Theories of Social Change

A new millennium provides an opportunity to consider *social change,* which we have defined as significant alteration over time in behavior patterns and culture. Social change can occur so slowly as to be almost undetectable to those it affects, but it can also happen with breathtaking rapidity. As Table 11–2 shows, some changes that have occurred in U.S. society over the past century and a half have been relatively slow or slight; others have been rapid or striking in magnitude.

Explanations of social change are clearly a challenge in the diverse and complex world we inhabit today. Nevertheless, theorists from several disciplines have sought to analyze social change. In some instances, they have examined historical events to arrive at a better understanding of contemporary changes. We will review three theoretical approaches to change—evolutionary, functionalist, and conflict theory—and then take a look at global social change.

Table 11–2 The United States: A Changing Nation

Population	1850	1940	1960	2011
Total in millions	23.2	132.1	180.7	313.2
Percentage under age 15	41%	25%	31%	20%
Education	**1850**	**1940**	**1960**	**2008**
Percentage not completing high school	88%	18%	13%	14%
Percentage ages 19–24 enrolled in higher education	Under 1%	8%	40%	40%
Labor Force Participation	**1850**	**1940**	**1960**	**2009**
Men working in their 20s	94%	88%	86%	83%
Women working in their 20s	22%	39%	74%	72%
Health	**1850**	**1940**	**1960**	**2007**
Physicians per 100,000 population	176	133	150	271
Life expectancy at birth, in years	38	63	70	78.3
Technology	**1870**	**1940**	**1960**	**2007**
Copyrights issued	5,600	176,997	243,926	524,700
Patents issued	12,127	42,238	47,170	182,900
Family	**1890**	**1940**	**1960**	**2008**
Median age at first marriage	26	24	23	28
Men	22	22	20	26
Women	3.25	2.7	3.65	2.12
Number of children born per family				

NOTE: Data are comparable, although definitions vary. Definition of the United States changes between 1850 and 1940 and between 1940 and 1960. Most recent physician data are for 2006. Earliest date for children born per family is 1905.

SOURCE: Author, based on federal data collected in American Community Survey 2009:Table B12007; Bureau of Labor Statistics 2010b:Table 3; Bureau of the Census 2009a:9, 12, 76, 111, 148, 500; B. Hamilton et al. 2009; Kreider 2005:8; Sutch and Carter 2006:1–28/29, 391, 401–402, 440, 541, 685, 697, 709, 2–441/442, and 3–424/425, 427/428.

Think About It
Which of the social changes shown in this table surprises you the most? Which category do you think will change the most in the next 20 years?

EVOLUTIONARY THEORY

The pioneering work of Charles Darwin (1809–1882) in biological evolution contributed to 19th-century theories of social change. Darwin's approach stresses a continuing progression of successive life forms. For example, human beings came at a later stage of evolution than reptiles and represent a more complex form of life. Social theorists seeking an analogy to this biological model originated *evolutionary theory,* in which society is viewed as moving in a definite direction. Early evolutionary theorists generally agreed that society was progressing inevitably to a higher state. As might be expected, they concluded in ethnocentric fashion that their own behavior and culture were more advanced than those of earlier civilizations.

Auguste Comte (1798–1857), a founder of sociology, was an evolutionary theorist of social change. He saw human societies as moving forward in their thinking from mythology to the scientific method. Similarly, Émile Durkheim ([1893] 1933) maintained that society progressed from simple to more complex forms of social organization.

Today, evolutionary theory influences sociologists in a variety of ways. For example, it has encouraged sociobiologists to investigate the behavioral links between humans and other animals. It has also influenced human ecology, the study of the interaction between communities and their environment (Maryanski 2004).

FUNCTIONALIST THEORY

Functionalist sociologists focus on what *maintains* a system, not on what changes it. This statement might seem to suggest that functionalists can offer little of value to the study of social change. Yet as the work of sociologist Talcott Parsons demonstrates, functionalists have made a distinctive contribution to this area of sociological investigation.

Parsons (1902–1979), a leading proponent of functionalist theory, viewed society as being in a natural state of equilibrium. By "equilibrium," he meant that society tends toward a state of stability or balance. Parsons would view even prolonged labor strikes or civilian riots as temporary disruptions in the status quo rather than as significant alterations in social structure. Therefore, according to his *equilibrium model,* as changes occur in one part of society, adjustments must be made in other parts. If adjustments are not made, society's equilibrium will be threatened.

Taking an evolutionary approach, Parsons (1966) maintained that four processes of social change are inevitable. The first, *differentiation,* refers to the increasing complexity of social organization. The change from "medicine man" to physician, nurse, and pharmacist is an illustration of differentiation in the field of health care. This process is accompanied by *adaptive upgrading,* through which social institutions become more specialized. The division of physicians into obstetricians, internists, surgeons, and so forth is an example of adaptive upgrading.

The third process identified by Parsons is the *inclusion* into society of groups that were once excluded because of such factors as gender, race, and social class background. Medical schools have practiced inclusion by admitting increasing numbers of women and African

Americans. Finally, Parsons suggested that societies experience *value generalization,* the development of new values that tolerate and legitimate a greater range of activities. The acceptance of preventive and alternative medicine is an example of value generalization: our society has broadened its view of health care. All four processes identified by Parsons stress consensus—societal agreement on the nature of social organization and values (B. Johnson 1975; Wallace and Wolf 1980).

Though Parsons's approach explicitly incorporates the evolutionary notion of continuing progress, the dominant theme in his model is balance and stability. Society may change, but it remains stable through new forms of integration. For example, in place of the kinship ties that provided social cohesion in the past, society develops laws, judicial processes, and new values and belief systems.

Functionalists assume that social institutions will not persist unless they continue to contribute to society's well-being. This assumption leads functionalists to conclude that altering institutions will threaten societal equilibrium. Critics note that the functionalist approach virtually disregards the use of coercion by the powerful to maintain the illusion of a stable, well-integrated society (Gouldner 1960).

CONFLICT THEORY

The functionalist perspective minimizes the significance of change. It emphasizes the persistence of social life and sees change as a means of maintaining social equilibrium (or balance). In contrast, conflict theorists contend that social institutions and practices persist because powerful groups have the ability to maintain the status quo. Change has crucial significance, since it is needed to correct social injustices and inequalities.

Karl Marx accepted the evolutionary argument that societies develop along a particular path. However, unlike Comte and Spencer, he did not view each successive stage as an inevitable improvement over the previous one. Society, according to Marx, proceeds through a series of stages, each of which exploits a class of people. Ancient society exploited slaves; the estate system, or feudalism, exploited serfs; modern capitalist society exploits the working class. Ultimately, through a socialist revolution led by the proletariat, human society will move toward the final stage of development: a classless communist society, or "community of free individuals," as Marx described it in *Das Kapital* in 1867 (see Bottomore and Rubel 1956:250).

As we have seen, Marx had an important influence on the development of sociology. His thinking offered insights into such institutions as the economy, the family, religion, and government. The Marxist view of social change is appealing because it does not restrict people to a passive role in responding to inevitable cycles or changes in material culture. Rather, Marxist theory offers a tool to those who wish to seize control of

summingUP

Table 11–3 Sociological Perspectives on Social Change

Evolutionary	Social change moves society in a definite direction, frequently from simple to more complex.
Functionalist	Social change must contribute to society's stability. Modest adjustments must be made to accommodate social change.
Conflict	Social change can correct social injustices and inequalities.

the historical process and gain their freedom from injustice. In contrast to functionalists' emphasis on stability, Marx argues that conflict is a normal and desirable aspect of social change. In fact, change must be encouraged as a means of eliminating social inequality (Lauer 1982).

One conflict sociologist, Ralf Dahrendorf (1959), has noted that the contrast between the functionalist perspective's emphasis on stability and the conflict perspective's focus on change reflects the contradictory nature of society. Human societies are stable and long-lasting, yet they also experience serious conflict. Dahrendorf found that the functionalist and conflict approaches were ultimately compatible, despite their many areas of disagreement. Indeed, Parsons spoke of new functions that result from social change, and Marx recognized the need for change so that societies can function more equitably.

Table 11–3 summarizes the differences between the three major theories of social change.

Use Your Sociological Imagination

Which theory of social change do you find most convincing? Why?

GLOBAL SOCIAL CHANGE

We are living at a truly dramatic time in history to consider global social change. Maureen Hallinan (1997), in her presidential address to the American Sociological Association, asked those present to consider just a few of the recent political events: the collapse of communism; terrorist attacks in various parts of the world, including the United States; the dismantling of the welfare system in the United States; revolution and famine in Africa and Eastern Europe; the spread of AIDS; and the computer revolution. Just a few months after her remarks came the first verification of the cloning of a complex animal, Dolly the sheep.

In this era of massive social, political, and economic change, is it possible to predict change? Some technological changes seem obvious, but the collapse of Communist governments in the former Soviet Union and Eastern Europe in the early 1990s took people by surprise. Prior to the Soviet collapse, however, sociologist Randall Collins (1986, 1995), a conflict theorist, had observed a crucial sequence of events that most observers had missed. In seminars as far back as 1980, and in a book published in 1986, Collins had argued that Soviet expansionism had resulted in an overextension of resources, including disproportionate spending on military forces. Such an overextension will strain a regime's stability. Moreover, geopolitical theory suggests that nations in the middle of a geographic region, such as the Soviet Union, tend to fragment into smaller units over time. Collins predicted that the coincidence of social crises on several frontiers would precipitate the collapse of the Soviet Union.

And that is just what happened. In 1979 the success of the Iranian revolution had led to an upsurge of Islamic fundamentalism in nearby Afghanistan, as well as in Soviet republics with substantial Muslim populations. At the same time, resistance to Communist rule was growing, both throughout Eastern Europe and within the Soviet Union itself. Collins had predicted that the rise of a dissident form of communism within the Soviet Union might facilitate the breakdown of the regime. Beginning in the late 1980s, Soviet leader Mikhail Gorbachev chose not to use military power and other types of repression to crush dissidents in Eastern Europe. Gorbachev offered plans for democratization and social reform of Soviet society, and seemed willing to reshape the Soviet Union into a loose federation of somewhat autonomous states. But in 1991, six republics on the western periphery declared their independence, and within months the entire Soviet Union had formally disintegrated into Russia and a number of other independent nations.

In her address, Hallinan (1997) cautioned that we need to move beyond restrictive models of social change—both the linear view of evolutionary theory and the assumptions about equilibrium within functionalist theory. She and other sociologists have looked to the "chaos theory" advanced by mathematicians to see erratic events as an integral part of change. Hallinan noted that upheavals and major chaotic shifts do occur, and that sociologists must learn to predict their occurrence, as Collins did with the collapse of the Soviet Union. Imagine, for instance, the dramatic nonlinear social change that will result from major innovations in communications and biotechnology, a topic we will discuss later in this chapter.

Resistance to Social Change

Efforts to promote social change are likely to meet with resistance. In the midst of rapid scientific and technological innovation, many people become frightened by the demands of an ever-changing society. Moreover, certain individuals and groups have a stake in maintaining the status quo.

Social economist Thorstein Veblen (1857–1929) coined the term *vested interests* to refer to those people or groups who will suffer in the event of social change. For example, in 2010 President Obama proposed scuttling NASA's Constellation project, whose primary goal was to return humans to the moon. Although many people expressed disappointment with the decision to abandon manned space flights, key opposition came from just 27 members of Congress. All represented districts in Alabama and Texas that were home to large suppliers to the project. Ironically, many of those representatives had gone on record as opponents of large federal spending projects. In general, those with a disproportionate share of society's wealth, status, and power, such as members of Congress and representatives of big business, have a vested interest in preserving the status quo (Friedman 2010; Veblen 1919).

ECONOMIC AND CULTURAL FACTORS

Economic factors play an important role in resistance to social change. For example, meeting high standards for the safety of products and workers can be expensive for manufacturers. Conflict theorists argue that in a capitalist economic system, many firms are not willing to pay the price of meeting strict safety standards. They may resist social change by cutting corners or by pressuring the government to ease regulations.

Communities, too, protect their vested interests, often in the name of "protecting property values." The cry "not in my backyard" is often heard when people protest landfills, prisons, nuclear power facilities, and even bike trails and group homes for people with developmental disabilities. The targeted community may not challenge the need for the facility but may simply insist that it be located elsewhere. The "not in my backyard" attitude has become so common that it is almost impossible for policy makers to find acceptable locations for such facilities as hazardous waste dumps (Jasper 1997).

Like economic factors, cultural factors frequently shape resistance to change. William F. Ogburn (1922) distinguished between material and nonmaterial aspects of culture. *Material culture* includes inventions, artifacts, and technology; *nonmaterial culture* encompasses ideas, norms, communications, and social organization. In music, for instance, the instruments musicians play and the CDs they record are aspects of material culture; their style of playing, such as rap, and the rules of pitch and rhythm they follow are aspects of nonmaterial culture. Ogburn pointed out that one cannot devise methods for controlling and utilizing a new technology before its introduction. Thus, nonmaterial culture typically must respond to changes in material culture. Ogburn introduced the term **culture lag** to refer to the period of maladjustment when the nonmaterial culture is still struggling to adapt to new material conditions. One example of culture lag is the questions that have been raised by the rapid, uncontrolled growth of the Internet—whether to regulate it, and if so, to what degree.

In certain cases, changes in material culture can strain the relationships between social institutions. For example, new means of birth control have been developed in recent decades. Large families are no longer

Use Your Sociological Imagination

What kind of change do you find the hardest to accept? The easiest?

economically necessary, nor are they commonly endorsed by social norms. But certain religious faiths, among them Roman Catholicism, continue to extol large families and to disapprove most methods of limiting family size, such as contraception and abortion. This gap in values represents a lag between aspects of material culture (technology) and nonmaterial culture (religious beliefs). Conflicts may emerge between religion and other social institutions, such as government and the educational system, over the dissemination of birth control and family-planning information (Riley et al. 1994a, 1994b).

RESISTANCE TO TECHNOLOGY

Technological innovations are examples of changes in material culture that have often provoked resistance. The Industrial Revolution, which took place largely in England during the period 1760 to 1830, was a scientific revolution focused on the application of nonanimal sources of power to labor tasks. As the revolution proceeded, societies relied more and more on new inventions that facilitated agricultural and industrial production, and on new sources of energy such as steam. In some industries, the introduction of power-driven machinery reduced the need for factory workers and made it easier for factory owners to cut wages.

Strong resistance to the Industrial Revolution emerged in some countries. In England, beginning in 1811, masked craft workers took extreme measures: They raided factories and destroyed some of the new machinery. The government hunted these rebels, known as **Luddites,** and banished or hung them. In a similar effort in France, angry workers threw their wooden shoes (*sabots*) into factory machinery to destroy it, giving rise to the term *sabotage.* While the resistance of the Luddites and the French workers was short-lived and unsuccessful, they have come to symbolize resistance to technology over the last two centuries.

Are we now in the midst of a second Industrial Revolution, with a contemporary group of Luddites resisting? Many sociologists believe that we are living in a *postindustrial society.* When this era began is difficult to pinpoint exactly. Generally, it is viewed as having begun in the 1950s, when for the first time the majority of workers in industrial societies became involved in services rather than in the actual manufacturing of goods (D. Bell 1999; Fiala 1992).

Just as the Luddites resisted the Industrial Revolution, people in many countries have resisted postindustrial technological changes. The term *neo-Luddites* refers to those who are wary of technological innovations and who question the incessant expansion of industrialization, the increasing destruction of the natural and agrarian world, and the "throw-it-away" mentality of contemporary capitalism, with its resulting pollution of the environment.

A new slang term, *urban amish,* refers specifically to those who resist technological devices that have become part of our daily lives, such as cell phones. These people insist that whatever the presumed benefits of industrial and postindustrial technology, such technology has distinctive social costs and may represent a danger to both the future of the human species and our planet (Bauerlein 1996; Rifkin 1995; Sale 1996; Slack and Wise 2007; Snyder 1996; Urban Dictionary 2010).

Other people will resist a new technology because they find it difficult to use or because they suspect that it will complicate their lives. Both these objections are especially true of new information and media technologies. Whether it is TiVo, the iPhone, or even the latest digital camera, many consumers are leery of these so-called "must-have" items.

In 2007 the Pew Research Center released a report that sorted U.S. residents into 10 categories based on their use of information and communications technologies (ICTs) (see Table 11–4). According to the report, about 31 percent of the adult population falls into the top

Table 11–4 Contours of Communication

Omnivores: 8% of American adults constitute the most active participants in the information society, consuming information goods and services at a high rate and using them as a platform for participation and self-expression.

The Connectors: 7% of the adult population surround themselves with technology and use it to connect with people and digital content. They get a lot out of their mobile devices and participate actively in online life.

Lackluster Veterans: 8% of American adults make up a group who are not at all passionate about their abundance of modern ICTs. Few like the intrusiveness their gadgets add to their lives and not many see ICTs adding to their personal productivity.

Productivity Enhancers: 9% of American adults happily get a lot of things done with information technology, both at home and at work.

Mobile Centrics: 10% of the general population are strongly attached to their cell phones and take advantage of a range of mobile applications.

Connected but Hassled: 9% of American adults fit into this group. They have invested in a lot of technology, but the connectivity is a hassle for them.

Inexperienced Experimenters: 8% of adults have less ICT on hand than others. They feel competent in dealing with technology, and might do more with it if they had more.

Light but Satisfied: 15% of adults have the basics of information technology, use it infrequently, and it does not register as an important part of their lives.

Indifferents: 11% of adults have a fair amount of technology on hand, but it does not play a central role in their daily lives.

Off the Net: 15% of the population, mainly older Americans, is off the modern information network.

NOTE: From a Pew Internet and American Life Project survey conducted in April 2006.

SOURCE: Horrigan 2007:vii.

Think About It
What category would you place yourself in?

4 categories, from the "Omnivores," who use these devices as a means of self-expression, to the "Productivity Enhancers," who use them to get the job done. Middle-of-the-road users, who represent about 20 percent of the population, take advantage of new technologies but aren't as excited about them. They range from the "Mobile Centrics," who are strongly attached to their cell phones, to the "Connected but Hassled." Close to half the people in the nation have few if any technology devices, or if they do, they are not wedded to them. Typically, younger people embrace technological change more than older people, who tend either to be indifferent toward new technologies or to find them annoying.

Such concerns are worth remembering as we turn to our technological future and its possible impact on social change.

Technology and the Future

Technology is cultural information about how to use the material resources of the environment to satisfy human needs and desires. Technological advances—the airplane, the automobile, the television, the atomic bomb, and more recently the computer, the fax machine, and the cellular phone—have brought striking changes in our cultures, our patterns of socialization, our social institutions, and our day-to-day social interactions. Technological innovations are, in fact, emerging and being accepted with remarkable speed. In the following sections we will examine various aspects of our technological future and consider their overall impact on social change, including the strains they will bring. We will focus in particular on recent developments in computer technology—especially their effects on global offshoring and censorship—and biotechnology.

COMPUTER TECHNOLOGY

The last decade witnessed an explosion of computer technology in the United States and around the world. Its effects were particularly noteworthy with regard to the Internet, the world's largest computer network. In 2008 the Internet reached 1.8 billion users, compared to just 50 million in 1996 (Internet World Stats 2010).

The Internet evolved from a computer system built in 1962 by the U.S. Defense Department to enable scholars and military researchers to continue their government work even if part of the nation's communications system were destroyed by a nuclear attack. A generation ago, it was difficult to gain access to the Internet without holding a position at a university or a government research laboratory. Today, however, virtually anyone can reach the Internet with a phone line, a computer, and a modem. People buy and sell cars, trade stocks, auction off items, research new medical remedies, vote, and track down long-lost friends online—to mention just a few of the thousands of possibilities.

Unfortunately, not everyone can get onto the information highway, especially not the less affluent. Moreover, this pattern of inequality is global. The core nations that Immanuel Wallerstein described in his world-systems analysis have a virtual monopoly on information technology; the peripheral nations of Asia, Africa, and Latin America depend on the core nations both for technology and for the information it provides. For example, North America, Europe, and a few industrialized nations in other regions possess almost all the world's *Internet hosts*— computers that are connected directly to the worldwide network.

Recently, however, some developing nations have begun to benefit from the ease with which information—particularly business information—can be transferred around the world instantaneously. In semiperiphery countries like India, where a growing segment of the workforce speaks English and is computer literate, multinational corporations have been opening new offices, creating well-paid service and professional jobs that boost the local economy. This business approach is not new; U.S. firms have been *outsourcing* certain types of work for generations. For example, moderate-size businesses such as furniture stores and commercial laundries have long relied on outside trucking firms to make deliveries to their customers. The new trend toward *offshoring* carries this practice one step further, by transferring other types of work to foreign contractors. Now, even large companies are turning to overseas firms, many of them located in developing countries.

Global Offshoring   At home, offshoring has become the latest tactic in the time-worn business strategy of raising profits by reducing costs. A 2007 report showed that 75 percent of the world's 2,000 largest companies are engaged in offshoring (Weier 2007).

Because offshoring, like outsourcing in general, tends to improve the efficiency of business operations, it can be viewed as functional to society. Offshoring also increases economic interdependence in the production of goods and services, both among enterprises located just across town from one another and among those across the globe.

Conflict theorists charge that this aspect of globalization furthers social inequality. While moving high-tech work to India does help to lower a company's costs, the impact on those technical and service workers who are displaced is clearly devastating (see Table 11–5). Certainly, middle-class workers in industrial countries are alarmed by the trend. Though economists favor some assistance for workers who have been displaced by offshoring, they oppose broad-based efforts to block the practice.

There is a downside to offshoring for foreigners, as well. Although outsourcing is a significant source of employment for India's upper-middle class, hundreds of millions of other Indians have seen little to no positive impact from the trend. Most households in India do not possess any form of high technology: only about 1 out of 14 have a telephone,

Table 11–5 Occupations Most Vulnerable to Offshoring

Rank	Occupation
1	Computer programming
2	Data entry
3	Electrical and electronics drafting
4	Mechanical drafting
5	Computer and information science, research
6	Actuarial science
7	Mathematics
8	Statistics
9	Mathematical science (all other)
10	Film and video editing

SOURCE: Bureau of Labor Statistics data cited in Hira 2008; Moncarz et al. 2008.

and just 3 out of 1,000 a computer. Instead of improving these people's lives, the new business centers have siphoned water and electricity away from those who are most in need. Even the high-tech workers are experiencing negative consequences. Many suffer from stress disorders such as stomach problems and difficulty sleeping; more than half quit their jobs before the end of a year. On the other hand, the new call centers have brought significant improvements in India's infrastructure, particularly in telecommunications and power generation. The long-term impact of offshoring on India and other developing nations is difficult to predict (Waldman 2004a, 2004b, 2004c).

Privacy and Censorship in a Global Village   As the description of the spying billboard at the beginning of this chapter showed, recent advances in computer technology have made it increasingly easy for business firms, government agencies, and even criminals to retrieve and store information about everything from our buying habits to our Web-surfing patterns. In public places, at work, and on the Internet, surveillance devices now track our every move, be it a keystroke or an ATM withdrawal. At the same time that these innovations have increased others' power to monitor our behavior, they have raised fears that they might be used for undemocratic purposes. In short, new technologies threaten both our privacy and our freedom from censorship (O'Harrow Jr. 2005).

In recent years, concern about the criminal misuse of personal information has been underscored by the accidental loss of some huge databases. In 2006, for example, the theft of a laptop computer from the home of an employee of the Veterans' Administration compromised the names, Social Security numbers, and dates of birth of up to 26.5 million veterans. Unfortunately, technologies that facilitate the sharing of information have also created new types of crime.

From a sociological point of view, the complex issues of privacy and censorship can be considered illustrations of culture lag. As usual, the material culture (technology) is changing faster than the nonmaterial culture (norms for controlling the use of technology). Too often, the result is an anything-goes approach to the use of new technologies.

Legislation regarding the surveillance of electronic communications has not always upheld citizens' right to privacy. In 1986, the federal government passed the Electronic Communications Privacy Act, which outlawed the surveillance of telephone calls except with the permission of both the U.S. attorney general and a federal judge. Telegrams, faxes, and e-mail did not receive the same degree of protection, however. In 2001, one month after the terrorist attacks of September 11, Congress passed the USA PATRIOT Act, which relaxed existing legal checks on surveillance by law enforcement officers. Federal agencies are now freer to gather data electronically, including credit card receipts and banking records (Eckenwiler 1995).

Sociologists' views on the use and abuse of new technologies differ depending on their theoretical perspective. Functionalists take a generally positive view of the Internet, pointing to its manifest function of facilitating communication. From their perspective, the Internet performs the latent function of empowering those with few resources—from hate groups to special interest organizations—to communicate with the masses. Conflict theorists, in contrast, stress the danger that the most powerful groups in a society will use technology to violate the privacy of the less powerful. Indeed, officials in the People's Republic of China have attempted to censor online discussion groups and Web

Though the USA PATRIOT Act was intended to protect citizens from terrorism, in practice it has raised concerns about the potential violation of their privacy.

postings that are critical of the government. The same abuses can occur in the United States, civil liberties advocates remind us, if citizens are not vigilant in protecting their right to privacy (Magnier 2004).

Another source of controversy is the widespread use of GPS devices to track the location of cars or even people, not to mention the electronic tracking of handheld communications devices. Technology allows you to tweet your whereabouts to your friends, but should others, including the government, be able to home in on you? Put another way, is your location at any given moment covered by the Fourth Amendment to the U.S. Constitution, which protects your right to privacy? Both public opinion and court rulings on this question remain divided. The issue is yet another example of culture lag, or the time it takes for society to reconcile a new technology with traditional cultural values and behavior (Zipp 2009).

If anything, people seem to be less vigilant today about maintaining their privacy than they were before the information age. Young people who have grown up browsing the Internet seem to accept the existence of the "cookies" and "spyware" they may pick up while surfing. They have become accustomed to adult surveillance of their conversation in electronic chat rooms. Many see no risk in providing personal information about themselves to the strangers they meet online. Little wonder that college professors find their students do not appreciate the political significance of their right to privacy (Turkle 2004).

Do you hold strong views regarding the privacy of your electronic communications? If your safety were in jeopardy, would you be willing to sacrifice your privacy?

BIOTECHNOLOGY AND THE GENE POOL

Another field in which technological advances have spurred global social change is biotechnology. Sex selection of fetuses, genetically engineered organisms, cloning of sheep and cows—these have been among the significant yet controversial scientific advances in the field of biotechnology in recent years. George Ritzer's concept of McDonaldization applies to the entire area of biotechnology. Just as the fast-food concept has permeated society, no phase of life now seems exempt from therapeutic or medical intervention. In fact, sociologists view many aspects of biotechnology as an extension of the recent trend toward the medicalization of society, discussed in Chapter 10. Through genetic manipulation, the medical profession is expanding its turf still further (Clarke et al. 2003).

Today's biotechnology holds itself out as totally beneficial to human beings, but it is in constant need of monitoring. As we will see, biotechnological advances have raised many difficult ethical and political questions, among them the desirability of tinkering with the gene pool, which could alter our environment in unexpected and unwanted ways (Weinstein and Weinstein 1999).

One startling biotechnological advance is the possibility of altering human behavior through genetic engineering. Fish and plant genes have already been mixed to create frost-resistant potato and tomato crops. More recently, human genes have been implanted in pigs to provide humanlike kidneys for organ transplants.

One of the latest developments in genetic engineering is gene therapy. Geneticists working with mouse fetuses have managed to disable genes that carry an undesirable trait and replace them with genes carrying a desirable trait. Such advances raise staggering possibilities for altering animal and human life forms. Still, gene therapy remains highly experimental and must be considered a long, long shot (Kolata 1999).

The debate on genetic engineering escalated in 1997 when scientists in Scotland announced that they had cloned a sheep. After many unsuccessful attempts, they had finally been able to replace the genetic material of a sheep's egg with DNA from an adult sheep, creating a lamb that was a clone of the adult. The very next year, Japanese researchers successfully cloned cows. These developments raised the possibility that in the near future, scientists may be able to clone human beings.

William F. Ogburn probably could not have anticipated such scientific developments when he wrote of culture lag 70 years earlier. However, the successful cloning of sheep illustrates again how quickly material culture can change, and how nonmaterial culture moves more slowly in absorbing such changes.

While cloning grabs the headlines, controversy has been growing concerning genetically modified (GM) food. This issue arose in Europe but has since spread to other parts of the world, including the United States. The idea behind the technology is to increase food production and make agriculture more economical. But critics use the term *Frankenfood* (as in "Frankenstein") to refer to everything from breakfast cereals made from genetically engineered grains to "fresh" GM tomatoes. Members of the anti-biotech movement object to tampering with nature, and are concerned about the possible health effects of GM food. Supporters of genetically modified food include not just biotech companies, but those who see the technology as a way to help feed the burgeoning populations of Africa and Asia (World Health Organization 2009).

Another form of biotechnology with a potentially wide-ranging impact is the Human Genome Project. This effort involves teams of scientists around the world in sequencing and mapping all 20,000 to 25,000 human genes in existence, collectively known as the *human genome.* Supporters say that the resulting knowledge could revolutionize doctors' ability to treat and even prevent disease. But sociologists worry about the ethical implications of such research.

Try to imagine the world 100 years from now. On balance, is it a world in which technology contributes to or threatens people's well-being? In what ways?

Sociology Matters

Sociology matters because it helps you to understand the social change you encounter.

- Have you had any experience working in a social movement? If so, what kind of social change were you hoping to support? What resources did the movement try to mobilize? Who were the vested interests who opposed the movement?

- Have you yourself experienced culture lag, or have you observed it in others? If so, what kind of change caused the lag—was it a new technology, or some other kind of change? Did you notice a generational difference in the way people responded to the change? Did you see any open resistance to it?

- Have new technologies helped you in any significant way, and if so, how? On balance, do you see new technologies as a benefit or a threat to society? Explain.

CHAPTER RESOURCES

Summary

Social movements are a form of collective behavior that promotes **social change,** or a significant alteration over time in behavior patterns and culture. This chapter examined social movements, sociological theories of social change, resistance to social change, and the impact of **technology** on social change.

1. A group will not mobilize into a **social movement** unless its members believe they can end their **relative deprivation** only through collective action.

2. The success of a social movement depends in good part on effective **resource mobilization.** Increasingly, social movements are using **technology**—including the Internet—to mobilize their resources.

3. Early advocates of the **evolutionary theory** of social change believed that society was progressing steadily and inevitably toward a higher state.

4. Talcott Parsons, a leading advocate of functionalist theory, thought that **social change** would always return society to a natural state of equilibrium, or balance. Conflict theorists see change more as a necessity in correcting social injustices and inequities.

5. In general, those with a disproportionate share of society's wealth, status, and power, called **vested interests,** will resist social change and attempt to preserve the status quo.

6. A period of maladjustment, called **culture lag,** occurs when a nonmaterial culture strains to adapt to new material conditions.

7. The Internet, the world's largest computer network, has revolution-ized communications and commercial activity around the world.

8. Though developing nations typically have little access to new technologies, some semiperiphery nations have begun to benefit from the **offshoring** of service and professional jobs once done in core nations.

9. New computer and video technologies have compromised our privacy and facilitated government censorship.

10. Advances in biotechnology have raised difficult ethical questions about genetic engineering.

www.mhhe.com/schaefersm5e
Visit the Online Learning Center for *Sociology Matters* to access quizzes, review activities, and other learning tools.

Key Terms

culture lag, 311

equilibrium
   model, 307

evolutionary
   theory, 307

false
   consciousness, 303

Luddites, 312

new social
   movements, 304

offshoring, 315

relative
   deprivation, 301

resource
   mobilization, 302

social change, 300

social movements, 300

technology, 314

vested interests, 310

Appendix   Careers in Sociology

For the last two decades the number of U.S. college students who have graduated with a degree in sociology has risen steadily (see Figure 1). In this appendix we'll consider some of the options these students have after completing their undergraduate education.

How do students first learn about the sociological perspective on society? Some may take a sociology course in high school. Others may study sociology at community college, where 40 percent of all college students in the United States are enrolled. Indeed, many future sociology majors first develop their sociological imaginations at a community college.

An undergraduate degree in sociology doesn't just serve as excellent preparation for future graduate work in sociology. It also provides a strong liberal arts background for entry-level positions in business, social services, foundations, community organizations, not-for-profit groups, law enforcement, and many government jobs. A number of fields—among them marketing, public relations, and broadcasting—now

Figure 1
Sociology Degrees Conferred in the United States by Gender

Source: Department of Education 2006.

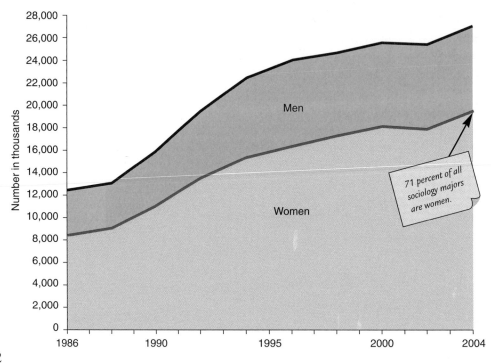

require investigative skills and an understanding of the diverse groups found in today's multiethnic and multinational environment. Moreover, a sociology degree requires accomplishment in oral and written communication, interpersonal skills, problem solving, and critical thinking—all job-related skills that may give sociology graduates an advantage over those who pursue more technical degrees. Consequently, while few occupations specifically require an undergraduate degree in sociology, such academic training can be an important asset in entering a wide range of occupations.

Figure 2 summarizes the occupations of college graduates with BA or BS degrees in sociology. It shows that the areas of social services, administration, management, and sales and marketing offer major career opportunities for sociology graduates. Undergraduates who know where their career interests lie are well advised to enroll in sociology courses and specialties best suited to those interests. For example, students hoping to become health planners would take a class in medical sociology; students seeking employment as social science research assistants would focus on courses in statistics and methods. Internships, such as placements at city planning agencies and survey research organizations, afford another way for sociology students to prepare for careers. Studies show that students who choose an internship placement have less trouble finding jobs, obtain better jobs, and enjoy greater job satisfaction than students without internship placements (American Sociological Association 2009; Salem and Grabarek 1986).

Many college students view social work as the field most closely associated with sociology. Traditionally, social workers received their undergraduate training in sociology and allied fields such as psychology and counseling. After some practical experience, social workers would

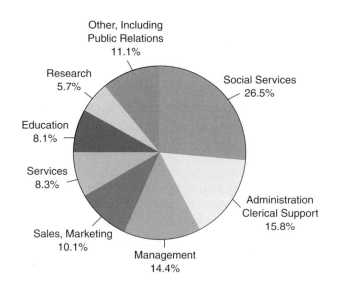

Other, Including
Public Relations
11.1%

Research
5.7%

Education
8.1%

Services
8.3%

Sales, Marketing
10.1%

Management
14.4%

Social Services
26.5%

Administration
Clerical Support
15.8%

Figure 2

Occupations of Graduating Sociology Majors

NOTE: *Based on a national survey conducted in early 2007 of 1,800 graduates of the year 2005.*
SOURCE: Table 1 in Spalter-Roth and Van Vooren 2008a.

generally seek a master's degree in social work (MSW) to be considered for supervisory or administrative positions. Today, however, some students choose (where it is available) to pursue a bachelor's degree in social work (BSW). This degree prepares graduates for direct service positions, such as caseworker or group worker.

Many students continue their sociological training beyond the bachelor's degree. More than 250 universities in the United States have graduate programs in sociology that offer PhD and/or master's degrees. These programs differ greatly in their areas of specialization, course requirements, costs, and the research and teaching opportunities available to graduate students. About 61 percent of the graduates are women (American Sociological Association 2005, 2010a).

Higher education is an important source of employment for sociologists with graduate degrees. About 83 percent of recent PhD recipients in sociology seek employment in colleges and universities. These sociologists teach not only majors committed to the discipline but also students hoping to become doctors, nurses, lawyers, police officers, and so forth (American Sociological Association 2005).

Use Your Sociological Imagination

Did you know that as a student at Princeton University, Michelle Obama majored in sociology? She used that degree as a stepping-stone to Harvard law school. Read her senior thesis at www.politico.com/news/stories/0208/8642.html.

Sociologists who teach in colleges and universities may use their knowledge and training to influence public policy. For example, sociologist Andrew Cherlin (2003) has commented on the debate over proposed federal funding to promote marriage among welfare recipients. Citing the results of two of his studies, Cherlin questioned the potential effectiveness of such a policy in strengthening low-income families. Because many single mothers choose to marry someone other than the father of their children—sometimes for good reason—their children often grow up in stepfamilies. Cherlin's research shows that children who are raised in stepfamilies are no better off than those in single-parent families. He sees government efforts to promote marriage as a politically motivated attempt to foster traditional social values in a society that has become increasingly diverse.

For sociology graduates interested in academic careers, the road to a PhD (or doctorate) can be long and difficult. This degree symbolizes competence in original research; each candidate must prepare a book-length study known as a dissertation. Typically, a doctoral student in sociology will engage in four to seven years of intensive work, including the time required to complete the dissertation. Yet even this effort is no guarantee of a job as a sociology professor.

The good news is that over the next 10 years, the demand for instructors is expected to increase because of high rates of retirement among faculty from the baby-boom generation, as well as the anticipated slow but steady growth in the college student population in the United States. Nonetheless, anyone who launches an academic career must be prepared for considerable uncertainty and competition in the college job market (American Sociological Association 2009).

Of course, not all people working as sociologists teach or hold doctoral degrees. Take government, for example. The Census Bureau relies on people with sociological training to interpret data for other government agencies and the general public. Virtually every agency depends on survey research—a field in which sociology students can specialize—in order to assess everything from community needs to the morale of the agency's own workers. In addition, people with sociological training can put their academic knowledge to effective use in probation and parole, health sciences, community development, and recreational services. Some people working in government or private industry have a master's degree (MA or MS) in sociology; others have a bachelor's degree (BA or BS).

Currently, about 15 percent of the members of the American Sociological Association use their sociological skills outside the academic world, whether in social service agencies or in marketing positions for business firms. Increasing numbers of sociologists with graduate degrees are employed by businesses, industry, hospitals, and nonprofit organizations. Studies show that many sociology graduates are making career changes from social service areas to business and commerce. For an undergraduate major, sociology is excellent preparation for employment in many parts of the business world (Spalter-Roth and Van Vooren 2008b).

Whether you take a few courses in sociology or actually complete a degree, you will benefit from the critical thinking skills developed in this discipline. Sociologists emphasize the value of being able to analyze, interpret, and function within a variety of working situations—an asset in virtually any career. Moreover, given rapid technological change and the expanding global economy, all of us will need to adapt to substantial social change, even in our own careers. Sociology provides a rich conceptual framework that can serve as a foundation for flexible career development and assist you in taking advantage of new employment opportunities.

Glossary

Numbers following the definitions indicate pages where the terms were identified. Consult the index for further page references.

Absolute poverty: A standard of poverty based on a minimum level of subsistence that no family should be expected to live below. (145)

Achieved status: A social position attained by a person largely through his or her own efforts. (78, 130)

Affirmative action: Positive efforts to recruit members of subordinate groups or women for jobs, promotions, and educational opportunities. (181)

Agrarian society: The most technologically advanced form of preindustrial society, in which members are engaged primarily in the production of food but increase their crop yield through such technological innovations as the plow. (90)

Anomie: Émile Durkheim's term for the loss of direction felt in a society when social control of individual behavior has become ineffective. (110)

Anomie theory of deviance: A theory developed by Robert Merton that explains deviance as an adaptation either of socially prescribed goals or of the norms governing their attainment, or both. (111)

Anticipatory socialization: Processes of socialization in which a person "rehearses" for future positions, occupations, and social relationships. (71)

Applied sociology: The use of the discipline of sociology with the specific intent of yielding practical applications for human behavior and organizations. (32)

Argot: Specialized language used by members of a subculture. (45)

Ascribed status: A social position that is "assigned" to a person by society without regard for the person's unique talents or characteristics. (78, 130)

Authority: Power that has been institutionalized and is recognized by the people over whom it is exercised. (246)

Basic sociology: Sociological inquiry conducted with the objective of gaining a more profound knowledge of the fundamental aspects of social phenomena. Also known as *pure sociology*. (33)

Bilateral descent: A kinship system in which both sides of a person's family are regarded as equally important. (218)

Birthrate: The number of live births per 1,000 population in a given year. Also known as the *crude birthrate*. (266)

Bourgeoisie: Karl Marx's term for the capitalist class, or the owners of the means of production. (133)

Brain drain: The immigration to the United States and other industrialized nations of skilled workers, professionals, and technicians who are desperately needed in their home countries. (279)

Bureaucracy: A component of formal organization in which rules and hierarchical ranking are used to achieve efficiency. (93)

Capitalism: An economic system in which the means of production are held largely in private hands, and the main incentive for economic activity is the accumulation of profits. (133, 252)

Caste: A hereditary system of rank, usually religiously dictated, that tends to be fixed and immobile. (131)

Causal logic: The relationship between a condition or variable and a particular consequence, with one event leading to the other. (23)

Census: An enumeration, or counting, of a population. (266)

Charismatic authority: Max Weber's term for power made legitimate by a leader's exceptional personal or emotional appeal to his or her followers. (247)

Class: A term used by Max Weber to refer to a group of people who have a similar level of wealth and income. (135)

Class consciousness: In Karl Marx's view, a subjective awareness of common vested interests and the need for collective political action to bring about social change. (134)

Class system: A social ranking based primarily on economic position in which achieved characteristics can influence social mobility. (131)

Classical theory: An approach to the study of formal organizations in which workers are viewed as being motivated almost entirely by economic rewards. (97)

Clinical sociology: The use of the discipline of sociology with the specific intent of altering social relationships or restructuring social institutions. (33)

Closed system: A social system in which there is little or no possibility of individual mobility. (150)

Code of ethics: The standards of acceptable behavior developed by and for members of a profession. (31)

Cognitive theory of development: Jean Piaget's theory that children's thought progresses through four stages of development. (63)

Colonialism: The maintenance of political, social, economic, and cultural domination over a people by a foreign power for an extended period. (154)

Color-blind racism: The use of the principle of race neutrality to defend a racially unequal status quo. (178)

Communism: As an ideal type, an economic system in which all property is communally owned and no social distinctions are made on the basis of people's ability to produce. (254)

Community: A spatial or political unit of social organization that gives people a sense of belonging. (268)

Concentric-zone theory: A theory of urban growth devised by Ernest Burgess that sees growth in terms of a series of rings radiating from the central business district. (273)

Conflict perspective: A sociological approach that assumes that social behavior is best understood in terms of conflict or tension between competing groups. (17)

Conformity: Going along with peers—individuals of our own status, who have no special right to direct our behavior. (104)

Contact hypothesis: An interactionist perspective that states that interracial contact between people of equal status engaged in a cooperative task will reduce prejudice. (176)

Content analysis: The systematic coding and objective recording of data, guided by some rationale. (30)

Control group: Subjects in an experiment who are not introduced to the independent variable by the researcher. (29)

Control variable: A factor held constant to test the relative impact of an independent variable. (26)

Correlation: A relationship between two variables in which a change in one coincides with a change in the other. (24)

Counterculture: A subculture that conspicuously and deliberately opposes certain aspects of the larger culture. (46)

Credentialism: An increase in the lowest level of education needed to enter a field. (238)

Crime: A violation of criminal law for which some governmental authority applies formal penalties. (119)

Cultural relativism: The evaluation of a people's behavior from the perspective of their own culture. (41)

Cultural transmission: A school of criminology that argues that criminal behavior is learned through social interactions. (113)

Cultural universal: A general practice found in every culture. (40)

Culture: The totality of learned, socially transmitted customs, knowledge, material objects, and behavior. (38)

Culture industry: The worldwide media industry that standardizes the goods and services demanded by consumers. (40)

Culture lag: William F. Ogburn's term for the period of maladjustment when the nonmaterial culture is still struggling to adapt to new material conditions. (44, 311)

Culture shock: The feeling of surprise and disorientation that people experience when they witness cultural practices different from their own. (46)

Culture war: The polarization of society over controversial elements of culture. (53)

Curanderismo: Traditional Latino folk practices for holistic health care and healing. (285)

Death rate: The number of deaths per 1,000 population in a given year. Also known as the *crude death rate.* (267)

Degradation ceremony: An aspect of the resocialization process within total institutions, in which people are subjected to humiliating rituals. (72)

Deindustrialization: The systematic, widespread withdrawal of investment in basic aspects of productivity, such as factories and plants. (259)

Demography: The scientific study of population. (264)

Dependency theory: An approach to global stratification that contends that industrialized nations exploit developing countries for their own gain. (155)

Dependent variable: The variable in a causal relationship that is subject to the influence of another variable. (23)

Deviance: Behavior that violates the standards of conduct or expectations of a group or society. (108)

Differential association: A theory of deviance proposed by Edwin Sutherland that holds that violation of rules results from exposure to attitudes favorable to criminal acts. (113)

Diffusion: The process by which a cultural item spreads from group to group or society to society. (43)

Discovery: The process of making known or sharing the existence of some aspect of reality. (42)

Discrimination: The denial of opportunities and equal rights to individuals and groups based on some type of arbitrary bias. (179)

Dominant ideology: A set of cultural beliefs and practices that help to maintain powerful social, economic, and political interests. (54)

Double consciousness: The division of an individual's identity into two or more social realities. (13)

Downsizing: Reductions taken in a company's workforce as part of deindustrialization. (259)

Dramaturgical approach: A view of social interaction popularized by Erving Goffman that examines people as if they were theatrical performers. (62)

Dysfunction: An element or process of a society that may actually disrupt the social system or reduce its stability. (16)

Economic system: The social institution through which goods and services are produced, distributed, and consumed. (252)

Education: A formal process of learning in which some people consciously teach while others adopt the social role of learner. (235)

Egalitarian family: An authority pattern in which spouses are regarded as equals. (218)

Elite model: A view of society as being ruled by a small group of individuals who share a common set of political and economic interests. (248)

Environmental justice: A legal strategy based on claims that racial minorities and the lower classes are subjected disproportionately to environmental hazards. (295)

Equilibrium model: Talcott Parsons's functionalist view of society as tending toward a state of stability or balance. (307)

Estate system: A system of stratification under which peasants were required to work land leased to them by nobles in exchange for military protection and other services. Also known as *feudalism.* (131)

Esteem: The reputation that a specific person has earned within an occupation. (140)

Ethnic group: A group that is set apart from others primarily because of its national origin or distinctive cultural patterns. (168)

Ethnocentrism: The tendency to assume that one's own culture and way of life represent the norm or are superior to all others. (40, 178)

Ethnography: The study of an entire social setting through extended systematic observation. (28)

Evolutionary theory: A theory of social change that holds that society is moving in a definite direction. (175)

Experiment: An artificially created situation that allows the researcher to manipulate variables. (29)

Experimental group: Subjects in an experiment who are exposed to an independent variable introduced by a researcher. (29)

Exploitation theory: A Marxist theory that views racial subordination in the United States as a manifestation of the class system inherent in capitalism. (307)

Expressiveness: A concern for the maintenance of harmony and the internal emotional affairs of the family. (195)

Extended family: A family in which relatives—such as grandparents, aunts, or uncles—live in the same home as parents and their children. (215)

False consciousness: A term used by Karl Marx to describe an attitude held by members of a class that does not accurately reflect its objective position. (134, 303)

Family: A set of people related by blood, marriage (or some other agreed-upon relationship), or adoption who share the primary responsibility for reproduction and caring for members of society. (214)

Feminist perspective: A sociological approach that views inequity in gender as central to all behavior and organization. (18)

Feminization of poverty: A trend in which women constitute an increasing proportion of the poor people of the United States. (146)

Fertility: The level of reproduction in a society. (264)

Folkway: A norm governing everyday social behavior whose violation raises comparatively little concern. (49)

Force: The actual or threatened use of coercion to impose one's will on others. (246)

Formal norm: A norm that generally has been written down and specifies strict punishment of violators. (49)

Formal organization: A group designed for a special purpose and structured for maximum efficiency. (93)

Formal social control: Control carried out by authorized agents, such as police officers, physicians, school administrators, employers, military officers, and managers of movie theaters. (107)

Functionalist perspective: A sociological approach that emphasizes the way that the parts of a society are structured to maintain its stability. (15)

Fundamentalism: Rigid adherence to fundamental religious doctrines, often accompanied by a literal application of scripture or historical beliefs to today's world. (228)

Gemeinschaft: A term used by Ferdinand Tönnies to describe a small, close-knit community, often found in a rural area, in which strong personal bonds unite members. (88)

Gender role: Expectations regarding the proper behavior, attitudes, and activities of males or females. (65, 190)

Generalized other: A term used by George Herbert Mead to refer to the attitudes, viewpoints, and expectations of society as a whole that a child takes into account in his or her behavior. (60)

Gesellschaft: A term used by Ferdinand Tönnies to describe a community, often urban, that is large and impersonal, with little commitment to the group or consensus on values. (88)

Glass ceiling: An invisible barrier that blocks the promotion of a qualified individual in a work environment because of the individual's gender, race, or ethnicity. (180, 203)

Global warming: The significant rise in the earth's surface temperatures that occurs when industrial gases like carbon dioxide turn the planet's atmosphere into a virtual greenhouse. (289)

Globalization: The worldwide integration of government policies, cultures, social movements, and financial markets through trade and the exchange of ideas. (43, 156)

Goal displacement: Within a bureaucracy, overzealous conformity to official regulations. (96)

Group: Any number of people with similar norms, values, and expectations who interact with one another on a regular basis. (81)

Growth rate: The difference between births and deaths, plus the difference between immigrants and emigrants, per 1,000 population. (268)

Hate crime: A criminal offense committed because of the offender's bias against a race, religion, ethnic group, national origin, or sexual orientation. (178)

Hawthorne effect: The unintended influence of observers or experiments on subjects of research. (29)

Health: As defined by the World Health Organization, a state of complete physical, mental, and social well-being, and not merely the absence of disease and infirmity. (276)

Hidden curriculum: Standards of behavior that are deemed proper by society and are taught subtly in schools. (238)

Homophobia: Fear of and prejudice against homosexuality. (190)

Horizontal mobility: The movement of an individual from one social position to another of the same rank. (150)

Horticultural society: A preindustrial society in which people plant seeds and crops rather than merely subsist on available foods. (90)

Human ecology: An area of study that is concerned with the interrelationships between people and their spatial setting and physical environment. (272)

Human relations approach: An approach to the study of formal organizations that emphasizes the role of people, communication, and participation within a bureaucracy and tends to focus on informal groups. (97)

Hunting-and-gathering society: A preindustrial society in which people rely on whatever foods and fibers are readily available in order to survive. (90)

Hypothesis: A speculative statement about the relationship between two or more variables. (23)

Ideal type: A construct or model that serves as a measuring rod against which actual cases can be evaluated. (11, 94)

Impression management: A term used by Erving Goffman to refer to the altering of the presentation of the self in order to create distinctive appearances and satisfy particular audiences. (62)

Incidence: The number of new cases of a specific disorder occurring within a given population during a stated period, usually a year. (282)

Income: Salaries and wages. (130)

Independent variable: The variable in a causal relationship that, when altered, causes or influences a change in a second variable. (23)

Industrial city: A city characterized by relatively large size, open competition, an open class system, and elaborate specialization in the manufacturing of goods. (270)

Industrial society: A society that depends on mechanization to produce its goods and services. (91)

Infant mortality rate: The number of deaths of infants under one year of age per 1,000 live births in a given year. (267)

Influence: The exercise of power through a process of persuasion. (246)

Informal norm: A norm that generally is understood but is not precisely recorded. (49)

Informal social control: Control that people use casually to enforce norms. (106)

In-group: Any group or category to which people feel they belong. (83)

Innovation: The process of introducing a new idea or object to a culture through discovery or invention. (42)

Institutional discrimination: The denial of opportunities and equal rights to individuals and groups that results from the normal operations of a society. (180)

Instrumentality: An emphasis on tasks, a focus on more distant goals, and a concern for the external relationship between one's family and other social institutions. (195)

Interactionist perspective: A sociological approach that generalizes about everyday forms of social interaction. (19)

Intergenerational mobility: Changes in the social position of children relative to their parents. (150)

Interview: A face-to-face or telephone questioning of a respondent to obtain desired information. (27)

Intragenerational mobility: Changes in a person's social position within his or her adult life. (150)

Invention: The combination of existing cultural items into a form that did not exist before. (42)

Kinship: The state of being related to others. (217)

Labeling theory: A theory that attempts to explain why certain people are viewed as deviants. (115)

Laissez-faire: A form of capitalism in which businesses compete freely, with minimal government intervention in the economy. (252)

Language: An abstract system of word meanings and symbols for all aspects of culture; includes gestures and other nonverbal communication. (47)

Latent function: An unconscious or unintended function; hidden purpose. (17)

Law: Governmental social control. (49, 107)

Life chances: Max Weber's term for people's opportunities to provide themselves with material goods, positive living conditions, and favorable life experiences. (148)

Life expectancy: The median number of years a person can be expected to live under current mortality conditions. (268)

Life-course approach: A research orientation in which sociologists and other social scientists look closely at the social factors that influence people throughout their lives, from birth to death. (71)

Looking-glass self: A concept used by Charles Horton Cooley to emphasize that the self is the product of our social interactions with other people. (59)

Luddites: Rebellious craft workers in 19th-century England who destroyed new factory machinery as part of their resistance to the Industrial Revolution. (312)

Macrosociology: Sociological investigation that concentrates on large-scale phenomena or entire civilizations. (14)

Manifest function: An open, stated, and conscious function. (17)

Master status: A status that dominates others and thereby determines a person's general position within society. (79)

Material culture: The physical or technological aspects of our daily lives. (44)

Matriarchy: A society in which women dominate in family decision making. (218)

Matrilineal descent: A kinship system that favors the mother's relatives. (218)

Matrix of domination: The cumulative impact of oppression because of race, gender, and class, as well as religion, sexual orientation, disability, and age. (197)

McDonaldization: The process through which the principles of the fast-food restaurant have come to dominate certain sectors of society, both in the United States and throughout the world. (43)

Mechanical solidarity: A collective consciousness that emphasizes group solidarity, characteristic of societies with minimal division of labor. (87)

Microfinancing: Lending small sums of money to the poor so they can work their way out of poverty. (257)

Microsociology: Sociological investigation that stresses the study of small groups, often through experimental means. (14)

Modernization: The far-reaching process through which developing nations move from traditional or less developed institutions to those characteristic of more developed societies. (159)

Modernization theory: The functionalist view that modernization and development will gradually improve the lives of people in developing nations. (160)

Monogamy: A form of marriage in which one woman and one man are married only to each other. (216)

Monopoly: Control of a market by a single business firm. (253)

Morbidity rate: The incidence of disease in a given population. (282)

Mores: Norms deemed highly necessary to the welfare of a society. (49)

Mortality rate: The incidence of death in a given population. (282)

Multinational corporation: A commercial organization that is headquartered in one country but does business throughout the world. (156)

Multiple masculinities: A variety of male gender roles, including nurturing-caring and effeminate-gay roles, that men may play along with their more pervasive traditional role of dominating women. (193)

Multiple-nuclei theory: A theory of urban growth developed by Chauncey D. Harris and Edward Ullman that views growth as emerging from many centers of development, each of which reflects a particular urban need or activity. (274)

Natural science: The study of the physical features of nature and the ways in which they interact and change. (4)

Neocolonialism: Continuing dependence of former colonies on foreign countries. (154)

New social movements: Organized collective activities that address values and social identities as well as improvements in the quality of life. (304)

New urban sociology: An approach to urbanization that considers the interplay of local, national, and worldwide forces and their effect on local space, with special emphasis on the impact of global economic activity. (275)

Nonmaterial culture: Customs, beliefs, philosophies, governments, and patterns of communication, as well as ways of using material objects. (44)

Nonverbal communication: The sending of messages through the use of posture, facial expressions, and gestures. (20)

Norm: An established standard of behavior maintained by a society. (48)

Nuclear family: A married couple and their unmarried children living together. (215)

Obedience: Compliance with higher authorities in a hierarchical structure. (104)

Objective method: A technique for measuring social class that assigns individuals to classes on the basis of criteria such as occupation, education, income, and place of residence. (140)

Observation: A research technique in which an investigator collects information through direct participation in and/or closely watching a group or community under study. (28)

Offshoring: The transfer of work to foreign contractors. (315)

Open system: A social system in which the position of each individual is influenced by his or her achieved status. (150)

Operational definition: An explanation of an abstract concept that is specific enough to allow a researcher to assess the concept. (22)

Organic solidarity: A collective consciousness that rests on mutual interdependence, characteristic of societies with a complex division of labor. (88)

Organized crime: The work of a group that regulates relations between various criminal enterprises involved in various illegal activities. (121)

Out-group: A group or category to which people feel they do not belong. (83)

Patriarchy: A society in which men dominate in family decision making. (218)

Patrilineal descent: A kinship system that favors the father's relatives. (218)

Personality: The individual characteristics, attitudes, needs, and behaviors that set one person apart from another. (38)

Peter Principle: A principle of organizational life originated by Laurence J. Peter, according to which every employee within a hierarchy tends to rise to his or her level of incompetence. (97)

Pluralist model: A view of society in which many competing groups within the community have access to government officials, so that no single group is dominant. (250)

Politics: In Harold D. Lasswell's words, "who gets what, when, and how." (245)

Polyandry: A form of polygamy in which a woman may have several husbands at the same time. (216)

Polygamy: A form of marriage in which an individual may have several husbands or wives simultaneously. (216)

Polygyny: A form of polygamy in which a husband may have several wives at the same time. (216)

Postindustrial city: A city in which global finance and the electronic flow of information dominate the economy. (271)

Postindustrial society: A society whose economic system is engaged primarily in the processing and control of information. (91)

Postmodern society: A technologically sophisticated society that is preoccupied with consumer goods and media images. (92)

Power: The ability to exercise one's will over others. (135, 246)

Power elite: A term used by C. Wright Mills for a small group of military, industrial, and government leaders who control the fate of the United States. (248)

Preindustrial city: A city with only a few thousand residents that is characterized by a relatively closed class system and limited social mobility. (269)

Prejudice: A negative attitude toward an entire category of people, often an ethnic or racial group. (178)

Prestige: The respect and admiration that an occupation holds in a society. (140)

Prevalence: The total number of cases of a specific disorder that exist at a given time. (282)

Primary group: A small group characterized by intimate, face-to-face association and cooperation. (82)

Professional criminal: A person who pursues crime as a day-to-day occupation. (120)

Proletariat: Karl Marx's term for the working class in a capitalist society. (133)

Protestant ethic: Max Weber's term for the disciplined work ethic, this-worldly concerns, and rational orientation to life emphasized by John Calvin and his followers. (225)

Qualitative research: Research that relies more on what scientists see in the field or in naturalistic settings than on statistical data. (28)

Quantitative research: Research that collects and reports data primarily in numerical form. (27)

Questionnaire: A printed or written form used to obtain information from a respondent. (27)

Racial formation: A sociohistorical process in which racial categories are created, inhibited, transformed, and destroyed. (167)

Racial group: A group that is set apart from others because of obvious physical differences. (168)

Racial profiling: Any arbitrary action initiated by an authority based on race, ethnicity, or national origin rather than on a person's behavior. (176)

Racism: The belief that one race is supreme and all others are innately inferior. (178)

Random sample: A sample for which every member of the entire population has the same chance of being selected. (24)

Rational-legal authority: Max Weber's term for power made legitimate by law. (247)

Reference group: Any group that individuals use as a standard in evaluating themselves and their own behavior. (83)

Relative deprivation: The conscious feeling of a negative discrepancy between legitimate expectations and present actualities. (301)

Relative poverty: A floating standard of deprivation by which people at the bottom of a society, whatever their lifestyles, are judged to be disadvantaged in comparison with the nation as a whole. (145)

Reliability: The extent to which a measure produces consistent results. (25)

Religion: According to Émile Durkheim, a unified system of beliefs and practices relative to sacred things. (222)

Religious belief: A statement to which members of a particular religion adhere. (228)

Religious experience: The feeling or perception of being in direct contact with the ultimate reality, such as a divine being, or of being overcome with religious emotion. (229)

Religious ritual: A practice required or expected of members of a faith. (229)

Research design: A detailed plan or method for obtaining data scientifically. (27)

Resocialization: The process of discarding former behavior patterns and accepting new ones as part of a transition in one's life. (71)

Resource mobilization: The ways in which a social movement utilizes such resources as money, political influence, access to the media, and personnel. (302)

Rite of passage: A ritual marking the symbolic transition from one social position to another. (70)

Role conflict: The situation that occurs when incompatible expectations arise from two or more social positions held by the same person. (80)

Role strain: The situation that occurs when the same social position imposes conflicting demands and expectations. (81)

Role taking: The process of mentally assuming the perspective of another in order to respond from that imagined viewpoint. (60)

Sample: A selection from a larger population that is statistically representative of that population. (24)

Sanction: A penalty or reward for conduct concerning a social norm. (50, 102)

Science: The body of knowledge obtained by methods based on systematic observation. (4)

Scientific management approach: Another name for the *classical theory* of formal organizations. (97)

Scientific method: A systematic, organized series of steps that ensures maximum objectivity and consistency in researching a problem. (21)

Second shift: The double burden—work outside the home followed by child care and housework—that many women face and few men share equitably. (204)

Secondary analysis: A variety of research techniques that make use of previously collected and publicly accessible information and data. (29)

Secondary group: A formal, impersonal group in which there is little social intimacy or mutual understanding. (82)

Self: According to George Herbert Mead, a distinct identity that sets one apart from others. (58)

Serial monogamy: A form of marriage in which a person may have several spouses in his or her life, but only one spouse at a time. (216)

Sexism: The ideology that one sex is superior to the other. (199)

Sexual harassment: Behavior that occurs when work benefits are made contingent on sexual favors. (200)

Sick role: Societal expectations about the attitudes and behavior of a person viewed as being ill. (277)

Significant other: A term used by George Herbert Mead to refer to those individuals who are most important in the development of the self, such as parents, friends, and teachers. (61)

Slavery: A system of enforced servitude in which some people are legally owned by other people. (130)

Social change: Significant alteration over time in behavior patterns and culture. (300)

Social control: Techniques and strategies for preventing deviant behavior in any society. (102)

Social disorganization theory: The theory that increases in crime and deviance can be attributed to the absence or breakdown of communal relationships and social institutions, such as the family, school, church, and local government. (114)

Social epidemiology: The study of the distribution of disease, impairment, and general health status across a population. (282)

Social inequality: A condition in which members of a society enjoy different amounts of wealth, prestige, or power. (130)

Social institution: An organized pattern of beliefs and behavior centered on basic social needs. (86, 210)

Social interaction: The ways in which people respond to one another. (76)

Social mobility: The movement of individuals or groups from one position in a society's stratification system to another. (149)

Social movements: Organized collective activities to bring about or resist fundamental change in an existing group or society. (300)

Social network: A series of social relationships that links a person directly to others, and through them, indirectly to still more people. (84)

Social role: A set of expectations for people who occupy a given social position or status. (80)

Social science: The study of various aspects of human society. (5)

Social structure: The way in which a society is organized into predictable relationships. (76)

Socialism: An economic system in which the means of production and distribution are collectively rather than privately owned. (253)

Socialization: The process through which people learn the attitudes, values, and behaviors appropriate for members of a particular culture. (38)

Societal-reaction approach: Another name for *labeling theory*. (115)

Society: A fairly large number of people who live in the same territory, are relatively independent of people outside it, and participate in a common culture. (39)

Sociobiology: The systematic study of how biology affects human social behavior. (55)

Sociocultural evolution: The process of change and development in human societies that results from the interplay of continuity, innovation, and selection. (90)

Socioeconomic status: A measure of social class that is based on income, education, and occupation. (142)

Sociological imagination: An awareness of the relationship between an individual and the wider society, both today and in the past. (3)

Sociology: The scientific study of social behavior and human groups. (3, 275)

Status: A term used by sociologists to refer to any of the full range of socially defined positions within a large group or society. (78)

Status group: A term used by Max Weber to refer to people who have the same prestige or lifestyle, independent of their class positions. (135)

Stereotype: An unreliable generalization about all members of a group that does not recognize individual differences within the group. (168)

Stigma: A label society uses to devalue members of a certain social group. (109)

Stratification: The structured ranking of entire groups of people that perpetuates unequal economic rewards and power in a society. (130)

Subculture: A segment of society that shares a distinctive pattern of customs, rules, and traditions that differs from the pattern of the larger society. (44)

Survey: A study, generally in the form of an interview or questionnaire, that provides researchers with information about how people think and act. (27)

Symbol: A gesture, object, or language that forms the basis of human communication. (59)

Symbolic ethnicity: An emphasis on such concerns as ethnic food or political issues rather than on deeper ties to one's ethnic heritage. (171)

Teacher-expectancy effect: The impact that a teacher's expectations about a student's performance may have on the student's actual achievements. (241)

Technology: Cultural information about how to use the material resources of the environment to satisfy human needs and desires. (44, 90, 314)

Theory: In sociology, a set of statements that seeks to explain problems, actions, or behavior. (7)

Total fertility rate (TFR): The average number of children born alive to any woman, assuming that she conforms to current fertility rates. (71)

Total institution: A term coined by Erving Goffman to refer to institutions that regulate all aspects of a person's life under a single authority, such as prisons, the military, mental hospitals, and convents. (71)

Tracking: The practice of placing students in specific curriculum groups on the basis of their test scores and other criteria. (239)

Traditional authority: Legitimate power conferred by custom and accepted practice. (247)

Trained incapacity: The tendency of workers in a bureaucracy to become so specialized that they develop blind spots and fail to notice obvious problems. (95)

Transnational crime: Crime that occurs across multiple national borders. (123)

Urban ecology: An area of study that focuses on the interrelationships between urban residents and their environment. (272)

Urbanism: A term used by Louis Wirth to describe distinctive patterns of social behavior evident among city residents. (271)

Validity: The degree to which a measure or scale truly reflects the phenomenon under study. (25)

Value: A collective conception of what is considered good, desirable, and proper—or bad, undesirable, and improper—in a culture. (51)

Variable: A measurable trait or characteristic that is subject to change under different conditions. (23)

Verstehen: The German word for "understanding" or "insight"; used by Max Weber to stress the need for sociologists to take into account the subjective meanings people attach to their actions. (11)

Vertical mobility: The movement of a person from one social position to another of a different rank. (150)

Vested interests: Thorstein Veblen's term for those people or groups who will suffer in the event of social change and who have a stake in maintaining the status quo. (310)

Victimization survey: Questioning of ordinary people, not police officers, to determine whether they have been victims of crime. (125)

Victimless crime: The willing exchange among adults of widely desired, but illegal, goods and services. (120)

Vital statistics: Records of births, deaths, marriages, and divorces that are gathered through a registration system maintained by governmental units. (266)

Wealth: An inclusive term encompassing all a person's material assets, including land, stocks, and other property. (130)

White-collar crime: Illegal acts committed in the course of business activities. (121)

White privilege: Rights or immunities granted to people as a particular benefit or favor simply because they are White. (165)

World-systems analysis: Immanuel Wallerstein's view of the global economic system as divided between certain industrialized nations that control wealth and developing countries that are controlled and exploited. (154, 275)

References

Abercrombie, Nicholas, Stephen Hill, and Bryan Turner. 1980. *The Dominant Ideology Thesis.* London: George Allen Unwin.

———, Bryan S. Turner, and Stephen Hill, eds. 1990. *Dominant Ideologies.* Cambridge, MA: Unwin Hyman.

Aberle, David E., A. K. Cohen, A. K. Davis, M. J. Leng, Jr., and F. N. Sutton. 1950. "The Functionalist Prerequisites of a Society" *Ethics* 60 (January): 100–111.

Addams, Jane. 1910. *Twenty Years at Hull-House.* New York: Macmillan.

———. 1930. *The Second Twenty Years at Hull-House.* New York: Macmillan.

Adler, Patricia A., and Peter Adler. 2003. "The Promise and Pitfalls of Going into the Field." *Contexts* (Spring):41–47.

———, and ———. 2004. *Paradise Laborers: Hotel Work in the Global Economy.* Ithaca, NY: Cornell University Press.

———, and ———. 2007. "The Demedicalization of Self-Injury: From Psychopathology to Sociological Deviance." *Journal of Contemporary Ethnography* 36 (October):537–570.

———, and ———. 2008b. "The Cyber Worlds of Self-Injurers: Deviant Communities, Relationships, and Selves." *Symbolic Interaction* 31 (1):33–56.

———, ———, and John M. Johnson. 1992. "Street Corner Society Revisited." *Journal of Contemporary Ethnography* 21 (April):3–10.

———, 2007. "The Demedicalization of Self-Injury: From Psychopathology to Sociological Deviance." *Journal of Contemporary Ethnography* 36 (October):537–570.

———. 2008a. "Of Rhetoric and Representation: The Four Faces of Ethnography." *Sociological Quarterly* (No. 1).

Adorno, Theodor. [1971] 1991. *The Culture Industry.* London: Routledge.

Alain, Michel. 1985. "An Empirical Validation of Relative Deprivation." *Human Relations* 38 (8):739–749.

Alba, Richard D. 1990. *Ethnic Identity: The Transformation of White America.* New Haven, CT: Yale University Press.

Allen, Bem P. 1978. *Social Behavior: Fact and Falsehood.* Chicago: Nelson-Hall.

Allport, Gordon W. 1979. *The Nature of Prejudice.* 25th anniversary ed. Reading, MA: Addison-Wesley.

Alzheimer's Association. 2010. *2010 Alzheimer's Disease Facts and Figures.* Chicago: Alzheimer's Association.

American Academy of Cosmetic Surgery. 2008. "2007 Procedural Survey Reveals a Two-Year Increase in Age of Patients Seeking Cosmetic Surgery." Press release. Accessed at www.cosmeticsurgery.org/media/pr_031308.pdf.

American Community Survey. 2009. "2008 American Community Survey." Accessed at http://factfinder.census.gov.

American Federation of Teachers. 2007. *Survey and Analysis of Teacher Salary Trends 2005.* Washington, DC: AFT.

American Psychological Association. 2008. "Being Gay Is Just as Healthy as Being Straight." Accessed February 25 (http://www.apa.org).

American Sociological Association. 1997. *Code of Ethics.* Washington, DC: American Sociological Association. Available at www.asanet.org/members/ecoderev.html.

———. 2005. "Need Today's Data Yesterday." Accessed December 17 (www.asanet.org).

———. 2009. *21st Century Careers with an Undergraduate Degree in Sociology.* Washington, DC: ASA.

———. 2010a. *2010 Guide to Graduate Departments of Sociology.* Washington, DC: ASA.

Andersen, Margaret. 2007. *Thinking About Women: Sociological Perspectives on Sex and Gender.* 7th ed. New York: Allyn and Bacon.

Ansell, Amy E. 2008. "Color Blindness." Pp. 320–321, vol. 1, in *Encyclopedia of Race, Ethnicity, and Society,* edited by Richard T. Schaefer. Thousand Oaks, CA: Sage.

Arias, Elizabeth. 2004. "United States Life Tables, 2002." *National Vital Statistics Report,* November 10.

Armer, J. Michael, and John Katsillis. 1992."Modernization Theory." Pp. 1299–1304 in *Encyclopedia of Sociology,* vol. 4, edited by Edgar F. Borgatta and Marie L. Borgatta. New York: Macmillan.

Association of Theological Schools. 2010. "2009–2010 Annual Data Tables: Table 2-12A." Accessed April 17 (www.ats.edu/Resources/Publications/Documents/AnnualDataTables/2009-10AnnualDataTables.pdf).

Astin, Alexander, Sarah A. Parrott, William S. Korn, and Linda J. Sax. 1994. *The American Freshman: Thirty Year Trends.* Los Angeles: Higher Education Research Institute.

The Atlantic. 2008. "Engineers for Osama." 301 (January/February):26.

Azumi, Koya, and Jerald Hage. 1972. *Organizational Systems.* Lexington, MA: Heath.

Babad, Elisha Y., and P. J. Taylor. 1992. "Transparency of Teacher Expectancies Across Language, Cultural Boundaries." *Journal of Educational Research* 86:120–125.

Bainbridge, William Sims. 2007. "The Scientific Research Potential of Virtual Worlds." *Science* 317 (July 27):472–476.

Barboza, David. 2008. "Reform Stalls in Chinese Factories." *New York Times,* January 5, pp. B1, B6.

Barrionuevo, Alexei. 2008. "Amazon's 'Forest Peoples' Seek Role in Striking Global Climate Agreements." *New York Times,* April 6, p. 6.

Barton, Bernadette. 2006. *Stripped: Inside the Lives of Exotic Dancers.* New York: New York University Press.

Bauerlein, Monika. 1996. "The Luddites Are Back." *Utne Reader* (March/April):24, 26.

Bauman, Kurt J. 1999. "Extended Measures of Well-Being: Meeting Basic Needs." *Current Population Reports,* ser. P-70, no. 67. Washington, DC: U.S. Government Printing Office.

Beagan, Brenda L. 2001. "'Even If I Don't Know What I'm Doing I Can Make It Look Like I Know What I'm Doing': Becoming a Doctor in the 1990s." *Canadian Review of Sociology and Anthropology* 38:275–292.

Becker, Howard. 1963. *The Outsiders: Studies in the Sociology of Deviance.* New York: Free Press.

———. 1973. *The Outsiders: Studies in the Sociology of Deviance.* Rev. ed. New York: Free Press.

Beeghley, Leonard. 1978. *Social Stratification in America: A Critical Analysis of Theory and Research.* Santa Monica, CA: Goodyear Publishing.

Beisel, Nicola, and Tamara Kay. 2004. "Abortion, Race, and Gender in Nineteenth-Century America." *American Sociological Review* 69(4):498–518.

Bell, Daniel. 1999. *The Coming of Post-Industrial Society: A Venture in Social Forecasting.* With new foreword. New York: Basic Books.

Bell, Wendell. 1981."Modernization." Pp. 186–187 in *Encyclopedia of Sociology.* Guilford, CT: DPG Publishing.

Beller, Emily. 2009. "Bringing Intergenerational Social Mobility Research into the Twenty-First Century: Why Mothers Matter." *America Sociological Review* 74 (August):507–528.

Benford, Robert D. 1992. "Social Movements." Pp. 1880–1887 in *Encyclopedia of Sociology,* vol. 4, edited by Edgar F. Borgatta and Marie Borgatta. New York: Macmillan.

Bergen, Raquel Kennedy. 2006. *Marital Rape: New Research and Directions.* Harrisburg, PA: VAW Net.

Berger, Peter, and Thomas Luckmann. 1966. *The Social Construction of Reality.* New York: Doubleday.

Berman, Paul. 2003. *Terror and Liberalism.* New York: W.W. Norton.

Black, Donald. 1995. "The Epistemology of Pure Sociology." *Law and Social Inquiry* 20 (Summer):829–870.

Blank, Rebecca M. 2008. "Presidential Address: How to Improve Poverty Measurement in the United States." *Journal of Policy Analysis and Management* 27 (2):233–254.

Blau, Peter M., and Otis Dudley Duncan. 1967. *The American Occupational Structure.* New York: Wiley.

Blauner, Robert. 1972. *Racial Oppression in America.* New York: Harper and Row.

Blumer, Herbert. 1955. "Collective Behavior." Pp. 165–198 in *Principles of Sociology,* 2d ed., edited by Alfred McClung Lee. New York: Barnes and Noble.

Bonilla-Silva, Eduardo. 2004. "From Bi-Racial to Tri-Racial: Towards a New System of Racial Stratification in the USA." *Ethics and Racial Studies* 27 (November):931–950.

———. 2006. *Racism Without Racists.* Lanham: Rowman and Littlefield.

Borjas, George S., Jeffrey Grogger, and Gordon H. Hanson. 2006. "Immigration and African-American Employment Opportunities: The Response of Wages, Employment, and Incarceration to Labor Supply Shocks." Working paper 12518. Cambridge MA: National Bureau of Economic Research.

Bottomore, Tom, and Maximilien Rubel, eds. 1956. *Karl Marx: Selected Writings in Sociology and Social Philosophy.* New York: McGraw-Hill.

Bourdieu, Pierre, and Jean-Claude Passerson. 1990. *Reproduction in Education, Society and Culture,* 2d ed. London: Sage. Originally published as *La reproduction.*

Bowles, Samuel, and Herbert Gintis. 1976. *Schooling in Capitalistic America: Educational Reforms and the Contradictions of Economic Life.* New York: Basic Books.

Brannon, Robert. 1976. "Ideology, Myth, and Reality: Sex Equality in Israel." *Sex Roles* 6:403–419.

Bray, James H., and John Kelly. 1999. *Stepfamilies: Love, Marriage, and Parenting in the First Decade.* New York: Broadway Books.

Breines, Winifred. 2007. "Struggling to Connect: White and Black Feminism in the Movement Years." *Contexts* 6 (Winter):18–24.

Brettell, Caroline B., and Carolyn F. Sargent. 2005. *Gender in Cross-Cultural Perspective,* 4th ed. Upper Saddle River, NJ: Prentice Hall.

Brimmer, Andrew F. 1995. "The Economic Cost of Discrimination against Black Americans." Pp. 9–29 in *Economic Perspectives in Affirmative Action,* edited by Margaret C. Simms. Washington, DC: Joint Center for Political and Economic Studies.

Britannica Online. 2010. "Worldwide Adherents of All Religions by Six Continental Areas. Mid-2009." Accessed April 10.

Broder, John M. 2009. "5 Nations Forge Pact on Climate; Goals Go Unmet." *New York Times,* December 19, pp. A1, A10.

Brown, David K. 2001. "The Social Sources of Educational Credentialism: Status Cultures, Labor Markets, and Organizations." *Sociology of Education* 74 (Extra Issue):19–34.

Browne, Irene, ed. 2001. *Latinas and African American Women at Work: Race, Gender, and Economic Inequlity.* New York: Russell Sage Foundation.

Buchanan, Joy. 2008. "Medicine Meets a Culture Gap." *USA Today,* February 14, p. 9D.

Buchmann, Claudia, Thomas A. DiPrete, and Anne McDaniel. 2008. "Gender Inequalities in Education." *Annual Review of Sociology* 34:319–337.

Bullard, Robert, D. 1993. *Dumping in Dixie: Race, Class, and Environmentalist Quality.* 2d ed. Boulder, CO: Westin Press.

Bulle, Wolfgang F. 1987. *Crossing Cultures? Southeast Asian Mainland.* Atlanta: Centers for Disease Control.

Bureau of Labor Statistics. 2010b. "Labor Force Statistics from the Current Population Survey." Accessed April 23 (www.bls.gov/cps/#tables).

Bureau of the Census. 1975. *Historical Statistics of the United States, Colonial Times to 1970.* Washington, DC: U.S. Government Printing Office.

———. 1996. "Percent Distribution of Projected Households by Type: 1995 to 2010." Released May 1996. Accessed March 1, 2006 (www.census.gov).

———. 2004a. *Statistical Abstract of the United States, 2004–2005.* Washington, DC: U.S. Government Printing Office.

———. 2007a. *Statistical Abstract of the United States 2008.* Washington D.C.: U.S. Government Printing Office.

———. 2008b. "Total Midyear Population for the World: 1900–2050." (Data updated 3-27-2008.) Accessed April 9 (www.census.gov).

———2009a. *Statistical Abstract of the United States 2010.* Washington, DC: U.S. Government Printing Office.

———. 2009e. "Historical Tables on Income Inequality." Accessed February 20, 2010 (www.census.gov/hhes/www/income/incomestats.html#incomeineq).

———. 2010d. International Programs: World POPClock Projection: Accessed July 12 at http://www.census.gov/ipc/www/popclockworld.html.

Burger, Jerry M. 2009. "Replicating Milgram: Would People Still Obey Today?" *American Psychologist* 64 (January):1–11.

Burgess, Ernest W. 1925. "The Growth of the City." Pp. 47–62 in *The City,* edited by Robert E. Park, Ernest W. Burgess, and Roderick D. McKenzie. Chicago: University of Chicago Press.

Burkeman, Oliver. 2007. "Virtual World Wakes Up to Violent Protest." *Manchester Guardian,* February 16, p. 6.

Calhoun, Craig. 1998. "Community without Propinquity Revisited." *Sociological Inquiry* 68 (Summer):373–397.

Call, V. R., and Teachman, J. D. 1991. "Military Service and Stability in the Family Life Course." *Military Psychology* 3:233–250.

Cameron, Deborah. 2007. *The Myth of Mars and Venus.* Oxford: Oxford University Press.

Caplan, Ronald L. 1989. "The Commodification of American Health Care." *Social Science and Medicine* 28 (11):1139–1148.

Carbon Trust. 2010. "About the Carbon Trust." Accessed April 27 (www.carbontrust.co.uk/about-carbon-trust/pages/default.aspx).

Carty, Win. 1999. "Greater Dependence on Cars Leads to More Pollution in World's Cities."*Population Today* 27 (December):1–2.

Castells, Manuel. 2010a. *The Rise of the Network Society.* 2nd ed. With a new preface. Malden, MA: Wiley-Blackwell.

———. 2010b. *The Power of Identity.* 2nd ed. With a new preface. Malden, MA: Wiley-Blackwell.

———. 2010c. *End of Millennium.* 2nd ed. With a new preface. Malden, MA: Wiley-Blackwell.

Catalyst. 2009a. *2008 Catalyst Census of Women Corporate Officers and Top Earners of the* Fortune *500.* New York: Catalyst.

———. 2009b. *Women in U.S. Management.* New York: Catalyst.

Center for American Women and Politics. 2010. *Fact Sheet: Women in the U.S. Congress 2010 and Statewide Elective Women 2010.* Rutgers, NJ: CAWP.

Center for Corporate Diversity. 2008. "Nordic 500, 2006–2008." Accessed March 17 (www.managementwomen.no).

Centers for Disease Control. 2009. "HIV/AIDS in the United States." Updated August 2009. Accessible at www.cdc.gov/hiv.

Chambliss, William. 1973. "The Saints and the Roughnecks." *Society* 11 (November/December):24–31.

Chase-Dunn, Christopher, and Peter Grimes. 1995. "World-Systems Analysis." Pp. 387–417 in *Annual Review of Sociology,* 1995, edited by John Hagan. Palo Alto, CA: Annual Reviews.

———, Yukio Kawano, and Benjamin D. Brewer. 2000. "Trade Globalization Since 1795: Waves of Integration in the World System." *American Sociological Review* 65 (February):77–95.

Cherlin, Andrew J. 2003. "Should the Government Promote Marriage?" *Contexts* 2 (Fall):22–29.

Christakis, Nicholas A., and James Fowler. 2009. *Connected: The Amazing Power of Social Networks and How They Shape Our Lives.* New York: Harper.

Chu, Henry. 2007. "English Divides India's Call-Centre Hub." *Guardian* 176 (February 16):3.

Chung, Esther K., Leny Mathew, Amy C. Rothkopt, Irma T. Elo, James C. Cayne, and Jennifer F. Culhane. 2009. "Parenting Attitudes and Infant Spanking: The Influence of Childhood Experiences." *Pediatrics* 124 (August):278–286.

Clark, Candace. 1983. "Sickness and Social Control." Pp. 346–365 in *Social Interaction: Readings in Sociology,* 2d ed., edited by Howard Robboy and Candace Clark. New York: St. Martin's.

Clarke, Adele E., Janet K. Shim, Laura Maro, Jennifer Ruth Fusket, and Jennifer R. Fishman. 2003. "Bio Medicalization: Technoscientific Transformations of Health, Illness, and U.S. Biomedicine." *American Sociological Review* 68 (April):161–194.

Coates, Rodney. 2008. "Covert Racism in the USA and Globally." *Sociology Compass* 2:208–231.

Cockerham, William C. 2009. *Medical Sociology.* 11th ed. Upper Saddle River, NJ: Prentice Hall.

Cohen, Patricia. 2010. "Indian Tribes Go in Search of Their Lost Languages." *New York Times* (April 6), pp.1, 5.

Cole, Mike. 1988. *Bowles and Gintis Revisited: Correspondence and Contradiction in Educational Theory.* Philadelphia: Falmer.

Coleman, Isobel. 2004. "The Payoff from Women's Rights." *Foreign Affairs* 83 (May/June):80–95.

Collins, Patricia Hill. 2000. *Black Feminist Thought: Knowledge, Consciousness, and the Politics of Empowerment.* Revised 10th Anniv. 2d ed. New York: Routledge.

Collins, Randall. 1975. *Conflict Sociology: Toward an Explanatory Sociology.* New York: Academic.

———. 1980. "Weber's Last Theory of Capitalism: A Systematization." *American Sociological Review* 45 (December):925–942.

———. 1986. *Weberian Sociological Theory.* New York: Cambridge University Press.

———. 1995. "Prediction in Macrosociology: The Case of the Soviet Collapse." *American Journal of Sociology* 100 (May):1552–1593.

Collura, Heather. 2007. "Roommate Concerns Fed by Facebook." August 8, p. 6D.

Commission on Civil Rights. 1976. *A Guide to Federal Laws and Regulations Prohibiting Sex Discrimination.* Washington, DC: U.S. Government Printing Office.

———. 1981. *Affirmative Action in the 1980s: Dismantling the Process of Discrimination.* Washington, DC: U.S. Government Printing Office.

Commoner, Barry. 1971. *The Closing Circle.* New York: Knopf.

———. 1990. *Making Peace with the Planet.* New York: Pantheon.

———. 2007. "At 90, an Environmentalist from the 70's Still Has Hope." *New York Times,* June 19, p. D2.

Commonwealth Fund. 2008. *Why Not the Best?* New York: Commonwealth Fund.

Conley, Dalton. 2010. *Being Black, Living in the Red.* 10th anniversary edition: Berkeley: University of California Press.

Connell, R.W. 1987. *Gendered Power: Society, the Person, and Sexual Politics.* Stanford, CA: Stanford University Press.

————. 2002. *Gender.* Cambridge, UK: Polity Press.

————. 2005. *Masculinities.* 2d ed. Berkeley: University of California Press.

Conrad, Peter. 2007. *The Medicalization of Society: On the Transformation of Human Conditions into Treatable Disorders.* Baltimore, MD: Johns Hopkins University.

————. 2009a. *The Medicalization of Society: On the Transformation of Human Conditions into Treatable Disorders.* 11th ed. Baltimore, MD: Johns Hopkins University.

————. 2009b. *The Sociology of Health and Illness: Cultural Perspectives.* 8th ed. New York: Worth.

Cooley, Charles. H. 1902. *Human Nature and the Social Order.* New York: Scribner.

Coontz, Stephanie. 2006. "A Pop Quiz on Marriage." *New York Times,* February 19, p. 12.

Cooper, Richard T. 1998. "Jobs Outside High School Can Be Costly, Report Finds." *Los Angeles Times,* November 6, p. A1.

Corbett, Christianne, Catherine Hill, and Andresse St. Rose. 2008. *Where the Girls Are: The Facts About Gender Equity in Education.* Washington, DC: American Association of University Women.

Coser, Lewis A. 1977. *Masters of Sociological Thought: Ideas in Historical and Social Context.* 2d ed. New York: Harcourt, Brace and Jovanovich.

Couch, Carl. 1996. *Information Technologies and Social Orders.* Edited with an introduction by David R. Maines and Shing-Ling Chien. New York: Aldine de Gruyter.

Council on Scientific Affairs. 1999. "Hispanic Health in the United States." *Journal of the American Medical Association* 265 (January 9):248–252.

Cox, Oliver C. 1948. *Caste, Class, and Race: A Study in Social Dynamics.* Detroit: Wayne State University Press.

Cross, Simon, and Barbara Bagilhole. 2002. "Girls' Jobs for the Boys? Men, Masculinity and Non-Traditional Occupations." *Gender, Work, and Organization* 9 (April):204–226.

Cuff, E. C., W. W. Sharrock, and D.W. Francis, eds. 1990. *Perspectives in Sociology.* 3d ed. Boston: Unwin Hyman.

Cullen, Francis T., Jr., and John B. Cullen. 1978. *Toward a Paradigm of Labeling Theory,* ser. 58. Lincoln: University of Nebraska Studies.

Currie, Elliot. 1985. *Confronting Crime: An American Challenge.* New York: Pantheon.

————. 1998. *Crime and Punishment in America.* New York: Metropolitan Books.

Curry, Timothy Jon. 1993. "A Little Pain Never Hurt Anyone: Athletic Career Socialization and the Normalization of Sports Injury." *Symbolic Interaction* 26 (Fall):273–290.

Curtiss, Susan. 1977. *Genie: A Psycholinguistic Study of a Modern Day "Wild Child."* New York: Academic Press.

————. 1985. "The Development of Human Cerebral Lateralization." Pp. 97–116 in *The Dual Brain,* edited by D. Frank Benson and Eran Zaidel. New York: Guilford.

Dahl, Robert A. 1961. *Who Governs?* New Haven, CT: Yale University Press.

Dahrendorf, Ralf. 1959. *Class and Class Conflict in Industrial Sociology.* Stanford, CA: Stanford University Press.

Darwin, Charles. 1859. *On the Origin of Species.* London: John Murray.

Davis, James A., Tom W. Smith, and Peter V. Marsden. 2009. *General Social Surveys, 1972–2008: Cumulative Codebook.* Chicago: National Opinion Research Center.

Davis, Kingsley. 1940. "Extreme Social Isolation of a Child." *American Journal of Sociology* 45 (January):554–565.

———. 1947. "A Final Note on a Case of Extreme Isolation." *American Journal of Sociology* 52 (March):432–437.

———. [1949] 1995. *Human Society.* Reprint, New York: Macmillan.

———, and Wilbert E. Moore. 1945. "Some Principles of Stratification." *American Sociological Review* 10 (April):242–249.

Davis, Nanette J. 1975. *Sociological Constructions of Deviance: Perspectives and Issues in the Field.* Dubuque, IA: Wm. C. Brown.

De Anda, Roberto M. 2004. *Chicanas and Chicanos in Contemporary Society.* 2d ed. Lanham, MD: Rowman and Littlefield.

Death Penalty Information Center. 2010. "Executions by State." Accessed November 11 at http://www.deathpenaltyinfo.org/number-executions-state-and-region-1976.

Deegan, Mary Jo, ed. 1991. *Women in Sociology: A Bio-Bibliographical Sourcebook.* Westport, CT: Greenwood.

———. 2003. "Textbooks, the History of Sociology, and the Sociological Stock of Knowledge." *Sociological Theory* 21 (November):298–305.

Deibert, Ronald J., John Palfrey, Rafal Rohozinski, and Jonathan Zittrain. 2008. *Access Denied: The Practice and Policy of Global Internet Filtering.* Cambridge, MA: MIT Press.

DeNavas-Walt, Carmen, Bernadette D. Proctor, and Jessica C. Smith. 2009. "Income, Poverty, and Health Insurance Coverage in the United States: 2008." Pp. 60–236 in *Current Population Survey.* Washington DC: U.S. Government Printing Office.

DeParle, Jason. 2007. "Migrant Money Flow: A $300 Billion Current." *New York Times,* November 18, Work section, p. 3.

Department of Commerce. 2010. "Observations from the Interagency Technical Working Group on Developing a Supplemental Poverty Measure." Accessible at www.census.gov/hhes/www/povmeas/SPM_TWGobservations.pdf.

Department of Education. 2006. *Integrated Postsecondary Education Data Systems, Completions, 1995–2004.* Washington, DC: NCES.

Department of Energy. 2004. *Permanent Markers Implementation Plan.* Carlsbad, NM: Carlsbad Field Office, Department of Energy.

Department of Homeland Security. 2006. *The Federal Response to Hurricane Katrina: Lessons Learned.* Washington, DC: U.S. Government Printing Office.

Department of Justice. 2009. Uniform Crime Reports, 2008. Accessible at www.fbi.gov/about-us/cjis/ucr/ucr.

Department of Labor. 1995a. *Good for Business: Making Full Use of the Nation's Capital.* Washington, DC: U.S. Government Printing Office.

———. 1995b. *A Solid Investment: Making Full Use of the Nation's Human Capital.* Washington, DC: U.S. Government Printing Office.

Deutsch, Francine M. 2007. "Undoing Gender." *Gender and Society* 21 (February):106–127.

Di Carlo, Matthew, and Nate Johnson, with Pat Cochran. 2008. *Survey and Analysis of Teacher Salary Trends 2007.* Washington, DC: American Federation of Teachers.

Diehl, William C., and Esther Prins. 2008. "Unintentional Outcomes in Second Life: Intercultural Literacy and Cultural Identity in a Virtual World." *Language and Intercultural Communication* 8(2):101–116.

Dobbin, Frank, and Jiwook Jung. 2010. "Corporate Board Gender Diversity and Stock Performance: The Competence Gap or Institutional Investor Bias?" *North Carolina Law Review* (forthcoming).

Domhoff, G. William. 1978. *Who Really Rules? New Haven and Community Power Reexamined.* New Brunswick, NJ: Transaction.

———. 2006. *Who Rules America?* 5th ed. New York: McGraw-Hill.

———. 2010. *Who Rules America?* 6th ed. New York: McGraw-Hill.

Dorn, Stan. 2008. *Uninsured and Dying Because of It.* Washington, DC: Urban Institute.

Dougherty, Kevin, and Floyd M. Hammack. 1992. "Education Organizations." Pp. 525, 541 in *Encyclopedia of Sociology,* vol. 2, edited by Edgar F. Borgatta and Marie L. Borgatta.

Dovidio, John F. 2001. "On the Nature of Contemporary Prejudice: The Third Wave." *Journal of Social Issues* 57 (No. 4):829–849.

Doyle, James A. 1995. *The Male Experience.* 3d ed. Dubuque, IA: Brown & Benchmark.

Dream Act Portal. DAP 2010. "Welcome to the DREAM Act Portal." Accessed December 7 at http://dreamact.info/.

DuBois, W. E. B. [1900] 1969. "To the Nations of the World." Pp. 19–23 in *An ABC of Color,* edited by W. E. B. DuBois. New York: International Publishers.

———. [1899] 1995. *The Philadelphia Negro: A Social Study.* Philadelphia: University of Pennsylvania Press.

———. [1903] 1961. *The Souls of Black Folks: Essays and Sketches.* New York: Fawcett.

———. [1903] 2003. *The Negro Church.* Walnut Creek, CA: Alta Mira Press.

———. [1935] 1962. *Black Reconstruction in America 1860–1880.* New York: Athenaeum.

Duneier, Mitchell. 1994a. "On the Job, but Behind the Scenes." *Chicago Tribune,* December 26, pp. 1, 24.

———. 1994b. "Battling for Control." *Chicago Tribune,* December 28, pp. 1, 8.

Dunlap, Riley E. 1993. "From Environmental to Ecological Problems." Pp. 707–738 in *Introduction to Social Problems,* edited by Craig Calhoun and George Ritzer. New York: McGraw-Hill.

———, and William R. Catton, Jr. 1983. "What Environmental Sociologists Have in Common." *Sociological Inquiry* 53 (Spring):113–135.

Durden, T. Elizabeth, and Robert A. Hummer. 2006. "Access to Healthcare Among Working-Aged Hispanic Adults in the United States." *Social Science Quarterly* 87 (December):1319–1343.

Durkheim, Émile. [1893] 1933. *Division of Labor in Society.* Translated by George Simpson. Reprint, New York: Free Press.

———. [1895] 1964. *The Rules of Sociological Method.* Translated by Sarah A. Solovay and John H. Mueller. Reprint, New York: Free Press.

———. [1897] 1951. *Suicide.* Translated by John A. Spaulding and George Simpson. Reprint, New York: Free Press.

———. [1912] 2001. *The Elementary Forms of Religious Life.* A new translation by Carol Cosman. New York: Oxford University Press.

Eckenwiler, Mark. 1995. "In the Eyes of the Law." *Internet World* (August):74, 76–77.

The Economist. 2004. "Veil of Tears." January 15.

The Economist. 2006a. "The World's Largest Economies." (April 1):84.

——— 2008. "A Ravenous Dragon: A Special Report on China's Quest for Resources." (March 15):1–22.

Edwards, John. 2008. "Building One America." *Pathways* (March):8–10.

Ehrenreich, Barbara. 2001. *Nickel and Dimed: On (Not) Getting By in America.* New York: Metropolitan.

Ehrlich, Paul R. 1968. *The Population Bomb.* New York: Ballantine.

———, and Anne H. Ehrlich. 1990. *The Population Explosion.* New York: Simon and Schuster.

———, and Katherine Ellison. 2002. "A Looming Threat We Won't Face." *Los Angeles Times,* January 20, p. M6.

Ellison, Brandy. 2008. "Tracking." Pp. 301–304, vol. 2, in *Encyclopedia of Race, Ethnicity, and Society,* edited by Richard T. Schaefer. Thousand Oaks, CA: Sage.

Engels, Friedrich. [1884] 1959. "The Origin of the Family, Private Property, and the State." Pp. 392–394, excerpted in *Marx and Engels: Basic Writings on Politics and Philosophy,* edited by Lewis Feuer. Garden City, NY: Anchor.

Entine, Jon, and Martha Nichols. 1996. "Blowing the Whistle on Meaningless 'Good Intentions.'" *Chicago Tribune,* June 20, sec. 1, p. 21.

Epstein, Cynthia Fuchs. 1999. "The Major Myth of the Women's Movement." *Dissent* (Fall):83–111.

Etaugh, Claire. 2003. "Witches, Mothers and Others: Females in Children's Books." *Hilltopics* (Winter): 10–13.

Etzioni, Amitai. 1964. *Modern Organization.* Englewood Cliffs, NJ: Prentice Hall.

FAIR 2010 "The DREAM Act Amnesty Bill Resurfaces in Congress" Accessed November 22 at http://www.fairus.org/site/PageServer?pagename= dream_act_amnesty.

Faith, Nazila. 2005. "Iranian Cleric Turns Blogger in Campaign for Reform." *New York Times,* January 16, p. 4.

Farr, Grant M. 1999. *Modern Iran.* New York: McGraw-Hill.

Farrell, Amy, and Jack McDevitt. 2010. "Identifying and Measuring Racial Profiling by the Police." *Sociology Compass* 4:77–88.

Favreault, Melissa. 2008. "Discrimination and Economic Mobility." Washington, DC: Economic Mobility Project. Also accessible at http://www.economicmobility.org/reports_and_research/literature_reviews?id=0004.

Feagin, Joe R. 1983. *The Urban Real Estate Game: Playing Monopoly with Real Money.* Englewood Cliffs, NJ: Prentice Hall.

Featherman, David L., and Robert M. Hauser. 1978. *Opportunity and Change.* New York: Aeodus.

Ferber, Abby L., and Michael S. Kimmel. 2008. "The Gendered Face of Terrorism." *Sociology Compass* 2:870–887.

Ferree, Myra Marx. 2005. "It's Time to Mainstream Research on Gender." *Chronicle of Higher Education* 51 (August 21):B10.

———, and David A. Merrill. 2000. "Hot Movements, Cold Cognition: Thinking about Social Movements in Gendered Frames." *Contemporary Society* 29 (May):454–462.

Feuer, Lewis S., ed. 1959. *Karl Marx and Friedrich Engels: Basic Writings on Politics and Philosophy.* Garden City, NY: Doubleday.

Fiala, Robert. 1992. "Postindustrial Society." Pp. 1512–1522 in *Encyclopedia of Sociology,* vol. 3, edited by Edgar F. Borgatta and Marie L. Borgatta. New York: Macmillan.

Fields, Jason. 2004. "America's Families and Living Arrangements: 2003." *Current Population Reports,* ser. P-20, no. 553. Washington, DC: U.S. Government Printing Office.

Fields, Jessica. 2005. "'Children Having Children': Race, Innocence, and Sexuality Education." *Social Problems* 52 (4):549–571.

Fine, Gary C. 2008. " Robbers Cave." Pp. 1163–1164, vol. 3, in *Encyclopedia of Race, Ethnicity, and Society,* edited by Richard T. Schaefer. Thousand Oaks, CA: Sage.

Fine, Gary. 2004. "Forgotten Classic: The Robbers Cave Experiment." *Sociological Forum* 19 (December):663–666.

Finkel, Steven E., and James B. Rule. 1987. "Relative Deprivation and Related Psychological Theories of Civil Violence: A Critical Review." *Research in Social Movements* 9:47–69.

Fitzgerald, Kathleen J. 2008. "White Privilege." Pp. 1403–1405, vol. 3, in *Encyclopedia of Race, Ethnicity, and Society,* edited by Richard T. Schaefer. Thousand Oaks, CA: Sage.

———, and Diane M. Rodgers. 2000. "Radical Social Movement Organization: A Theoretical Model." *The Sociological Quarterly* 41 (4):573–592.

Flacks, Richard. 1971. *Youth and Social Change.* Chicago: Markham.

Fletcher, Connie. 1995. "On the Line: Women Cops Speak Out." *Chicago Tribune Magazine,* February 19, pp. 14–19.

Flynn, Laurie J. 2008. "MySpace Mind-Set Finally Shows Up at the Office." *New York Times* April 9, sect. H, p. 7.

Fonseca, Felicia. 2008. "Dine College on Quest to Rename Navajo Cancer Terms." *News from Indian Country* 22 (January 7): 11.

Forbes. 2010. "The World's Billionaires." Accessed July 12 at http://www.forbes.com/lists/2010/10/billinoaires-2010_The-Worlds-Billionaires_Rand.html.

Fouché, Gladys. 2008. "Norway's Gender Deadline Passes." *The Guardian Weekly,* April 1, p. 15.

Franke, Richard Herbert, and James D. Kaul. 1978. "The Hawthorne Experiments: First Statistical Interpretation." *American Sociological Review* 43 (October):623–643.

Freese, Jeremy. 2008. "Genetics and the Social Science Explanation of Individual Outcomes." *American Journal of Sociology* 114 (Suppl.):51–535.

Freidson, Eliot. 1970. *Profession of Medicine.* New York: Dodd, Mead.

French, Howard B. 2004. "China's Textbooks Twist and Omit History." *New York Times,* December 6, p. A10.

French, Howard W. 2008. "Lines of Grinding Poverty, Untouched by China's Boom." *New York Times,* January 13, p. 4.

Fridlund, Alan J., Paul Erkman, and Harriet Oster. 1987. "Facial Expressions of Emotion: Review of Literature 1970–1983." Pp. 143–224 in *Nonverbal Behavior and Communication,* 2d ed., edited by Aron W. Seigman and Stanley Feldstein. Hillsdale, NJ: Lawrence Erlbaum Associates.

Friedman, Louis. 2010. "NASA's Down to Earth Problem." *Star-Telegram* (Ft. Worth) March 28. Accessible at www.star-telegram.com.

Friedrichs, David O. 1998. "New Directions in Critical Criminology and White Collar Crime." Pp. 77–91 in *Cutting the Edge,* edited by Jeffrey Ross. Westport, CT: Praeger.

Frosch, Dan. 2008. "Its Native Tongue Facing Extinction, Arapaho Tribe Teaches the Young." (October 17), p. A14.

Furstenberg, Frank, and Andrew Cherlin. 1991. *Divided Families: What Happens to Children When Parents Part.* Cambridge, MA: Harvard University Press.

Fuwa, Makiko. 2004. "Macro-Level Gender Inequality and the Division of Household Labor in 22 Countries." *American Sociological Review* 69 (December):751–767.

Gallup. 2009c. "Religion." Accessed April 9 (www.gallup.com).

Gallup Opinion Index. 1978. "Religion in America, 1977–1978." 145 (January).

Gambetta, Diego, and Steffen Hertog. 2007. "Engineers of Jihad." Sociology Working Papers (University of Oxford) 2007–10. Accessed June 2008 (www.sociology.ox.ac.uk/swp.html).

Gamson, Joshua. 1989. "Silence, Death, and the Invisible Enemy: AIDS Activism and Social Movement 'Newness.'" *Social Problems* 36 (October):351–367.

Gans, Herbert J. 1979. "Symbolic Ethnicity: The Future of Ethnic Groups and Cultures in America." *Ethnic and Racial Studies* 2 (January):1–20.

———. 1995. *The War against the Poor: The Underclass and Antipoverty Policy.* New York: Basic Books.

Gardner, Gary, Erik Assadourian, and Radhika Sarin. 2004. "The State of Consumption Today." Pp. 3–21 in *State of the World 2004,* edited by Brian Halweil and Lisa Mastny. New York: W.W. Norton.

Garfinkel, Harold. 1956. "Conditions of Successful Degradation Ceremonies." *American Journal of Sociology* 61 (March):420–424.

Garner, Roberta. 1996. *Contemporary Movements and Ideologies.* New York: McGraw-Hill.

Garreau, Joel. 1991. *Edge City: Life on the New Frontier.* New York: Doubleday.

Gauette, Nicole. 1998. "Rules for Raising Japanese Kids." *Christian Science Monitor,* October 14, pp. B1, B6.

Gecas, Victor. 1982. "Socialization." Pp. 1863–1872 in *Encyclopedia of Sociology,* vol. 4, edited by Edgar F. Borgatta and Marie L. Borgatta. New York: Macmillan.

Geist, Claudia. 2005. "The Welfare State and the Home: Regime Differences in the Domestic Division of Labour." *European Sociological Review 2005* 21(1):23–4.

Gerth, H. H., and C. Wright Mills. 1958. *From Max Weber: Essays in Sociology.* New York: Galaxy.

Gilley, Brian Joseph. 2006. *Becoming Two-Spirit: Gay Identity and Social Acceptance in Indian Country.* Lincoln: University of Nebraska Press.

Giordano, Peggy C. 2003. "Relationships in Adolescence." Pp. 257–281 in *Annual Review of Sociology, 2003,* edited by Karen S. Cook and John Hagan. Palo Alto, CA: Annual Reviews.

———, Stephen A. Cernkovich, and Alfred DeMaris. 1993. "The Family and Peer Relations of Black Adolescents." *Journal of Marriage and Family* 55 (May):277–287.

Giroux, Henry A. 1988. *Schooling and the Struggle for Public Life: Critical Pedagogy in the Modern Age.* Minneapolis: University of Minnesota Press.

Goering, Laurie. 2007. "The First Refugees of Global Warming." *Chicago Tribune,* May 2, pp. 1, 25.

———. 2008. "Women Urge Larger Role in Easing World's Ills." *Chicago Tribune,* March 11, p. 11.

Goffman, Erving. 1959. *The Presentation of Self in Everyday Life.* New York: Doubleday.

———. 1961. *Asylums: Essays on the Social Situation of Mental Patients and Other Inmates.* Garden City, NY: Doubleday.

———. 1963. *Stigma: Notes on Management of Spoiled Identity.* Englewood Cliffs, NJ: Prentice Hall.

Gottdiener, Mark, and Joe R. Feagin. 1988. "The Paradigm Shift in Urban Sociology." *Urban Affairs Quarterly* 24 (December):163–187.

———, and Ray Hutchison. 2010. *The New Urban Sociology.* 4th ed. Boulder, CO: Westview.

Gould, Larry A. 2002. "Indigenous People Policing Indigenous People: The Potential Psychological and Cultural Costs." *Social Science Journal* 39:171–188.

Gouldner, Alvin. 1960. "The Norm of Reciprocity." *American Sociological Review* 25 (April):161–177.

Government Accountability Office. 2003. "Women's Earnings: Work Patterns Partially Explain Difference Between Men's and Women's Earnings." Washington, DC: U.S. Government Printing Office.

Gramsci, Antonio. 1929. *Selections from the Prison Notebooks.* Antonio Gramsci. Edited and translated by Quintin Hoare and Geoffrey Nowell Smith. London: Lawrence and Wishort.

Greeley, Andrew M. 1989. "Protestant and Catholic: Is the Analogical Imagination Extinct?" *American Sociological Review* 54 (August):485–502.

Greenhouse, Linda. 1998. "High Court Ruling Says Harassment Includes Same Sex." *New York Times,* March 5, pp. A1, A17.

Greenhouse, Steven. 2008b. "Millions of Jobs of a Different Collar." *New York Times,* March 26.

Groza, Victor, Daniela F. Ileana, and Ivor Irwin. 1999. *A Peacock or a Crow: Stories, Interviews, and Commentaries on Romanian Adoptions.* Euclid, OH: Williams Custom Publishing.

Hacker, Andrew. 1964. "Power to Do What?" Pp. 134–146 in *The New Sociology,* edited by Irving Louis Horowitz. New York: Oxford University Press.

Hallinan, Maureen T. 1997. "The Sociological Study of Social Change." *American Sociological Review* 62 (February):1–11.

Hamilton, Anita. 2007. "Is Facebook Overrated?" *Time,* December 3, pp. 46–48.

Hamilton, Brady E., Joyce A. Martin, and Stephanie J. Ventura. 2009. "Births: Preliminary Data for 2007." *National Vital Statistics Reports* 57(12).

Hamm, Steve. 2007. "Children of the Web." *BusinessWeek,* July 2, pp. 50–56, 58.

Harris, Chauncey D., and Edward Ullman. 1945. "The Nature of Cities." *Annals of the American Academy of Political and Social Science* 242 (November):7–17.

Haub, Carl, and Mary Mederius Kent. 2009. *2009 World Population Data Sheet.* Washington, DC: Population Reference Bureau.

———. *2010 World Population Data Sheet.* Washington DC: Population Reference Bureau.

Haviland, William A., Harald E. L. Prins, Dana Walrath, and Bunny McBride. 2005. *Cultural Anthropology—The Human Challenge.* New York: McGraw-Hill.

———. 2011. *Cultural Anthropology—The Human Challenge.* 13th ed. Belmont, CA: Thompson Higher Education.

Hawkins, Darnell F., et al. 2000. "Race, Ethnicity, and Serious and Violent Juvenile Offending." *Juvenile Justice Bulletin* (June):107.

Heckert, Druann, and Amy Best. 1997. "Ugly Duckling to Swan: Labeling Theory and the Stigmatization of Red Hair." *Symbolic Interaction* 20 (4):365–384.

Hedley, R. Alan. 1992. "Industrialization in Less Developed Countries." Pp. 914–920 in *Encyclopedia of Sociology,* vol. 2, edited by Edgar F. Borgatta and Marie L. Borgatta. New York: Macmillan.

Heilman, Madeline E. 2001. "Description and Prescription: How Gender Stereotypes Prevent Women's Ascent up the Organizational Ladder." *Journal of Social Issues* 57 (4):657–674.

Hendershott, Anne. 2002. *The Politics of Deviance.* San Francisco, CA: Encounter Books.

Henly, Julia R. 1999. "Challenges to Finding and Keeping Jobs in the Low-Skilled Labor Market." *Poverty Research News* 3 (1):3–5.

Herring, Hubert B. 2006. "A Teacher's Year, A C.E.O.'s Day: The Pay's Similar." *New York Times,* September 5, p. 2.

Hewlett, Sylvia Ann, and Carolyn Buck Luce. 2005. "Off-Ramps and On-Ramps: Keeping Talented Women on the Road to Success." *Harvard Business Review* (March):43–53.

Hickman, Jonathan. 2002. "America's 50 Best Corporations for Minorities." *Fortune* 146 (July 8):110–120.

Hill, Michael R., and Susan Hoecker-Drysdale, eds. 2001. *Harriet Martineau: Theoretical and Methodological Perspectives.* New York: Routledge.

Hira, Ron. 2008. "An Overview of the Offshoring of U.S. Jobs." Pp. 14–15 in Marlene A. Lee and Mark Mather. "U.S. Labor Force Trends." *Population Bulletin* 63 (June).

Hitlin, Steven, and Jane Allyn Piliavin. 2004. "Values: Reviving a Dormant Concept." Pp. 359–393 in *Annual Review of Sociology, 2004,* edited by Karen S. Cook and John Hagan. Palo Alto, CA: Annual Reviews.

Hochschild, Arlie Russell. 1990. "The Second Shift: Employed Women Are Putting in Another Day of Work at Home." *Utne Reader* 38 (March/April): 66–73.

———. 2005. *The Commercialization of Intimate Life: Notes from Home and Work.* Berkeley: University of California Press.

———, with Anne Machung. 1989. *The Second Shift: Working Parents and the Revolution at Home.* New York: Viking Penguin.

Hoffman, Lois Wladis. 1985. "The Changing Genetics/Socialization Balance." *Journal of Social Issues* 41 (Spring):127–148.

Homans, George C. 1979. "Nature versus Nurture: A False Dichotomy." *Contemporary Sociology* 8 (May):345–348.

hooks, bell. 1994. "Black Students Who Reject Feminism." *The Chronicle of Higher Education,* 60 (July 13): A44.

Horkheimer, Max, and Theodor Adorno. [1944] 2002. *Dialectic of Enlightenment.* Palo Alto, CA: Sanford University Press.

Horowitz, Helen Lefkowitz. 1987. *Campus Life.* Chicago: University of Chicago Press.

Horrigan, John B. 2007. *A Typology of Information and Communication Technology Users.* Washington, DC: Pew Internet and American Life Project.

Howard, Judith A. 1999. "Border Crossings between Women's Studies and Sociology." *Contemporary Sociology* 28 (September):525–528.

Hughes, Everett. 1945. "Dilemmas and Contradictions of Status." *American Journal of Sociology* 50 (March):353–359.

Hughlett, Mike. 2008. "Sitting Pretty." *Chicago Tribune,* September 14, sec. 5, pp. 1, 7.

Hunter, Herbert M., ed. 2000. *The Sociology of Oliver C. Cox: New Perspectives: Research in Race and Ethnic Relations,* vol. 2. Stamford, CT: JAI Press.

Hunter, James Davison. 1991. *Culture Wars: The Struggle to Define America.* New York: Basic Books.

Huntington, Samuel P. 1993. "The Clash of Civilizations?" *Foreign Affairs* 72 (Summer): 22–49.

Hurn, Christopher J. 1985. *The Limits and Possibilities of Schooling* 2d ed. Boston: Allyn and Bacon.

Hyde, Janet Shibley. 2005. "The Gender Similarities Hypothesis." *American Psychologist* 60 (No. 6):581–592.

Inglehart, Ronald, and Wayne E. Baker. 2000. "Modernization, Cultural Change, and the Persistence of Traditional Values." *American Sociological Review* 65 (February):19–51.

Intercom. 1978. "Populandia: A Country Is Born." *Intercom* 6 (January):9.

International Crime Victim Survey. 2004. *Nationwide Surveys in the Industrialized Countries.* Accessed February 20 (www.ruljis.leidenuniv.nl/ group/jfcr/ www/icvs).

International Fund for Agricultural Development 2007. *Sending Money Home: Worldwide Remittance Flows to Developing and Transition Countries.* Rome: IFAD. Accessible at www.ifad.org.

International Gay and Lesbian Human Rights Commission. 2010. Home page. Accessed February 11 (www.iglhrc.org).

International Monetary Fund. 2000. *World Economic Outlook: Asset Prices and the Business Cycle.* Washington, DC: International Monetary Fund.

Internet Crime Complaint Center. 2007. "The Internet Crime Complaint Center Hits 1 Million!" Accessed January 12, 2008 (http://www.ic3.gov/ media/2007/070613.htm).

Internet World Stats. 2010. "Usage and Population Statistics" and "Internet World Users by Language." Accessed April 23 (www.internetworldstats.com).

Isaacs, Julia B. 2007a. *Economic Mobility of Families Across Generations.* Washington, DC: Economic Mobility Project, Pew Charitable Trusts.

———. 2007b. *Economic Mobility of Men and Women.* Washington, DC: Economic Mobility Project.

———. Isabel V. Sawhill, and Ron Haskins. 2008. *Getting Ahead or Losing Ground: Economic Mobility in America.* Washington, DC: Pew Charitable Trust.

ITOPF. 2006. "Statistics: International Tanker Owners Pollution Federation Limited." Accessed May 2 (www.itopf.com/stats.html).

Jackson, Elton F., Charles R. Tittle, and Mary Jean Burke. 1986. "Offense-Specific Models of the Differential Association Process." *Social Problems* 33 (April):335–356.

Jackson, Philip W. 1968. *Life in Classrooms.* New York: Holt.

Jacobe, Dennis. 2008. "Half of Public Favors the Environment over Growth." Accessed April 9 (www.gallup.com).

Jain, Saranga, and Kathleen Kurz. 2007. *New Insights on Preventing Child Marriage: A Global Analysis of Factors and Programs.* Washington, DC: International Center for Research on Women.

Jänttii, Markus. 2009. "Mobility in the United States in Comparative Perspectives." *Focus* 26 (Fall).

Jasper, James M. 1997. *The Art of Moral Protest: Culture, Biography, and Creativity in Social Movements.* Chicago: University of Chicago Press.

Jenkins, Matt. 2008. "A Really Inconvenient Truth." *Miller-McCure* 1 (March–April):38–41.

Jenkins, Richard. 1991. "Disability and Social Stratification." *British Journal of Sociology* 42 (December):557–580.

Jensen, Gary F. 2003. "Social Disorganization Theory in R. A. Wright." *Encyclopedia of Criminology.* New York: Fitzroy Dearborn.

Johnson, Benton. 1975. *Functionalism in Modern Sociology: Understanding Talcott Parsons.* Morristown, NJ: General Learning.

Johnson, Tallese D. 2008. "Maternity Leave and Employment Patterns of First-Time Mothers: 1961–2003." *Current Population Reports,* ser. P-70, no. 113. Washington, DC: U.S. Government Printing Office.

Jones, James T., IV. 1988. "Harassment Is Too Often Part of the Job." *USA Today,* August 8, p. 5D.

Jones, Nicholas A. 2005. *We the People of More Than One Race in the United States.* Census 2000 Special Reports, CENSR-22. Washington, DC: U.S. Government Printing Office.

Juhasz, Anne McCreary. 1989. "Black Adolescents' Significant Others." *Social Behavior and Personality* 17 (2):211–214.

Kahn, Joseph. 2006. "Where's Mao? Chinese Revise History Books." *New York Times,* September 1, pp. A1, A6.

Kalev, Alexandra. 2009. "Cracking the Glass Cages? Restructuring and Ascriptive Inequality at Work." *American Journal of Sociology* 114 (May):1591–1643.

Kalita, S. Mitra. 2006. "On the Other End of the Line."*Washington Post National Weekly Edition,* January 9, pp. 20–21.

Kambayashi, Takehiko. 2008. "Japanese Men Shout the Oft-Unsaid 'I Love You.'" *Christian Science Monitor,* February 13.

Karney, Benjamin R., and John S. Crown. 2007. *Families Under Stress: An Assessment of Data, Theory, and Research on Marriage and Divorce in the Military.* Santa Monica, CA: RAND.

Katovich, Michael A. 1987. Correspondence. June 1.

Katz, Michael. 1971. *Class, Bureaucracy, and the Schools: The Illusion of Educational Change in America.* New York: Praeger.

Kennickell, Arthur B. 2009. *Ponds and Streams: Wealth and Income in the U.S., 1989 to 2007.* Washington, DC: Federal Reserve Board.

Kerbo, Harold R. 2006. *World Poverty: The Roots of Global Inequality and the Modern World System.* New York: McGraw-Hill.

———. 2009 *Social Stratification and Inequality: Class Conflict in Historical, Comparative, and Global Perspective.* 6th ed. New York: McGraw-Hill.

Kimmel, Michael. 2006. "A War Against Boys?" *Dissent* (Fall):65–70.

———. 2008. *The Gendered Society.* 3d ed. New York: State University of New York at Stony Brook.

King, Meredith L. 2007. *Immigrants in the U.S. Health Care System.* Washington, DC: Center for American Progress.

Kitchener, Richard F. 1991. "Jean Piaget: The Unknown Sociologist." *British Journal of Sociology* 42 (September):421–442.

Kleiner, Art. 2003. "Are You In with the In Crowd?" *Harvard Business Review* 81 (July):86–92.

Kochhar, Rakesh. 2006. "Growth in the Foreign-Born Workforce and Employment of the Natural Born." Washington, DC: Pew Hispanic Center.

———. 2008. *Latino Workers in the Ongoing Recession: 2007–2008.* Washington, DC: Pew Hispanic Center.

Kohut, Andrew, et al. 2005. *American Character Gets Mixed Reviews: 16-Nation Pew Global Attitudes Survey.* Washington, DC: Pew Global Project Attitudes.

———. 2007. *Global Unease with Major World Powers: Rising Environmental Concern in 47-Nation Survey.* Washington, DC: Pew Global Project Attitudes.

Kokmen, Leyla. 2008. "Environmental Justice for All." *Utne Reader* (March–April):42–46.

Kolata, Gina. 1999. *Clone: The Road to Dolly and the Path Beyond.* New York: William Morrow.

Koolhaas, Rem, et al. 2001. *Mutations.* Barcelona, Spain: Actar.

Kottak, Conrad. 2011 *Anthropology: Appreciating Human Diversity.* 14th edition. New York: McGraw-Hill.

Kreider, Rose M. 2005. "Number, Timing, and Duration of Marriages and Divorces: 2001." *Current Population Reports,* pp. 70–97. Washington, DC: U.S. Government Printing Office.

Kwong, Jo. 2005. "Globalization's Effects on the Environment." *Society* 42 (January/February):21–28.

Landtman, Gunnar. [1938] 1968. *The Origin of Inequality of the Social Class.* New York: Greenwood (original edition 1938, Chicago: University of Chicago Press).

Lang, Robert E., and Jennifer B. LeFurgy. 2007. *Boomburbs: The Rise of America's Accidental Crisis.* Washington, DC: Brookings Institution.

Langewiesche, William. 2002. *American Ground: Unbuilding the World Trade Center.* New York: North Point Press.

Lasswell, Harold D. 1936. *Politics: Who Gets What, When, How.* New York: McGraw-Hill.

Laszewski, Chuck. 2008. "The Sociologists' Take on the Environment." *Contexts* 7 (Spring):20–24.

Lauer, Robert H. 1982. *Perspectives on Social Change.* 3d ed. Boston: Allyn and Bacon.

Laumann, Edward O., John H. Gagnon, Robert T. Michael, and Stuart Michaels. 1994b. *The Social Organization of Sexuality: Sexual Practices in the United States.* Chicago: University of Chicago Press.

Leavell, Hugh R., and E. Gurney Clark. 1965. *Preventive Medicine for the Doctor in His Community: An Epidemiologic Approach.* 3d ed. New York: McGraw-Hill.

Lengermann, Patricia Madoo, and Jill Niebrugge-Brantley. 1998. *The Women Founders: Sociology and Social Theory, 1830–1930.* Boston: McGraw-Hill.

Lenski, Gerhard. 1966. *Power and Privilege: A Theory of Social Stratification.* New York: McGraw-Hill.

Levine, Nancy. 1988. *The Dynamics of Polyandry: Kinship, Domesticity, and Population on the Tibetan Border.* Chicago: University of Chicago Press.

Lewin, Tamar. 1998. "Debate Centers on Definition of Harassment." *New York Times,* March 22, pp. A1, A20.

Lindsey, Linda L. 2005. *Gender Roles: A Sociological Perspective.* Upper Saddle River, NJ: Prentice Hall.

Lipson, Karen. 1994. "'Nell' Not Alone in the Wilds." *Los Angeles Times,* December 19, pp. F1, F6.

Liptak, Adam. 2008. "Inmate Court in U.S. Dwarfs Other Nations." *New York Times,* April 23, pp. A1, A14.

Long, Sharon K., and Paul B. Masi. 2009. *Access to and Affordability of Care in Massachusetts as of Fall 2008: Geographic and Racial/Ethnic Differences.* Washington, DC: Urban Institute.

Lukacs, Georg. 1923. *History and Class Consciousness.* London: Merlin.

Lumpe, Lora. 2003. "Taking Aim at the Global Gun Trade." *Amnesty Now* (Winter):10–13.

Lynas, Mark. 2008. *Six Degrees: Our Future on a Hotter Planet.* Washington, DC: National Geographic.

Lynn, Barry C. 2003. "Trading with a Low-Wage Tiger." *The American Prospect* 14 (February):10–12.

MacDorman, Marian, et al. 2005. "Explaining the 2001–2002 Infant Mortality Increase: Data from the Linked Death/Infant Death Data Set." *National Vital Statistics Reports* 53 (January 24).

Machalek, Richard, and Michael W. Martin. 2010. "Evolution, Biology and Society: A Conversation for the 21st-Century Sociology Classroom." *Teaching Sociology* 38 (1):35–45.

Mack, Raymond W., and Calvin P. Bradford. 1979. *Transforming America: Patterns of Social Change.* 2d ed. New York: Random House.

Magnier, Mark. 2004. "China Clamps Down on Web News Discussion." *Los Angeles Times,* February 26, p. A4.

Maguire, Brendan. 1988. "The Applied Dimension of Radical Criminology: A Survey of Prominent Radical Criminologists." *Sociological Spectrum* 8 (2):133–151.

Malcolm X, with Alex Haley. 1964. *The Autobiography of Malcolm X.* New York: Grove.

Malthus, Thomas Robert, Julian Huxley, and Frederick Osborn. [1824] 1960. *Three Essays on Population.* Reprint. New York: New American Library.

Martin, Susan E. 1994. "Outsider Within the Station House: The Impact of Race and Gender on Black Women Politics." *Social Problems* 41 (August):383–400.

Martineau, Harriet. [1837] 1962. *Society in America.* Edited, abridged, with an introductory essay by Seymour Martin Lipset. Reprint. Garden City, NY: Doubleday.

———. [1838] 1989. *How to Observe Morals and Manners.* Philadelphia: Leal and Blanchard. Sesquentennial edition, edited by M. R. Hill, Transaction Books.

Marubbio, M. Elise. 2006. *Killing the Indian Maiden: Images of Native American Women in Film.* Lexington, University Press of Kentucky.

Marx, Karl. [1844] 1964. "Contribution to the Critique of Hegel's Philosophy of Right." In *On Religion,* Karl Marx and Friedrich Engels. New York: Schocker Books.

———. [1847] 1955. *Selected Work in Two Volumes.* Reprint, Moscow: Foreign Languages Publishing House.

Maryanski, Alexandra R. 2004. "Evaluation Theory." Pp. 257–263 in *Encyclopedia of Social Theory,* edited by George Ritzer. Thousand Oaks, CA: Sage.

Masuda, Takahiko, Phoebe C. Ellsworth, Batja Mesquita, Janxin Leu, Shigehito Tanida, and Ellen Van de Veerdonk. 2008. "Attitudes and Social Cognition—Placing the Face in Context: Cultural Differences in the Perception of Facial Emotion." *Journal of Personality and Social Psychology* 94 (No. 3): 365–381.

Matsushita, Yoshiko. 1999. "Japanese Kids Call for a Sympathetic Ear." *Christian Science Monitor,* January 20, p. 15.

Mays, Vickie M., Susan D. Cochran, and Namdi W. Barnes. 2007. "Race, Race-Based Discrimination, and Health Outcomes Among African Americans." *Annual Review of Psychology* 58:201–225.

McFalls, Joseph A., Jr. 2003. "Population: A Lively Introduction." *Population Bulletin* 58 (December).

McGrath, Kristin. "Status Update: Facebook Logs 500 Million Members." *USA Today* (July 22), p. 3D.

McGurty, Eileen Maura. 2000. "Warren County, NC, and the Emergence of the Environmental Justice Movement: Unlikely Coalitions and Shared Meanings in Local Collective Action." *Society and Natural Resources* 13:373–387.

McIntosh, Peggy. 1988. "White Privilege and Male Privilege: A Personal Account of Coming to See Correspondence Through Work and Women's Studies." Working Paper No. 189, Wellesley College Center for Research on Women, Wellesley, MA.

McKinlay, John B., and Sonja M. McKinlay. 1977. "The Questionable Contribution of Medical Measures to the Decline of Mortality in the United States in the Twentieth Century." *Milbank Memorial Fund Quarterly* 55 (Summer): 405–428.

McNeil, Donald G. 2004. "Plan to Battle AIDS Worldwide Is Falling Short." *New York Times,* March 28, pp. 1, 14.

Mead, George H. 1934. In *Mind, Self and Society,* edited by Charles W. Morris. Chicago: University of Chicago Press.

———. 1964a. In *On Social Psychology,* edited by Anselm Strauss. Chicago: University of Chicago Press.

———. 1964b. "The Genesis of the Self and Social Control." Pp. 267–293 in *Selected Writings: George Herbert Mead,* edited by Andrew J. Reck. Indianapolis: Bobbs-Merrill.

Mead, Margaret. [1935] 2001. *Sex and Temperament in Three Primitive Societies.* New York: Perennial, Harper-Collins.

Mehl, Matthias R., Simine Vazire, Nairán Ramírez-Esparza, Richard B. Slatcher, and James W. Pennebacker. 2007. "Are Women Really More Talkative Than Men?" *Science* 317 (July 6):82.

Melia, Marilyn Kennedy. 2000. "Changing Times." *Chicago Tribune,* January 2, sec. 17, pp. 12–15.

Mertion, Robert. 1968. *Social Theory and Social Structure.* New York Free Press.

———, and Alice S. Kitt. 1950. "Contributions to the Theory of Reference Group Behavior." Pp. 40–105 in *Continuities in Social Research: Studies in the Scope and Methods of the American Soldier,* edited by Robert K. Merton and Paul L. Lazarsfeld. New York: Free Press.

Michels, Robert. 1915. *Political Parties.* Glencoe, IL: Free Press (reprinted 1949).

Microfinance Information Exchange. 2008. *MicroBanking Bulletin* 17 (Autumn).

———. 2009. "Growth of Numbers of Borrowers and Savers." Accessed April 20 (www.themix.org/node/936).

Milgram, Stanley. 1963. "Behavioral Study of Obedience." *Journal of Abnormal and Social Psychology* 67 (October):371–378.

———. 1975. *Obedience to Authority: An Experimental View.* New York: Harper and Row.

Mills, C. Wright. [1959] 2000a. *The Sociological Imagination. 40th Anniversary Edition: New Afterword by Todd Gitlin.* New York: Oxford University Press.

———. [1956] 2000b. *The Power Elite.* New Edition. Afterword by Alan Wolfe. New York: Oxford University Press.

Moen, Phyllis, and Patricia Roehling. 2005. *The Career Mystique: Cracks in the American Dream.* Lanham, MD: Rowman and Littlefield.

Moncarz, Roger J., Michael G. Wolf, and Benjamin Wright. 2008. "Service-Providing Occupations, Offshoring, and the Labor Market." *Monthly Labor Review* (December): 71–86.

Moore, Wilbert E. 1967. *Order and Change: Essays in Comparative Sociology.* New York: Wiley.

———. 1968. "Occupational Socialization." Pp. 861–883 in *Handbook of Socialization Theory and Research,* edited by David A. Goslin. Chicago: Rand McNally.

Morehouse Medical Treatment and Effectiveness Center. 1999. *A Synthesis of the Literature: Racial and Ethnic Differences in Access to Medical Care.* Menlo Park, CA: Henry J. Kaiser Family Foundation.

Morris, Aldon. 2000. "Reflections on Social Movement Theory: Criticisms and Proposals." *Contemporary Sociology* 29 (May):445–454.

Morse, Arthur D. 1967. *While Six Million Died: A Chronicle of American Apathy.* New York: Ace.

Mosley, J., and E. Thomson. 1995. Pp. 148–165 in *Fatherhood: Contemporary Theory, Research and Social Policy,* edited by W. Marsiglo. Thousand Oaks, CA: Sage.

Mosisa, Abraham T. 2006. "Foreign-Born Workforce, 2004: A Visual Essay." *Monthly Labor Review* (July): 48–55.

Mueller, G. O. 2001. "Transnational Crime: Definitions and Concepts." Pp. 13–21 in *Combating Transnational Crime: Concepts, Activities, and Responses,* edited by P. Williams and D. Vlassis. London: Franklin Cass.

Murdock, George P. 1945. "The Common Denominator of Cultures." Pp. 123–142 in *The Science of Man in the World Crisis,* edited by Ralph Linton. New York: Columbia University Press.

———. 1949. *Social Structure.* New York: Macmillan.

———. 1957. "World Ethnographic Sample." *American Anthropologist* 59 (August): 664–687.

Murray, Velma McBride, Amanda Willert, and Diane P. Stephens. 2001. "The Half-Full Glass: Resilient African American Single Mothers and Their Children." *Family Focus,* June, pp. F4–F5.

Nakao, Keiko, and Judith Treas. 1994. "Updating Occupational Prestige and Socioeconomic Scores: How the New Measures Measure Up." *Sociological Methodology* 24:1–72.

Nash, Manning. 1962. "Race and the Ideology of Race." *Current Anthropology* 3 (June):285–288.

National Advisory Commission on Criminal Justice. 1976. *Organized Crime.* Washington, DC: U.S. Government Printing Office.

National Organization for Men Against Sexism. 2008. Home page. Accessed February 25 (www.nomas.org).

Navarro, Mirey. 2005. "When You Contain Multitudes." *New York Times,* April 24, pp. 1, 2.

Newport, Frank. 2010. "Americans' Global Warming Concerns Continue to Drop." March 11. Accessed April 27 (www.gallup.com/poll/126560/Americans-global-warming-concerns-continue-drop.aspx).

Nielsen, Joyce McCarl, Glenda Walden, and Charlotte A. Kunkel. 2000. "Gendered Heteronormativity: Empirical Illustrations in Everyday Life." *Sociological Quarterly* 41 (2):283–296.

Nolan, Patrick, and Gerhard Lenski. 2009. *Human Societies: An Introduction to Macrosociology.* 11th ed. Boulder, CO: Paradigm.

Noonan, Rita K. 1995. "Women Against the State: Political Opportunities and Collective Action Frames in Chile's Transition to Democracy." *Sociological Forum* 10:81–111.

Nordhaus, Ted, and Michael Shellenberger. 2007. *Break Through: From the Death of Environmentalism to the Politics of Possibility.* Boston: Houghton Mifflin.

Norris, Pippa, and Ronald Inglehart. 2004. *Sacred and Secular: Religion and Politics Worldwide.* Cambridge: Cambridge University Press.

North Carolina Department of Environment and Natural Resources. 2008. "Warren County PCB Landfill Fact Sheet." Accessed April 9 (http://www.wastenotnc.org/WarrenCo_Fact_Sheet.htm).

Oberschall, Anthony. 1973. *Social Conflict and Social Movements.* Englewood Cliffs, NJ: Prentice Hall.

O'Connor, Anne-Marie. 2004. "Time of Blogs and Bombs." *Los Angeles Times,* December 27, pp. E1, E14–E15.

Office of Immigration Statistics. 2008. "2007 Yearbook of Immigration Statistics." Washington, DC: U.S. Department of Homeland Security.

Office of Justice Programs. 1999. "Transnational Organized Crime." *NCJRS Catalog* 49 (November/December):21.

Ogburn, William F. 1922. *Social Change with Respect to Culture and Original Nature.* New York: Huebsch (reprinted 1966, New York: Dell).

————, and Clark Tibbits. 1934. "The Family and Its Functions." Pp. 661–708 in *Recent Social Trends in the United States,* edited by Research Committee on Social Trends. New York: McGraw-Hill.

Ogunwole, Stella V. 2006. *We the People: American Indians and Alaska Natives in the United States.* Censr-28. Washington, DC: U.S. Government Printing Office.

O'Harrow, Jr., Robert. 2005. "Mining Personal Data." *Washington Post National Weekly Edition* (February 6), pp. 8–10.

Okano, Kaori, and Motonori Tsuchiya. 1999. *Education in Contemporary Japan: Inequality and Diversity.* Cambridge: Cambridge University Press.

Oliver, Melvin L., and Thomas M. Shapiro. 2006. *Black Wealth/White Wealth: New Perspectives on Racial Inequality.* 2nd ed. New York: Routledge.

————, 2008. "Sub-Prime as a Black Catastrophe." *American Prospect* (October):A9–A11.

Omi, Michael, and Howard Winant. 1994. *Racial Formation in the United States,* 2d ed. New York: Routledge.

OpenNet Initiative. 2008. Home Page. Accessed January 12 (http://opennet.net).

Orfield, Gary, and Chungmei Lee. 2007. *Historic Reversals, Accelerating Resegregation, and the Need for New Integration Strategies.* Los Angeles: Civil Rights Project, UCLA.

Orum, Anthony M., and John G. Dale. 2009. *Political Sociology: Power and Participation in the Modern World.* 3rd ed. New York: Oxford University Press.

Pacific Institute. 2010a. *Cleaning the Waters: A Focus on Water Quality Solutions.* Nairobi, Kenya: Pacific Institute.

Pacific Institute. 2010b. "Water Conflict Chronology." Accessed April 19 (www.worldwater.org/chronology.html).

Pager, Devah. 2003. "The Mark of a Criminal Record." *American Journal of Sociology* 108 (March):937–975.

————. 2007. *Marked: Race, Crime, and Funding Work in an Era of Mass Incarceration.* Chicago: University of Chicago Press.

————, Bruce Weston, and Bart Bonikowski. 2009. "Discrimination in a Low-Wage Labor Market: A Field Experiment." *American Sociological Review* 74 (October):777–799.

Park, Robert E. 1916. "The City: Suggestions for the Investigation of Human Behavior in the Urban Environment." *American Journal of Sociology* 20 (March):577–612.

————. 1936. "Succession, an Ecological Concept." *American Sociological Review* 1 (April):171–179.

Parsons, Talcott. 1951. *The Social System.* New York: Free Press.

————. 1966. *Societies: Evolutionary and Comparative Perspectives.* Englewood Cliffs, NJ: Prentice Hall.

————. 1975. "The Sick Role and the Role of the Physician Reconsidered." *Milbank Medical Fund Quarterly Health and Society* 53 (Summer):257–278.

————, and Robert Bales. 1955. *Family: Socialization and Interaction Process.* Glencoe, IL: Free Press.

Passero, Kathy. 2002. "Global Travel Expert Roger Axtell Explains Why." *Biography,* July, pp. 70–73, 97–98.

Pennachio, Dorothy L. 2004. "Cultural Competence: Caring for Chinese, Japanese and Korean Patients." *Medical Economics* (July 9). Accessed April 30, 2008 (http://www.medicaleconomics.com).

———. 2005. "Cultural Competence: Caring for Your Muslim Patients." *Medical Economics* (May 6). Accessed April 30, 2008 (http://www.medicaleconomics.com).

Perrow, Charles. 1986. *Complex Organizations.* 3d ed. New York: Random House.

Peter, Laurence J., and Raymond Hull. 1969. *The Peter Principle.* New York: Morrow.

Petersen, William. 1979. *Malthus.* Cambridge, MA: Harvard University Press.

Pew Internet Project. 2008. "Demographics of Internet Users." Accessed April 18 (http://www.pewinternet.org/trends/User_Demo_2.15.08.htm).

Phillips, E. Barbara. 1996. *City Lights: Urban–Suburban Life in the Global Society.* New York: Oxford University Press.

Phillips, Susan A. 1999. *Wallbangin': Graffiti and Gangs in L.A.* Chicago: University of Chicago Press.

Piaget, Jean. 1954. *The Construction of Reality in the Child.* Translated by Margaret Cook. New York: Basic Books.

Picca, Leslie Houts, and Joe Feagin. 2007. *Two Faces of Reason: Frontstage and Backstage.* New York: Routledge.

Piller, Charles. 2006. "An Alert Unlike Any Other." *Los Angeles Times,* May 3, pp. A1, A8.

Pinderhughes, Dianne. 1987. *Race and Ethnicity in Chicago Politics: A Reexamination of Pluralist Theory.* Urbana: University of Illinois Press.

Pinderhughes, Raquel. 2008. "Green Collar Jobs." Accessed June 29 (www.urbanhabitat.org/node/528).

Pinkerton, James P. 2003. "Education: A Grand Compromise." *Atlantic Monthly* 291 (January/February):115–116.

Polletta, Francesca, and James M. Jasper. 2001. "Collective Identity and Social Movements." Pp. 283–305 in *Annual Review of Sociology, 2001,* edited by Karen S. Cook and Leslie Hogan. Palo Alto, CA: Annual Reviews.

Population Reference Bureau. 1996. "Speaking Graphically." *Population Today* 24 (June/July):b.

Pryor, John H., Sylvia Hurtado, Linda De'Angelo, Laura Palucki Blake, and Serge Tram. 2009. *The American Freshman: National Norms for Fall 2009.* Los Angeles: Higher Education Research Institute, UCLA.

Pryor, John H., Sylvia Hurtado, Victor B. Saenz, José Luis Santos, and William S. Korn. 2007. *The American Freshman: Forty Year Trends.* Los Angeles: Higher Education Research Institute, UCLA.

Quillian, Lincoln. 2006. "New Approaches to Understanding Racial Prejudice and Discrimination." *Annual Review of Sociology* 32:299–328.

Quinney, Richard. 1970. *The Social Reality of Crime.* Boston: Little, Brown.

———. 1974. *Criminal Justice in America.* Boston: Little, Brown.

———. 1979. *Criminology.* 2d ed. Boston: Little, Brown.

———. 1980. *Class, State and Crime.* 2d ed. New York: Longman.

Ramet, Sabrina. 1991. *Social Currents in Eastern Europe: The Source and Meaning of the Great Transformation.* Durham, NC: Duke University Press.

Rand, Michael R. 2008. "Criminal Victimization, 2007." *Bureau of Justice Statistics Bulletin* (December).

Raybon, Patricia. 1989. "A Case for 'Severe Bias.'" *Newsweek* 114 (October 2):11.

Rennison, Callie. 2002. *Criminal Victimization 2001. Changes 2000–01 with Trends 1993–2001.* Washington, DC: U.S. Government Printing Office.

Revkin, Andrew C. 2007. "Wealth and Poverty, Drought and Flood: Report from Four Fronts in the War on Warming." *New York Times,* April 3, pp. D4–D5.

Rideout, Victoria K., Ulla G. Foehr, and Donald F. Roberts. 2010. "Generation M: Media in the Lives of 8–18 Year-Olds." Kaiser Family Foundation. Accessible at www.kff.org/entmedia/mh012010pkg.cfm.

Rieker, Patricia R., and Chloe E. Bird. 2000. "Sociological Explanations of Gender Differences in Mental and Physical Health." Pp. 98–113 in *Handbook of Medical Sociology,* edited by Chloe E. Bird, Peter Conrad, and Allan Fremont. New York: Prentice Hall.

Rifkin, Jeremy. 1995. "Afterwork." *Utne Reader* (May/June):52–62.

Riley, Matilda White, Robert L. Kahn, and Anne Foner. 1994a. *Age and Structural Lag.* New York: Wiley InterScience.

———, Robert L. Kahn, and Anne Foner, in association with Karin A. Mock. 1994b. "Introduction: The Mismatch between People and Structures." Pp. 1–36 in *Age and Structural Lag,* edited by Matilda White Riley, Robert L. Kahn, and Anne Foner. New York: Wiley InterScience.

Ritzer, George. 2002. *McDonaldization: The Reader.* Thousand Oaks, CA: Pine Forge Press.

———. 2011. *The McDonaldization of Society 6.* Thousand Oaks CA: Pine Forge Books.

Roberts, J. Timmons, Peter E. Grines, and Jodie L. Mañale. 2003. "Social Roots of Global Environmental Change: A World-Systems Analysis of Carbon Dioxide Emissions." *Journal of World-Systems Research* 9 (Summer):277–315.

Robertson, Roland. 1988. "The Sociological Significance of Culture: Some General Considerations." *Theory, Culture, and Society* 5 (February):3–23.

Rose, Arnold. 1951. *The Roots of Prejudice.* Paris: UNESCO.

Rosenberg, Douglas H. 1991. "Capitalism." Pp. 33–34 in *Encyclopedic Dictionary of Sociology,* 4th ed., edited by Dushkin Publishing Group. Guilford, CT: Dushkin.

Rosenfeld, Richard. 2004. "The Case of the Unsolved Crime Decline." *Scientific American* (February).

Rosenthal, Elisabeth. 2009. "Obama's Backing Increases Hopes for Climate Pact." *New York Times,* December 1, pp. 1, 10.

Rosenthal, Robert, and Lenore Jacobson. 1968. *Pygmalion in the Classroom.* New York: Holt.

———, and Lenore Jacobson. 1992. *Pygmalion in the Classroom: Teacher Expectations and Pupils' Intellectual Development.* Newly expanded edition. Bancy Felin, UK: Crown House.

Rossides, Daniel W. 1997. *Social Stratification: The Interplay of Class, Race, and Gender.* 2d ed. Upper Saddle River, NJ: Prentice Hall.

Roszak, Theodore. 1969. *The Making of a Counter-Culture.* Garden City, NY: Doubleday.

Ruane, Janet M., and Karen A. Cerulo. 2004. *Second Thoughts: Seeing Conventional Wisdom Through the Sociological Eye.* Thousand Oaks, CA: Pine Forge.

Ryan, William. 1976. *Blaming the Victim.* Rev. ed. New York: Random House.

Rymer, Russ. 1993. *Genie: An Abused Child's Flight from Science.* New York: HarperCollins.

Sacks, Peter. 2007. *Tearing Down the Gates: Confronting the Class Divide in American Education.* Berkeley: University of California Press.

Sagarin, Edward, and Jose Sanchez. 1988. "Ideology and Deviance: The Case of the Debate over the Biological Factor." *Deviant Behavior* 9 (1):87–99.

Said, Edward W. 2001. "The Clash of Ignorance." *The Nation* (October 22).

Sale, Kirkpatrick. 1996. *Rebels against the Future: The Luddites and Their War on the Industrial Revolution* (with a new preface by the author). Reading, MA: Addison-Wesley.

Salem, Richard, and Stanislaus Grabarek. 1986. "Sociology B.A.s in a Corporate Setting: How Can They Get There and of What Value Are They?" *Teaching Sociology* 14 (October):273–275.

Sallaz, Jeffrey J., and Jane Zavisca. 2007. "Boundaries in American Sociology, 1980–2004." Pp. 21–41 in *Annual Review of Sociology 2007.* Palo Alto, CA: Annual Reviews.

Sampson, Robert J., and W. Byron Groves. 1989. "Community Structure and Crime: Testing Social-Disorganization Theory." *American Journal of Sociology* 94 (January):774–802.

Samuelson, Paul A., and William D. Nordhaus. 2010. *Economics.* 19th ed. New York: McGraw-Hill.

Sanchanta, Mariko. 2010. "Starbucks Plans Major China Expansion." *Wall Street Journal* (April 13).

Sanday, Peggy Reeves. 2002. *Women at the Center: Life in a Modern Matriarchy.* Ithaca, NY: Cornell University Press.

———. 2008. Home page. Accessed March 15 (http://www.sas.upenn.edu/~psanday/)

Sanders, Edmund. 2004. "Coming of Age in Iraq." *Los Angeles Times,* August 14, pp. A1, A5.

Sanyal, Paromita. 2009. "From Credit to Collective Action: The Role of Microfinance in Promoting Women's Social Capital and Normative Influence." *American Sociological Review* 74 (August):529–550.

Sawhill, Isabel, and John E. Morton. 2007. *Economic Mobility: Is the American Dream Alive and Well?* Washington, DC: Economic Mobility Project, Pew Charitable Trusts.

Sayer, Liana C., Suzanne M. Bianchi, and John P. Robinson. 2004. "Are Parents Investing Less in Children? Trends in Mothers' and Fathers' Time with Children." *American Journal of Sociology* 110 (July):1–43.

Schaefer, Richard T. 2011. *Race and Ethnicity in the United States.* 12th ed. Census Update. Upper Saddle River, NJ: Prentice Hall.

———, and William Zellner. 2011. *Extraordinary Groups.* 9th ed. New York: Worth.

Scharnberg, Kirsten. 2007. "Black Market for Midwives Defies Bans." *Chicago Tribune,* November 25, pp. 1, 10.

Scherer, Ron. 2010b. "For Jobless, Online Friends Can Be Lifelines." *Christian Science Monitor,* March 25, p. 21.

Schnaiberg, Allan. 1994. *Environment and Society: The Enduring Conflict.* New York: St. Martin's

Schulman, Gary I. 1974. "Race, Sex, and Violence: A Laboratory Test of the Sexual Threat of the Black Male Hypothesis." *American Journal of Sociology* 79 (March): 1260–1272.

Schur, Edwin M. 1965. *Crimes without Victims: Deviant Behavior and Public Policy.* Englewood Cliffs, NJ: Prentice Hall.

———. 1968. *Law and Society: A Sociological View.* New York: Random House.

———. 1985. "'Crimes without Victims': A 20 Year Reassessment." Paper presented at the annual meeting of the Society for the Study of Social Problems.

Schwartz, Howard D., ed. 1987. *Dominant Issues in Medical Sociology.* 2d ed. New York: Random House.

Schwartz, Shalom H., and Anat Bardi. 2001. "Value Hierarchies Cultures: Taking a Similarities Perspective." *Journal of Cross-Cultural Perspective* 32 (May):268–290.

Scott, Alan. 1990. *Ideology and the New Social Movements.* London: Unwin Hyman.

Scott, Gregory. 2001. "Broken Windows behind Bars: Eradicating Prison Gangs through Ecological Hardening and Symbolic Cleansing." *Corrections Management Quarterly* 5 (Winter):23–36.

Scott, W. Richard, 2008. *Institutions and Organizations: Ideas and Interests.* 3rd. ed. Thousand Oaks CA: Sage Publications.

Second Life. 2008. "Economic Statistics." Accessed January 8 (http://secondlife.com/whatis/economy_stats.php).

Seidman, Steven. 2002. *Beyond the Closet: The Transformation of Gay and Lesbian Life.* New York: Routledge.

Semuels, Alana. 2007. "Second Life Proves Hard Sell." *Chicago Tribune,* July 23, p. 5.

Sengupta, Somini. 2004. "For Iraqi Girls, Changing Land Narrows Lines." *New York Times,* June 27, pp. A1, A11.

Sernau, Scott. 2001. *Worlds Apart: Social Inequalities in a New Century.* Thousand Oaks, CA: Pine Forge Press.

Shah, Anup. 2009. "Climate Justice and Equity." October 4. Accessed December 12 (www.globalissues.org/print/articles/231).

Shapley, Dan. 2010. "So How Big Was the BP Oil Spill?" *The Daily Green* (May 28). Accessed August 2 at http://www.thedailygreen.com.

Shaw, Claude, and Henry D. McKay. 1942. *Juvenile Delinquency and Urban Areas.* Chicago: University of Chicago Press.

Shenon, Philip. 1995. "New Zealand Seeks Causes of Suicides by Young." *New York Times,* July 15, p. 3.

Shin, Hyon, and Robert A. Kominski. 2010. *Language Use in the United States.* Washington DC: U.S. Printing Office.

Sicular, Terry, Ximing Yue, Bjorn Gustafsson, and Shi Li. 2006. *The Urban-Rural Income Gap and Inequality in China.* Research Paper No. 2006/135, United Nations University—World Institute for Development Economic Research.

Simpson, Sally. 1993. "Corporate Crime." Pp. 236–256 in *Introduction to Social Problems,* edited by Craig Calhoun and George Ritzer. New York: McGraw-Hill.

Sisson, Carmen K. 2007. "The Virtual War Family." *Christian Science Monitor* (May 29).

Sjoberg, Gideon. 1960. *The Preindustrial City: Past and Present.* Glencoe, IL: Free Press.

Slack, Jennifer Daryl, and J. Macgregor Wise. 2007. *Culture + Technology.* New York: Peter Lang.

Slavin, Barbara. 2007. "Child Marriage Rife in Nations Getting U.S. Aid." *USA Today,* July 17, p. 6A.

Sloan, Allan. 2009. "What's Still Wrong with Wall Street." *Time,* November 9, pp. 24–29.

Smelser, Neil. 1963. *The Sociology of Economic Life.* Englewood Cliffs, NJ: Prentice Hall.

Smith, David A. 1995. "The New Urban Sociology Meets the Old: Rereading Some Classical Human Ecology." *Urban Affairs Review* 20 (January):432–457.

———, and Michael Timberlake. 1993. "World Cities: A Political Economy/ Global Network Approach." Pp. 181–207 in *Urban Sociology in Transition,* edited by Ray Hutchison. Greenwich, CT: JAI Press.

Smith, David M., and Gary J. Gates. 2001. *Gay and Lesbian Families in the United States: Same-Sex Unmarried Partner Households.* Washington, DC: Human Rights Campaign.

Smith, Michael Peter. 1988. *City, State, and Market.* New York: Basil Blackwell.

Smith, Tom W. 2009. *Religious Change around the World.* Chicago: NORC/ University of Chicago.

Snyder, Thomas D. 1996. *Digest of Education Statistics 1996.* Washington, DC: U.S. Government Printing Office.

Sorenson, John, Robert Winkle, Victoria Brewer, and Jones Marquart. 1999. "Capital Punishment and Deterrence: Examining the Effect of Executions on Murder in Texas." *Crime and Delinquency* 45:481–493.

Sorokin, Pitirim A. [1927] 1959. *Social and Cultural Mobility.* New York: Free Press.

Southern Poverty Law Center. 2009. "10 Ways to Fight Hate on Campus." Accessed March 20 (www.tolerance.org/campus).

Spalter-Roth, Roberta, and Nicole Van Vooren. 2008a. "What Are They Doing with a Bachelor's Degree in Sociology?" Washington, DC: American Sociological Association. Accessible at http:asanet.org/galleries/research/ASAresearchbrief_corrections.pdf.

———. 2008b. "Skills, Reasons, and Jobs. What Happened to the Class of 2005." Washington, DC: American Sociological Association. Accessible at http://asanet.org.

Spitzer, Steven. 1975. "Toward a Marxian Theory of Deviance." *Social Problems* 22 (June):641–651.

Squires, Gregory D., ed. 2002. *Urban Sprawl: Causes, Consequences and Policy Responses.* Washington, DC: Urban Institute.

Starr, Paul. 1982. *The Social Transformation of American Medicine.* New York: Basic Books.

Steffensmeier, Darrell, and Stephen Demuth. 2000. "Ethnicity and Sentencing Outcomes in U.S. Federal Courts: Who Is Punished More Harshly?" *American Sociological Review* 65 (October):705–729.

Stockard, Janice E. 2002. *Marriage in Culture.* Belmont, CA: Thomson Wadsworth.

Sturtevant, William C., and Jessica R. Cattelino. 2004 "Florida Seminole and Miccosukee." In *Handbook of North American Indians (Southeast).* R. D. Fogelson, ed. Pp. 429–449, Vol. 14. Washington, DC: Smithsonian Institution Press.

Sugimoto, Yoshio. 1997. *An Introduction to Japanese Society.* Cambridge: Cambridge University Press.

Sullivan, Harry Stack. [1953] 1968. *The Interpersonal Theory of Psychiatry.* Edited by Helen Swick Perry and Mary Ladd Gawel. New York: Norton.

Sullivan, Kevin. 2006. "Bridging the Digital Divide." *Washington Post National Weekly Edition* 25 (July 17):11–12.

Sum, Andrew, Paul Harrington, and Ishwar Khatiwada. 2006. *The Impact of New Immigrants on Young Native-Born Workers, 2000–2005.* Washington, DC: Center for Immigration Studies.

Sumner, William G. 1906. *Folkways.* New York: Ginn.

Sutch, Richard, and Susan B. Carter. 2006. *Historical Statutes of the U.S.: Earliest Time to the Present.* Cambridge, England: Cambridge University Press.

Sutherland, Edwin H. 1937. *The Professional Thief.* Chicago: University of Chicago Press.

———. 1940. "White-Collar Criminality." *American Sociological Review* 5 (February):1–11.

———. 1949. *White Collar Crime.* New York: Dryden.

———. 1983. *White Collar Crime: The Uncut Version.* New Haven, CT: Yale University Press.

———, Donald R. Cressey, and David F. Luckenbill. 1992. *Principles of Criminology.* 11th ed. New York: Rowman and Littlefield.

Swatos, William H., Jr., ed. 1998. *Encyclopedia of Religion and Society.* Lanham, MD: Alta Mira.

Swidler, Ann. 1986. "Culture in Action: Symbols and Strategies." *American Sociological Review* 51 (April):273–286.

Szasz, Andrew. 1994. *EcoPopulism: Toxic Waste and the Movement for Environmental Justice.* Minneapolis: University of Minnesota Press.

Szasz, Thomas S. 2010. *The Myth of Mental Illness: Foundations of a Theory of Personal Conduct.* New York: HarperCollins.

Talbot, Margaret. 1998. "Attachment Theory: The Ultimate Experiment." *New York Times Magazine,* May 24, pp. 4–30, 38, 46, 50, 54.

Tannen, Deborah. 1990. *You Just Don't Understand: Women and Men in Conversation.* New York: Ballantine.

Taylor, Dorceta E. 2000. "The Rise of the Environmental Justice Paradigm." *American Behavioral Scientist* 43 (January):508–580.

Taylor, Verta. 1999. "Gender and Social Movements: Gender Processes in Women's Self-Help Movements." *Gender and Society* 13:8–33.

———. 2004. "Social Movements and Gender." Pp. 14348–14352 in *International Encyclopedia of the Social and Behavioral Sciences.*

———, Nancy Whittier, and Leila J. Rupp. 2007. *Feminist Frontiers.* 7th ed. New York: McGraw-Hill.

Thomas, Gordon, and Max Morgan Witts. 1974. *Voyage of the Damned.* Greenwich, CT: Fawcett Crest.

Thomas, William I. 1923. *The Unadjusted Girl.* Boston: Little, Brown.

Threadcraft, Shatema. 2008. "Welfare Queen." In *Encyclopedia of Race, Ethnicity and Society,* edited by Richard T. Schaefer. Thousand Oaks, CA: Sage.

Tierney, John. 1990. "Betting the Planet." *New York Times Magazine,* December 2, pp. 52–53, 71, 74, 76, 78, 80–81.

———. 2003. "Iraqi Family Ties Complicate American Efforts for Change." *New York Times,* September 28, pp. A1, A22.

Tilly, Charles. 1964. *The Vendée.* Cambridge, MA: Harvard University Press.

———. 1993. *Popular Contention in Great Britain 1758–1834.* Cambridge, MA: Harvard University Press.

———. 2003. *The Politics of Collective Violence.* New York: Cambridge University Press.

———. 2004. *Social Movements, 1768–2004.* Boulder, CO: Paradigm.

Tönnies, Ferdinand. [1887] 1988. *Community and Society.* Rutgers, NJ: Transaction.

Touraine, Alain. 1974. *The Academic System in American Society.* New York: McGraw-Hill.

Traynor, Ian. 2008. "Europe Expects Flood of Climate Refugees." *The Guardian Weekly* (March 14):1–2.

Trotter III, Robert T., and Juan Antonio Chavira. 1997. *Curanderismo: Mexican American Folk Healing.* Athens, GA: University of Georgia Press.

Tuchman, Gaye. 1992. "Feminist Theory." Pp. 695–704 in *Encyclopedia of Sociology,* vol. 2, edited by Edgar F. Borgatta and Marie L. Borgatta. New York: Macmillan.

Tumin, Melvin M. 1953. "Some Principles of Stratification: A Critical Analysis." *American Sociological Review* 18 (August):387–394.

———. 1985. *Social Stratification.* 2d ed. Englewood Cliffs, NJ: Prentice Hall.

Turkle, Sherry. 2004. "How Computers Change the Way We Think." *Chronicle of Higher Education* 50 (January 30):B26–B28.

Twenge, Jean M. 2009. "Change Over Time in Obedience: The Jury's Still Out, But It Might Be Decreasing." *American Psychologist* 64 (1):28–31.

United Nations Development Fund for Women. 2009. *Who Answers to Women?* New York: UNIFEM.

United Nations Development Programme. 2007. *Fighting Climate Change: Human Solidarity in a Divided World. Human Development Report 2007/2008.* New York: United Nations Development Programme.

United Nations Framework Convention on Climate Change. 2010. Home page. Accessed April 19 (http://unfcc.int).

United Nations Office on Drugs and Crime. 2005. "The United Nations Convention Against Transnational Organized Crime and Its Protocols." Accessed March 18, 2005 (www.unodc.org).

United Nations Population Division. 2004b. "Population Division Homepage: World Percentage Urban." Accessed October 4 (http://esa.un.org/unpp/p2kOdata.asp).

Urban Dictionary. 2010. "Urban Amish." Accessed April 28 (www.urbandictionary.com/define.php?term=urban%20amish).

U.S. Trade Representative. 2007. "Trade Promotion Authority Delivers Jobs, Growth, Prosperity, and Security at Home." January 31 Fact Sheet. Accessed February 19 (www.ustr.gov).

van den Berghe, Pierre. 1978. *Race and Racism: A Comparative Perspective.* 2nd ed. New York: Wiley.

Veblen, Thorstein. [1899] 1964. *Theory of the Leisure Class.* New York: Macmillan. New York: Penguin.

————. 1919. *The Vested Interests and the State of the Industrial Arts.* New York: Huebsch.

Velásquez, Carmen, and P. Rafael Hernandez-Arias. 2009. *Voices from the Communities: Community Health Assets and Needs Assessment.* Chicago: Alivio Medical Center and Stearns Center for Community-Based Service Learning.

Velasquez-Manoff, Moises. 2009. "Could Water Scarcity Cause International Conflict?" *Christian Science Monitor,* October 26.

Walder, Andrew G. 2009. "Political Sociology and Social Movements." *Annual Review of Sociology.* 35:393–412.

Waldman, Amy. 2004a. "India Takes Economic Spotlight, and Critics Are Unkind." *New York Times,* March 7, p. 3.

————. 2004b. "Low-Tech or High, Jobs Are Scarce in India's Boom." *New York Times,* May 6, p. A3.

————. 2004c. "What India's Upset Vote Reveals: The High Tech Is Skin Deep." *New York Times,* May 15, p. A5.

Wallace, Ruth A., and Alison Wolf. 1980. *Contemporary Sociological Theory.* Englewood Cliffs, NJ: Prentice Hall.

Wallerstein, Immanuel. 1974. *The Modern World System.* New York: Academic Press.

————. 1979a. *Capitalist World Economy.* Cambridge, England: Cambridge University Press.

————. 1979b. *The End of the World as We Know It: Social Science for the Twenty-First Century.* Minneapolis: University of Minnesota Press.

————. 2000. *The Essential Wallerstein.* New York: The New Press.

————. 2004. *World-Systems Analysis: An Introduction.* Durham, NC: Duke University Press.

Wallis, Claudia. 2008. "How to Make Great Teachers." *Time* 171 (February 25):28–34.

Wang, Meiyan, and Fand Cai. 2006. *Gender Wage Differentials in China's Urban Labor Market.* Research Paper No. 2006/141. United Nations University World Institute for Development Economics Research.

Weber, Max. [1913–1922] 1947. *The Theory of Social and Economic Organization.* Translated by A. Henderson and T. Parsons. New York: Free Press.

————. [1904] 2009. *The Protestant Ethic and the Spirit of Capitalism.* 4th ed. Translation by Stephen Kalberg. New York: Oxford University Press.

Wechsler, Henry, J. E. Lee, M. Kuo, M. Seibring, T. F. Nelson, and H. Lee. 2002. "Trends in College Binge Drinking During a Period of Increased Prevention Efforts: Findings from Four Harvard School of Public Health College Alcohol Surveys: 1993–2001." *Journal of American College Health* 50 (5):203–217.

————, Mark Seibring, I-Chao Liu, and Marilyn Ahl. 2004. "Colleges Respond to Student Binge Drinking: Reducing Student Demand or Limiting Access." *Journal of American College Health* 52 (4):159–168.

Weden, Margaret M. 2007. *Twentieth Century U.S. Racial Inequalities in Mortality.* Santa Monica, CA: RAND.

Weeks, John. 2008. *Population: An Introduction to Concepts and Issues.* 10th ed. Belmont, CA: Wadsworth.

Weier, Mary Hayes. 2007. "The Second Decade of Offshore Outsourcing: Where We're Headed." *InformationWeek* (November 3). Accessed June 6, 2008 (www.informationweek.com).

Weinberg, Daniel H. 2004. *Evidence from Census 2000 About Earnings by Detailed Occupation for Men and Women.* CENSR-15. Washington, DC: U.S. Government Printing Office.

———. 2007. "Earnings by Gender: Evidence from Census 2000." *Monthly Labor Review* (July/August):26–34.

Weinstein, Deena, and Michael A. Weinstein. 1999. "McDonaldization Enframed." Pp. 57–69 in *Resisting McDonaldization,* edited by Barry Smart. London: Sage.

Weitz, Rose. 2007. *The Sociology of Health, Illness, and Heath Care.* 4th ed. Belmont, CA: Thomson.

Wentling, Tre, Elroi Windsor, Kristin Schilt, and Betsy Lucal. 2008. "Teaching Transgender." *Teaching Sociology* 36 (January):49–57.

Wells-Barnett, Ida B. 1970. *Crusade for Justice: The Autobiography of Ida B. Wells.* Edited by Alfreda M. Duster. Chicago: University of Chicago Press.

West, Candace, and Don H. Zimmerman. 1987. "Doing Gender." *Gender and Society* 1 (June):125–151.

Whyte, William Foote. 1981. *Street Corner Society: Social Structure of an Italian Slum.* 3d ed. Chicago: University of Chicago Press.

Wickman, Peter M. 1991. "Deviance." Pp. 85–87 in *Encyclopedic Dictionary of Sociology,* 4th ed., edited by Dushkin Publishing Group. Guilford, CT: Dushkin.

Wilford, John Noble. 1997. "New Clues Show Where People Made the Great Leap to Agriculture." *New York Times,* November 18, pp. B9, B12.

Wilkinson, Alec. 2007. "No Obstacles." *New Yorker* (April 16): 106–108, 110, 112–114, 116.

Wills, Jeremiah B., and Barbara J. Risman. 2006. "The Visibility of Feminist Thought in Family Studies." *Journal of Marriage and Family* 68 (August):690–700.

Wilson, Barbara J., Stacy L. Smith, W. James Porter, Dale Kunkel, Daniel Linz, Carolyn M. Colvin, and Edward Donnerstein. 2002. "Violence in Children's Television Programming: Assessing the Risks." *Journal of Communication* 52 (March):5–35.

Wilson, Edward O. 2000. *Sociobiology: The New Synthesis.* Cambridge, MA: Belknap Press, Harvard University Press.

Wilson, John. 1973. *Introduction to Social Movements.* New York: Basic Books.

———. 1978. *Religion in American Society: The Effective Presence.* Englewood Cliffs, NJ: Prentice Hall.

Wilson, William J. 1996. *When Work Disappears: The World of the New Urban Poor.* New York: Knopf.

———. 1999. *The Bridge over the Racial Divide: Rising Inequality and Coalition Politics.* Berkeley: University of California Press.

Winant, Howard B. 1994. *Racial Conditions: Politics, Theory, Comparisons.* Minneapolis, MN: University of Minnesota Press.

———. 2006. "Race and Racism: Towards a Global Future." *Ethnic and Racial Studies* 29 (September):986–1003.

Winslow, Robert W., and Sheldon X. Zhang. 2008a. *Criminology: A Global Perspective.* New York: Pearson Prentice Hall.

———. 2008b. "Crime and Society: A Comparative Tour of the World." Accessed January 28 (www-rohan.sdsu.edu/faculty/rwinslow.)

Wirth, Louis. 1928. *The Ghetto.* Chicago: University of Chicago Press.

———. 1931. "Clinical Sociology." *American Journal of Sociology* 37 (July):49–60.

———. 1938. "Urbanism as a Way of Life." *American Journal of Sociology* 44 (July):1–24.

Wolf, Naomi. 1992. *The Beauty Myth: How Images of Beauty Are Used Against Women.* New York: Anchor.

Wood, Daniel B. 2010. "Fewer Illegal Immigrants in U.S." *Christian Science Monitor,* March 1, p. 19.

World Bank. 2000. *World Development Report 2000/2001.* Washington, DC: World Bank.

———. 2009. *World Development Indicators 2009.* Washington, DC: World Bank.

———. 2010a. *World Development Indicators 2010.* Washington, DC: World Bank.

——— 2010b. *World Development Report 2010: Development and Climate Change.* Washington, DC: World Bank.

World Health Organization. 2008. *World Development Indicators 2008.* Washington, DC: World Bank.

———. 2009. "Biotechnology (GM Foods)." Accessed May 11 (www.who.int/foodsafety/biotech/en/).

———. 2010. "Suicide Prevention." Accessed July 10 at http://www.who.int/mental_health/prevention/en/.

World Resources Institute. 1998. *1998–1999 World Resources: A Guide to the Global Environment.* New York: Oxford University Press.

Wortham, Robert A. 2008. "DuBois, William Edward Burghardt." Pp. 423–427, vol. 1, in *Encyclopedia of Race, Ethnicity, and Society,* edited by Richard T. Schaefer. Thousand Oaks CA: Sage.

Wright, Erik Olin, David Hachen, Cynthia Costello, and Joy Sprague. 1982. "The American Class Structure." *American Sociological Review* 47 (December):709–726.

Yamagata, Hisashi, Kuang S. Yeh, Shelby Stewman, and Hiroko Dodge. 1997. "Sex Segregation and Glass Ceilings: A Comparative Statistics Model of Women's Career Opportunities in the Federal Government over a Quarter Century." *American Journal of Sociology* 103 (November):566–632.

Yinger, J Milton. 1974. "Religion, Sociology of." Pp. 604–613 in *Encyclopaedia Britannica,* vol. 15. Chicago: Encyclopedia Britannica.

Zang, Xiaowei. 2002. "Labor Market Segmentation and Income Inequality in Urban China." *Sociological Quarterly* 43 (1):27–44.

Zellner, William M. 1995. *Counter Cultures: A Sociological Analysis.* New York: St. Martin's Press.

Zimbardo, Philip G. 2007. "Revisiting the Stanford Prison Experiment: A Lesson in the Power of the Situation." *Chronicle of Higher Education* 53 (March 20):B6, B7.

Zimbardo, Philip G., Robert L. Johnson, and Vivian McCann. 2009. *Psychology: Core Concepts.* 6th ed. Boston: Allyn and Bacon.

Zipp, Yvonne. 2009. Courts Divided on Police Use of GPS Tracking. *Christian Science Monitor,* May 15.

Zittrain, Jonathan, and John Palfrey. 2008. "Reluctant Gatekeepers: Corporate Ethics on a Filtered Internet." Pp. 103–122 in *Access Denied,* edited by Ronald Deibert, John Palfrey, Rafal Rohozinski, and Jonathan Zittrain. Cambridge, MA: The MIT Press.

Zola, Irving K. 1972."Medicine as an Institution of Social Control." *Sociological Review* 20 (November):487–504.

———. 1983. *Socio-Medical Inquiries.* Philadelphia: Temple University Press.

Zweigenhaft, Richard L., and G. William Domhoff. 1998. *Diversity in the Power Elite: How It Happened, Why It Matters.* 2d ed. New York: Rowman and Littlefield.

Credits

Chapter 10: P. 267 Figure 10–1 from Carl Haub. 2010. *World Population Data Sheet 2010.* Used by permission of Population Reference Bureau. P. 271 Table 10–1 based on Gideon Sjoberg. 1960. *The Preindustrial City: Past and Present*:323–328. Copyright © 1960 by The Free Press; copyright renewed 1988 by Gideon Sjoberg. Adapted with permission of The Free Press, a division of Simon & Schuster Adult Publishing Group. All rights reserved. And based on E. Barbara Phillips. 1996. *City Lights: Urban-Suburban Life in the Global Society,* 2/e:132–135. Copyright © 1981 by E. Barbara Phillips and Richard T. LeGates, 1996 by E. Barbara Phillips. Used by permission of Oxford University Press, Inc. P. 273 Figure 10–2 Figure from Chauncy D. Harris & Edward Ullman. 1945. "The Nature of Cities" in *Annals of the American Academy of Political and Social Science,* Volume 242, November 1945. P. 290 Cartoon by Joseph Farris. Reprinted by permission of Miller-McCune and Joseph Farris. P. 294 Cartoon by Signe Wilkinson. Used with permission of Signe Wilkinson and the Washington Post Writers Group in conjunction with the Cartoonist Group. All rights reserved.

Chapter 11: P. 300 Figure 11–1 adapted from *The Economist,* "The future is another country." © The Economist Newspaper Limited, London, July 24, 2010. P. 313 Table 11–4 Table adapted from John B. Horrigan, *A Typology of Information and Communication Technology Users,* May 7, 2007, pp. 5–11, www.pewinternet.org/ Reports/2007/A-Typology-of-Information-and-Communication-Technology-Users. aspx. Pew Internet & American Life Project. P. 317 Cartoon © Matt Wuerker. Reprinted by permission.

PHOTO CREDITS

CO 1: U.S. Cost Guard photo by Petty Officer 3rd Class Patrick Kelley; **CO 2:** Courtesy of Alice Tejkalová; **CO 3:** C Squared Studios/Getty Images; **CO 4:** © image 100/ Corbis; **CO 5:** Greg Wood/AFP/Getty Images; **CO 6:** Corbis © image 100/Corbis; **CO 7:** © Digital Vision/Getty Images; **CO 8:** Don Smetzer/Stone/Getty Images; **CO 9:** Getty Images; **CO 10:** David Madison/Getty Images; **CO 11:** Hiroko Masuike/ *The New York Times*/Redux Pictures.

Index

Note: Page numbers followed by *f* indicate figures; those followed by *t* indicate tables.